In conclusion, t
an economic and so
vertising, disaggreg;
tors, and includes
appendices that go to the heart of the
economic study of advertising. An extensive bibliography completes the text.

JULIAN L. SIMON is professor of economics and of marketing at the University of Illinois.

**Issues
in the Economics
of Advertising**

Issues
in the Economics
of Advertising

Julian L. Simon

UNIVERSITY OF ILLINOIS PRESS

Urbana Chicago London

Contents

List of Tables

List of Figures

Introduction

In the nineteenth century the great economists paid little or no attention to advertising. And for good reason, because mass advertising clearly had little economic or social importance before the twentieth century. In the twentieth century most mainstream economists also have had little to say about advertising. Perhaps this is because the classical writers bequeathed no categories within which the subject of advertising could be fitted easily. Or it may be that the subject really has little importance to the economy as a whole. One of the purposes of this book is to find out whether the latter is true.

Some twentieth-century economists, however, have concluded that advertising has important effects on a developed industrial economy, while others have at least considered that the matter is worth study.[1] But paucity of basic knowledge of how advertising works, both at the level of the firm and at higher levels of aggregation, has prevented the subject from advancing very much. And major obstacles have hindered the investigation of advertising's social and economic role. For example,

the introduction of dynamic conditions into our analysis necessitates a considerable change in the statement of optimal conditions. The difference is not one of principle, but it is nevertheless important. Judged purely on statical grounds, monopolies or a patent system may appear as unmitigated evils, and certainly inferior to atomistic competition and free trade. But in a dynamical world these judgments may have to be reversed; viz. the infant industry argument for protection, the stimulus to large scale research which only a monopolist can afford, the (alleged) necessity to hold out incentives to inventors, etc. Indeed the measure of support which capital-

---

[1] "Such topics as the economic serviceability of advertising, the reaction of an unstable price level upon production, the effect of various systems of public regulation [should be studied by the National Bureau]" (Mitchell, p. 30).

ism commands is most importantly related to precisely these factors of development [Samuelson, 1947, p. 253].

Advertising well illustrates Samuelson's point because the most important of its causes and effects are very long run and are entwined with culture and tastes. For this reason Kaldor (1950) concluded that the effects of advertising are mostly either not knowable or are trivial. As a specific illustration, Kaldor threw up his hands at the investigation of the effect of advertising on the consumption function. And with even the one aspect of advertising that Kaldor thought could be studied successfully — the effect of advertising upon industrial concentration — dynamic processes confuse the issue. To illustrate, if one considers a *given size* economy at time t, it might (or might not) be true that there would be more competitors at that time if the society permits advertising than if it does not. But if one does not assume a given size economy, one must also consider the possibility that if two same-size economies begin at time t − k, one with and one without advertising, the two economies may well grow at different rates due to advertising, and be different sizes at time t. If so, the static comparison of equal-size economies at time t is misleading.

Another example of how long-run considerations obscure the issue is the social question of whether advertising enriches or corrupts human values. Not only is there no obvious way of assessing the relevant dynamic causal processes, but there are no satisfactory measurements even for static comparisons. How does one compare the degree of materialism in the U.S. to that in the U.S.S.R. or to that in a nonliterate tribe? (In some nonliterate tribes anthropologists report high individualistic concern with personal property and wealth.) Furthermore, it fags the brain even to think about evaluating the effect of advertising, *ceteris paribus*, when there may be no mass media, let alone any advertising, in one of the societies to be compared.

A second obstacle to the successful study of advertising is the scientific urge to bring all subtypes of a phenomenon under the same theoretical blanket. This urge has led writers, almost without exception,[2] to discuss whether advertising raises prices or lowers prices, whether advertising does or does not increase consumption, whether advertising enslaves the mind or promotes freedom, and so on. But as we shall see, any and all possible effects of advertising may be found in some subtype of advertising in the complex economy. It may be possible eventually to say on balance what the overall effect is of advertising on prices or output on quality. Up until now, however, there have not been, except for

[2] Borden is the notable exception (1942, pp. 46–47).

Borden (1942), many careful studies of the workings of advertising in the various industries and trade channels; and until we have information on the segments we cannot make statements about the whole.[3]

A third obstacle to the understanding of advertising's economic effects has been disappearing fast. Students of the subject were formerly hamstrung by ignorance of the microeconomics of advertising. A leading example has been our ignorance about the lagged relationship of advertising to sales that is so important in many industries. Everyone knew that much of advertising's effect is spread out over time, but no one knew how to measure the distributed effect. This lacuna in knowledge blocked Borden's attempts to go much beyond crude statistical description in his case studies of oranges, cigarettes, towels, and the other industries he studied. But in the last ten years much has been learned about the mechanism of advertising as a selling device, and therefore we are now in a better position to understand advertising's industrial and macro economics.

The obstacles have not completely prevented scholars from investigating the economics of advertising. From the early times of advertising's importance in the United States there have been serious articles written about it. The first piece I know of with a title like "Economics of Advertising" was that of Harris in 1893. Many of the observations in that piece are not much different from those of learned observers today. Sherman's 1900 article is still very useful today. And by 1924 a panel at the American Economic Association meetings which included papers by F. Clark, Hotchkiss, and Moriarty, and discussion by Cherington and Copeland (all 1925), said most of the things which are said now.[4]

There have also been a fair number of book-length attempts to cover the entire subject of advertising in the economy. Most of these have either been the work of amateurs (some of them talented amateurs, however) or exercises in special pleading written with the aim of justifying or damning advertising. Both types of work have generally brought forth little new knowledge. But there have also been a handful of serious and valuable books. Perhaps the first was by Vaile (1927) and an excellent beginning it was. Where Vaile did not then say what one would say today, it is probably because he had relatively little data and

---

[3] Gibbs said that it is often easier to understand the whole than its parts. However, this is not one of those cases, I am convinced.

[4] Those interested in a bibliography of evaluative articles on advertising may find many listed in the bibliography in Chamberlin (1962), keyed under "Selling Costs." Most of this extensive literature is repetitive and a waste of time, however. Many of the articles dealing with the various specialized aspects of the subject of the economies of advertising are touched on in the appropriate chapters of this book, or are listed in the bibliography here.

no Keynsian theory available to him. Among the other books since then have been those by Baster (1935), Bishop (1944a), Lever (1947), Taplin (1960), and Harris and Seldon (1962).

In 1948 Kaldor and Silverman pulled together "the main facts about advertising in their relation to the national economy" of Great Britain (p. xiii). Kaldor (1950) followed this empirical work with a long but pithy article that rounded up many important theoretical arguments, especially those that arose in the context of Keynsian macroeconomics. And Telser's recent encyclopedia article is a short but comprehensive review of the issues (1968).

But surely the high point in the literature that surveys the economics of advertising is Borden's *The Economic Effects of Advertising,* which has already been referred to above. That work benefited from an author who understood the important theoretical issues but who also understood the practice of advertising. Perhaps most important, however, Borden gathered a vast amount of facts and quantitative data. Though many of the appropriate econometric devices were not then used to make the data yield up all its secrets, the book provided a far more comprehensive picture of advertising in the economy than was previously available — and nothing better has been done since.[5]

Now a few words about the present book. It is not a comprehensive survey of present knowledge. It does not describe the work of other writers except where that is groundwork for the argument. (However, most important work that has been done in the field is at least referred to somewhere in the book, and more is included in the bibliography.) The book tackles those problems in the economics of advertising that I have thought would most benefit from attention at this time. Many important issues are not covered. Some issues are not touched on because it would be folly to approach them at this stage of the game. Basic material is lacking to support investigation of many of the more complex problems. Other issues are left alone because they were settled long ago; unfortunately, this latter category is not very large. Though coverage is selective, however, the various investigations mostly relate to and depend upon each other.

Advertising is, among other things, a sociological subject, a psychological subject, and an anthropological subject. But this volume restricts itself to the examination of advertising as an *economic* entity. Such matters as the content of advertisements, the communications

---

[5] Perhaps Backman's recent book (1967) should be mentioned for completeness because of its wide circulation, but it is primarily a survey of materials already in the literature, and it is mostly confined to the single issue of the effect of advertising on competition among enterprises.

character of media and audiences, and the noneconomic societal effects of advertising are not dealt with except in occasional asides. And my views on the managerial economics of advertising are covered in another book to appear soon (Simon, 1970).

It would have been good if this book could have been a study of all promotion rather than of just advertising. Outside salesmen (as distinguished from sales clerks, who do little promotion), public relations, store display, and other promotional forms are conceptually very similar to advertising, and they are quantitatively much more important in the economy than is advertising. Data on these other promotional forms is almost totally lacking, however, and therefore the best one can do is wave a hand at the issue and suggest that most of the analysis of advertising also applies to the other promotional forms.

Now a forward look. Microeconomic studies of the advertising industry comprise the first part of the book. Chapter 1 investigates whether or not there are ever increasing returns to advertising, i.e., whether doubling the advertising can ever more than double the sales; this is a basic parameter that enters into much of the subsequent work. Then the amount that firms spend for advertising, and the determinants of the advertising expenditure, are the subject of a series of four chapters. Theoretical treatment is in Chapters 2 to 4, and Chapter 5 is an empirical study of the matter. Chapter 6 includes a study of advertising-agency mergers (done in collaboration with Harold W. Johnson) and two studies of the advertising-rate structure (one done in collaboration with Ian Bowers), rounding out Part One.

Part Two studies the macroeconomics of advertising. Chapter 7 takes a broad view of human economy and society, examining how and why advertising evolves as the economy develops. Chapter 8 discusses various theories about the effect of advertising on the propensity to consume, and examines available evidence that helps discriminate between the theories. Chapter 9 takes up the relationship of advertising to industrial concentration, first surveying previous theoretical and empirical work and then presenting new empirical evidence. Chapter 10 is a case study of a complex issue in advertising and society, cigarette advertising. And Chapter 11 offers an economic and social appraisal of advertising, disaggregated by major sectors.

There are also several appendices that are important to the rest of the book. Appendix A discusses why the Chamberlinian notion of product differentiation — so often dragged into analyses of advertising — is meaningless, confusing, and unnecessary. Then Appendix B (written in collaboration with George Crain) discusses the ratio of advertising to sales which is commonly used in research on advertising; we arrived at the conclusion that this ratio is seldom a useful measure and always a treacherous one. Appendix C (written in collaboration with Leslie Golembo) analyzes the history of the diffusion of an innovation in advertising, the January White Sale. Appendix D is a brief bibliographical essay on sources of advertising data, written with the assistance of Eleanor Blum. Appendix E lists some studies on advertising that seem to be worth doing and that I hope someone does.

The sole financial support for this research came from modest grants by the Research Board of the University of Illinois for research assistance with a couple of empirical chapters. I am very grateful for that assistance. This fact is also relevant in another connection. Because of the source of support, the conclusions should be safe from the charge that they were affected by the financial backing for the work.

I am grateful to many people for taking the time to read and comment on various chapters, at various stages of their development. The following list is far from complete: William Baumol, Appendix A; Royall Brandis, Appendix A; Louis Bucklin, Chapters 2 to 4; Robert Ferber, Chapter 8; James Ferguson, Chapter 6; Fritz Machlup, Appendix A; Vincent Norris, Chapter 10; Lee Preston, Appendix B; Robert Resek, Appendix A; John Stewart, Chapter 1; George Stigler, Appendix A; Lester Telser, Chapters 1 to 4; and Thomas Yancey, Chapter 8. Darrell B. Lucas read the entire book thoroughly and made many useful comments. Harold Johnson and Ian Bowers were good enough to allow me to publish our joint work here as Sections A and C of Chapter 6, as were George Crain with Appendix B and Leslie Golembo with Appendix C. And unknown journal readers have made many helpful suggestions. Vikram Dutt, Lawrence Miller and Kiyoshi Nagata were helpful research assistants. Carole S. Appel has been as competent and faithful an editor as a book could hope to have, for which I am grateful indeed.

I also thank the editors of the following journals for allowing me to use in revised form materials originally published as articles: *Journal of Advertising Research*, Chapter 1 and Appendix B; *Quarterly Journal of Economics*, Chapter 4; *Bulletin of the Oxford Institute of Economics and Statistics*, Chapter 6 (Section A); *Journal of Political Economy*, Chapter 6 (Section B); *Kyklos*, Chapter 8; *Illinois Business Review*, Chapter 10; *Ethics*, Appendix A; *The Journal of Business*, Appendix C.

PART ONE:

Microeconomics of Advertising

1

Can Double
the Advertising
Produce Double
the Sales?

INTRODUCTION

The subject of this chapter is, to speak loosely, the relative efficiency of smaller and larger quantities of advertising. More precisely, this chapter inquires whether there are ever increasing marginal returns in advertising, i.e., whether an increase in advertising will ever produce a more-than-proportional increase in sales. In other words, we ask whether doubling the amount of advertising ever more than doubles sales.

Discussion of this matter is sometimes muddled by a blurred distinction between (1) the marginal productivity of different physical quantities of advertising, e.g., the sales produced by a half-page versus a full-page advertisement; and (2) the marginal productivity of different amounts of money spent for advertising, e.g., the sales produced by the first $1,000 spent for advertising versus the second $1,000. Unfortunately the available data are sometimes in physical quantities and sometimes in money costs. This distinction cannot be maintained in the work, though an attempt is made to keep the two ideas unconfused.

The subject of this chapter is part of an interrelated set of questions concerning the size of the advertising expenditures of firms. To avoid confusion we must first survey these questions. The simplest question is that which is covered in this chapter and Appendix B, and the answer to it is of particular interest to firms. This is the question of the effect on sales of variations in the amount of advertising, but without concurrent expansion of the rest of the firm. That is, the firm asks whether, with the same sales force and the same plant, it can get more than twice as many orders from double the advertising. Of course the firm plans on increasing production to fill the larger number of orders, but the management decision under discussion is only whether to increase the amount of advertising, other changes being reflexive. To repeat, though the answer to this question affects the answers to the other questions that follow, it is only firms who are interested in the answer to this question for its own sake.

The next question may also be seen from the point of view of the firm. If the firm enlarges the overall size of the operation, including the advertising budget but not the advertising budget alone, will the firm be more successful? This is the question of economies of scale. The firm does not just plan on producing whatever sales the advertising creates. Rather, it decides on a plant size, an advertising budget, a sales force, etc., as one integrated interacting whole in which the amount of the advertising budget is not independent of the plant size (e.g., the firm will consider how much advertising is needed to sell most or all of the output of each plant size under consideration, as well as the converse).

The question of economies of scale in an industry, with advertising compared to without advertising, may be of interest to the society too, but it need not be. If the nature of the industry is such that a firm that sells, say, a million units yearly can operate as efficiently as any larger unit, and if the yearly sales of the industry are 20 million units, it need not be of concern to the society that a one-million unit firm has an advantage over a 200,000 unit firm. This is because in this case economies of scale do not rule out competition among a good many firms. If, however, the situation is such that the firm size that operates most efficiently is so large that there is only room for one or a handful of firms, the society may be concerned. And if the nature of advertising contributes to the ability of the large firm to operate more efficiently, society may worry about advertising. (It should be clear that if there are increasing marginal returns, it would be one possible case of economies of scale, in that the bigger firm would have an advantage over the smaller firm on this basis alone.)

The issue of economies of scale per se is not one that we can or will do much with here. This is because it is exceedingly difficult to determine which sizes of firms are most efficient (see Stigler, 1958). And without knowing which sizes of firms are most efficient one obviously cannot learn much about how important the instrument of advertising is in the efficiency of various size firms.

The third question concerning advertising and firm size is the most general. This is the question of how important advertising is in the achievement of market power — the power to extract noncompetitive profits from the society. If the economies of scale are such that one or a few firms can dominate an industry by being much more efficient than smaller firms, then market power arises from this source. But there may be other causes of market power than what are ordinarily thought of as economies of scale. These tangled matters are the subject of Chapter 9.

More specifically, now, this chapter surveys the evidence on the marginal productivity of advertising. The purpose is to increase our knowledge of the form of the advertising-response function, and more specifically, to learn whether there are any increasing returns in advertising. This chapter comes first because its conclusion is used in many later chapters. For example, increasing returns might be an important force toward oligopoly and industrial concentration. Kaldor (1950, p. 14) sounds the alarm: ". . . this process of concentration might go on indefinitely (or until complete monopoly is established) so long as the basic assumption, that a larger expenditure on advertising exercises a greater 'pulling power' than a smaller expenditure . . . remains valid. . ." an issue which is discussed at length in Chapter 9. The possibility of increasing returns also affects the planning of advertisers in their decisions about whether they should concentrate or disperse their

FIGURE 1–1. INCREASING AND DECREASING RETURNS IN ADVERTISING RESPONSE FUNCTIONS

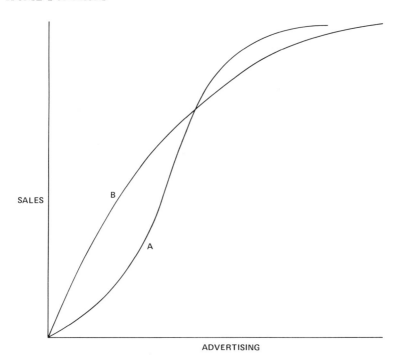

advertising expenditure geographically, over time periods, among media, among copy approaches, and into unit sizes of advertisements. And the form of the advertising-sales relationship is especially important in the next three chapters, which offer some theory of how much is spent for advertising under various conditions.

The issue here is only whether there are increasing returns for a given firm advertising a given product. In geometric terms the question is whether the advertising-sales response function has the shape of curve A or of curve B in Figure 1-1. Not considered here are the advantages which may flow from (1) joint advertising of several products, (2) joint use of a common brand name for several products,[1] (3) store distribution induced by advertising, or (4) multiproduct volume-discount purchases of advertising time and space.[2] That is, this chapter deals only with the comparative-statics problem, which assumes that all other things remain the same. The other issues mentioned as (1)–(4) above deal with the effect of advertising when compounded with structural changes in firm and market behavior, and they go beyond the matter of the marginal productivity of advertising. Some of the more important of these structural changes are discussed in Chapter 9, "Advertising and Market Power," as part of the more general issue of economies of scale.

Ideally the analysis would assess the total effect of a given advertising expenditure, over the entire time that it continues to produce sales, in the spirit of a distributed-lag model. Unhappily, the available data seldom allow such a complete analysis, but rather are mostly restricted to the current period.

Excluded from the discussion are those sales attributable to merchandising efforts other than advertising, i.e., those sales that would have taken place independently of the level of advertising expenditure. Advertising, personal selling, and other merchandising efforts are often joint in their effect, of course. This joint effect could be taken account of but it would obscure the argument.

Most economists have simply assumed that there are increasing re-

[1] "We may be able to derive additional value from the Clorox name for other new and related products . . ." (internal Proctor & Gamble memo, quoted in U.S., F.T.C., 1963, p. 3). What is puzzling, however, is that there is *so little* use of the common brand name by multiproduct firms instead of such unconnected names as "Bold," "Tide," "Kent," etc. There is an unfortunate lack of published research on the effect of common brand names.

[2] That multiproduct volume discounts have been important has been made very clear by the Federal Trade Commission study of the acquisition of Clorox by Proctor & Gamble (1963) and by the Blake-Blum study of television advertising rates (1965). But Blank (1968) argues that such discount effects no longer exist in network television.

turns in advertising, for a variety of theoretical economic and psychological reasons (e.g., Bain, 1956a; Borden, 1942, pp. 426–7; Chamberlin, 1962, pp. 133–4; Dean, 1951c, p. 357; Dorfman and Steiner, 1954; Howard, 1957, pp. 330–6; Marshall, 1961, p. 282). Marketing and operations researchers have generally agreed (e.g., Vidale and Wolfe, 1957; Zentler and Ryde, 1956), as has the Federal Trade Commission in its decision against Proctor & Gamble in the Clorox case (1963). Advertising practitioners quite generally believe that increasing returns exist, at least in some cases. And the advertising-trade press has been virtually unanimous in backing the idea of increasing returns. The relevant arguments will now be reviewed briefly.

The basic argument *against* the existence of increasing returns has been the progressive diminution of unreached prospects. Stigler (1961) and Ozga (1960) have built analyses of information economics around this idea. Also, the most important cause of increasing returns in manufacturing — indivisibilities of capital goods and organization — is not present in advertising. With minor exceptions an advertiser can purchase advertising space or time in any quantity he wishes, and though there may be discount effects, there are no important discontinuous jumps from level to level.

The most powerful argument *in favor* of increasing returns is psychological. It and other arguments for increasing returns were summed up by Chamberlin (1962, pp. 133–134):

1. . . . Control of the buyer's consciousness must be gained, and while it is being gained additional expenditure yields increasing returns.
2. . . . Improvement in the organization of the expenditure as its total amount is increased . . . the employment of more resources means greater specialization in their use.
3. . . . The most effective media may be those whose use requires a large outlay. As expenditure increases, then, a shift may take place to continually more effective media, so that a tendency to increasing returns is imparted to the cost curve.
4. . . . The most effective choice of media may involve the use of several in combination. . . .

Clearly there are arguments on both sides of the question, and there are no reasonable estimates of the effects of any of these forces. Therefore it is fruitless to hope for a satisfactory deductive answer about the advertising response function's shape, let alone a quantified answer about the magnitude of the sum of these forces. It is necessary to resort to the empirical evidence.

The only general treatment of this subject is the chapter on "Selling Costs" in a National Bureau of Economic Research (1943) study, which emphasized the paucity of relevant data and the consequent impossibility of arriving at conclusions at that time. That study also gave thought to the problems faced by an investigation of the advertising-sales relationship, and emphasized that data of various types — time-series, cross-sectional, and others — would be needed in order to arrive at satisfactory conclusions. In fact, although there is an enormous amount of published data and discussion, when considered closely most or all of the literature either proves unsatisfactory in method or does not bear directly upon the problem. This chapter considers only that small fraction of the literature that promises to provide some reasonably valid clues. (The reader should also be forewarned that the author began this study with the hypothesis that increasing returns do not exist in advertising, and this preconception could have biased the choice of literature to cite.)

First, studies of the advertising-sales relationship in various industries will be surveyed. Then aggregate advertising-sales cross-sectional investigations will be mentioned briefly. Next, various sorts of studies using psychological proxies for sales will be surveyed, including evidence from studies of various sizes of advertisements and various amounts of repetition. Last, a recent extensive experimental study will be examined in some detail.

SURVEY OF THE EVIDENCE FROM SALES

Proprietary Drugs

Roberts (1947) measured the effect of varying numbers of advertisement-carrying magazines upon the individual drug purchases of a cross section of consumers. He related the number of advertisement-bearing issues received by individual members of a national panel to their recorded purchases, holding constant the effect of important demographic variables.

Roberts found that "the resulting curve shows plainly the effect of diminishing returns," (p. 142) at all points on the curve. However, the number of magazine exposures is not a perfect index of a firm's expenditures, and Roberts' techniques had other unfortunate but unavoidable loopholes, especially the absence of a measure of prior sales.

Palda (1964) investigated the advertising-sales relationship for Lydia Pinkham's Vegetable Compound from 1908 to 1960. He fitted many regressions, lagged and nonlagged, to the data, and found that a distributed-lag model with the logarithm of advertising as an independent variable gave the best predictions. This result "tends to confirm the operation of decreasing returns to a variable factor."

Lydia Pinkham is a very small advertiser compared to the giants in the proprietary drug industry. This fact makes Palda's finding particularly useful for our purposes here.

Cigarettes

Telser (1962b) thoroughly investigated the relation of sales to advertising for the three largest cigarette brands before World War II. He took into account the lagged effects of advertising, and fitted regressions to the advertising-sales relationship. He found that "the regression estimates . . . support the hypothesis that the advertising outlays were large enough to place the firms in the region of decreasing marginal effectiveness of advertising" (pp. 479–80).

Telser's conclusion is interesting more as a confirmation than as a discovery, however; one would hardly expect the largest advertisers to stop advertising at a point of increasing returns, if such a point exists. Nor does this finding about the largest brands tell us whether they are operating at a lower per-unit cost than is possible at greatly lower levels of advertising expenditure.

Liquor-Brand Advertising Expenditures

In a distributed-lags regression analysis of liquor-brand advertising (1969a), this writer found that a logarithmic transformation of the advertising variable produced the best fit to the observations, which implies diminishing returns. This agrees with the findings of Telser in cigarettes and Palda for Lydia Pinkham tonic, whose methods this study followed in many respects. Furthermore, there were found to be higher advertising coefficients for the smaller advertisers than for the larger advertisers, which also suggests no increasing returns.

Whisky

A national advertiser should spend, say, $100,000 to advertise one brand rather than $50,000 on advertising for each of two brands if there are increasing returns over that range of expenditures. And if the advertiser is acting correctly, the smallest expenditure spent to advertise one brand of a multibrand firm is at least large enough so that returns are diminishing at that point.

Liquor distributors commonly market several brands of each type of distilled spirits, however. Here are the brands of just one type of liquor, blended whisky, sold by just one firm, Schenley, and the prices of a fifth of each in New York City in 1962:

B.P.R. Reserve 86°	$3.88
Wilken Family 86°	3.96
Gibson's Diamond 8 86°	3.99

V.S.R. 3 Feathers 86°	4.29
Cream of Kentucky 80°	4.30
Golden Wedding 86°	4.30
Park & Tilford Carriage	4.33
Schenley Reserve 86°	4.79
Sir John by Schenley 86°	5.40

Schenley also markets several other brands of blended whiskies in other states. And of course Schenley also markets dozens of brands of rye, bourbon, gin, vodka, bonded whiskey, and other distilled beverages.

This proliferation of brands cannot be explained by objective differences in the products themselves. All available evidence indicates that consumers cannot distinguish blends when taken straight. And even professional tasters cannot distinguish between brands when taken as mixed drinks.

Nor does price lining explain the multitude of brands. Notice that there are several brands at each of several price levels.

By the logic given above, this evidence suggests that if there are any increasing returns in advertising whiskies, they must be present only at very low expenditure levels.

Fluid Milk

The American Dairy Association (in cooperation with the Department of Agriculture) ran a well-controlled experiment on the effect of several levels of promotional expenditure upon fluid milk sales (Clement et al., 1965). The base expenditure level was two cents per capita per year, the present normal level. The experimental treatments were 15 cents and 30 cents per capita. The 15-cent expenditure (13 cents above the base level) raised sales 4.5 percent above the base sales level, and the 30-cent expenditure (28 cents above base) raised sales 5.9 percent over base. Therefore the incremental effect of the 15-cent level is $\frac{.045}{\$.13} = .034$, much higher than the incremental effect of the 30-cent level, $\frac{.059 - .045}{\$.28 - \$.13} = .009$. Over the range of this experiment there are diminishing marginal returns.

An Industrial Product

Weinberg (1960a) analyzed the records of an unidentified industrial-goods manufacturer. Applying a time-series method to market-share and advertising-share data, he found that within the range of the firm's manufacturing capacity (which was between 14 and 22 percent of industry capacity) advertising-response efficiency declined logarithmically as a function of advertising expenditure. This is evidence against increasing returns.

Cross Section of Retailers

Mitchell (1941) surveyed 13,000 retailers and found that for all types of stores, holding size of city constant, the larger stores had higher ratios of advertising to sales. This evidence goes to the more general question of advertising-related economies of scale rather than marginal returns, because it is surely true that even if stores are larger because they advertise more, stores also advertise more because they are larger. However, if one makes the heroic assumption that the returns to all other retail-store factors of production are constant or increasing, these data can be used for inferences about returns to advertising. If this assumption is reasonable, and if one could assume *ceteris paribus* for the size classes, Mitchell's data imply that there are no increasing returns. However, the reasons why smaller or larger stores might advertise more or less are so many that it is not reasonable to assume *ceteris paribus*, and hence no strong conclusion should be drawn from these data.

Cross Section of Industrial Advertisers

Kolliner (1963) surveyed 900 industrial advertisers who sold materials, equipment, and supplies, and whose sales volume ranged from under $1 million to over $25 million. Kolliner's data show an inverse relationship between "advertising as a percent of sales expense" and "sales expense as a percent of sales." This relationship seems to hold for firms of several different sizes.

On the face of it, Kolliner's study implies economies of scale. However, his variables do not correspond well to the appropriate model, i.e., advertising as independent variable and sales as dependent variable, in addition to the lack of *ceteris paribus* in such cross-sectional comparisons.

General Cross-Sectional Studies

The relationship between size-class of firm and proportion of sales revenue spent for advertising was investigated for 109 industries, a 50 percent sample of U.S. three-digit industries, by Simon and Crain (see Appendix B). The results were thoroughly mixed, the relationship being positive in half the industries and negative in the others. This might indicate either that economies of scale are present in some industries and not in others, *or* that cross-sectional data by size-class are not capable of throwing light on the problem, especially advertising-sales ratio data. The latter is more likely, we judged.

Mail-Order Studies

Mail-order data are as nearly perfect as economic data can be. The relationship between advertising and sales is completely measurable. No links in the logical relationship need to be estimated with judgment, as is the case, say, when one uses readership data to gauge the ultimate sales payoff. And in the mail-order business there are no other merchandising efforts that work jointly with advertising, as is the case with dealer-sold products, and which may obscure the effect of advertising.

The mail-order distribution system is dissimilar in many important respects from other marketing systems, however, and the concept of marginal returns is somewhat different for mail order than for consumer advertising.[3] For general advertising, a larger expenditure usually means more of the same — more repetitions of the message in the same media, and perhaps larger advertisements. For mail order, a larger expenditure's main effect is to enlarge the media schedule with more magazines and mailing lists. And in mail order, unlike general advertising, it is possible to make a very accurate ladder of advertising-media opportunities from best to worst. The response function, therefore, is a function of successively poorer media opportunities, as well as of increased repetition and increased size of advertisement.

Just after the turn of the century, W. A. Shryer was the proprietor of a mail-order correspondence course in managing a collection-and-credit service, and he was also an advertising "counselor." In a book (1912) that was probably the first quantitative study of advertising, Shryer discussed the "cumulative advertising effect" theory put forth by the magazine-advertising-space salesmen. The space salesman's argument was (and still is) that an advertiser must advertise constantly until, like the rock that is finally split by successive drops of water, sales rise greatly. The underlying logical model of "cumulative advertising effect" is that two advertisements have more than twice the effect of a single advertisement.

Shryer adduced the results of literally thousands of keyed advertisements to prove, conclusively, that: "The first insertion of a tried piece of copy in a new medium will pay better, in every way, than any subsequent insertion of the same copy in the same magazine" (1912, p. 347). In other words, returns decrease with repetition. Shryer exhibited data on the results from repeated ads for a magazine-subscription campaign in which the average cost per inquiry from the first ad in a pair

---

[3] It may be very important that mail-order sales do not require store distribution. A larger non–mail-order advertiser could have an advantage even if his advertising produces less consumer response per dollar if stores simply choose to stock the biggest-selling brands. In this way absolute size of advertising expenditures could wipe out the greater efficiency of smaller advertisers' advertising. In other words, store stocking may institute a real threshold effect. See Chapter 9 for a fuller discussion of this issue.

was $.85, compared to a cost of $1.91 from the second insertion. (See Table 1-1, which also includes data on some advertisements that were not repeated. Also, a small part of the effect in this table may have been seasonal.) More comprehensive data than these (Table 1-1) have not been published since then, to my knowledge.

Table 1-1. Repeated Mail-Order Advertisement Results

Date Run	Medium	Cost of Advertisement	Number of Orders	Cost per Order
March	Technical World	$ 40.00	51	$0.79
April	Technical World	40.00	20	2.00
Feb. 19	Saturday Evening Post	250.00	338	.79
March 6	Saturday Evening Post	250.00	181	1.38
March	Circle	30.00	10	3.00
April	Circle	30.00	3	10.00
Feb. 19	Literary Digest	45.00	58	.77
March 19	Literary Digest	62.50	35	1.79
Feb. 3	Chicago Journal	12.00	17	.71
March 3	Chicago Journal	27.00	13	2.08
Feb. 6	Chicago Examiner	90.00	258	.35
Feb. 27	Chicago Examiner	90.00	94	.95
March 6	Chicago Examiner	90.00	57	1.58
March 13	Chicago Examiner	90.00	25	3.60
Feb. 6	New York American	112.50	131	.86
March 6	New York American	112.50	71	1.58
Feb. 13	Chicago Inter Ocean	15.00	20	.75
March 6	Chicago Inter Ocean	33.75	29	1.16
Feb. 15	New York Journal	49.00	62	.79
March 8	New York Journal	112.50	53	2.12
Feb. 27	San Francisco Examiner	30.00	67	.45
March 20	San Francisco Examiner	42.50	9	4.71
Feb. 27	Minneapolis Journal	11.00	21	.52
March 13	Minneapolis Journal	24.75	2	12.37
March 27	Minneapolis Journal	24.75	1	24.75
Feb. 27	Philadelphia Times	12.00	22	.55
March 20	Philadelphia Times	27.00	3	9.00
Feb. 27	Los Angeles Examiner	10.00	16	.62
March 13	Los Angeles Examiner	22.50	11	2.22
Feb. 27	Chicago Tribune	30.00	72	.42
March 20	Chicago Tribune	67.50	9	7.50
Feb. 27	Boston Post	20.00	32	.63
March 13	Boston Post	45.00	7	6.43
Feb. 20	St. Louis Post-Dispatch	20.00	38	.53
March 13	St. Louis Post-Dispatch	45.00	26	1.73
Feb. 20	Cincinnati Enquirer	18.00	24	.75
March 20	Cincinnati Enquirer	40.50	8	5.06

Results from a campaign for a "popular publication" to sell subscriptions.
Source: Shryer 1912, pp. 82-83.

Virtually all published mail-order data corroborate Shryer's finding. Schwab (1950) estimated that a second (full-page) insertion within 30 to 90 days will pull 70 to 75 percent as much as the original advertisement. The third insertion within a short time will pull only 45 to 50 percent as much.

Shryer also found that smaller advertisements produce more returns per dollar spent for advertising than do larger advertisements (see Table 1–2). This finding is corroborated by other published accounts, with some few exceptions discussed below. Studies reported by Rudolph (1936) indicate that half-page advertisements pull about 70 percent as many returns as full pages.

Table 1-2. Cost per Inquiry, by Size of Advertisement

Five-line classified	$ .30
Seven-line display	.53
16-line display	.70
56-line display	.76
Half-page display	.92

Source: Shryer, 1912, pp. 171-175.

There are large and predictable differences in profitability among the media available to advertise any given mail-order product. Direct-mail mail-order firms have an especially sharp gradient in advertising-media opportunities available to them. The "house list" always "outpulls" any rented list by a large margin, for example. (The National Research Bureau, which sells business letters and business information, told about a campaign in which the response for the house list was 14 percent, while for the most profitable outside lists response was a maximum of 4 percent [Stone, 1955].) The direct-mail practice of testing small samples of large lists before the full mailing also makes it possible to rank the opportunities into a ladder with high discrimination. Such a ladder of opportunities is equivalent to an operational advertising-response function that is perceived by the firm as having monotonically diminishing returns to added advertising investments.

EVIDENCE FROM NON-SALES DATA

Most studies of the effect of advertising employ non-sales measures of behavior as proxies for sales. These non-sales measures may or may not be good indicators of sales, and they provide no way to estimate the total dollars of sales that the advertisement produces. Despite these defects we shall examine the best of these data for the light they may shed on the shape of advertising-response functions. (For a thoughtful and exhaustive analysis of this literature, see Copland [1958].)

Size of Advertisements

Three pieces of evidence on the effectiveness of various sizes of advertisements in magazines are as follows: (1) *Coupon tests* of magazine advertisements follow the mail-order pattern: a half page produces about 70 percent as many coupon inquiries as does a full page (Starch, 1959a). (2) Rudolph (1936) showed that the readership score for a half page is 55 to 60 percent as high as that of a full-page advertisement. (3) In a dummy magazine experiment, Strong (1914) found that recall did not increase proportionately to the increase in size. The relative recall value for a quarter page was 1.0, a half page 1.5, and a full page 2.2. Similar results were found for advertisements that were shown twice and four times at monthly intervals.

Television commercials were studied by Schwerin (Hoffman, 1963, p. 70), and showed the following results, using the 60-second commercial as a standard:

	60-second commercials	*20-second commercials*
Effectiveness	100	83
Brand name recall	100	92
Sales point recall	100	71

Capitman also found that on many different measures efficiency per second decreases from 20 to 40 to 60 seconds (*Media/Scope*, October, 1964, pp. 64–65).

In a laboratory experiment Wheatley (1968) compared 30-second and 60-second commercials for a food product. The results were as follows, clearly indicating diminishing returns:

Audience Response to Test Commercials

Criteria	*30-Second Commercial in Clutter Position*	*60-Second Commercial in Clutter Position*	*60-Second Commercial in Island Position*
Adjective check list score	23.08	31.12	28.61
Brand identification	78.48	79.59	85.25
Mean number of sales points recalled	1.08	1.24	1.30
Product desire score	3.43	3.47	3.53
Pre-post attitude change score	9.90	12.83	13.23
Sample size	79	49	61

Source: Wheatley, 1968, p. 200.

In the other direction, however, Schwerin's lottery-choice method showed the highest "competitive preference change" per second for commercials of 11 to 29 seconds. Commercials of 10 seconds or less in length did worse by this measure than the 11 to 29–second commercials (the sample size is unknown), a fact which can be interpreted as evidence of increasing returns. However, commercials so short are not even considered to be real alternatives by advertisers, and are not included in any other tests. Apparently the 20-second commercial is relatively much more effective than the one-minute commercial. The dollar efficiency must also be greater, despite the stiff discounts for the larger time unit. Furthermore, three 20-second commercials will be seen by a much greater unduplicated audience than a single one-minute commercial.

To summarize, none of the cited studies shows any strong evidence of increasing returns with increased size of advertisement.

Repetition of Advertisements

Starch (1959d) and Britt (1956) have each reported that "noted" scores remain about the same for repeated advertisements. However, neither researcher used any device to adjust downward for readers who really saw the advertisement the first time it appeared but who said they saw it in the second issue, a confusion which is very likely to occur frequently. Therefore it seems likely that the reported results really indicate a drop-off in scores rather than the lack of drop-off which those writers concluded they had found.

Politz (1960) investigated the effect of repeated advertising-page exposure upon "brand familiarity," "brand claim familiarity," and "willingness to buy." On a Monday an interviewer hand-delivered a magazine containing four advertisements, and asked respondents for editorial criticism of articles. On Wednesday the interviewer again delivered an identical issue containing the original four advertisements, plus four new ones. At that time subjects were asked to reread the issue. On Friday they were tested on recall. Results: the repeated advertisements did almost twice as well on two measurement dimensions, and did more than twice as well on the other two, the latter apparently indicating increasing returns.

The four new (nonrepeated) advertisements had the benefit of less forgetting time. But the repeated advertisements had the advantage of being exposed in the first reading of the issue, as well as in the second reading. This could have constituted an enormous advantage, indeed, and might well account for the observed effect. A replication of this experiment that splits the nonrepeated advertisement between the first and second readings, and controls for forgetting by testing one group for recall after only a single magazine exposure, would be very valuable.

A Politz survey for *Look* (1964) found that incremental "message registration" decreases with number of magazine advertisements. For an average set of advertisements, the first insertion produced an increment of 3.7 million readers, the second insertion produced an increment of 3.2 million readers (6.9 — 3.7), the third produced 2.6(9.5 — 6.9), the fourth produced 2.1 (11.6 — 9.5). The comparison of the various insertions is biased somewhat because some forgetting surely took place between the monthly insertions, but there is no way to assess the size of the bias. Politz also shows similar effects with a recall measurement over 13 insertions. But again the extent of decay bias is unknown.

In still another study (1965) Politz showed that for "Familiarity with Product," "Rating of Product Quality," and "Susceptibility to Prescribe Product," six insertions for prescription drugs in *Modern Medicine*, a magazine sent only to doctors, produced less incremental effect than did three insertions. It is reasonable to expect that decay bias should not be important on such variables as these. Both this and the 1964 study suggest no increasing returns with the repetition of advertisements, subject to the forgetting bias and assuming that incremental frequency discounts are not as great as the incremental decrease in efficiency.

Starch (1959b) provided massive evidence that the rate of coupon returns drops off with the repetition of print advertisements. The relative rate for the first advertisement was 100, the second 76, the third 63.

Zielske (1959) mailed 1 to 13 advertisements, at weekly or monthly intervals, to women who were tested on recall of the advertising after the last advertisement had arrived. For advertisements mailed monthly, there appear to be increasing returns over the range of the first few advertisements, using reader-memory-weeks as an index.

Zielske's study is ingenious and persuasive. It has the very great virtue of measuring the total effect of each advertisement over time, by summing the strength of the advertising impression over time until the impression has disappeared. This is unlike most studies of advertising impression which measure the effect of an advertisement at a single point in time, without taking into account the subsequent changes in the advertising impression. There are, however, reservations about Zielske's conclusion about increasing returns that stem from small sample sizes for the individual group, a somewhat peculiar mode of bringing the advertisement to the attention of the audience, and a first exposure to all advertisements in the same week, a week which could have been particularly poor for seasonal reasons.

Adams (1916, pp. 229, 230, 235) prepared a dummy magazine in which a given advertisement appeared once, twice, or four times. After exposure he tested for memory, obtaining these results:

Number of Times Different Advertisements for Brand Appeared

	Once	*Twice*	*Four times*
Quarter page	1.0	1.6	2.8
Half page	1.0	1.2	2.6
Full page	1.0	1.7	2.3

When Adams varied the ads for the same brands, rather than repeating them identically, the value of the repeated appearances increased dramatically:

Number of Times Different Advertisements for Brand Appeared

	Once	*Twice*	*Four times*
Quarter page	1.0	2.9	5.3
Half page	1.0	2.7	3.7
Full page	1.0	2.3	3.2

Though Adams' experiments are old and apply only to print media, they remain the soundest experimental research that has been done until now. Laboratory evidence of this type suffers from the limitation that subjects are in an unnatural, forced-exposure situation. On the other hand, laboratory experiments benefit from having the situation almost completely controlled, and thus presumably are not confounded by extraneous factors.

To summarize this section, studies of repetition using non-sales measures of advertising response — except for one dimension of Politz's study — show a lack of increasing returns. And Politz's method was probably biased strongly in favor of the repeated advertisements.

The Response Function in New Food Products[4]

Stewart (1964) recently published the results of by far the largest controlled study of advertising effects that has yet been reported:

Perhaps the most important finding from the study was that it did require substantial repetition to achieve efficient purchase results. In contrast to the rapid rise in brand awareness, there was a time lag before the awareness transformed into purchase behavior. For instance, the lowest advertising costs per "extra" purchases did not occur until the fifteenth consecutive weekly advertisement had appeared. Thus, under the conditions of this particular test, a short campaign of only three or four insertions

---

[4] I appreciate helpful communication with Professor John B. Stewart in the preparation of this section.

was quite inefficient, while sustained repetition increased the efficiency of the expenditures [1964, abstract].

Because the continual exposure made good use of the favorable state of awareness achieved by the first four exposures, the cost per extra trier (of Chicken Sara Lee) was lowest where advertising was continued and highest where it was stopped quickly [1964, p. 293].

These results are the most weighty reported evidence *for* increasing returns in advertising. Therefore, it is worthwhile to examine this report in some detail.

The design of the study follows Zielske's design. A schedule of 0, 4, 8, and 20 consecutive weekly newspaper insertions for each of two new products — Chicken Sara Lee and Lestare, a dry bleach — went into matched quarters of Fort Wayne. Six thousand personal interviews evaluated the advertising impact of the different exposure schedules. New samples were drawn from each market area without replacement during successive interviewing periods, so that the total effect of the advertising could be measured over time, in a unit such as "percent-a-ware-days" (PAD). Such a concept is appropriate and useful, unlike measures of impact at a single point in time. (Analogously, if one wants to estimate the cost of winter heating, knowledge of the temperature on the coldest day in the winter, or on an arbitrarily chosen date, will not help much. What one wants is a measure like "degree-days.")

Stewart measured advertising effect on several different dimensions, including awareness (aided recall), product knowledge, attitudes, and purchases. In this and in other ways the study was well thought out and apparently carefully executed. However, though the matched-areas design may have been a wise tactical choice, it has the very important drawback that all comparisons are subject to question about whether the result is a true change in the dependent variable or reflects an imperfection in area matching. For Lestare, for example, Stewart found that "In the long run (22 weeks) the effects created by four exposures resulted in a poorer state than would have existed with no advertising at all" (1964, p. 284). Unlike Stewart, I believe that this result is probably an artifact of the matching, or a random result of small sample size, rather than a true finding about the nature of advertising effects. This would cast doubt on the sample matching. But because the samples were matched, no statistical test can help us judge between these explanations.

The relevant question here is whether Stewart's main conclusion — that increased repetition results in increased returns — follows from his data, and that we shall now consider.

There were eight relevant comparisons — four types of measurements for each of two products. In four of the comparisons — those for product knowledge and attitude toward the brand for each of the two brands — the evidence is very strongly against an increase in efficiency with repetition, i.e., against increasing returns. On brand awareness, the evidence from Chicken Sara Lee is against increased efficiency, but Stewart interprets the data for Lestare as showing increased efficiency. On purchasing, the Lestare data showed nothing, but Stewart interprets the Chicken Sara Lee evidence as showing increasing efficiency. The Lestare-awareness and Chicken Sara Lee–purchase evidence, which constitute the only possible support for Stewart's conclusion, will now be discussed separately in some detail.[5]

Lestare Brand Awareness

Up to week 22, by Stewart's method, the number of PAD above the no-exposure group was 220 and 519 for the four-exposure and eight-exposure groups, respectively (1964, p. 125). Taken at face value, these figures indicate a tiny advantage in efficiency for the eight-exposure group. But the PAD are apparently computed from smoothed envelope curves, and deductions of PAD are made where the no-exposure group apparently had higher awareness than the four- and eight-exposure groups. Without these deductions, the four-exposure group would show a slight advantage.

A more serious defect is the shapes of the curves. The four-exposure and eight-exposure curves are drawn convex downwards and upwards respectively, without theoretical justification. At termination, therefore, the four-exposure curve is increasing while the eight-exposure curve is decreasing, and any extrapolation would show an enormous advantage for the four-exposure group, and no increasing returns. These data are certainly too flimsy, and the method of interpretation too arbitrary, to support any belief in increasing returns.

Chicken Sara Lee Purchasing

Table 1-3 shows the data for the number of people in each sample who said they had purchased Chicken Sara Lee once or more, up to the time of interview.

There is no completely satisfactory way to summarize these data, but the table below seems not unreasonable:

1. Number-of-exposures group	0	4	8	20
2. Purchasers	7	16	28	35
3. Sample size	1315	1406	1896	1903

[5] Comparisons for the 20-exposure group will not be made because interviewing ceased after 22 weeks, a considerable handicap for the 20-exposure data.

4. Purchasers per capita (2) ÷ 3	.0053	.0114	.0148	.0184
5. Marginal purchasers per capita per incremental exposure (successive differences from row (4), divided by successive differences from row (1).		.0015	.0008	.0003
6. Efficiency = (4) ÷ (1)		.0028	.0018	.0009

The results in rows 4 and 5 show that four exposures are more efficient than eight exposures, though the samples are ludicrously small in terms of the number of purchasers (row 2).

Table 1-3. Chicken Sara Lee Experimental Data

Interview week	Group(s) by number of exposures	Sample size	Purchasers
1	0	124	0
2	4, 8, 20	324	1
3	0	236	0
4	4, 8, 20	327	4
5	0	243	1
6	4	259	2
7	0	121	1
8	8, 20	565	9
9	0	128	1
10	8	231	6
11	4	223	4
12	20	234	7
13	0	132	1
14	0		
15	8	252	3
16	20	224	8
17	0	133	2
18			
19	8	197	5
20	20	229	6
21	0	198	1
22	4	274	5

Source: Stewart, 1964, ˈp. 260.

It seems to me, then, that on balance Stewart's data are strong evidence against increased returns rather than for it. The two of the eight comparisons that Stewart interpreted as showing increasing returns show no such thing (as re-analyzed above), and six of the eight were unquestionably against increasing efficiency with repetition (as Stewart's text notes).

CONCLUSIONS

There is not one single piece of strong evidence to support the general belief that increasing returns exist in advertising. A very few studies suggest that there are increasing returns, but their evidence is weak. Individually, the items of evidence against increasing returns are also weak, except for mail-order tests. But there are a great many studies that show diminishing marginal returns, and I feel their collective weight is much greater than that of the evidence supporting increasing returns.

Both sales and psychological studies suggest that the shape of the advertising-response function is invariably concave downward, i.e., that there are no S-curve and no increasing returns in advertising a given product by a given firm. By my reading of the evidence the efficiency of advertising expenditures always decreases, even at the lowest levels, with increased repetition and with increased size of advertisements (though total profits may continue to rise, of course). Furthermore, there is no published case where bulk discounts made larger expenditures increasingly efficient.

Mail-order data are conclusive against increasing returns, but mail order is a specialized form of marketing.

Increasing returns might be present in some situations though not in others, and the possibility in any given situation will always exist no matter what the weight of evidence for or against. But as the evidence mounts up the possibility becomes increasingly remote.

Threshold effects and increasing returns to repetition and size constitute a monstrous myth, I believe, but a myth so well entrenched that it is almost impossible to shake.

Perhaps the best test for increasing returns would be controlled advertising experiments beaming the same advertising in different quantities to samples of several geographical test areas. If increasing returns really exist, they would show up clearly in such investigations. An even more promising approach selectively blacks out television commercials or magazine advertisements (Towers et al., 1962). However, sound conclusions on this subject will require a considerable mass of good data, collected in several ways and developed from different product situations. Even as massive an attack as that mounted by Stewart does not necessarily yield sufficient data for reasonable conclusions.

Even if there are not increasing returns for individual brands, they may exist for firms that advertise several products. The most important economies may stem from using common brand names for several products, obtaining bulk discounts from multiproduct advertising expenditures, achieving good store distribution, and acquiring advertising know-how. These and related matters are discussed in Chapter 9.

2

The Influence
of Demand Dimensions
upon Advertising
Expenditures

INTRODUCTION

Kaldor stated that the two most interesting issues in the economics of advertising are (1) the effect of advertising on the general welfare, and (2) an explanation of why advertising is done in the various amounts in which it is done (Kaldor, 1950, p. 1). Kaldor tackled the first of these issues, though he did not exhaust the subject. The second issue has received little attention, theoretically or empirically, despite the fact that the "function" of advertising and other promotion in our society is a favorite question of social commentators, and also of such economists as Marshall, Knight, Stigler, and Bain. And upon examination of the elusive concept of "function" the most likely empirical approach to it turns out to be an inquiry into the causal conditions under which there is more and less promotion.

Let us begin with a brief review of relevant literature. Chamberlin (editions from 1933 to 1962) worked out the theory of the equilibrium amount of promotion, taking into account the shape of the production function, variation in the product, and number and behavior of rivals. But it is difficult to derive from his analysis any statements that can be tested empirically.

Telser has discussed the matter in a series of papers (1961, 1964, 1966, 1968). Taking the question to be the differences in the ratio of advertising to sales among different products, Telser couched his explanation primarily in terms of the price elasticity of the demand curve faced by the sellers, plus the market size, the number of sellers, and the supposed product differentiation. Telser's analysis does seem successful for some products, but he notes that there are many types of products for which the amount of advertising done cannot easily be explained in this way.

Telser took a theorem by Dorfman and Steiner (1954) as his point of departure. That theorem states that at the point of optimization the price elasticity will be equal to the marginal value product of advertising. Telser's extension of this analysis leads to the prediction "that heavily advertised products should exhibit lower price elasticities than little advertised products" (Telser, 1961, p. 198).[1]

Bain examined the ratio of advertising to sales for various industries, relative to the number of firms, the structure of competition, and degree of product differentiation. He concluded that the amount of advertising is positively correlated with degree of product differentiation and extent of barriers to entry (Bain, 1959).

In his massive study of advertising in several industries, Borden (1942) examined in great detail the reasons for the amounts of advertising done by various firms in the various industries. Though Borden did hazard some general statements, his most general conclusion is that there is immense variation within industries as to amounts of advertising by various firms, and that this variation can only be explained by a multitude of complex factors and the interaction among them. This detailed institutional study seems to me to have enormous merit, not only for the factual knowledge that it provides, but also for emphasizing the complexity even at the cost of reducing generalizations and theory. But Borden's study does not provide many useful predictive statements.

This chapter and the following two consider the effect of the individual variables that influence the amount of promotion. This chapter discusses the effects of various demand variables. Chapter 3 discusses cost and cost-structure variables. And Chapter 4 studies the effect of competition: market structure, numbers of competitors, and competitive product variation.

These chapters differ from previous work in several ways:

1. Instead of attempting to explain absolute levels of advertising (promotion) for a product or firm, or the absolute size of its advertising-sales ratio, explanation of only changes or differences in those variables is attempted.[2] This departs from almost everything that has been

---

[1] I do not find this conclusion persuasive because Telser intends his price elasticity only to be that at the equilibrium price-maximizing point. I think, however, that the shape of the function at other points is also relevant, and I think that this is also implicit in Telser's analysis. But clarification of this matter would require a long argument.

[2] "Instead of giving a complete explanation of the 'determination' of output, prices, and employment by the firm, marginal analysis really intends to explain the effects which certain *changes* in conditions may have upon the action of the firm" (Machlup, 1963, p. 150).

said on the subject since at least the turn of the century, when Sherman discussed the topic with considerable wisdom and in terms that sound quite contemporary (Sherman, 1900). Telser's recent work (1961, 1965, 1968) has carried this tradition furthest. I believe it is crucial to shift the examination away from the amount of advertising for particular products and toward the study of changes in various other variables, holding product constant. The central difficulty in making a valid interproduct analysis is that *ceteris paribus* conditions are violated on every hand. For example, differences in the number of sellers, price elasticity (if it can be estimated), and size of market do not even scratch the surface of the differences between fresh potatoes and canned potatoes; among pasteurized milk, evaporated milk, and powdered milk; and between any kind of milk and distilled liquor, etc. It is hoped, however, that the kind of analysis that we shall attempt here will provide help for later *ceteris paribus* analyses of interproduct differences.

2. Elasticity of demand with respect to price is not used as an independent variable because it is several levels too abstract and aggregated for the purposes here. For example, the price elasticity for a product is affected not only by the sensitivity of given individuals to price differences, but also by changes in the number of individuals in the market. Several of the lower-level components that make up the price elasticity will figure importantly in the analysis, however.

3. Purely economic variables are used as much as possible, avoiding psychological variables such as "prestige," "conspicuous consumption," and "glamor," which Bain uses for example, or statements such as "These products serve delicate needs and consumers are often firmly attached to particular brands to avoid risking health or beauty on untried alternatives" (Telser, 1961, p. 199). In particular, the frequently used concept of product differentiation is not used here. This is because on close inspection the notion turns out to be logically meaningless, a discovery that came out of the attempt to use the concept in the work of this group of chapters. This argument is given at length in Appendix A.

4. Instead of restricting the discussion to advertising as the dependent variable, wherever possible the subject is the more inclusive concept: promotion. "Promotion" here means aggressive contact by a seller that is initiated with the intent to sell goods. This concept obviously includes all advertising. It also includes most of what salesmen do (though some kinds of services performed by some salesmen, e.g. store clerks, are not promotion), window display, publicity, and the display of goods so that potential customers can examine them, including trade fairs. The promotion concept does not include product-quality changes or price changes. The product, with its given quality and at a

given price, is taken as fixed in this discussion, just as it is in the majority of promotional decisions that are made by firms. The discussion also excludes mechanical servicing, delivery, credit, and other marketing functions. We focus on the work done by the seller and not on the work of obtaining market information that is done by buyers, even though the latter is often a relevant consideration.

The reasons for treating all promotion together are as follows. There is a high cross-elasticity of substitution among the various activities included here under promotion. For example, an increase in the cost of traveling salesmen may cause a large shift of expenditures from the sales force to advertising. Furthermore, there is a low cross-elasticity of substitution between any of these activities and other marketing activities, with the occasional exception of price changes and quality changes, including consumer services.[3] And unlike other marketing functions, the cost of promotion does not depend upon the number of units sold as does transportation, for example, which may be treated in exactly the same way as a production cost.

Conceptually this study resembles studies in industrial organization, whose underlying assumption is, as Bain summarizes Mason, "that there may be a determinate association between objectively ascertainable characteristics of market structure and price results. Accordingly [Mason] advanced the hypothesis that the objective market situation is primarily determining, in the sense that different individuals placed in the same situation would make price policy decisions in approximately the same way" (Bain, 1948, p. 156). Many studies have used prices as data, but remarkably few have used advertising or promotion expenditures as data, despite the fact that changes in both quantities affect consumption, and despite the substitutability of price changes and promotion under some (but only some) conditions. One cannot justify the present neglect of this question on the grounds of triviality. I would guess that the outlay for promotional effort in the United States was about $51 billion in 1967 ($17 billion for advertising), though the sum is very hard to estimate. This estimate includes only those items that are included in our definition of promotion above, and does not include the huge items for inside-the-store nonpromotional sales clerks, transportation, and warehousing.[4]

---

[3] Telser expressed much the same idea: ". . . commodities differ much less with respect to the proportion of their price representing the total cost of informing and persuading consumers than with respect to relative advertising expenditures. . . . Thus a more inclusive measure of selling costs would reveal less differences among commodities than a less inclusive measure such as advertising outlays" (1961, p. 1, mimeo).

[4] The amount spent for advertising is reasonably accurate. But the estimates for such items as sales promotion are wildly disparate, e.g., Spratlen estimated

The effects of the independent variables upon the promotional mix, and upon the locus of promotion within the marketing channel, will be discussed only as peripheral issues where the argument seems to be reasonably straightforward and uncomplicated. The effect of some of these and other independent variables upon the form and content of the advertising message is discussed elsewhere (Simon, 1970).

Before beginning the analysis in this chapter and the following two, this assumption needs to be made explicit: at all times the discussion refers to a firm (or to an industry of such firms) whose demand curve is not *both* infinitely elastic *and* unalterably so. That is, the discussion does not apply to firms in perfectly competitive industries in which a firm cannot escape perfect competition by affecting the shape of its demand curve with product variation, advertising, service, location, or any other such device. We shall talk only about firms (or about industries of such firms) whose demand curves now slope or can be made to

---

$2.6 billion for sales promotion in 1958 (in Matthews et al., 1964, p. 337), whereas Robinson estimated $10 billion in 1965 (*Advertising Age*, July 26, 1965). The latter is a sales-promotion executive, however, and in the absence of a published method of estimation, one naturally wonders whether he has a stake in a high estimate.

Premiums of all sorts were estimated at $3.2 billion for 1967, including trading stamps, $739 million, and sales incentives, $600 million (*Advertising Age*, September 23, 1968, p. 50, quoting from *Incentive Marketing Facts*, published by Bill Publications).

Sales work, which is the largest item at issue, is also hard to estimate. Spratlen estimated $15.8 billion for salaries only for 1958 (Spratlen, 1962, quoted by Matthews et al., 1964, p. 337). But for 227 *industrial-product* firms surveyed by McGraw-Hill, the following proportions of sales were spent for relevant categories: salesmen's salaries, commission, travel, and entertainment, 7 percent; advertising and sales promotion, 2.2 percent; salaries and operating expenses of advertising and sales departments, 4.4 percent (*Media/Scope*, September, 1964, p. 24).

Machlup (1962, pp. 384–385) estimated that in 1950, 3.62 percent of the civilian labor force (2.1 million people) were "knowledge-producing sales workers," that is, salesmen other than "hucksters, peddlers, and all persons in retail trade (who) are excluded because they are less specialized in 'sales talk' than in handling the merchandise sold" (p. 383). The estimate was only 2.74 percent for 1959 (1.8 million people) but the estimate for 1959 is less accurate because 1950 was a census year. And Machlup estimates only $5,924 million income for such sales workers in 1950 (p. 391). Brink and Kelley (1963, p. 10) estimated 1.2 million outside salesmen in 1955. They conclude that the most reasonable ratio of total promotion to advertising expenditures is between 3 and 4 to 1 (1963, p. 14). (Their discussion of this matter is excellent.) Borden (1942, Table 106) is relevant but difficult to interpret. The only comprehensive source of industry-by-industry selling costs is in FTC (1944), but no aggregate estimate was given. Hauk (1965, p. 216, quoted in Economists Advisory Group, 1967, p. 18) estimated that advertising was 36 percent of aggregate selling costs in 1958.

All in all, I judge that the most likely ratio of total promotion to advertising expenditures is between 2.5 and 3.5 — say 3 — or $51 billion in 1967.

slope. This implies that entry to the industry not be perfectly easy, due to the need for fixed investment or to some other frictional barrier to entry. In practice this includes almost all manufacturers and retail stores. It excludes mostly farmers and hawkers, and perhaps some wholesalers.

1. Potential Buyers of Product (not Brand) as a Proportion of Geographic Population

Consider an upward shift of the advertising-response function from PP_1 to PP_2 in Figure 2-1, representing an increase in the probability of purchase by a random individual in a given geographic market, price and total population remaining constant. The shift may stem from such an exogeneous change as an improvement in the product (e.g., a lengthening in the lifetime of a patented gadget) or a change in the population's taste for the specific product (e.g., the upsurge in interest in guitar-playing in the mid-1960s). Such a shift not only might raise the response function at all points, but it might well raise it by at least an

FIGURE 2–1. ADVERTISING RESPONSE FUNCTIONS

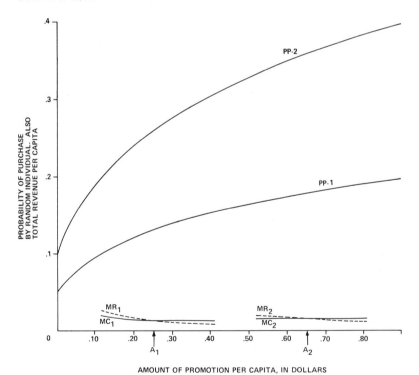

AMOUNT OF PROMOTION PER CAPITA, IN DOLLARS

absolute amount or even proportionally at all levels of promotion. (The illustrative example will be the latter.) [5] The discussion is now from the point of view of the industry as a whole, rather than the point of view of one among several sellers.

Figure 2-1, intended now to represent a monopolized industry, needs some explaining: (a) each point on PP_1 and PP_2 shows the probability of purchase (vertical axis) of a random person at a given level of per capita promotion (horizontal axis); (b) because total revenue (TR) = purchase probability (PP) × price × number of people,[6] and the latter two quantities are constant, the revenue-cost relationships may be drawn in the same diagram with a different scale; and (c) an intersection of marginal cost (MC) with marginal revenue (MR) is an optimum expenditure for advertising.

If PP_1 and PP_2 have shapes as in Figure 2-1, a shift from PP_1 to PP_2 would result in an increase in promotion from A_1 to A_2. This may be seen most clearly in Table 2-1, which includes a linear physical-production function. Table 2-2 shows exactly the same information but converts it from a per capita basis to more familiar aggregate quantities, assuming a community of 1,000 people.

It is not necessarily the case that the promotion level is higher where the purchase probability is greater. Figure 2-2 illustrates a possible case in which an increase in proportion of users from PP_2 to PP_3 might be associated with a decrease in the amount of promotion,[7] assuming the function is that of a monopolist. This might be true of a product the market for which becomes "mature" as preferences and habits concerning the product become fixed, *and* in which "saturation" is at hand (i.e., all potential customers are already actual customers). Or if PP_2 represents a retail service newly entered into a community, especially where the service will be the only one of its kind — say an office-machine store in a small town — the response function might shift from PP_2 to PP_3 as the store becomes established in the community. The shift in slope of the function and the reduction in sensitivity to promotion would then make a lower level of promotion more profitable — say A_3, which is less than A_1.

[5] All the response functions drawn in the figures in this chapter are logarithmic functions, in accord with what I take to be the consensus of the relevant empirical work (e.g., Telser, 1961; Palda, 1964; see Chapter 1 of this book).

[6] This assumes that all purchasers purchase the same quantity, at the same intervals between purchases. This assumption could be dropped at the cost of further complexity.

[7] These functions have the same shapes as those in Figure 2–1. PP_3 is simply a raised PP_1. This means that the MC-MR intersections are at the same levels of advertising as in Figure 2–1.

Table 2-1. Hypothetical Advertising Response Functions for an Individual

1 Amount of Promotion Per Capita	2 Probability of Purchase by Individual	3 Total Revenue Per Capita	4 Production Cost Per Capita	5 Advertising Cost Per Capita	6 Total Cost	7 Net Profit Per Capita	8 Marginal Revenue	9 Marginal Cost
				PP_1				
$.00	$.050	$ .50	$ .20	$.00	$ .20	$ .30	$.50	$.20
.10	.095	.95	.38	.10	.48	.47	.45	.28
.20	.122	1.22	.48	.20	.68	.54	.27	.20
→ .30 *	.140	1.40	.56	.30	.86	.54	.18	.18 ←*
.40	.155	1.55	.62	.40	1.02	.53	.15	.16
.50	.166	1.66	.67	.50	1.17	.49	.11	.15
.60	.176	1.76	.71	.60	1.31	.45	.10	.14
.70	.185	1.85	.74	.70	1.44	.41	.09	.13
.80	.193	1.93	.77	.80	1.57	.36	.08	.13
.90	.200	2.00	.80	.90	1.70	.30	.07	.13
				PP_2				
.00	.100	1.00	.40	.00	.40	.60	1.00	.40
.10	.190	1.90	.76	.10	.86	1.04	.90	.46
.20	.243	2.43	.97	.20	1.17	1.26	.53	.31
.30	.280	2.81	1.12	.30	1.42	1.39	.38	.25
.40	.309	3.10	1.24	.40	1.64	1.46	.29	.22
.50	.333	3.33	1.34	.50	1.84	1.49	.23	.20
.60	.353	3.54	1.41	.60	2.01	1.53	.21	.17
→ .70 *	.371	3.71	1.48	.70	2.18	1.53	.17	.17 ←*
.80	.386	3.86	1.54	.80	2.34	1.52	.15	.16
.90	.400	4.00	1.60	.90	2.50	1.50	.14	.16

*Optimizing Promotion Expenditure

Table 2-2. Hypothetical Advertising Response Functions for a Market

Amount of Promotion	Probability of Purchase by Individual	Total Revenue	Production Cost	Advertising Cost	Total Cost	Net Profit	Marginal Revenue	Marginal Cost
				PP₁				
$000	.050	$500	$200	$000	$200	$300	$500	$200
100	.095	951	380	100	480	471	451	280
200	.122	1220	480	200	680	540	269	200
* → 300	.140	1550	580	300	860	690	330	180 ←*
400	.155	1550	620	400	1020	530	0	160
500	.166	1660	670	500	1170	490	110	150
600	.176	1760	710	600	1310	450	100	140
700	.185	1850	740	700	1440	410	90	130
800	.193	1930	770	800	1570	360	80	130
900	.200	2000	800	900	1700	300	70	130
				PP₂				
000	.100	1000	400	000	400	600	1000	400
100	.190	1903	760	100	860	1040	903	460
200	.243	2431	970	200	1170	1260	528	310
300	.280	2806	1120	300	1420	1380	375	250
400	.309	3097	1240	400	1640	1450	291	220
500	.333	3334	1340	500	1840	1490	237	200
600	.353	3535	1410	600	2010	1525	201	170
* → 700	.371	3709	1480	700	2180	1529	174	170 ←*
800	.386	3862	1540	800	2340	1520	153	160
900	.400	4000	1600	900	2500	1500	138	160

*Optimizing Promotion Expenditure

The first finding, then, is slightly surprising: an upward shift of a monopolist's advertising-response function for a given geographic area has an indeterminate effect on total promotion unless one can specify the shapes of the functions.

FIGURE 2–2. ADVERTISING RESPONSE FUNCTIONS

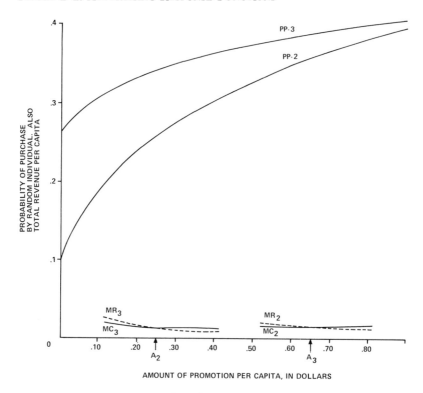

AMOUNT OF PROMOTION PER CAPITA, IN DOLLARS

Now assume that there are several competing firms within the industry, one of which has the first response function of PP_1^F shown in Figure 2-3 which goes along with the corresponding industry function PP_1^I. Consider a shift in the industry's function from PP_1^I to PP_2^I the geometry of which implies an increase in the optimum amount of advertising for the industry (in similar manner to the demonstration in Figure 2-1). There is no reason to think that the same effect will not be reflected downward to the individual firm's advertising amounts. But more: from the geometry of these plausible curves, it is reasonable to think that the firms' functions PP_1^F and PP_2^F are more advertising-elastic than is the industry's function, just as firms' demand functions with respect to price are more elastic than the industry function.[8] If so, an upward shift in the industry function which would dictate a smaller advertising expenditure for a monopolist (as in Figure 2-2) might still

FIGURE 2–3. ADVERTISING RESPONSE FUNCTIONS

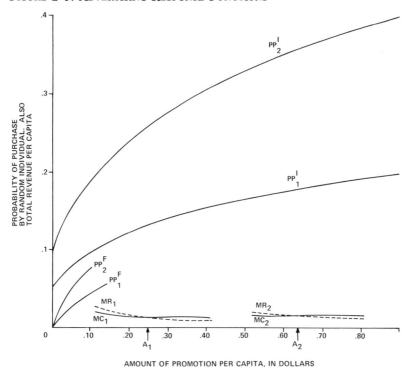

AMOUNT OF PROMOTION PER CAPITA, IN DOLLARS

lead to unchanged or increased expenditures for individual firms in oligopoly or polypoly.

[8] This assumes that other things are equal, especially an unchanged amount of promotion by competitors, as the firm in question considers various promotion levels. (The problem of competitive interaction among firms is discussed in Chapter 4.) The reason the advertising elasticity is greater for the firm with competition is that the prospective buyer is presented with closer (perhaps even perfect) physical substitutes, and hence a given change in advertising should have a greater effect. If the firm in question does no advertising at all while its competitors advertise, it is reasonable to think that its sales will be zero. This is not the case with a product as a whole for which there are no perfect physical substitutes. This reasoning could probably be given in more precise form with indifference curves, showing that a given amount of revolution around a point produces more change in a shallowly convex indifference curve (one where the products are close substitutes) than in a more convex indifference curve, but I do not think that the point is sufficiently in doubt to be worth the effort.

Notice that if a firm sets its advertising budget as a fixed percentage of observed or expected sales,[9] an upward response-curve shift will automatically result in more promotion.

Borden argued that advertising could not and should not be used "against trends," but rather in conjunction with them. We can now formulate a more precise statement of his principle: if the response function for the firm is like PP_1^F as exogenous forces shift the advertising-response function progressively upward, increased advertising will be profitable. (It is necessary to remember, however, that the firm might have a response function that shifts as from PP_2 to PP_3 in Figure 2-3, in which case the upward sales trend should cause less advertising.)

Else (1966) provides some relevant though aggregated evidence. For 33 "inexpensive, nondurable consumer goods of the kind that most households might buy at fairly frequent intervals" (p. 93) he regressed each good's advertising-sales ratio (using checking-service data to estimate advertising expenditures) on the total amount of manufacturer sales of the good, and on the number of firms advertising a brand of the good. The coefficient for amount of manufacturer sales was negative, suggesting that (with number of brands held constant) a larger amount of sales is related to less advertising. (But remember that the measure of advertising used by Else is the tricky advertising-sales ratio; see Appendix B.)

Effect of Consumer-Usage Change in Geographic Markets on the Promotion Mix. Ceteris paribus, the more potential buyers that are within a given geographic area (which is the same thing in this case as a higher probability of purchase by a random individual), the more economical is the operation of a retail outlet. And as retail outlets become more economical there will be more of them and more total promotion by them. Among other effects, more promotion by retailers will lead unequivocally to less price dispersion,[10] because retailers sometimes or often advertise the price of merchandise.

An increase in the number of potential buyers in a geographic area may also lead to increased promotion by the brand-owner. One must then ask whether the increase in retail promotion will be proportionally more or less than the brand-owners' increase. Unless there is reason to

[9] This is not a very rational policy even though it is common. For a better policy see Simon (1965a).

[10] Surprisingly, however, Preston found "that food products are not in general cheaper or even more uniformly priced when 'everyone' is advertising them than at other times, although products are likely to be somewhat lower and more uniform in price when they are repeatedly featured in the most prominent ad positions" (1963, p. 50). But I would interpret Preston's data as being for a system that has had a very long time to converge to equilibrium.

believe that there are comparably large economies for the brand-owner, I would expect the amount of retail promotion to increase relative to brand-owner promotion, and hence, retail promotion would come to be a larger proportion of total promotion as the number of potential buyers increases. Furthermore, retail-advertising budgets are very flexible because retailers have accurate knowledge of the response their advertising gets, and retail budgets must therefore increase quickly as the marginal revenue curve shifts to the right. This suggests that an increased demand in a geographic area will lead to an increase in retail promotion relative to national advertisers who may maintain a constant advertising-sales ratio and adjust more slowly to a change in conditions in any particular market. This jibes with the demand for national advertising being observed to be less price-elastic than the demand for local advertising.[11] The available aggregate data on retailer- and manufacturer-advertising data do not seem to support this speculation, however (see page 190, Chapter 7, postscript). But increased geographic density may have been so slight over the period of the IRS data (1954 to 1964) as to be swamped by other effects.

The most determinate case is that in which the probability of purchase in the earlier period was not sufficient to support a retailer of, say, cameras or sporting goods or scientific equipment. Mail-order firms then fill the needs of customers. In a later period when the probability of purchase is great enough to support a retailer, mail-order promotion into the area will be less.

The proportion of face-to-face selling to total promotion will also change, by a similar argument. The efficiencies of face-to-face selling increase with the density of potential buyers, replacing mail-order selling and reducing the burden on national advertising.

2. Potential Buyers of Product (Distinguished from Brand) as a Proportion of the Audience in a Given Advertising Medium

By the same reasoning as in Section 1 above, an increase in the number of potential buyers in the audience of a given advertising medium will lead to an increased amount of promotion for the product in that medium, if there are multiple noncooperating firms in the industry.

Consider the shift from PP_5 to PP_6 in Figure 2-4. In the latter case given amounts of advertising produce more revenue, and hence there will be an increase in promotion, for each firm and for the industry as a whole.[12] The response function is shown passing through the origin for

---

[11] See Chapter 6 for discussion of this matter.

[12] Again these are the same curves as PP_1 and PP_2, with the same marginal functions and points of intersection. So the optimal amounts of advertising are the same.

two reasons. First, the focus of this section is mostly on the individual firm. Second, and more important, *with respect to sales produced by that medium* the response function certainly does pass through the origin. That is, if one does not advertise in that medium there will certainly be no incremental sales (*ceteris paribus*) from that medium.

It is possible that a high response function in one period may imply a

FIGURE 2–4. ADVERTISING RESPONSE FUNCTIONS

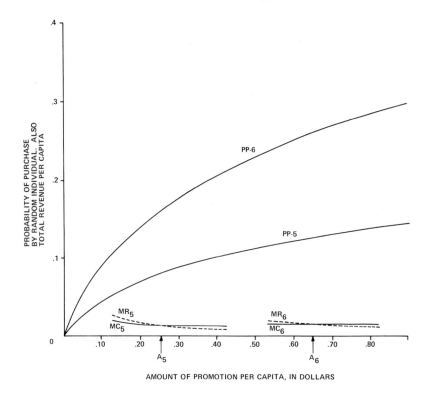

AMOUNT OF PROMOTION PER CAPITA, IN DOLLARS

low response function in the next, i.e., a saturation effect. It may be that *Playboy* is a poorer advertising medium for stereo hi-fi sets (in 1969) than is *Popular Mechanics* because a very large proportion of *Playboy* readers already own stereo hi-fi sets. This suggests only that the observed function in one period is not necessarily an accurate source of evidence for drawing the function for the next period. Repeat-purchase items are not subject to a saturation effect, by their very definition as repeatedly bought goods. But it is possible that a monopolist might face consecutive situation PP_7 and PP_8 as in Figure 2-5 below, for cigarettes, perhaps. If so, the higher response function (PP_8) might imply less advertising. But such a shift is likely to happen only in the long run. (However, single-period geometric analysis is not useful for the understanding of such changes over time. The more appropriate tools are multi-period analysis using the calculus, or more simply, multi-period tabular arithmetic analysis of a few plausible alternatives.)

FIGURE 2–5. ADVERTISING RESPONSE FUNCTIONS

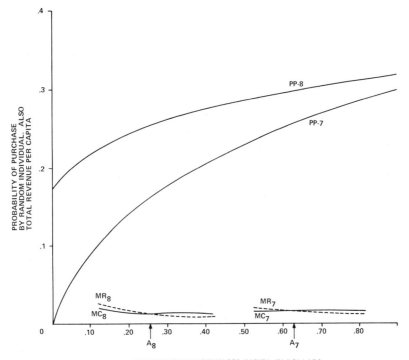

AMOUNT OF PROMOTION PER CAPITA, IN DOLLARS

As with geographic markets, an increase in promotion in one medium due to an increased number of prospects in it logically should not result in a *ceteris paribus* decrease of promotion in other media, as long as the media are independent. But in the short run a firm may decide to increase promotion in a given medium within the framework of a promotion-budget constraint, in which case the increase in one medium must imply a decrease elsewhere. In the intermediate and long run, however, the overall appropriation will be set on the basis of this new market knowledge and hence the total amount of promotion will in-

crease if there is an increase in any one medium due to increased potential buyers in its audience.

The behavior of mail-order firms confirms these predictions. Media
used by mail-order firms can be considered independent of each other
for the purposes of mail-order firms; their advertising-response curves
pass through the origin and hence are not steep; and mail-order firms
do not restrict themselves to a fixed advertising budget. Therefore,
when there is an increase in response from a given medium, the mail-
order firm invariably increases expenditures in that medium with no
change elsewhere; hence a total increase in expenditures occurs.

The same analysis holds for a decrease in media rates, in absolute
terms or in terms of cost per thousand. The analysis also holds for the
appearance of a new medium. In both cases an increase in total expenditures must result.

*Effects of Product-Usage Change of Advertising Medium's Audience
on the Promotion Mix.* Though the analysis for the amount of *total* promotion is similar for advertising-media markets and for geographic
markets, there are some differences in the way that positive changes in
these variables affect the promotion mix. Manufacturer advertising
probably will rise, and retail promotion may actually decrease; if advertising "presells" the customer there is less room for selling-promotion
by retailers. For example, if advertisements that carry information
about appliances are increased in one or more media, there is less of an
informational job for the retailer to do.

Furthermore, the more that the manufacturer presells his product
with advertising, the greater is his ability to force retail distribution, because customers will ask the retailer for the advertised product. The
stronger the position achieved by the manufacturer in this way, the less
the markup he will allow the retailer in fair trade or other situations
in which he has some control over the retail price, especially when he
advertises the price. We have evidence for this in the higher markups
that retailers demand and receive on little-advertised brands, and the
higher markups they take on their own private-label merchandise
(Preston, 1963, pp. 37–39). Retailers can sell a given amount of an advertised brand with less of their own promotional effort, and therefore
their break-even markup falls, the markup that is acceptable to them
at equilibrium also is lower, and we can expect price competition among
retailers to force a decrease in the actual markup. That retailers do indeed spend more personal selling time on unadvertised brands gets
some corroboration from a small study (Hatcher, 1942).

A similar analysis applies to the promotional mix of the retailer

alone. As his advertising media become more efficient, and as he therefore increases the amount of his advertising, he will decrease the
amounts of his promotion other than advertising. One might test the hypothesis that within a given group of similar retail stores, holding size
and price line constant, those that can advertise at cheaper rates will advertise more and will be more largely self-service stores than stores in
areas where advertising is more expensive. One such test might be to
compare the rare towns in which there are two competing evening
newspapers, e.g., Champaign-Urbana, Illinois, against matched towns
in which there is only one newspaper and hence (presumably) higher

FIGURE 2–6. SPOT TV COST PER 1,000 TV HOMES BY TV MARKET SIZE

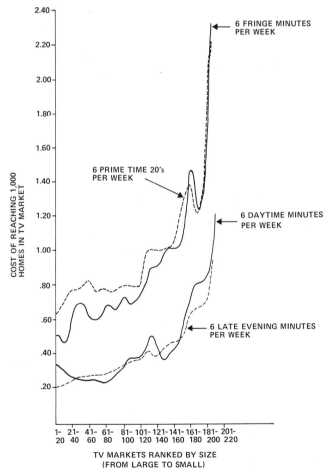

Source: *Media/Scope*, August, 1964.

advertising rates. (But see Chapter 6, Study C, on advertising rates as a function of number of newspapers.)

3. Increase in Absolute Population of a Given Market, Proportions of Everything Remaining as Before

As distinguished from Section 1, which dealt with changes in the composition of geographic markets, size remaining constant, this section deals with expansion of markets whose composition remains the same.

For a brand-owner, an increase in the total size of a market will cause a proportional increase in the amount of promotion, if all else remains equal, just as there will be twice as much total promotion in two (equal-size) markets together as in one of them alone. But in per cap-

Table 2-3. Milline Rates of Weekday Newspapers (in 1943)

Circulation Size Group	Milline Rates
500,000 and over	$1.33
300,000 - 500,000	1.56
100,000 - 300,000	2.05
50,000 - 100,000	2.46
25,000 - 50,000	3.58
10,000 - 25,000	5.01
5,000 - 10,000	7.32
Under 5,000	10.37

Source: Borden et al., 1944, p. 441.

ita terms an increase in the total size of a market affects nothing except through the costs of promotion per capita, which decrease; the cost per thousand of television and newspaper advertising is much lower in larger markets, as shown in Figure 2-6 and Table 2-3 respectively.

This cost decrease should lead to an increase in the brand-owner's promotion in the market, which is consistent with the observed higher amounts of national spot television in the larger markets (Table 2-4), the larger number of national grocery brands advertising in larger cities (Table 2–5), and the larger amounts of linage and larger advertisements used for six categories of consumer goods in larger cities (Tables 2-6a and 2-6b).

For a retailer, the immediate short-run effect of an increase in total market size is an increased number of potential customers for the same expenditures on window displays, merchandise display, and point-of-purchase advertising. The effect is the same as if the total market remained the same but the promotion curve shifted to the right, and the shift is relatively greater than for the manufacturer. But the longer-run result is that more competitors enter to get in on the profitable situation, which leads to smaller markups and lower prices in larger cities.

Table 2-4. Spot Billings per Television Family in 1963

Market[a]	Television Families July, 1963[b] (in 000)	Spot Billings per Television Family 1963	1968
New York	5,558	$13.35	$20.66
Los Angeles	3,112	14.46	26.73
Chicago	2,319	16.42	27.51
Philadelphia	2,103	11.94	17.41
Boston	1,820	10.73	18.17
Detroit	—[c]	—	—
San Francisco	1,425	11.79	26.10
Cleveland	1,311	11.34	17.00
Pittsburgh	1,252	11.46	14.89
Washington	916	11.89	16.53
St. Louis	853	12.00	18.50
Baltimore	789	10.71	13.18
Dallas–Ft. Worth	775	10.30	17.46
Cincinnati	759	8.17	11.74
Minneapolis–St. Paul	758	9.66	15.39
Providence	713	7.61	7.72
Miami	677	10.83	18.25
Milwaukee	652	11.92	16.03
Kansas City	616	11.20	16.22
Sacramento–Stockton	605	9.25	12.44
Seattle–Tacoma	599	11.48	16.73
Atlanta	598	9.33	15.67
Buffalo–Niagara Falls	585	15.02	19.96
Grand Rapids–Kalamazoo	560	8.46	11.40
Houston–Galveston	522	14.47	20.29
Memphis	499	7.33	9.11
Columbus, O.	488	12.42	14.84
Tampa–St. Petersburg	488	9.21	12.55
Portland, Ore.	478	11.02	15.32
Syracuse	470	9.59	11.43
Asheville, N.C.–Greenville– Spartanburg, S.C.	449	4.52	7.50
Nashville	447	5.89	8.04
New Orleans	440	10.19	13.64
Albany–Schenectady–Troy	428	10.53	12.58
Louisville	423	9.70	10.94
Greensboro–Winston Salem– High Point, N.C.	397	6.59	7.09
Denver	380	13.25	16.62
Wichita–Hutchinson	354	5.89	6.57
Oklahoma City–Enid	351	11.52	15.36
San Antonio	348	7.55	10.67
Orlando–Daytona Beach	339	4.80	8.64
Davenport–Rock Island	334	6.94	7.10
Rochester, N.Y.	331	7.87	9.42
Tulsa	328	8.24	10.51
Omaha	326	9.61	10.27
Norfolk–Portsmouth– Newport–New Hampton	315	7.55	7.21
Cedar Rapids–Waterloo	308	5.08	7.91

(Continued)

Table 2-4. (Continued)

Market[a]	Television Families July, 1963[b] (in 000)	Spot Billings per Television Family 1963	Spot Billings per Television Family 1968
Richmond–Petersburg	305	$ 4.67	$ 7.21
Shreveport, L.A.–Texarkana	299	5.23	6.80
Scranton–Wilkes Barre	293	5.11	6.95
Salt Lake City–Ogden–Provo	269	7.13	9.84
Spokane	266	7.55	8.22
Phoenix	258	10.70	15.63
Madison	251	5.69	7.31
Knoxville	248	5.58	8.17
Little Rock	239	5.36	7.23
Binghamton	237	5.48	4.99
Columbia, S.C.	229	3.84	6.59
Greenville, S.C.–Wash., N.C.	219	4.57	4.77
Evansville, Ind.–Henderson, Ky.	218	4.52	5.77
Chattanooga	211	4.52	5.48
Fresno	196	11.19	11.19
Youngstown	177	6.31	5.64
Peoria	169	8.09	8.64
Ft. Wayne	169	8.37	8.50
Beaumont–Port Arthur	168	5.05	5.67
Albuquerque	168	4.73	6.38
South Bend–Elkhart	144	6.27	6.46
Charleston, S.C.	144	3.43	3.94
Honolulu	144	7.72	11.06
Bakersfield	143	5.80	4.99
Amarillo	124	4.96	5.96
Tucson	112	6.00	7.36
El Paso	111	7.16	6.72
Colorado Springs–Pueblo	100	5.76	8.15
Las Vegas–Henderson	55	5.16	3.58

Source: *Advertising Age,* August 24, 1964, p. 58; February 3, 1969, p. 61.

[a]   Excludes T.V. areas where the FCC billing figures represent a combination of two or more markets with varying set counts.

[b]   Source: *Television Magazine,* July, 1963.

[c]   Data for Detroit have been excluded inasmuch as the FCC total for that market does not include billings for station CKLW-TV. Excluding CKLW-TV, billings per family came to $8.61 in 1963.

Table 2-5. Number of Grocery Advertising Accounts Using Newspaper Space in 104 Cities, Ranked by Population

City	Population, 1940	No. of Accounts, 1941	City	Population, 1940	No. of Accounts, 1941
New York	7,454,995 (1)	273 (2)	Omaha	223,844 (38)	177 (26)
Chicago	3,396,808 (2)	269 (3)	Dayton	210,718 (39)	117 (59)
Philadelphia	1,931,334 (3)	280 (1)	Syracuse	205,967 (40)	224 (16)
Detroit	1,623,452 (4)	262 (4)	Oklahoma City	204,424 (41)	219 (18)
Los Angeles	1,504,277 (5)	247 (9)	San Diego	203,341 (42)	123 (53)
Cleveland	878,336 (6)	245 (10)	Worcester	193,694 (43)	121 (55)
Baltimore	859,100 (7)	232 (13)	Richmond	193,042 (44)	121 (56)
St. Louis	816,048 (8)	214 (20)	Fort Worth	177,662 (45)	107 (64)
Boston	770,816 (9)	262 (5)	Jacksonville	173,065 (46)	121 (57)
Pittsburgh	671,659 (10)	259 (6)	Miami	172,172 (47)	187 (25)
Washington	663,091 (11)	248 (8)	Youngstown	167,720 (48)	126 (49)
San Francisco	634,536 (12)	248 (7)	Nashville	167,402 (49)	169 (31)
Milwaukee	587,472 (13)	230 (14)	Hartford	166,267 (50)	157 (36)
Buffalo	575,901 (14)	232 (12)	New Haven	160,605 (51)	126 (48)
New Orleans	494,537 (15)	164 (33)	Des Moines	159,819 (52)	139 (42)
Minneapolis	492,370 (16)	151 (39)	Flint	151,543 (53)	89 (73)
Cincinnati	455,610 (17)	204 (22)	Salt Lake City	149,934 (54)	125 (50)
Newark	429,760 (18)	155 (37)	Yonkers	142,598 (55)	75 (85)
Kansas City	399,178 (19)	174 (28)	Tulsa	142,157 (56)	103 (68)
Indianapolis	386,972 (20)	210 (21)	Scranton	140,404 (57)	118 (58)
Houston	384,514 (21)	152 (38)	Albany	130,577 (58)	218 (19)
Seattle	368,302 (22)	234 (11)	Trenton	124,697 (59)	84 (78)
Rochester	324,975 (23)	145 (40)	Spokane	122,001 (60)	159 (35)
Denver	322,412 (24)	134 (45)	Fort Wayne	118,410 (61)	106 (65)
Louisville	319,077 (25)	132 (46)	Camden	117,536 (62)	112 (62)
Columbus	306,087 (26)	167 (32)	Erie	116,955 (63)	84 (79)
Portland, Ore.	305,394 (27)	226 (15)	Fall River	115,428 (64)	78 (84)
Atlanta	302,288 (28)	223 (17)	Wichita	114,966 (65)	114 (61)
Oakland	302,163 (29)	159 (34)	Knoxville	111,580 (66)	117 (59)
Dallas	294,734 (30)	193 (24)	Reading	110,568 (67)	85 (75)
Memphis	292,942 (31)	176 (27)	New Bedford	110,341 (68)	80 (83)
St. Paul	287,736 (32)	141 (41)	Tacoma	109,408 (69)	110 (63)
Toledo	282,349 (33)	137 (43)	Sacramento	105,958 (70)	131 (47)
Birmingham	267,583 (34)	170 (30)	Peoria	105,087 (71)	136 (44)
San Antonio	253,854 (35)	195 (23)	South Bend	101,268 (72)	106 (66)
Providence	253,504 (36)	172 (29)	Duluth	101,065 (73)	89 (74)
Akron	244,791 (37)	122 (54)	Evansville	97,062 (74)	85 (76)
El Paso	96,810 (75)	94 (69)	Fresno	60,685 (90)	124 (52)
Schenectady	87,549 (76)	125 (51)	New Rochelle	58,408 (91)	70 (91)
Wilkes-Barre	86,236 (77)	93 (70)	Muncie	49,720 (92)	72 (90)
Rockford	84,637 (78)	85 (77)	Jamestown	42,638 (93)	62 (97)
Harrisburg	83,893 (79)	93 (71)	White Plains	40,327 (94)	68 (92)
Winston-Salem	79,815 (80)	74 (88)	Albuquerque	35,449 (95)	75 (87)
Niagara Falls	78,029 (81)	42 (102)	Port Chester	23,073 (96)	66 (93)
Manchester	77,685 (82)	81 (82)	Hempstead	20,856 (97)	10 (104)
Troy	70,304 (83)	84 (80)	Freeport	20,410 (98)	49 (101)
Roanoke	69,287 (84)	83 (81)	Glens Falls	18,836 (99)	39 (103)
Mount Vernon	67,362 (85)	73 (89)	Peekskill	17,311 (100)	58 (99)
Johnstown	66,668 (86)	75 (86)	Modesto	16,379 (101)	57 (100)
Phoenix	65,414 (87)	103 (67)	Ossining	15,996 (102)	66 (94)
Atlantic City	64,094 (88)	58 (98)	Mamaroneck	13,034 (103)	65 (95)
Cedar Rapids	62,120 (89)	90 (72)	Tarrytown	6,874 (104)	65 (96)

Source: Borden, Taylor, Hovde, p. 105, originally from *Media Records*, 1941, pp. 146-182.

These lower prices may also result from the lower cost-per-thousand rates and consequent increased advertising as the market grows.

McNair's data on prewar department stores also fit (Table 2-7). Holding size of store constant, the larger the city the greater the advertising ratio.[13] But the data for smaller retailers show a somewhat differ-

Table 2-6a.　Newspaper Advertisement Size for Various Products
in Cities in Four Population Groups

Advertiser	Linage in Papers in Cities over 1,000,000	Linage in Papers in Cities of 100,000 to 500,000	Linage in Papers in Cities of 25,000 to 100,000	Linage in Papers in Cities under 25,000
Food				
Largest-size advertisement	1500	1264	1115	1243
Smallest-size advertisement	14	16	9	14
Average-size advertisement	175	147	159	142
Automobile				
Largest-size advertisement	1729	1260	2352	2352
Smallest-size advertisement	30	17	14	84
Average-size advertisement	820	461	513	325
Cosmetics				
Largest-size advertisement	488	262	196	108
Smallest-size advertisement	14	36	37	96
Average-size advertisement	122	97	79	102
Gasoline and Oil				
Largest-size advertisement	2079	2368	2008	1025
Smallest-size advertisement	54	3	29	56
Average-size advertisement	718	721	608	608
Cigarettes				
Largest-size advertisement	1740	1600	1428	1025
Smallest-size advertisement	7	45	45	45
Average-size advertisement	348	395	525	512
Cigars				
Largest-size advertisement	1600	1010	2408	495
Smallest-size advertisement	39	47	25	49
Average-size advertisement	366	210	235	84

Source: Duffy, 1951, p. 67

Table 2-6b.　Cigarette Advertising in Different-Size Cities

Population Groups	Average-Size Advertisement Used by Big-Four Cigarettes
1,000,000 and over	866 lines
100,000 to 500,000	797 lines
25,000 to 100,000	679 lines
25,000 and under	646 lines

Source: Duffy, 1951, p. 68.

[13] McNair's data for the postwar period show somewhat different results due to the development of multibranch department stores in big cities.

ent pattern, which requires explanation. Department stores, except for their branches, take the entire city as their market, whereas many other retailers do not. A neighborhood drugstore in Brooklyn does not serve Manhattan customers. Hence it is not unexpected when Mitchell's data (Table 2-8) for many types of retailers show that, holding size of store

**Table 2-7. Representative Figures for
Advertising Ratios for Department Stores – 1940**
(Expressed in percentages of net sales)
Classified According to Net Sales Volume and Size of City

City Pop. (in thousands)	Net Sales in Thousands									
	Less than $150	$150-$300	$300-$500	$500-$750	$750-$1000	$1000-$2000	$2000-$4000	$4000-$10000	$10000-$20000	$20,000 or more
Less than 15	1.9	2.0								
15 to 25	2.1	2.2	2.7							
25 to 50		3.2	2.75	2.5	2.85	2.85				
50 to 100				2.5	3.15	3.25	2.7			
100 to 250						3.5	3.2	2.85		
250 to 500							4.0	3.65	2.95	
500 to 1,000							5.1	4.15	3.45	
1,000 or more									4.6	3.5

Source: McNair, 1940. Taken from Lund, 1947, p. 271.

constant, the store in the "middle-sized" city (perhaps 100,000 population) spends a larger amount for advertising, relative to sales, than retailers in smaller and larger cities spend. In such categories as motor vehicles and coal and fuel, however, which are not limited to neighborhood markets, the increase of promotion with size of city is true for large cities also. This is corroborated by Forrest's data (Table 2-9), which show that most types of stores with sales of $100,000 to $200,000 spend a larger proportion of their budget in city-wide newspapers than in neighborhood papers, compared to stores with sales under $100,000. (The reader should here remember the very great drawbacks of advertising-sales ratio data, and the possibility that they are misleading; see Appendix B.)

Effect of Increased Market Size on the Promotion Mix. The promotion-mix response to changes in total market size is interesting. No theory tells whether the geographical or media effect will be greater, and hence there is no way to guess whether the retail or national advertising response will be greater. However, I have the impression that the overall retail promotional response in the form of private labels will be greater than the brand-owner's response. The retailer takes over the entire promotion job for a private label. In New York City private-label liquor sales are a large and growing segment of total liquor sales, a

Table 2-8. Advertising Ratios of Large and Small Retailers in Three Sizes of Cities – 32 Trades, 1939

(Advertising expenditures appear as percentages of net sales)

Population Less than 20,000

Annual Sales

Trade	Less than $10,000	$10,000 to $20,000	$20,000 to $30,000	$30,000 to $50,000	$50,000 to $100,000	$100,000 to $300,000	Over $300,000
Jewelry Stores	1.5	1.3	1.7	←— 2.2 —→	2.5	←— 2.3 —→	..
Shoe Stores	1.2	2.1	0.9	1.1	1.3	..	..
Drug Stores	0.5	0.7	1.5	1.1	1.8	2.1	..
Furniture Stores	0.8	1.0	1.0	1.5	←— 1.4 —→		..
Household Appliances	1.1	1.1	1.0	1.2	←— 2.0 —→		..
Men's Clothing	1.1	1.2	1.4	1.6	←— 2.0 —→		..
Florists and Nurseries	..	..	..	..	..	..	..
Family Clothing	0.8	1.0	1.1	1.5	←— 1.4 —→		..
Paint, Wallpaper, and Glass	←— 1.4	1.4	1.3	1.4	1.2	1.6	..
Women's Ready-to-Wear	1.0	1.2	1.3	1.4	←— 1.6 —→		..
Auto Accessories and Parts	1.5	1.0	1.0	0.9	←— 0.7 —→		..
Dry Goods, General Merchandise	0.6	0.7	1.2	1.0	1.5	2.0	..
Hardware	0.5	1.0	1.0	1.1	←— 1.1 —→		..
Stationery	..	0.9 ——→	→	→	→	→	..
Limited Price Variety	..	..	..	..	..	..	..
Service Stations	0.8	0.4	0.4	0.7 ——→	..	..	..
Bakery Shops	←— 0.7 —→		0.6	0.6	..	0.6	..
Coal and Other Fuel	←— 0.5 —→		0.7	0.6	0.6	0.6	..
Grocery Stores	0.1	0.6	0.7	0.7	0.6	0.8	..
Grocery and Meat Stores	0.2	0.5	0.5	0.6	0.6	0.6	..
Hardware and Farm Implements	←— 0.6 —→		←— 0.5 —→		0.6	..	..
Motor Vehicles	0.6	0.5	←— 0.8 —→		0.5	0.6	0.7
Restaurants, Eating Places	0.6	0.5	0.6	→	..	0.7	..
Confectionery	0.4	0.4	0.6	..	..	..	..

(Continued)

Table 2-8. (Continued)

Population Less than 20,000 (Continued)

Trade	Less than $10,000	$10,000 to $20,000	$20,000 to $30,000	$30,000 to $50,000	$50,000 to $100,000	$100,000 to $300,000	Over $300,000
Country General Stores	0.3	0.3	0.5	0.4	0.5	0.6 ——→	..
Lumber and Building Materials	0.3	0.2	0.4	0.4	0.5	←—— 0.5 ——→	..
Taverns and Bars	←—— 0.4 ——→			←—— 0.6 ——→			
Farm Implements	..	0.8	0.3	0.5	0.4	..	..
Filling Stations	0.4	0.4	0.4	0.5	0.6	0.4	..
Meat Markets	..	←—— 0.3 ——→		..	0.6 ——→		..
Farmers' Supply Stores	←—— 0.3 ——→		0.3	0.3	0.2	0.2	0.3
Groceries with Filling Stations	0.1	0.3	0.2	←—— 0.4 ——→		..	..

Population 20,000 to 100,000

Trade	Less than $10,000	$10,000 to $20,000	$20,000 to $30,000	$30,000 to $50,000	$50,000 to $100,000	$100,000 to $300,000	Over $300,000
Jewelry Stores	←—— 2.0 ——→			←—— 3.4 ——→	←—— 3.9 ——→		..
Shoe Stores	←—— 1.8 ——→			←—— 2.0 ——→	←—— 2.4 ——→		..
Drug Stores	←—— 0.6 ——→		0.5	←—— 1.2 ——→			..
Furniture Stores	←—— 1.0 ——→			1.5	2.4	3.4	
Household Appliances	←—— 2.3 ——→		2.4		2.2		
Men's Clothing	←—— 1.2 ——→			1.8	2.1	2.5	
Florists and Nurseries	..						..
Family Clothing	←—— 0.8 ——→			1.4	←—— 2.3 ——→		..
Paint, Wallpaper, and Glass	←—— 1.2 ——→				1.4		
Women's Ready-to-Wear	←—— 1.0 ——→				1.8		
Auto Accessories and Parts	←—— 2.0 ——→				1.0		
Dry Goods, General Merchandise	←—— 0.6 ——→			0.8		1.8	
Hardware	←—— 1.1 ——→			1.5		1.5	
Stationery	←—— 0.9 ——→				1.0		
Limited Price Variety	..						..
Service Stations	←—— 1.2 ——→			1.3		1.0	..

(Continued)

Table 2-8. (Continued)

Population 20,000 to 100,000 (Continued)

Trade	Less than $10,000	$10,000 to $20,000	$20,000 to $30,000	$30,000 to $50,000	$50,000 to $100,000	$100,000 to $300,000	Over $300,000
				Annual Sales			
Bakery Shops	..	← 0.6 →		..	..	..	..
Coal and Other Fuel	..	← 0.6 →		0.5	← 0.6 →		..
Grocery Stores	0.1	0.4	0.3	..	..	..	..
Grocery and Meat Stores	..	..	..	0.4	0.6	0.9	..
Hardware and Farm Implements	..	..	..	..	..	..	..
Motor Vehicles	..	← 0.5 →			0.6		0.8
Restaurants, Eating Places	..	..	← 0.8 →		..	..	..
Confectionery	..	..	..	..	..	..	..
Country General Stores	..	..	..	..	..	..	..
Lumber and Building Materials	..	← 0.5 →		..	0.6	← 0.5 →	
Taverns and Bars	← 0.6 →		..	..	..	..	..
Farm Implements	..	..	← 0.5 →		..	..	..
Filling Stations	..	..	← 0.4 →		← 0.9 →		..
Meat Markets	..	← 0.4 →		..	..	..	..
Farmers' Supply Stores	..	← 0.4 →		..	← 0.4 →		..
Groceries with Filling Stations	..	← 0.3 →		..	..	..	..

Population 100,000 to 500,000

Trade	Less than $10,000	$10,000 to $20,000	$20,000 to $30,000	$30,000 to $50,000	$50,000 to $100,000	$100,000 to $300,000	Over $300,000
Jewelry Stores	← 1.9 →		← 2.4 →		← 3.9 →		..
Shoe Stores	← 1.8 →		← 3.0 →		← 1.9 →		..
Drug Stores	← 0.7 →		0.3	← 0.4 →		3.8	..
Furniture Stores	← 0.8 →		← 1.4 →	1.9	2.4		..
Household Appliances	← 2.1 →		← 1.4 →	1.3		← 1.6 →	..
Men's Clothing	← 0.7 →		← 1.4 →		← 2.6 →		..
Florists and Nurseries	..	..	..	..	..	..	..
Family Clothing	← 1.2 →		← 0.6 →		← 1.9 →		..

(Continued)

Table 2-8. (Continued)

Population 100,000 to 500,000 (Continued)

Trade	Less than $10,000	$10,000 to $20,000	$20,000 to $30,000	$30,000 to $50,000	$50,000 to $100,000	$100,000 to $300,000	Over $300,000
Paint, Wallpaper, and Glass		← 0.7 →			1.1	→	..
Women's Ready-to-Wear	← 0.6 →		1.1		1.3	→	..
Auto Accessories and Parts	← 1.0 →			1.1	→		..
Dry Goods, General Merchandise	← 1.0 →		1.3		1.5	→	..
Hardware	← 0.4 →		1.0		0.5	→	..
Stationery	← 0.6 →			0.7	→		..
Limited Price Variety	..		..		..	..	..
Service Stations	← 0.5 →			0.4		..	..
Bakery Shops	← 0.5 →			0.8	→		..
Coal and Other Fuel	← 0.6 →	0.8			1.1	→	..
Grocery Stores	0.2		0.5	→	0.5	..	..
Grocery and Meat Stores	0.4		0.7	0.4		0.7	..
Hardware and Farm Implements	..		..			..	1.0
Motor Vehicles	← 0.8 →	0.5			0.7	0.9	→
Restaurants, Eating Places	← 0.8 →		0.4		1.0	→	..
Confectionery	← 0.2 →		..		..	..	..
Country General Stores	..		..		..	..	..
Lumber and Building Materials	← 0.9 →	0.4			0.6	← 0.7 →	..
Taverns and Bars	..		0.4	→	..	..	..
Farm Implements	..		..		..	..	..
Filling Stations	0.3	0.3	0.3	0.4	→	..	..
Meat Markets	← 0.9 →				0.6	0.6	→
Farmers' Supply Stores	..		..		..	0.4	..
Groceries with Filling Stations	← 0.4 →				..	..	..

Table 2-9. Advertising Ratios of Small and Medium-Size Retailers
by Kinds of Media, by Kind of Business, Ohio, 1945
(Annual Advertising Expenditure as a Percentage of Annual Sales)

Kind of Business	Newspaper City-wide	Newspaper Neighborhood	Shopping	Radio	Outdoor	Direct to Home	Direct in Store	Direct Mail	Average All Media
Annual Sales $100,000 or Less: Smaller Stores									
Drug	1.3	0.7	0.2	1.0	0.1	0.3	0.1	0.5	1.0
Furniture	2.1	1.1	0.8	0.9	0.3		0.1	1.1	2.5
Grocery	0.4	0.2	0.1	0.1	0.2	0.2	0.1	0.3	0.4
Hardware	0.5	0.7		0.1	0.1	0.5	0.1	0.4	0.8
Jewelry	3.2	0.4	0.5	0.6	0.5	0.4	0.9	0.7	3.4
Lumber	0.6	0.2	0.2	0.7	0.3			0.6	0.9
Men's-Boys' Clothing	1.6	0.1	0.2	1.5	0.2			0.1	1.8
Shoes	1.4	0.6					0.2	0.1	2.1
Women's Ready-To-Wear	1.8	0.5	0.2		0.2				1.2
Other	1.1	0.3	0.2	0.2	0.5	0.1	0.1	0.4	1.1
Annual Sales $100,0001–$200,000: Larger Stores									
Drug	1.4	0.1		0.6				0.1	1.2
Furniture	2.4		0.5						2.3
Grocery	0.5	0.4		0.8	0.2	0.1	0.1	0.3	0.5
Hardware	0.7	0.3			0.1		0.2		0.9
Jewelry	2.3	0.1		1.9	0.1				3.5
Lumber	0.8	0.3	0.1					0.1	0.9
Men's-Boys' Clothing	1.9			0.7				0.6	2.4
Shoes	2.7	0.4			0.4	0.2		0.5	3.1
Women's Ready-To-Wear	1.4	0.1							1.5
Other	0.6	0.6	0.2	0.5	0.2	0.1	0.1	0.5	1.1

Source: Forrest, 1949, p. 71.

much larger proportion than in the rest of New York State. Private labeling seems to be a direct function of the size of the retailer for obvious reasons, and the size of the retailer is a direct function of the total size of the market.

4. Increase in the Number of Physical Markets in Which a Firm Distributes

Section 3 dealt with an increase in the population of a particular geographically bounded market. This section deals with an increase in the size of the section of the country to which a manufacturer sells. This might be a local manufacturer spreading out to become regional or a regional manufacturer becoming national. This section does not apply to retailers except perhaps to retail chains as they expand.

Some evidence suggests that promotion may become more efficient as the number of markets increases. Network television is cheaper per thousand than smaller hookups, national editions of national magazines cost less per thousand than the regional editions, and there is less "waste circulation" in multimarket media audiences. Such efficiency in multimarket operations will lead to increased national promotion. This increase in the amount of "preselling" will then decrease the amount of retail promotion, by the argument given earlier.

5. Volume of Product per Customer in a Representative Geographic Market

The amount spent on a product by consumers is a function of the nature of a product: the average annual purchase per capita of shoelaces is not likely to exceed that of whiskey, no matter what else happens. But there can also be shifts in the per capita volume of use of a product: e.g., wine buyers may increase their annual purchases greatly, and non-wine-buyers may begin to buy wine. These changes result from changes in income or taste. (We shall here ignore changes that result from promotion of the sort that occurred in the frozen orange-juice concentrate industry [Henderson, 1961].)

A *ceteris paribus* increase in sales volume per capita means an increase in total volume for each firm. At the original promotional level for each firm the response will shift upward, perhaps proportionally, in which case the marginal revenue curve will shift to the right, leading to increased promotion. In the longer run, however, there will be an increase in the number of sellers in response to increased volume, and the summary effect on promotion expenditures is not immediately determinate. And over a very long period an increased sales volume might accompany or signal an increased state of information of buyers. For a monopolist this latter effect might actually cause a decrease in his advertising; this might be the case with advertising for home-use electric-

FIGURE 2–7. ADVERTISING RESPONSE FUNCTIONS

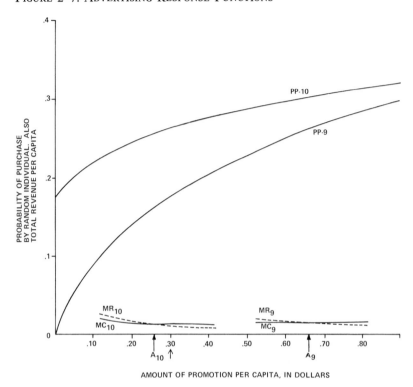

AMOUNT OF PROMOTION PER CAPITA, IN DOLLARS

ity, as seen in the shift from PP_9 to PP_{10} in Figure 2-7, which might accompany an increased volume per capita in the long run.

6. Income of Potential Purchasers

Assume that the product in question is one that people will buy more of if their incomes increase, price, amount of advertising, and tastes remaining the same. Then one may expect that the amount of advertising will increase as long as the demand increase faced by individual firms is at least as large at higher promotional levels than at lower levels, e.g., an absolute increase from PP_1 to PP_{12} or a proportional increase to PP_2 (Figure 2-8). The analysis is quite the same as in Section 1 above, and holds either if price remains the same or if price and advertising are both changed to a new joint optimum from an old joint optimum. (However, it is theoretically possible that advertising would actually decrease if the new response function were PP_{11}, rather than the more reasonable PP_2 or PP_{12}.) The fact that the absolute amounts, as well

FIGURE 2–8. ADVERTISING RESPONSE FUNCTIONS

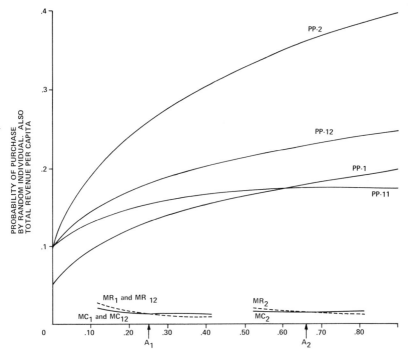

AMOUNT OF PROMOTION PER CAPITA, IN DOLLARS

as the proportions of advertising to sales, have increased secularly in such established products as liquor and aspirin as per capita income increased is consistent with the aforegoing proposition, though there are also many other forces that might also account for all or part of this increase, as discussed in this chapter and the following two.

This analysis is appropriate, however, only for a short-run income change over time. In the long run, or when considering a cross section of income classes, tastes may well be a function of income. The rich do not have a taste for some things that the poor prefer; beer and television are two examples. Intelligence, market knowledge, and self-confidence of consumers may also be positively associated with income, at least at the lower part of the distribution. And indeed, there is some evidence that working-class families are more likely to buy branded merchandise than cheaper private-label goods, as compared to middle-class people. To the extent that this is true, working-class families may be better targets for promotion than middle-class families.

7. The Effect of Product Price on Advertising Expenditures

At a price that exactly equals production costs there will be no promotion at all, because an advertising expenditure would immediately make the enterprise unprofitable. And at some price that is so high that no one will buy the product even with larger amounts of promotion — and there obviously is such a price for every commodity — there will also be no promotion. And if there is *some* price at which it is profitable to

FIGURE 2–9. RELATIONSHIP OF DEMAND FOR ONE BRAND TO PRICES OF OTHER BRANDS (HYPOTHETICAL)

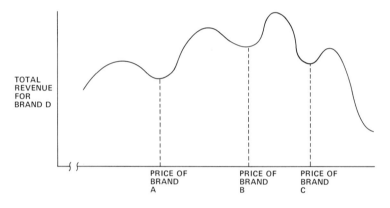

promote, it must therefore be true that some price rise will increase the amount spent for advertising, whereas another price rise — starting from a different point — will reduce the amount spent for advertising. The aforegoing is stated just to show that the effect of a price rise on promotion is indeterminate without further information.

A second simple observation: if the product is one which is already sold in several different brands at several different prices, the total revenue function of a potential brand, assuming any given level of advertising, may well have several inflection points, as shown in Figure 2-9. It is then intuitively obvious that the optimum level of promotion expenditures also rises and falls as one considers various prices from low to high.

Now let us consider whether Brand A or B or C in Figure 2-9 spends more for advertising, assuming that production costs are identical (e.g., bleaches, whiskies, gasolines). It is reasonable to assume that at any *given* level of advertising, the quantity sold will decrease with increasing price. (This assumes a long enough perspective so that all brands start from scratch. Obviously a brand that already has achieved a high degree of customer loyalty will sell more than a cheaper but less established brand in any given short time period.) It may quickly be seen that there is no general answer to this question about the effect of price on advertising expenditures. Consider the hypothetical data in Table 2-10 for the response function for a $6 price and for two alternative re-

Table 2-10. Hypothetical Advertising - Price Response Functions

Response Function	Price P_t	Quantity Sold Q_t	Total Revenue R_t	Pro- duction Cost M_t	Adver- tising Cost A_t	Total Cost C_t	Net Profit $N_t=R_t-C_t$
		Advertising Amount = A_t = $300					
	$6	800	$4800	$2400	$300	$2700	$2100
D	$7	700	$4900	$2100	$300	$2400	$2500
E	$7	700	$4900	$2100	$300	$2400	$2500
		A_t = $600					
	$6	1100	$6600	$3300	$600	$3900	$2700
D	$7	750	$5250	$2250	$600	$2850	$2400
E	$7	900	$6300	$2700	$600	$3300	$3000
		A_t = $900					
	$6	1199	$7194	$3597	$900	$4497	$2697
D	$7	795	$5565	$2385	$900	$3285	$2280
E	$7	990	$6930	$2970	$900	$3870	$3060

sponse functions for a $7 price. If response function D is the case, the optimum advertising amount is less ($$A_t = 300) for $7 than for $6 ($600), i.e., the net profit is higher for a $6 price. But for response function E the optimum amount is more ($900 and a $7 price). Which will be the case depends on the advertising and price elasticities at those particular prices and advertising expenditures.[14] If one thought it wise to specify the shapes of the functions, the answer would then be deter-

[14] At first one may think that either one of these elasticities alone may be sufficient, e.g.: "Advertising elasticity in particular can often be assumed to have a negative correlation with price elasticity. If the goods are cheap, so that the buyer does not have to be over-careful in making the purchase, it is easier to influence him by non-economic arguments. Emotive advertising then has a better chance of influencing the buyers, and in such cases the advertising elasticity has increased. The purchasers can better afford to follow their impulses, and thereby become easier victims of advertising" (Mickwitz, 1959, p. 45). But an advertising-response function would have to be convex downward to have constant elasticity, rather than the concave downward shape that is reasonable (Chapter 1). Hence the elasticity of advertising changes (downward) with more advertising, and it therefore does not make sense to talk of *the* advertising elasticity for a product, or about a correlation between advertising and price elasticities.

minate, but aside from constraining the response functions to be concave downward, I do not know of any reasonable specifications with general application.

So far the discussion has been about the effect of price on *absolute* amounts of advertising. But the example above also implies that the advertising-sales ratio also is not a determinate function of price unless the advertising-response functions are specified as to form.

The aforementioned two observations seem to run against common sense, which suggests that if a firm produces an article for $10 and sells

Table 2-11. Total Auto Advertising, and Advertising per Car Sold, in 1967, by Brand

	Unit Sales	Advertising Investment	Advertising Expenditure per Car Sold
American Motors (Rambler)	241,380	$11,749,959	$48.68
Chrysler-Imperial	222,512	7,389,908	33.21
Dodge	497,543	15,884,294	31.92
Plymouth	633,084	19,555,733	30.89
Ford	1,501,144	57,720,767	38.46
Lincoln-Continental	34,844	2,154,735	61.84
Mercury	298,757	16,433,595	55.01
Buick	567,824	17,783,753	31.32
Cadillac	208,112	8,548,000	41.07
Chevrolet	1,978,550	74,451,516	37.63
Oldsmobile	547,197	16,217,357	29.64
Pontiac	836,937	20,903,335	24.98

Source: *Advertising Age,* August 19, 1961, p. 81; and May 15, 1967, pp. N1-N30.

it for $20, it can then "afford" to spend up to $10 to gain another customer. That quantity is more than if the spread between production cost and selling price was, say, $15 — $10 = $5 rather than $20 — $10 = $10. And basing his observation on a survey, Lewis (1954, p. 4) noted that firms think this way: "Several firms indicated that they calculate back from the selling price in sales to see how much they can 'afford' to spend for promotion." But this spread is relevant only at the margin, and does not affect the total and average quantities in which we are interested here.

Not only does the relationship of advertising expenditure to price seem indeterminate in theory, but the empirical evidence also goes in both directions. One can find examples of products in which the low price lines promote the most, both in terms of promotion per unit sold and absolute promotion; but one can also find examples in which the medium and high price lines promote most. In the auto industry the cheapest American cars generally spend the most dollars for promotion, foreign cars (which are even cheaper) spend less, the highest-priced American cars spend less absolutely but more per unit sold, and Checker spends practically nothing (Table 2-11, especially last column; and Table 2-12). In the liquor industry the medium-priced brands spend the most total dollars, and the high-priced brands spend the most per unit sold. Lewis (1954, p. 4) did find, however, that "In general, sales costs tend to be higher on gross margin lines." This may indicate something about the most common shapes of advertising-response functions found at various selling prices.

It is relevant that various promotion-mix possibilities exist at each price. For example, of two brands whose retail prices are the same one may advertise more than the second, but the second may sell at a lower wholesale price to the retailer or offer "push money" to induce the retailer to promote the sale of his brand. The choice of such strategies involves important long-run versus short-run considerations. Manufacturer advertising may be a longer-term investment than lower wholesale prices or push money. On the other hand, retail customers created by push money may also develop brand loyalty based on their trials of the product, in the same way that advertising can create brand loyalty.

The evidence about the behavior of department stores is interesting in this connection. The higher the price line of goods sold in the department store, the smaller the store's ratio of advertising to sales. Edwards' and Howard's (1943) description of the lowest-price-line store provides both description and reasonable explanation of the phenomenon (note especially the last paragraph):

Promotional store. This is the bargain store, and virtually every sizable city in the United States numbers such a store among its retail establishments. It receives only a small proportion of [total] regular daily business; most of its customers come to the store in response to its advertised promotions. Customers rarely patronize the promotional store for their regular needs, having been trained to wait for its reduced-price sales, which are nearly continuous. The promotional store depends upon constant and powerful promotion for its existence.

This type of store usually merchandises from smaller stocks than does its more dignified competitors, capitalizing upon quicker turnover and larger volume at a lower mark-up. The sales force is less attentive, often encouraging the customer to serve herself. It offers fewer conveniences and courtesies than do its less promotional competitors. As a compensation for the scarcity of services, its prices are markedly lower.

For this store the operating statement will inevitably show a high advertising percentage — usually from 5 to 6 per cent, or higher [as compared to 1½ to 2½ percent for the "Non-promotional Store" and 3 to 4 percent for the "Semi-promotional Store"] [Edwards & Howard, 1943, p. 159].

Table 2-12. Total Auto Advertising in 1964

Company Brand	Total 1964 (in thousands of dollars)	Company Brand	Total 1964 (in thousands of dollars)
American Motors	$ 21,709.5	Buick	7,610.1
British Motors Corp./Hambro	1,399.9	Buick Special	429.1
Checker Motors	252.6	Buick Div.	2,122.2
Chrysler Corp.	60,275.6	Cadillac	5,897.7
Corporate Institutional	22,271.1	Chevrolet	24,157.5
Barracuda	1,041.8	Chevrolet Div.	4,721.9
Chrysler	6,128.5	Chevelle	3,855.1
Chrysler-Plymouth Div.	875.1	Chevy II	2,556.4
DeSoto	22.9	Corvair	6,948.1
Dart	3,569.0	Corvette	175.8
Dodge	12,032.3	Oldsmobile	10,151.5
Dodge Div.	226.6	Oldsmobile–F–85	1,890.7
Imperial	1,499.5	Pontiac	11,242.3
Plymouth	8,937.9	Pontiac Div.	169.4
Valiant	2,576.1	Tempest	2,980.3
Simca	1,094.8	Opel	1,340.3
Citroen Cars Corp.	119.6	Vauxhall	0.0
Fiat Motor Co.	591.5	Hoffman Motors	141.1
Ford Motor Co.	66,750.6	Jaguar Ltd.	334.8
Corporate Institutional	18,584.2	Kaiser Industries (Jeep)	2,707.7
Comet	5,193.6	Nissan Motor Co. (Datsun)	272.2
Ford	20,088.4	Peugot Inc.	82.9
Ford Div.	4,463.3	Renault Inc.	1,473.4
Falcon	2,388.3	Rolls-Royce Inc.	136.8
Lincoln	2,901.7	Rootes Motors	686.3
Lincoln-Mercury Div.	185.9	Rover Co.	125.9
Mercury	6,522.2	Saab	335.4
Meteor	0.0	Standard Triumph	777.9
Mustang	5,025.5	Studebaker Corp. (domestic)	669.3
Thunderbird	1,114.6	Toyota Motor Co.	123.5
English Fords	282.9	Volkswagen of America	8,356.4
General Motors Corp.	110,197.9	Volvo Inc.	1,101.1
Corporate Institutional	23,949.4	Grand Total	$268,730.3[a]

Source: *Printers' Ink,* July 9, 1965, p. 14.
a 1963 total — $241,131.2. Both grand totals exclude network radio.

And department stores spend far more on advertising particular goods in their basement than in the upstairs store, as shown in Table 2-13.

8. Amount of Information Available to the Advertiser about the Advertising-Response Function

If a change in a variable — e.g., any of the demand variables discussed above — is to affect the amount spent for promotion, the manager must come to be aware of the change in the variable. Up till now it has implicitly been assumed that the manager has available such information about changes in the relevant variables, but now we shall loosen that assumption and inquire into the effects of more or less information reaching the firm. That is, we now ask about the effects on promotional expenditures of more or less uncertainty about the effect of the promotion. We shall not consider the effects of accurate versus inaccurate information, or the effects of differences in information collected in different ways or based on different kinds of evidence, but only the effects of different amounts of information, *ceteris paribus*.

Some men pay to gamble, some pay to insure against loss. Different men, and therefore different firms, respond differently to risk because their preferences differ. And the extent of information available about customer response to advertising determines the risk of promotion. One can only deduce, then, that more customer-response information tends to reduce the variations in a firm's promotion outlays. And since men shift from pessimism to optimism and back again much more violently in the absence of information, we can also deduce that an increase in information will increase the stability and predictability of a firm's outlays.

Such mail-order firms as International Correspondence School are quite regular in their overall expenditures, as well as in their choice of media in which they advertise. This is because the sales volume created by each of their advertisements is measured perfectly, and hence the response to a given advertisement in any medium in any month is highly predictable. Department stores and other retailers are also remarkably stable in their choices of media, and in their daily and seasonal expenditure patterns, because they also can measure the effect of particular advertisements quite accurately. Neustadt data show this stability vividly, both for products whose total advertising is increasing and those for which it is not, as may be seen in Figure 2-10a and 2-10b. But national-brand advertisers, whose knowledge of the specific results of specific advertising is far inferior to mail-order firms and to retailers because of

Table 2-13. Typical Newspaper-Space-Cost and Total Publicity-Expense Percentages of Net Sales of 28 Departments in Department Stores with Annual Sales Volume of $2,000,000 to $5,000,000

(Figures for the 17 Departments That Spent the Highest and the 11 Departments That Spent the Lowest Percentages of Net Sales for Newspaper Space in 1940)

	Newspaper Space Costs, % of Net Sales	Total Publicity, % of Net Sales	Sales, % of Total Store	Profit or Loss, % of Net Sales
High				
Main Store:				
51-W Women's and Misses' Coats and Suits	3.8	6.3	3.0	5.8
53 Women's and Misses' Dresses	3.6	6.0	4.2	1.5
55 Girls' Wear	3.6	5.6	1.2	1.7
57 Aprons, House Dresses, and Uniforms	3.7	5.7	1.5	3.0
59 Furs	3.9	6.4	1.7	8.7
71 Furniture and Bedding	4.7	6.7	4.5	2.9
77-R Mechanical Refrigeration	3.6	5.2	1.4	4.7
77-O Other Major Household Appliances	3.8	5.4	1.0	4.6
78 Miscellaneous Housewares	4.1	5.6	2.2	1.2
84 Radios, Phonographs, and Records	4.5	6.3	0.7	3.6
Basement:				
110 Piece Goods, Domestics, Blankets, etc.	4.1	5.8	1.6	2.1
120 Small Wares	3.9	5.5	0.3	3.2
150-C Juniors', Misses', and Women's Coats and Suits	4.6	6.7	1.3	4.9
150-D Juniors', Misses', and Women's Dresses	4.3	6.3	1.5	0.3
157 Aprons, House Dresses and Uniforms	5.0	6.6	0.7	0.2
160 Men's and Boys' Wear	3.6	5.3	1.9	0.7
170 Home Furnishings	3.6	6.0	1.3	0.4
Low				
Main Store:				
21 Laces, Trimmings, and Ribbons	0.9	2.5	0.4	5.1
25-C Costume Jewelry	2.1	3.7	1.1	9.9
26 Umbrellas	1.4	2.8	0.2	6.6
28 Books and Stationery	1.9	3.7	2.0	3.1
31 Neckwear and Scarves	2.4	4.2	0.8	3.6
37-W Women's Hosiery	2.3	3.7	3.2	8.9
38 Knit Underwear	2.3	4.0	1.0	6.3
43 Infants' Wear	2.3	4.1	1.9	5.8
67 Men's and Boys' Shoes	2.4	4.3	0.7	2.2
73 Domestic Floor Coverings	2.4	4.2	2.2	2.3
96 Candy	1.7	3.4	0.6	0.9
Total Main Store	3.0	5.0	85.6	2.6
Total Basement	3.7	5.5	14.4	1.3
Total Store	3.1	5.0	100.0	2.5

Source: Edwards and Howard, 1943, p. 122. Originally from *1940 Departmental Merchandising and Operating Results of Department Stores and Specialty Stores,* published by the Controllers' Congress of the National Retail Dry Goods Association, New York, June 1941.

the much greater difficulties in advertising-response measurement, are much more mercurial in their media selections. They shift massive sums into television and out of magazines, or from *Look* to *Life* and back. One might also expect that the size of their advertising appropriations will vary more from year to year than retailers' appropriations, a hypothesis that I have not gathered data to test, however.

FIGURE 2–10a. PERCENTAGE OF YEARLY ADVERTISING EACH MONTH IN DEPARTMENT STORES: SILK AND WOOL DRESSES

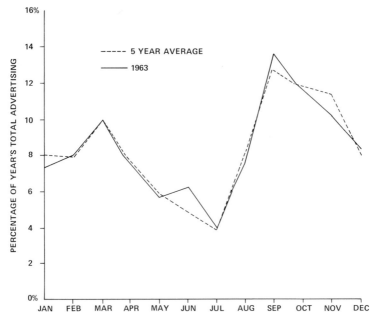

Source: *Neustadt Red Book*, 1963, p. 10.

Up till now we have considered only the *quantity* of advertising-response information available, implicitly assuming that the information (and the manager's estimate of response based on the information) is not systematically off in one direction or the other. But this need not be so. The manager's estimate might well be biased, either because the information-collecting procedure is biased or because the manager's calculation based on the raw data is unsound. Therefore it is worth considering briefly the effects of such biases.

One frequent source of bad managerial calculations is the failure to count in the lagged response to advertising. This is not entirely the manager's fault, because until recently no one had showed how to estimate lagged effects for advertising other than mail-order advertising (e.g., Zielske, 1959; Telser, 1962b). Failure to account for lagged effects biases *downward* an estimate of advertising response (unless the manager uses some rule of thumb to adjust his response estimate, e.g., attributing all of each year's sales to each year's advertising, a very bad rule if response is heavily lagged). The result of such a failure will be a

FIGURE 2–10b. PERCENTAGE OF YEARLY ADVERTISING EACH MONTH IN DEPARTMENT STORES: MADE-UP DRAPES

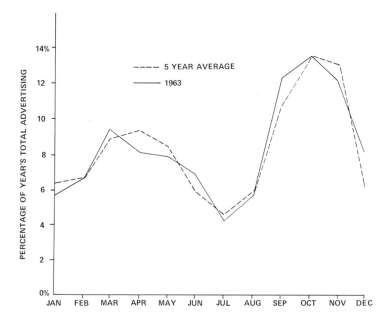

Source: *Neustadt Red Book*, 1963, p. 184.

lower expenditure for advertising than if response were estimated without bias.

A belief in increasing returns in advertising, or in a threshold effect, is another sort of bias. This belief is two-edged, either reducing to zero or raising upwards the advertising of would-be medium-sized or small advertisers.

9. Newness of Product in the Market

To the extent that advertising operates to pass information (news) from seller to buyer, it is reasonable to surmise that the longer a product has been on the market the less advertising there will be for it, because as time passes the news is no longer new.[15] The data for refrigerators in Table 2-14 shed empirical light on this proposition. The amount of advertising per refrigerator, as well as the amount of advertising as a proportion of retail sales of refrigerators, declined secularly from the introduction period onward.[16]

One might think that the depression caused a relative drop in refrigerator advertising. But the aggregate advertising-sales proportion (for all products in the economy) did not show nearly as much secular change as that for refrigerators, as seen in column 8. Nor does the drop in refrigerator advertising reflect a shift to more personal selling; in fact the opposite was true: "The reliance placed upon personal selling tended to be less with each year; more and more manufacturers counted upon advertising to bring consumers to retail establishments to buy" (Borden, 1942, p. 413). And because personal selling is more appropriate for situations where there is considerable information to talk about, it is indeed reasonable to believe that personal selling should decline relative to advertising as the product was no longer so new and as "the desirability of mechanical refrigeration was taken more for granted" (Borden, 1942, p. 413).

It may be true that the drop in refrigerator prices (which would, however, appear smaller if column 4 were corrected for the drop in price level during the 1930s) had causal influence in the drop in advertising, rather than just accompanying it. But even if this is true, it is still also true that the amount of advertising decreases as an innovation becomes less new.

[15] Telser recently presented the same hypothesis, but for very different reasons. He assumed that there is a "threshold of awareness" in consumers (i.e., economies of scale), and hence new products would have to be advertised enough to surmount the threshold once and for all" (1968, p. 5). In an earlier paper, however, Telser offered much the same explanation as given here (1965, pp. 9–10).

[16] This statement refers to the data limited to magazine advertising (column 5), but comparison of columns 5 and 6 for the period covered by column 6 indicates that column 5 is not a bad proxy for column 6. Even the figures in column 6 "fail to reflect the full extent of advertising and promotional expenditures devoted to refrigerators. Figures . . . submitted by several manufacturers show that the total [of advertising and promotional expenditures including cooperative advertising, dealer helps, administration, etc.] were two and one-half to three times the value of the traceable expenditures [column 6] . . ." (Borden, 1942, p. 404). But there is no reason to think that these data do not give a reliable relative indication of expenditures in various years. A shift toward retail advertising might cause some bias, but I doubt the likelihood of its being important here.

Table 2-14. Refrigerator Sales and Advertising

1	2	3	4	5	6	7	8
	Refrigerators Sold (in $1000s)	Retail Value of Refrigerators (in $1000s)	Average Retail Price per Unit in Current Dollars	Manufacturers' Advertising in Leading Magazines (in $1000s)	Manufacturers' Advertising in Four Media (Newspapers, farm magazines, chain radio) (in $1000s)	Magazine Advertising per Refrigerator (Col. 5÷Col. 2)	Magazine Advertising as a Proportion of Dollar Sales (Col. 6÷Col. 3)
1919				$ 38			
1920			$600	64			
1921	5	$ 2,750	550				
1922	12	6,300	525				
1923	18	8,550	475	45		$2.5000	
1924	30	13,500	450	114		3.8000	
1925	75	31,875	425	406		5.4133	
1926	205	79,950	390	1,111		5.4195	
1927	375	131,250	350	1,545		4.1200	
1928	535	178,690	334	2,075		3.8785	
1929	778	227,176	292	2,373	$6,012	3.0501	0.0264
1930	791	217,525	275	2,361	6,023	2.9848	0.0276
1931	906	233,748	258	3,105	7,368	3.4271	0.0315
1932	798	155,610	195	2,285	4,923	2.8634	0.0316
1933	1,016	172,720	170	1,126	3,135	1.1082	0.0181
1934	1,283	220,676	172	1,813	4,059	1.4130	0.0184
1935	1,568	253,648	162	2,165	4,531	1.3807	0.0178
1936	1,996	327,344	164	2,121	4,531	1.0626	0.0137
1937	2,310	395,010	171	2,422	5,377	1.0484	0.0136
1938	1,240	213,280	172	1,271	2,719	1.0250	0.0127
1939	1,840	309,120	168	1,612	3,385	0.8760	0.0109
1940	2,600	395,200	152				

Source: Borden, 1942, pp. 397, 400, 404, compiled by him from various trade sources.

For another example, Table 2-15 shows data on sales and advertising for television sets. It is quite clear that the proportion of retail advertising to sales was higher in earlier years than in later years. (Data on manufacturers' noncooperative advertising could not be obtained easily.)

Further empirical support for the hypothesis given above is found in the work of Comanor and Wilson (1967). In a sample of industries they found that the correlation between the mean advertising ratios for

Table 2-15. Television Set Production and Retail Advertising

1	2	3	4	5
Year	Sets Produced [a] (in 1000s)	Value [a] ($1000s)	Retail Advertising Linage for TV Sets (in 1000s)	Linage per Set (Col. 4 ÷ 2)
1947	179	$ 50		
1948	975	230	4,730	4.9
1949	3,000	580	14,808	4.9
1950	7,464	1,350	21,652	14.8
1951	5,385	957	18,761	3.5
1952	6,096	1,049	12,204	2.0
1953	7,216	1,230	10,303	1.4
1954	7,347	1,029	9,063	1.2
1955	7,757	1,071	9,700	1.3
1956	7,387	939	9,095	1.2
1957	6,399	833	6,538	1.0
1958	4,920	668	5,374	1.1
1959	6,349	896	6,344	1.0
1960	5,708	825	7,041	1.2
1961	6,178	835	6,199	1.0
1962	6,471	822	6,655	1.03

[a] N.B. Quite different estimates for production and value are given by *1964 Broadcasting Yearbook*, p. A-93, but either set of data shows the same effect under discussion in this section.
Sources: Production and Value Data *Television Fact Book*, 1964, p. 402; Advertising: *Neustadt Red Book*, 1963, p. 261.

industries, and the *rate of growth* of demand for the various industries, was .40; that correlation was higher than between the advertising-sales ratio and any other "structural" market variable they studied (p. 433, fn). What this suggests, then, is that while industries are growing they will advertise a lot. And it is reasonable to think that there is a relationship between an industry's demand growth and the extent of innovation in the industry, i.e., the amount of "newness" to be advertised.

The above discussion must be reconciled to the observed *increase* over time in absolute advertising expenditures for many products that are not innovations but rather have been a long time on the market, including beer, liquor, and soap. These products are certainly on a plateau with respect to new information, and one would therefore expect neither increase nor decrease in their advertising expenditures over time if all else remained constant. However, many factors that are likely to result in more advertising do not remain constant, especially on the demand side as discussed earlier in the chapter, e.g., increases in per capita income, increases in total population, and decreases in real media costs.

Increasing efficiency of advertising that comes with increased technological knowledge of the advertising process, and especially increased understanding of the lagged effect of advertising, may also contribute to increased advertising expenditures, as discussed earlier. Therefore, the increases over time in absolute advertising expenditures for such products as soap and beer do not conflict with the discussion of this section.

CONCLUSIONS

An increase in the proportion of users of a product (i.e., an upward shift in the response function) in a geographic market or an advertising medium probably will increase the promotion expenditures of a monopolist. But a decrease in promotion is also possible, especially if the increase in use heralds saturation of the market.

Because the response functions for representative firms are steeper than the industry's (or monopolist's) function, an increase in the proportion of product users will result in a bigger increase (or a smaller decrease) in amount of promotion if there are several competing advertisers than if the market is monopolized.

The higher the proportion of product users in a given geographic area, the larger the proportion of promotion that will be done by the retailer relative to the national brand-owner. The opposite is true of an increase in the proportion of product users in a particular national advertising medium.

An increase in geographic market size, *ceteris paribus*, leads to more advertising by the brand-owner and by the retailer also.

The greater the number of markets in which a firm sells, the lower will be its promotion costs on the average, and hence it will promote more in each market when it increases the number of markets it sells in.

An increase in sales volume per buyer may have many types of effects on promotion expenditures.

The less reliable the manager's information about the advertising-response function, the more variation may be expected in the firm's choice of advertising media and in the size of its advertising expenditure.

The effect of the brand's choice of selling price on the amount spent for advertising is indeterminate without specification of the shapes of the advertising-response functions.

The longer a new innovation is on the market, the less will be the amount of advertising per unit of sale.

In the short run the effect of an income rise is like any other change in probability of consumer purchase, but in the longer run the taste changes that accompany income changes may well alter the whole situation.

Postscript: On Advertising and the Business Cycle

This postscript digresses to consider whether President Eisenhower was correct (even if infelicitous in expression) when he stated that what the country needed most in the midst of a then-current recession was "more belly-to-belly selling."

In answer, this postscript is a short digression about the effect of advertising on the business cycle, a topic that has excited considerable interest among economists whose attention has turned to advertising ever since Vaile (1927) tackled the subject.[17] This discussion is located

[17] Even earlier, Sherman brought evidence to bear on the matter, "showing the number of pages of advertisements, and number of advertisements, in *Harper's Magazine*, since their first appearance in it in 1864, taking the month of October wherever a copy of that month's issue was accessible: —

Date	Pages of Ads	Number of Ads	Date	Pages of Ads	Number of Ads
1864	3¼	11	1885	11½	62
1865	2	5	1886	20	97
1866	3	19	1887	37	135
1867	6	30	1888	54	193
1868	7⅓	20	1889	48	237
1869	5⅓	35	1890	75	348
1870	4½	21	1891	113	409
1871	3½	30	1892	90	403
1872	2	20	1893	84	307
1873	1	7	1894	76	353
1874–80	No advertisements		1895	80	374
1881	Not accessible		1896	76	329
1882	1¼	15	1897	81	348
1883	8½	53	1898	83	330
1884	8	43	1899	112	322
			1900	110	294

"The effects of hard times on advertising could have no stronger illustration than the blank years 1874–80; and it is marked in the years following 1892" (Sherman, 1900, pp. 4–5).

where it is because the relevant variations in advertising expenditures over the business cycle are quite clearly caused by variations in demand, as will be seen shortly.

The relevant facts seem to be as follows:

1. Advertising expenditures generally follow the same course as the business cycle. This may be read in an excellent pioneering article by Wagner (1941), and in Blank (1962), or may be seen in Figures 2-11 and 2-12 (Borden's, pp. 718 and 720), 2-13 (Verdon et al., 1968, Chart 1), 2-14 to 2-16 (Yang, 1964, p. 26), or 3-4 and 3-6.

2. The variations over the business cycle in advertising expenditures for consumer durables are more violent than for consumer nondurables, just as sales of consumer durables vary more than does aggregated demand (see Yang's Figure 2-14, but note that the magnitudes shown are rates of change. The rates of change for advertising expenditures for the various product classes seem to be of about the same magnitudes as the rates of changes for the sales of those products. See Figure 2-14; also Figures 3-4 and 3-6 in Section 4, Chapter 3). *Total* advertising expenditures are somewhat more volatile than GNP, and of about the same volatility as the Index of Industrial Production (Wagner, 1941; Blank, 1963; Verdon et al., 1968). (Less aggregated data pertaining to the amount of year-to-year variation in firms' advertising expenditures are given in Chapter 5.)

3. The advertising cycle lags slightly behind the general business cycle observed for total production, consumers' goods production, employment, and other measures over 1924–38 by Wagner (1941), and for various measures observed over 1945–64 by Verdon et al. (1968). The latter estimate a lag of 3.75 months, and Wagner's estimates jibe with that.

Present-day businessmen are probably more likely to reduce advertising expenditures when sales go down than were businessmen when Vaile (1927) studied the matter, because businessmen understand advertising better now than then.[18] (Vaile found that a substantial number of firms increased their spending when sales went down.) This also suggests that businessmen are not likely to respond to moral suasion to increase rather than decrease advertising when times turn bad. In the other direction, to the extent that fixed costs increase in business, advertising may be expected to hold up or increase when sales go down. (This and other aspects of the cyclical behavior of individual firms, and of firms with different types of cost structures, are discussed in detail in

---

[18] See the advice of Dean (1950–51). But see also Keyser (1947) and Ramsdell (1931). The interested reader might find G. Collins (1948) useful.

FIGURE 2–11. RELATIONSHIP BETWEEN ADVERTISING AND BUSINESS ACTIVITY

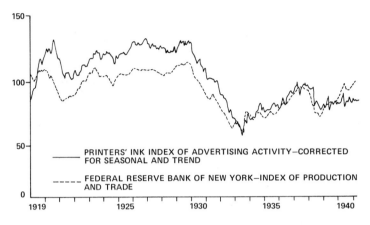

Source: Borden, 1942, p. 718.

FIGURE 2–12. RELATIONSHIP BETWEEN ADVERTISING ACTIVITY AND SALES OF GOODS AT RETAIL

Source: Borden, 1942, p. 720.

FIGURE 2–13. ADVERTISING EXPENDITURE, AND BUSINESS EXPANSIONS AND CONTRACTIONS

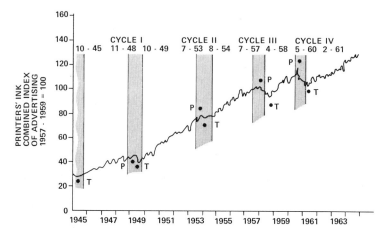

Notes: Vertical lines indicate reference cycle turning dates; contractionary phases shaded. *P* and *T* indicate CIA specific cycle turning dates; • shows reference cycle turning date corresponding to respective specific cycle date.

Source: Verdon et al., 1968, p. 10. Computed by them from basic time series in U.S. Department of Commerce, *Business Statistics*, 1963 and earlier editions, and *Survey of Current Business*, April, 1964, and April, 1965.

FIGURE 2–14. CHANGES IN CONSUMERS' NONDURABLE GOODS ADVERTISING AND SALES, OVER THE BUSINESS CYCLE

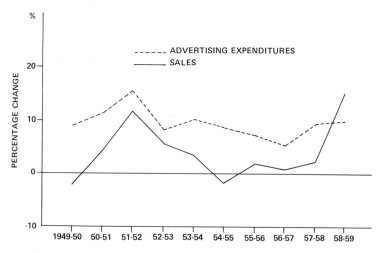

Source: Yang, 1964, p. 26.

FIGURE 2–15. CHANGES IN CONSUMERS' DURABLE GOODS ADVERTISING AND SALES, OVER THE BUSINESS CYCLE

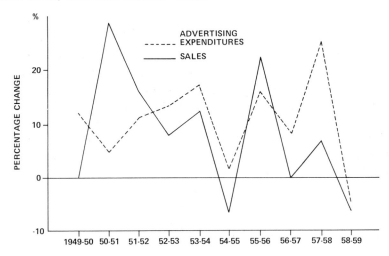

Source: Yang, 1964, p. 26.

FIGURE 2–16. CHANGES IN PRODUCERS' GOODS ADVERTISING AND SALES, OVER THE BUSINESS CYCLE

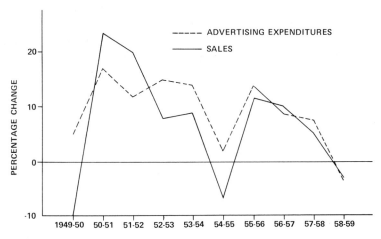

Source: Yang, 1964, p. 26.

Section 4 of Chapter 3.) But there is probably no reason to believe that fixed costs will be relatively more important in the future than at present.

The key question is how important advertising is in the business cycle. On this issue no one seems to have done any work except perhaps Dean (1951, p. 377). Those who have thought about the effect of advertising on business cycles have considered two aspects of advertising: (1) its direct effect on aggregate demand as an expenditure like any other expenditure; and (2) its possible indirect effect in stimulating people to buy other goods. I will peremptorily dismiss the latter possibility; my reasons for thinking that any effect of advertising on even the long-run propensity to consume is slight are given in Chapter 8, and the likelihood that advertising has any effect in the short run, i.e., over the length of a business cycle, I consider even slighter. If this view is correct, then all that remains to be considered is the effect of advertising as an expenditure like any other business or consumer expenditure that might rise or fall during the business cycle.

The total of advertising represents perhaps 2½ percent of U.S. production, and it is only one-third the size of privately purchased producers' durable equipment (see Table 2-16). Given that advertising is not much more volatile than GNP, the swing in advertising is not much more than 2½ percent of the swing in GNP over the business cycle. Therefore, even if the volume of advertising were rendered absolutely constant over the cycle, and even if a multiplier effect is reckoned in, perhaps 5 percent of the business-cycle effect would be eliminated. But nothing like complete constancy in advertising expenditures across the business cycle could be achieved with any conceivable manipulative device. (I completely dismiss as impossible the idea that the pattern could be reversed so far as to make advertising countercyclical.) And certainly there are other categories of goods that bulk much larger in the swing of economic activity — notably inventories and other business investment.

In considering a category of activity as a cyclical tool one wants to consider its controllability as well as its size. The categories to which one might most sensibly compare advertising are consumer durables and producer durables. And advertising seems to me to be less controllable than either. Perhaps the most important reason is that a drop in a firm's demand function during the business cycle makes it rational for the profit-maximizing firm to reduce its expenditure for advertising as purchasing declines. That is, advertising-sales response functions must fall when business is bad, and the maximizing advertising expenditure will then almost surely be lower (see Chapters 2 and 3). This is not the case with either consumer or producer durables, the purchase of neither of which is so predicated on contemporaneous conditions. So whereas it should be reasonably easy to induce a rational consumer or producer to shift his durable purchases from cyclical peaks to troughs with small cost or other incentives, it would take very large incentives even to keep advertisers from not shifting advertising expenditures away from troughs.

Table 2-16. Amounts Spent for Producer Durables and for Advertising

Year	1 Private Purchases of Producers' Durable Equipment (in billions)	2 Total U.S. Advertising (in billions)
1947	$15.9	$ 4.2
1948	18.1	4.9
1949	16.6	5.3
1950	18.7	5.9
1951	20.7	6.5
1952	20.2	7.2
1953	21.5	7.8
1954	20.6	8.1
1955	23.8	9.0
1956	26.5	9.7
1957	28.4	10.3
1958	25.0	10.4
1959	28.4	11.4
1960	30.3	11.9
1961	28.6	12.0
1962	32.5	12.9
1963	34.8	13.6
1964	39.7	14.6
1965	44.8	15.6
1966		16.8

Sources:
Column 1, *The National Income and Product Accounts of the United States, 1929-65*, pp. 84-85.
Column 2, *Advertising Age*, June 19, 1967, p. 88.

To restate the above point, a drop in advertising expenditures as business activity declines is really an objective consequence of a decline in sales rather than a psychological one. This is much less the case with consumer and producer durables. Hence it would be much harder to smooth out the advertising-expenditure fluctuations that accompany the business cycle.

(There is the further institutional matter that at least some portion of advertising budgets are set on some such rule-of-thumb basis as a proportion of sales, and hence advertising expenditures will vary automatically with the business cycle.)

These considerations of controllability, together with the previous considerations of the size of aggregate advertising expenditure and its likely effect on the short-run propensity to consume, lead me to doubt that advertising has, or could have, a very important role in the business cycle, one way or another.

3

The Effect
of Various Costs
upon Advertising
Expenditures

The previous chapter provided a general introduction to the investigation of the effect of various variables upon amounts of advertising expenditures, and it set forth the theory for the effects of various demand dimensions upon advertising. Chapter 4 will examine the effect of market structure (number of competitors) and product variations. This chapter studies the effects of changes in various kinds of costs and cost structures. The first sections deal with the cost of factors of production, the cost of advertising messages, and the cost of transportation. The treatment is brief and perhaps obvious, but apparently it has not been set forth before, except perhaps in hints by Borden (1942, Chapter XIX).[1] These first sections also provide underpinning for the last and major section on the effect of the proportion of fixed production costs to total production costs. That last section examines interesting phenomena of seasonal and cyclical shifts in advertising expenditures that are not so obvious in their explanation.

1. The Cost of Variable Factors of Production

In the short run following a decrease in a factor cost, selling price and number of competitors are fixed. The intersection of the appropriate marginal curves will therefore move to the right and hence promotion will increase. This effect is illustrated by the action of department stores when they heavily promote "special purchases."

In the somewhat longer run, especially in very competitive situations, wholesale and retail prices will follow factor costs down, perhaps to the

---

[1] Else (1966) also refers to the cost of advertising, but his meaning of "cost" and his general context are entirely different.

point of equilibrium at which manufacturers and retailers are netting the same total ("normal") profit as before, at the same percent markup as before, or even at the same absolute markup. The total profit will be at least no lower than before and perhaps larger. Sales will have increased due to the price reduction even if promotion has not yet increased.

In any of the above cases promotion should increase. Florists advertise those flowers that are cheapest at each particular season, and butchers the cheapest meat. These choices of merchandise to promote might be interpreted as "leaders" to "build traffic," or as mere choices of what to advertise with no increase in the particular retail budget. But with reference to the particular commodity, promotion is certainly higher than it would otherwise be. It is an empirical question whether the total retail budget is also increased if a particular kind of merchandise is reduced drastically in price.[2]

What about a rise in a factor-input cost? Is the process completely reversible? In a competitive retail situation, especially one in which retail prices are computed at least partly with rules of thumb as discussed by Holdren (1960), and Cyert and March (1963), factor prices will indeed affect retail prices directly. Retail promotion will be reduced if costs go up. Choice promotional display space will be given to other merchandise, and the product will not be chosen to be featured in advertising.[3] And in the short-run sticky-price manufacturing situation, selling prices are even less sticky on the up side than on the down side. There seems to be no theoretical reason not to expect that the promotion effect is reversible, or that less promotion will occur when factor prices increase.

2. Advertising Media Availability and Costs

Ceteris paribus, the marginal cost of advertising decreases as more media become available, or as the prices of media fall. Just as when the cost of any factor of production falls there should be an increase in total output, so the physical amount of promotion should increase as the cost of advertising decreases. On the other hand, the *dollar* volume of advertising might increase *or* decrease following a decrease in the price of advertising. The outcome depends upon the price elasticity

[2] In the even longer run, the number of firms will increase. The total effect on promotion of that change along with the others is not analyzed here. The similar case of the effect of a sales-tax change on advertising is discussed by Due (1959, pp. 348–352).

[3] But Preston found that some items are advertised that are the same price in all stores, including some items whose price is fixed by outside-the-store forces (1963, p. 50). This phenomenon is difficult to understand.

of demand for advertising, just as with any other good. And the relevant elasticity depends upon the importance in firms' budgets of the advertising medium or media in question. The demand for all advertising taken together is clearly less elastic than is the demand for a single radio station's time in a small town in Illinois, considering both the market in entirety and also almost every individual advertiser. And one would expect the demand for a trade magazine's space — especially the only trade magazine in a given line of business — to be less elastic than the demand for space in a consumer magazine, for which there are more close substitutes.

There do not seem to be any published estimates of any of these sorts of elasticities. But one may at least get a rough idea of the effects of differences in prices (per viewer) in different television markets upon sales of television time in those markets. It was shown in Figure 2-6 that the cost of six "fringe" television advertising minutes per week is less than 50 cents per thousand television homes in the largest urban market, and about 65 cents in the 75th largest market ($2.30 in the 200th largest market!). Table 2-4 shows the effect: national-advertiser expenditures per family in spot television are $13.35 in the largest market, around $5.00 in northern markets at the bottom of the size list, and as low as $3.43 in southern cities. Tables 2-3, 2-5, and 2-6 show the same pattern with newspaper rates; rates are lower in larger cities, and total advertising linage is also greatest there. There is no likely reason for these differences among cities in amount of advertising except the cost of the advertising.[4] And the implied elasticity is roughly in the neighborhood of unity.

An estimate of approximately unity for television prices in various markets does not, on the face of it, jibe with the observed data for television as a whole, which one expects a priori to have a lower price elasticity than individual markets. Total expenditures rose in much greater proportion than prices dropped from 1950, 1951, and 1952 to 1966, and the price rises in other media were nowhere near great enough to account for the effect (see Table 3-1 below). This would seem to imply a very high price elasticity for the television medium as a whole. But I would guess that progressively increasing advertiser familiarity with the new medium was responsible for a very large part of the increase in total television advertising.

An overall price elasticity of demand for advertising of unity is im-

---

[4] Differences in per capita income or per-family income might contribute to the differences, especially between southern and non-southern cities. But the variation among advertising expenditures is much greater than the variation among income levels. Furthermore, income levels are nowhere near so closely related to city size as are per-family advertising expenditures.

plied for a given firm if it adheres to a rule of spending a fixed proportion of sales for advertising. But this rule must be very short run, and is not used by many (or even most) firms.

Table 3-1. Advertising Cost Indices and Television Expenditures

	Advertising Expenditures on Television (in $1,000s)			Advertising Cost Indices			
				Television			
	Network	Spot	Local	Network	Spot	Magazines	Newspapers
1950	85	31	55	278	167	75	75
1951	181	70	82	167	120	78	79
1952	256	94	104	175	133	83	83
1965	1237	866	412	89	103	112	114

Source: Backman, 1968, pp. 178, 179, 199.

3. Availability and Cost of Transportation Facilities

In the simplest case the cost of transportation may be treated as a variable factor of production, and changes in its cost therefore have the same effect on the amount of promotion as do changes in the cost of any other factor. For example, a rise in the postage rate on books would have exactly the same effect on the Book-of-the-Month Club and its promotion expenditures as would a rise in the production cost of books. But this is an unusual example because the transportation cost of mailing books is the same no matter what the distance is to the addressee.

It is the graduation in the cost of transportation to more distant customers which distinguishes this section from Section 1 on the cost of variable factors of production. A change in transportation costs therefore affects the firm's relationship to distant customers more than its relationship to customers that are close at hand; a change in transportation cost therefore creates a larger price change to the distant customers.

Promotion is very much a creature of geographic distance between buyer and seller, because the closer the buyer and seller, the more likely is the buyer to be in full possession of relevant market information. (For justification of this statement see Chapter 7, Section 4.) Therefore, an increase (or decrease) in transportation cost, as measured by the cost per unit of sale to the average customer (i.e., a customer at an average distance from the seller), would induce a larger decrease (or increase) in promotion than would a similar change in cost per unit of other factors of production.

In other words, a very high cost of transportation limits the seller to a small geographic market, within which he has little need to promote, e.g., cement and brick firms. Of course, the element of geographic monopoly is inextricably intertwined in this consideration of transportation costs, but an important part of a geographic monoply is its monopoly of information, which reduces the need for promotion by the monopolist.

Mail-order selling is a particularly clear example of the importance of a system for transporting goods. This and other examples are discussed in a broader historical context in Chapter 7, Section 4.

A similar analysis applies to changes in the transportation cost for customers to *come* to a retail outlet. Nowadays dentists in Reno, Nevada, advertise in the classified telephone directory of Elko, Nevada, 293 miles away. (There is no speed limit on Nevada highways.) Harold's Club also takes promotional advantage of the twentieth-century ease of long-distance travel in the United States when it places its signs along roads thousands of miles from its location in Reno.

Improvement in customer transportation also leads to larger retail outlets — department stores for example — at the expense of local stores. And the Newark Bears and the Jersey City Giants, playing just across the Hudson River from the three New York City major league baseball clubs in those honest days before franchise moves, progressively lost fans to the major league clubs as transportation grew faster; at the same time, the major league clubs increased their advertising in New Jersey. This process was aided by the radio broadcast of major league games, another diminisher of the distance between buyer and seller.

The response of firms to changes in transportation costs, within reasonably short adjustment time periods, is quite consistent. There are few industries in which some of the brands are local or regional and others are national. And in many of those cases that do exist — beer, for example — the national brand is a multiple-plant operation which, on the production side, may function like a financial consolidation of regional manufacturers.

4. Proportion of Fixed Costs to Total Costs [5]

The proportion of fixed to total costs is important to almost a startling degree in influencing the amount of promotion. Differences in ratios of fixed cost to total cost affect promotion in two ways — directly by making for diminishing marginal costs, and indirectly by way of variations in demand. We shall treat the former aspect in this section, the latter aspect in the next section.

[5] Vaile (1931, p. 44) mentioned this factor in a single line.

We begin by noting that an increase in the proportion of fixed capital investment to variable costs will usually accompany a decrease of production costs.[6] This statement presupposes the operation of economic rationality, in the short run by rational calculation or in the somewhat longer run by trial and error. Insofar as the increase in capital investment implies a decrease in production cost, the same argument that applies to a decrease in factor costs leads us to expect an increase in promotion. This is a long-run estimate of the average over time for the firm. (Bookkeeping and depreciation problems can distort the issue. To the extent that a firm's accountants misstate the true economic picture, wrong decisions about promotion may occur.)

But the effect of technological change and increased capital investment goes beyond that of decreases in factor costs. An illustration of the direct effect of technology-caused diminishing marginal costs occurred early in the snowy early-winter evening when this paragraph was first being written. A circular came through the mail slot, an advertisement by an enterprising student offering to keep snow cleared from sidewalks and driveway for the entire winter at a single flat rate. I doubt that such a circular would have been distributed 10 years ago, or even 35 years ago in the depths of the depression. No student can himself shovel enough walks to make printed promotion necessary or useful. And the returns to the organizing work done by an entrepreneur hiring a gang of men probably would not be great enough to support such a promotion.

It was a technological development that caused this promotion. The student entrepreneur bought or rented a snow-clearing machine with which he can clean a good number of walks, and his production cost per sidewalk is far less than the opportunity cost of the homeowner. The situation therefore has these characteristics: The entrepreneur has the capacity to produce in quantity, and at a cost far less than the consumer's cost would be for doing the same job. But also, unless he does promote and get a lot of business he will not be able to recover his original investment or make a large profit on it.

Transportation service is another example of this phenomenon, and it is interesting to note that transportation services were among the earliest advertisers in English journals.[7] Low marginal cost for incremental passengers and freight on regularly scheduled runs was a very important condition for this advertising. Once a stagecoach or

[6] This statement is intended to apply over time and not cross-sectionally among areas, of course.

[7] "The first stage coach notices in England appeared in the year 1658, almost two centuries and a half ago" (Sherman, 1900, p. 12).

ship or train is scheduled for a trip, the marginal cost up to 100 per cent capacity is very small. Books are another commodity that was advertised very early and for which the marginal cost is low compared to average cost. As with transportation, there are major indivisibilities in book production that cause a very much lower cost for the 1,000th or 10,000th book compared to the average cost of the first few books that are produced. Hence there is heavy advertising.

5. Variations in Demand in High-Fixed-Cost Situations

The interaction of fluctuations in demand stemming from any of many sources, and the indivisibility and short-run inconvertibility of capital-goods investment, ensure that there will be variations over time in the point on a firm's cost curve at which the firm operates. In cruder terms, these forces ensure that there will be variations in the proportion of production "capacity" that is used from time to time. It should help to illuminate this matter if we perform the mental comparison of two firms that are operating at equal levels of capacity (measured in any sensible fashion) and at far less than full capacity. Assume the firms have different ratios of fixed costs to total costs, i.e., one may be more mechanized or automated than the other. The firm with the higher ratio will have a higher marginal net revenue (because its marginal cost is lower), and hence it will promote more. (The problem of the interrelation of production to promotion has been discussed in a managerial context by Dhrymes, 1962.)

The effect on the amount of promotion depends on the proportion of capacity in use both at peak times and at slack times, as well as on the structure of competition. For example, a one-minute car-wash that never approaches capacity at peak times, located in a town with five other car washes, is likely to promote vigorously in peak times; the large number of potential customers makes his promotion relatively efficient at that time. But a car wash that often reaches 100 percent capacity and that is located in a town in which it is either a monopolist or in which there are five other car washes, is likely to promote more heavily in slow times than in the peak season. (Car-washing services that have little or no capital investment and wash cars by hand do not *ever* promote.)

Department stores are especially troubled by this problem. Should a department store promote most heavily for slow days, slow seasons, slow years — or for busy days, busy seasons, good years? On slow days, incremental sales have a lower marginal production cost than on busy days, because salespeople and sales space are underoccupied. But on busy days a given amount of advertising will reach more people whose custom might be shifted from other stores.[8] Airlines that carry many tourists in travel seasons face a similar problem.

The actual promotional behavior of department stores throws some light on the problem.[9] Some seasonal fluctuations in demand are taken as given and immutable — Christmas buying in most departments, for example. In general, stores advertise more heavily in these busier seasons. But contrary to the general yearly pattern, advertising in December is less than proportional to sales relative to other months, and for some stores it is a low *absolute* advertising month (see Table 8-2). Such a promotional schedule for a given store is consistent with the following facts: (1) The store comes close enough to peak capacity in December so that the marginal production cost of additional sales would increase steeply. (2) Any given amount of advertising produces more incremental sales in busier seasons than in slack seasons. (3) There are diminishing marginal sales returns to advertising scale. If one is to allocate a given total amount of advertising expenditure throughout the year in such a way that the marginal returns will be the same in each period, expenditures will be higher in busier seasons. (4) The lower marginal production cost of sales in slower seasons raises the optimum promotional level in slow seasons higher than it would be if production costs were the same the year round. And this is exactly the pattern of promotion that trial and error seems to have recommended to Edwards and Howard:

[One should not waste] money in low-volume months by trying to force business when people are not inclined to buy. It erroneously curtails expenditures in months when business would normally be easy to get if sufficient publicity were used. [Nor should one go] to the opposite extremes of squandering money needlessly in high-volume months and of pinching pennies beyond the point of discretion in low-volume months. [Instead] publicity money should be spent to invite people to the store when they are naturally inclined to buy. It follows the course of least resistance by recognizing people's buying habits. . . . Generally a store will find it inadvisable, and often impossible, to distribute the seasonal expense-class appropriations to months in exact proportion to the percentages of the season's sales that the store plans to obtain in the different months. An illustration of the points that influence the distribution of the season's newspaper advertising appropriation to months will make this clear. The month of December contributes about 28 per cent of the fall season's

[8] It is an illustration of the strengths and weakness of the case-study system of teaching business administration that at least one problem of this sort appears in a 1937 casebook by Neil Borden (1937). More than 30 years later, we still have no theory to help solve the problem. Yet students grappled with the problem without theory, just as operating businessmen did then and do now.

[9] One might also learn much about the *capacities* of stores by backward deduction from their promotional behavior.

business (or about 15.8 per cent of the year's total business) in many stores. Most publicity directors agree that it would be unwise, and they have found it unnecessary, to spend 28 per cent of the fall season's newspaper advertising appropriation to attract December business. Usually they trim the December allotment and spend the difference in other months when it can be used to better advantage [1943, pp. 116–117].

It is instructive to compare the department-store seasonal pattern with the seasonal promotional pattern of mail-order firms, for whom fixed costs are a very small proportion of total costs. Promotion is a positive and sharp function of seasonal response, as may be seen in Table 3-2. The high level of promotion in November is because November magazine issues come out at the right time for mail-order Christmas sales. January, however, is the lowest-response month of the year for the type of novelty and gift goods advertised in *House Beauti-*

Table 3-2. Mail-Order Linage in *House Beautiful*

Month	1951		1952	
	Number of advertisements	Advertising linage	Number of advertisements	Advertising linage
January	90	658	87	5,786
February	188	12,982	183	12,032
March	175	11,564	209	13,486
April	213	15,434	270	18,928
May	278	18,922	306	21,114
June	249	15,680	256	16,888
July	104	6,876	126	8,228
August	91	6,412	109	7,776
September	221	15,524	260	17,244
October	431	30,720	490	36,223
November	887	62,338	986	68,871
December	531	35,694	530	34,424

Source: *House Beautiful* promotion literature.

ful. Response to a given amount of advertising undergoes much more gentle seasonal change than does the *amount* of advertising; it would be unusual for an advertisement in the best month to "pull" much more than twice as well as the poorest month. Yet this is translated into the enormous effect on amounts of promotion seen in Table 3-2.

Seasonal and daily shifts in demand are probably less important to manufacturers than to retailers because manufacturers can stockpile their products and thereby smooth out the peaks and troughs. The manufacturer can therefore ignore changes in marginal production cost from season to season. (If, indeed, his product is one that has large seasonal demand fluctuations, his promotion schedule will generally coincide with sales volume as seen in Figures 3-1, 3-2, and 3-3, for radios

FIGURE 3–1. REFRIGERATOR SALES AND ADVERTISING BY MONTH

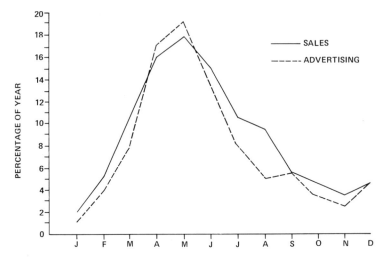

Source: Duffy, 1951, pp. 337–338.

FIGURE 3–2. RADIO SALES AND ADVERTISING BY MONTH

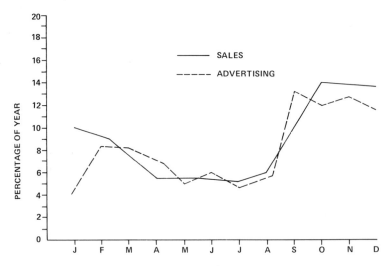

Source: Duffy, 1951, pp. 337–338.

FIGURE 3–3. GASOLINE SALES AND ADVERTISING BY MONTH

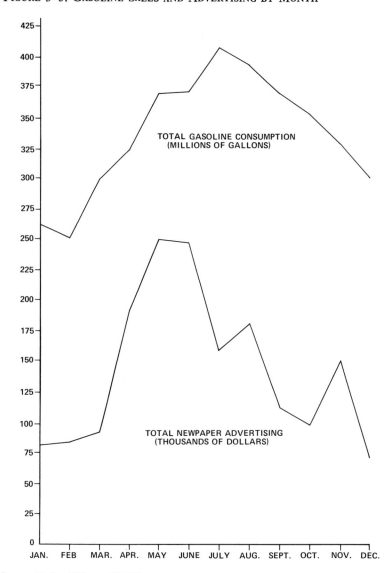

TOTAL GASOLINE CONSUMPTION
(MILLIONS OF GALLONS)

TOTAL NEWPAPER ADVERTISING
(THOUSANDS OF DOLLARS)

Source: Duffy, 1951, pp. 337–338.

and refrigerators and gasoline.) And of course manufacturers' advertising does not diminish in the very busiest season, unlike department stores, because manufacturers' production costs are unlikely to rise sharply in the busiest season, again unlike department stores.

The following anecdote demonstrates that stockpiling is far from a complete solution, however: "For years this company [Schaefer Brewing Company] confined its newspaper advertising to the spring, fall, and winter months, since a limited storage capacity prevented them from absorbing the tremendous demand for their product during the summer months. Now, however, that the company has adequate storage facilities, advertising is greatly intensified during the summer months" (Duffy, 1951, p. 335).

We would expect to find very large amounts of slack-time promotion for power utilities, whose product cannot be stored easily,[10] whose ratio of fixed to total costs is very high, and whose facilities are built close to peak capacity. Resort hotels should show similar patterns.

At this point we must consider the relationship between what is and what ought to be. The mail-order firm can and does calculate the profit and loss separately for each advertisement that is run, and only the rawest novice or the worst bumbler in mail order would fail to read these data correctly and use them as the basis for correct future action. It is reasonable to believe that our data for mail-order firms are instructive as to how mail-order firms *ought* to act in order to optimize. Measurement of the short-run and long-run response to advertisements is somewhat more difficult for the retailer, however, and it is less sure that what he does is what he ought to do. And manufacturers have much harder problems in advertising measurement; their measurement problem is often exceedingly complex, and a firm can do exactly the wrong thing for a relatively long time without finding out that it is clearly in error. The fact that Vaile (1927) was able to find, in a great many industries, manufacturing firms that increased *and* firms that decreased their promotion during the 1921 recession bears witness to the lack of clear knowledge by manufacturers about the correct direction of promotional response.[11]

Firms manipulate prices, too, in response to fluctuations in seasonal demand. But the direction of the price change is more predictable: a drop in demand and consequent operation at a lower proportion of ca-

---

[10] But at least one electricity utility has made a very large investment in a plant to pump water up a hill in off hours. The motors then become generators and the water is let flow back down for added capacity at peak times.

[11] I suppose one could also interpret this phenomenon in terms of strategies and counterstrategies, but that does not seem very plausible to me.

pacity almost surely produces lower rather than higher prices. (However, there are probably cases in which department stores offer special sales in busy periods to increase a *share* of an oligopolistic market.)

It is often said that price and advertising are alternative strategies for the firm; indeed, it may well be that when demand falls a firm may decide to choose either a price cut or an increase in promotion, or both. But during busy times a price rise and an increase in promotion may go together.

The *weekly* pattern of department-store promotion differs somewhat from city to city because the weekly sales pattern differs; the weekly sales pattern in turn is affected by differences in late-open days in various cities. But in general retail promotion and sales move together. Unlike the December drop below proportionality in seasonal advertising, the busiest day of the week gets the most advertising. This is consistent with the idea that during most weeks of the year stores operate at points on their production-cost curves well short of the steep-rise portion, even for the busy days of the week. The busiest day of an average week will have considerably lower sales than the busiest day in a December week. Duffy collected data that prove this point very nicely. At the time he was writing, in Jamaica (Long Island), New York City, and Newark, N.J., department stores stayed open until 9 P.M. on Friday, Thursday, and Wednesday, respectively. The amount of department-store linage was, in each case, heaviest on the day before the late-open day (Duffy, 1951, p. 340). Duffy also showed that in three major cities, "80 to 90 per cent of the weekly [food] volume occurs on Friday and Saturday" (1951, p. 341). And in each of these three cities, the newspaper linage for food on Thursday, preceding the busy days, was at least three times greater than the next heaviest day of the week (1951, p. 342).

The importance of the *cyclical* timing of promotion to the economy has already been discussed (Chapter 2, Postscript). But now we are in a position to discuss in microanalytic detail why one can reasonably expect a recession to result in more or less promotion for any given firm.

As noted before, Vaile (1927) found that there were some manufacturers who increased their advertising expenditures during the recession of 1921, as well as firms that took just the opposite course. It would seem, then, that we must temporarily jettison our usual assumption of automatic profit-maximizing rationality operating under conditions of sufficient (if not perfect) knowledge. It is likely that manufacturers lack ability to measure the effect of advertising and lack methods of calculating its long-run value, and it is reasonable that under such conditions we would find differences in managerial decisions about promotion in recessions. However, as industry knowledge of advertising increases we can expect increased unanimity of behavior, and, except for situations that meet the special criteria we have discussed above, we can expect less promotion in cyclical troughs than in peak periods.

Though some manufacturers have increased their expenditures as times became worse, and though some manufacturers even did so wisely, manufacturers and other national advertisers generally reduce their spending sharply in recessions (the solid line in Figure 3-4 shows this in national newspaper advertising from 1928 to 1939). And it is much easier for retailers than for manufacturers to measure the effect of their advertising, which suggests even greater unanimity of cyclical behavior among retailers than among manufacturers. I could not find relevant evidence to test this notion. However, the evidence is clear that the amount of retail promotion did fall from 1928 to 1932, from which time it rose slowly (figures 3-5, 3-6, and 3-7; and the drop in promotion expenditures is even greater than the figures show, because linage rather than dollars is shown there).

Though the absolute amounts spent for retail advertising decrease as sales decrease, there is evidence that the proportion of sales spent for advertising may increase (see Figure 3-4). (This is another example of how one can be misled by looking only at the advertising ratio.) It is a digression from our line of discussion to try to explain this phenomenon because our interest is in the absolute amounts of promotion. But part of the explanation may lie in the shift to cheaper price lines, which in department stores are advertised with a higher ratio of advertising to sales, *ceteris paribus* (see Chapter 2). The explanation may also depend on accounting practices; if the advertising appropriation is set with reference to costs, it makes a difference how the accountant charges for fixed costs.

Manufacturers Compared to Retailers

National advertising by manufacturers is more volatile seasonally than is retail advertising; Figure 3-8 shows data on New York City newspaper advertising over 1921–26. Considering Sunday linage only, the monthly index for national advertising ranged from 69 (August) to 124 (June), a larger spread than the range of 75 (July) to 113 (October) for retail advertisers (Crum, 1927, p. 168). This observation is consistent with manufactuers' ability to stockpile, as compared to retailers whose fixed capital in buildings and fixtures is completely time-bound in its utility.

National linage in New York City newspapers was also more volatile

FIGURE 3–4. NEWSPAPER ADVERTISING, DEPARTMENT STORE ADVER-
TISING, AND DEPARTMENT STORE SALES, OVER THE BUSINESS CYCLE

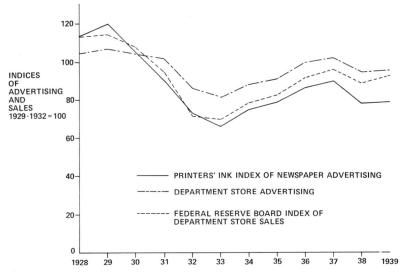

Source: Weld in *Printers' Ink*, July 26, 1940, p. 20.

FIGURE 3–5. DEPARTMENT STORE SALES AND TOTAL RETAIL SALES, OVER
THE BUSINESS CYCLE

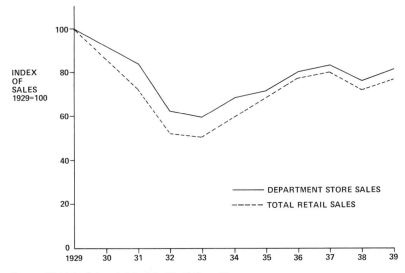

Source: Weld in *Printers' Ink*, July 26, 1940, p. 21.

FIGURE 3–6. NEWSPAPER ADVERTISING AND RETAIL SALES, OVER THE BUSINESS CYCLE

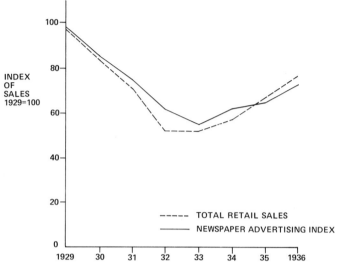

Source: Weld, in *Printers' Ink*, August 12, 1937, p. 50.

FIGURE 3–7. PERCENTAGE OF NET SALES SPENT ON ADVERTISING BY DEPARTMENT AND SPECIALTY STORES

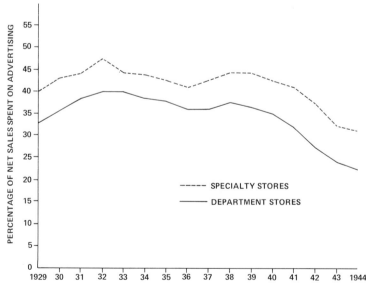

Source: Lund, 1947, p. 270.

cyclically than was retail advertising, from 1916 to 1922 and from 1921 to 1926, but the relative volatility was not so marked (Crum, 1927, p. 168). This makes sense when we remember that stockpiling is nowhere near as effective a strategy to smooth out cyclical variations as it is to smooth out seasonal variations. (Stockpiling aside, the ability to measure the effect of advertising is the other major difference between retailers and manufacturers, and this factor suggests high retail volatility, *ceteris paribus.*)

FIGURE 3–8. NATIONAL AND TOTAL NEW YORK NEWSPAPER ADVERTISING, OVER THE BUSINESS CYCLE

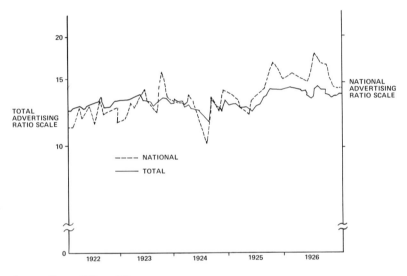

Source: Crum, 1927, p. 172.

Up until now this section has taken demand fluctuation as given. It has been assumed that the retailer faces a stable advertising-response function at any given moment. But promotion may alter these underlying demand conditions. For example, January and August white sales are creatures of heavy promotion that were, in turn, a result of unused physical and sales capacity. Over time, promotion has actually altered the timing of demand, as discussed in Chapter 8, Postscript.

CONCLUSIONS

Decreases in variable *factor* costs lead to increases in promotion expenditures. Promotion expenditures are also inversely related to advertising-*media* costs.

Amounts of promotion are related in a particularly sensitive way to costs of transportation of goods, because promotion influences sales at a distance from the seller.

A shift to a mode of production which has a higher ratio of fixed costs to total costs will lead to an increase in promotion because the more sharply diminishing marginal cost means that marginal sales give more net revenue. Hence the amount that should rationally be spent to attract the marginal customer rises, leading to a rise in the amount of promotion. Furthermore, a higher volume of sales is necessary to recapture the higher original investment, which also leads to more promotion.

Where fixed costs are substantial, promotion will fluctuate when demand varies. (If there are no fixed costs the situation is more likely to be one of perfect competition, and there will be no promotion for that reason.) Whether a decrease, say, in demand leads to an increase or a decrease in promotion depends on the combination of the degree to which marginal cost is reduced and the degree to which promotion is less efficient in obtaining response.

In addition to the influences of cost on promotion discussed in this chapter, the Postscript to Chapter 5 discusses how the size of the firm's existing plant influences the amount spent for promotion, which is really an argument about short-run fixed cost. Fixity of plant size is also the most important reason why a firm's market share in year t seems to influence its share of industry advertising expenditures in year t + 1.

A firm's cash position may also influence its advertising expenditure. A firm with much cash may view money as cheaper than a firm that is strapped for liquid capital and that would need to borrow (or might even be able to borrow more) to finance incremental advertising expenditures.

4

The Effect
of the Industry's
Competitive Structure
upon Advertising
Expenditures

The effect of advertising on industrial concentration and market structure has attracted considerable interest, and will be discussed in Chapter 9. But the converse question which is the subject of this chapter has received less attention, that is, the effect of market structure on advertising and promotion.[1] Discussion of this topic has heretofore concerned only the *number* of competitors in the market. And I could find only two theoretical statements — diametrically opposed — about the effect of numbers of firms on promotion: ". . . firms that have some monopoly power are more likely to advertise because they can obtain most of the increased sales stimulated by this advertising" (Telser, 1964, p. 551). And: ". . . when the production is all in the hands of one person or company, the total expenses involved are generally less than would have to be incurred if the same aggregate production were distributed among a multitude of comparatively small rival producers. They would have to struggle with one another for the attention of consumers, and would necessarily spend in the aggregate a great deal more on advertising in all its various forms than a single firm would . . ." (Marshall, 1961, p. 484). This chapter, however, considers the broader subject of *all* changes in the firm's competitive environment, of which a change in the number of firms is just one. Other types of change to be discussed include (speaking loosely for the moment) alterations

---

[1] The two questions cannot be separated completely, however. To see why, assume that advertising does lead to industrial concentration. If so, it could not also be the case that industrial concentration leads to *less* advertising unless the two opposing forces result finally in some equilibrium.

in the physical nature of competitors' *brands* that make them more or less homogeneous with what "our" firm sells, and the entry into the market of close-substitute *products*. (The distinction between "brands" and "product" is important in this section.) The reasons for treating the number of sellers in the same section with these other types of changes will become clear as we proceed.

The strategy of this chapter is to construct various types of promotion functions that might be appropriate for a particular type of firm in a particular competitive situation. Then the possible shifts that might occur in these promotion functions in response to various shifts in competitive situations are explored, and the effect on the amount of promotion is then deduced.

It is important to note that the chapter does not assume, or argue, or try to prove, that any particular function is appropriate for any particular type of firm or competitive situation, and the argument does not depend upon such assumptions. I do, however, speculate that given functions, *among* other functions, *might* fit particular types of firms. This is done only (1) to demonstrate that the case is possible and therefore must be considered, and (2) to ease the reader's burden by providing an intuitive basis for the argument. But if the reader decides that the function probably does not fit the actual example, this is not grounds for rejecting the argument. The argument would be rebutted, however, if it could be shown that *no* example *could* fit the abstract situation. The same is true of changes in competitive situations. I sometimes say that a particular type of shift in a function might be the result of some particular competitive change. If it really is not so, the argument is not damaged. I hope that this approach will become clearer as it is practiced in the next few pages.

Throughout the chapter, unless otherwise noted, it is assumed that all prices are constant. Also, the discussion of the sales response to promotion refers to the *entire response over time* that may be attributed to a particular quantity of advertising, i.e., to the sum of the present and lagged effects, properly discounted. This offers no conceptual difficulties, though the empirical problems are formidable (but can be overcome).

Case 1: Firms Whose Response Functions Pass Through the Origin

In this situation the response function facing Firm Alpha is PP_{14} in Figure 4-1. This might be the situation of a mail-order seller of pet monkeys, or a record club, or a correspondence course that teaches guitar-playing. We shall talk about the mail-order firm only, because no other type of firm comes to mind as facing a similar response function.

First let us analyze Apha's advertising in Medium A.[2] A response function such as PP_{14} in Figure 4-1 represents various *sizes* of advertisement in Medium A. The response function as drawn has these special properties: (1) it passes through the origin; if the firm does no advertising in Medium A, there will be no sales to the Medium A audience; and (2) it is concave downward without an inflection point, i.e. there are continually diminishing returns (see Chapter 1). It is also assumed that Alpha will advertise to the margin of profitability.

FIGURE 4–1. ADVERTISING RESPONSE FUNCTIONS

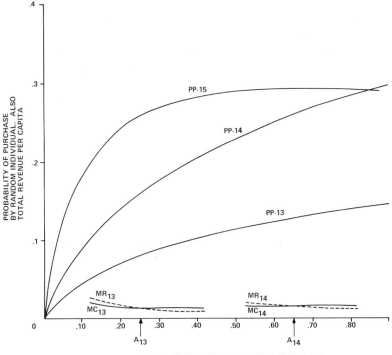

AMOUNT OF PROMOTION PER CAPITA, IN DOLLARS

Among the catalog of possible shifts of PP_{14} is a shift to PP_{13}. Such a shift might describe the new situation for Alpha if it were formerly the only firm advertising the product in Medium A, and another firm then entered with the same advertisement. (An identical advertisement by a

[2] Alpha's *overall* response function is the simple aggregate of such functions as PP_{14} in a number of media, and under easy assumptions of the order in which media are added to the advertising schedule (like a capital-budgeting ladder) the aggregate function therefore has the same shape and properties as this function for a single medium.

competitor would not occur, of course, but it saves complication in the argument.) The extent of the shift will depend upon the size of Beta's advertisement, but *any* shift in the direction of PP_{13} will result in a reduced promotion expenditure for Alpha because marginal revenue shifts to the left. (The slope of PP_{13} is less than the slope of PP_{14}.)[3]

If Beta's advertising message is identical to Alpha's, an advertisement half as large as the original advertisement of Alpha (two such advertisements being run now, one by each firm) should be at the break-even point. But if the two messages are slightly different, we can expect that the sum of them — equal in size to the sum of the original Alpha advertisement — will produce even more revenue than did the original Alpha advertisement. (This statement is based on technical knowledge of advertising but should be easy for the reader to believe. Two different advertisements produce more sales than two of the same advertisements.) And if they are above the break-even point one or both firms will increase promotion somewhat, and total promotion will then be greater than before.

To recapitulate: after the entry of Beta there is a determinate idealized equilibrium solution that can be deduced from the family of particular response functions of one firm, given various promotion levels of the other firm. At equilibrium the amount of promotion will be equal for the two firms; the advertisements will differ somewhat, each firm will spend more than half of what Alpha previously spent, and the total expenditure will therefore increase. And given monotonically diminishing returns, there is almost no set of assumptions under which the two firms would spend less in total than Alpha originally did. Only if each firm thought that the other would advertise much more than he really does could the total promotion decrease, and that would need be very temporary for reasons that we shall discuss later.

PP_{14} might also represent Alpha's response function if Alpha is one of two, or one of three, or one of four firms selling its product by mail order. A shift toward PP_{13} would then result from the entry of still another competitor, and the influences about the effect on Alpha's promotion (a reduction) and for the competitors taken together (an increase) will be the same as above. And the process should be reversible; the opposite predictions should hold if there are originally two firms and one

---

[3] This result follows for most reasonable functions that are concave downward without inflection points and that reach asymptotes. However, it is logically possible for the higher function to have a lesser slope at a particular level of advertising, as for example PP_{15} compared to PP_{13} as may be seen in Figure 4-1. (I am grateful to Leon E. Richartz for pointing this out to me.) This possible indeterminacy foreshadows the greater indeterminacies that come later — and which are the main point of the chapter.

ceases advertising (though that is not likely as long as its net revenue is greater than its advertising cost).

One might then ask why the number of firms does not multiply infinitely, using ever-smaller blocks of space but with an ever-increasing total expenditure for the firms together. The reason is that at some point the costs of production and organization on a small scale make the enterprise unprofitable.[4] It would not be profitable to operate a mail-order correspondence course on accounting (a large undertaking) with the sales volume obtained with ten-word classified ads. But for those mail-order businesses with zero fixed costs the number of firms can increase greatly. Examples are the large number of "book-finders" who advertise in classified ads in the *Saturday Review* and elsewhere, and the dozens of postage-stamp dealers who advertise in the classified columns of *Popular Science.*

If Beta and other firms sell products that affect the sales of Alpha but that are not physically identical[5] to Alpha's goods, we have a classic case of Chamberlin's monopolistic competition — or more precisely, competition among competitors who have downward-sloping demand curves because their products are not physically identical. The analysis above is still appropriate except that the shift in PP_{14} might well be smaller if the new competitor's product is not identical to "ours." Also, it may not be meaningful to discuss the total promotion for the two (or more) firms together because one might choose to consider them as not constituting an "industry." [6]

A shift from PP_{14} toward PP_{13} might also represent the result of Beta, a firm already advertising competitively to Alpha, changing the nature of its offer. If there is a way of objectively specifying a decrease in physical homogeneity in the products (or actually, in the physical description of the product in the advertisement), such a decrease might accompany a shift toward PP_{13}.

It is because a shift of PP_{14} might result either from a change in the number of sellers, or from a change in the nature of the products offered competitively, that both types of competitive changes are discussed together in the chapter.

The situation described above might also fit some dealer-sold products if the brands are physically identical, e.g., a general-purpose deter-

[4] E. H. Chamberlin also made this point somewhere, as does Telser (1964, p. 557).

[5] On the concept of physical identity in contrast to the concept of product differentiation see Appendix A.

[6] On this terminology, see Stigler's convincing (to me, anyway) attack (1949) on Chamberlin's "group" and on Chamberlin's rejection of the industry concept.

gent or beer or cigarette brand that is sold at advertised-brand prices. In the reasonably long run (or if the future is represented in the present by present-value calculations), the promotion curve does indeed pass through the origin. The saga of Sapolio and its decline (Tull, 1955, pp. 128–137) demonstrates this point.

A shift from PP_{14} to PP_{13} might well occur following the entry of a new brand of detergent, soap, or standard-blend cigarettes into the market. Such a shift would probably lead to less promotion by our representative firm, but whether or not the total for the industry would increase is not immediately obvious, though perhaps there is no reason for the analysis to differ from the mail-order situation above. (There is also no obvious prediction for the ratio of advertising to sales of our representative firm; the prediction about the absolute amount of promotion is a prediction about what happens at the margin, but the advertising ratio is an *average* quantity.)

A shift from PP_{14} to PP_{13} might also picture the effect on a brewery's promotion of the appearance of a new beer substitute such as malt liquor, or the effect on a washing-machine manufacturer of the appearance of an electronic clothes-cleaning machine. It is worth noting that the analysis does not require a distinction about whether what happens within the firm's environment is within its "Chamberlinian group" or outside its "group." We can simply lump together all those environmental changes that have the same effect upon the firm. This is unlike analyses that begin with the concept of the industry's price elasticity (or even the industry's promotion elasticity, though such analysis has not been done).

There are still other types of shifts of PP_{14} to which we can give meaning in terms of a change in competitive conditions. Again consider a representative firm selling a product physically homogeneous to several other brands: beer, bleach, nonfilter cigarettes. Assume that the firm changes its product away from physical homogeneity: perhaps becoming a dark beer, or adding a new active ingredient to the bleach, or adding a flavor (not menthol, but something else) to the cigarettes. (This is not identical to Chamberlin's concept of differentiation in that the latter includes "fancied" differences and advertising-created preferences for physically identical products; see Appendix A.) Such a product-innovation change might well shift the function at the zero-promotion level from S_0 to S_1, in Figure 4-2. Assume the analysis is being made some time after the product change takes place. There will now be some customers who can be expected to purchase the changed brand indefinitely without further promotion, because there is no exact substitute. The extent of the shift from S_0 to S_1 will depend upon how desirable the change is to some or all potential users.

Assuming competitors' prices and promotion amounts are constant — which is not contrary to fact in many situations — the new promotion function might be PP_1 or PP_{16}. If the innovation is of the sort that might lead participants in a preference panel to be able to distinguish the brand from other brands on the major dimension for which it is bought (taste for beer and cigarettes, effect on clothes or dishes or hands for a cleanser), and if some of the participants liked it more than the other homogeneous brands while other participants liked it less, the surety with which the product can be distinguished and the distribution of people into "like more" and "like less" would determine whether the shift would be to PP_1 or PP_{16}.

The geometry suggests that a shift to PP_1 (which has a lower slope than PP_{14}) would lead the firm to promote less, while a shift to PP_{16} (which has a higher slope than PP_{14}) would induce increased promo-

FIGURE 4–2. ADVERTISING RESPONSE FUNCTIONS

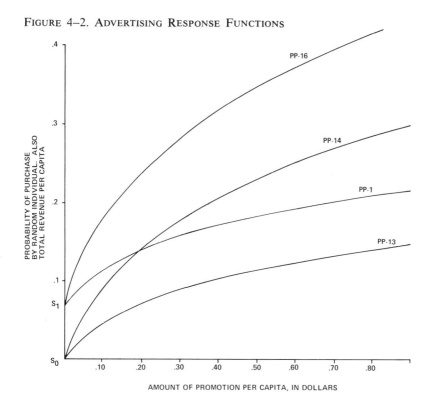

AMOUNT OF PROMOTION PER CAPITA, IN DOLLARS

tion. Which will actually occur depends upon the facts of the product change and the distribution of preferences. The indeterminacy of this prediction is the first of many findings that the effect of a change in competitive conditions is indeed quite indeterminate without specific knowledge of the promotion function. Adducing some technical advertising knowledge might improve the prediction somewhat, however. For example, assume that the proportion of blindfolded subjects preferring the brand to the almost physically homogeneous competitor's brand was in the same ratio as the firm's current market share. One could then expect that at the same expenditure level as before the change the firm's sales would be larger, because the very fact of physical product differences would improve the technical efficiency of its advertising by providing factual differences for the advertising to describe.

This analysis reveals the source of the common belief that physical homogeneity of product *causes* promotion expenditures to be large. At zero promotion the given firm will make no sales (PP_{13} or PP_{14}); promotion is indeed necessary to make sales in such a market environment. But this does not imply that a decrease in physical heterogeneity would cause an increase in promotion; a response function like PP_{13} does not necessarily lead to more advertising than PP_{16}. (PP_{13} has a lower slope than does PP_{16}.)

The matter of alterations in the physical product is illuminated by a spatial-location analogy in the tradition of Hotelling (1929) and Chamberlin (1962, Appendix A). Consider four retail stores that sell a given commodity, among many other commodities; assume that it is not obvious from their general assortments that they carry the product and they do not display the item, so a prospective customer would have zero probability of purchasing the item at Store Alpha unless Store Alpha advertises. If one store advertises a dollar's worth while the other stores do not promote at all, the promoting store gets 100 percent of the business.

Assume further that all four stores are in exactly the same location: four stalls in a public market, perhaps. Each store might then have a promotion-response function that goes through the origin, at any level of competitive promotion. Now consider several kinds of change. Assume that the four stores are located together in the middle of a uniformly dense population, but now one of the stores moves away. Its response might well shift from PP_{14} to PP_1. At low levels of promotion it will have *some* clientele — those people to whom it is closer than are the other three stores. But its potential at some *high* promotion level will be less than the other three stores, because its *average* distance from all potential customers is greater.

Next, consider a store that correctly forecasts a shift in the center of population and moves its location to a position that has a lower average distance than before from all potential customers. Its response function does not go through the origin, because the store is closer to some customers than is any other store. And at higher promotion levels it has an advantage with the average customer over the other stores. This might be represented by a shift toward PP_{16} from PP_{14}.

A last possibility is a store that moves further away from *all* potential customers, perhaps to a low-rent location much further out on the road than other roadside discount stores. Its function might shift from PP_1 to PP_{14}. This accords with the casual observation of the large amounts spent for advertising by outside-the-city highway shopping centers. The point of this spatial analogy is that alterations in physical products, toward or away from identity with competitive offerings, can cause either an increase or a decrease in the firm's promotion amount, depending on the particular facts of the case.

Case 2: Firms Whose Response Functions Are Positive at Zero Promotion Levels

Assume the response function facing Alpha is PP_2 (in Figure 4-3) which does not go through the origin. If Alpha does not promote at all it will have sales of S_2. The function is intended to describe a long-run equilibrium situation. The positive level of sales (S_2) shown at zero promotion indicates that in a static environment the firm's sales would be consistently at that level after many years of not advertising. It is not intended to represent the situation of a firm that had previously advertised and created "customer loyalty" such that in the first year of no advertising its custom would decay to X sales in the first year, something less than X sales in the second year, etc. In the case of firms whose custom does indeed decay slowly (e.g., cigarettes, at a rate of 15 to 20 percent per year prior to World War II, by Telser's estimate [1962]), one would construe the diagram differently.

PP_2 might represent a monopolist Alpha such as a patent-owning manufacturer, or a public utility, or a geographic monopolist such as the only movie house or taxi service in town. We now consider what happens if competition appears. When the second firm enters there is a whole family of response functions for each firm, one function for each level of promotion expenditure by the other firm. PP_{16} in Figure 4-3 might be the response function of one of the two firms if its competitor does not advertise at all. PP_{17} might be the response function for some fixed, positive level of promotion by the competition.

We can deduce as follows that if the competition does not advertise, then Alpha's new function PP_{16} will probably be steeper than its old function PP_2: (1) If Alpha, like Beta, does not promote, Alpha will have half the sales it previously would have had with no promotion, i.e., $\frac{S_2}{2} = S_1$. (2) If it advertises and Beta does not, Alpha can expect to diminish Beta's volume below $\frac{S_2}{2}$ and add that amount to its own sales, in addition to gaining the entire "industry" increment that is caused by positive amounts of promotion, as determined by PP_2. The slope of its new function, PP_{16}, must therefore be steeper than the function when it had a monopoly, PP_2. Hence, its promotion will be greater than before.

Another possible shift is from PP_2 to PP_{18}, which might be Alpha's response function if Alpha and new-entrant Beta spend the same amount for promotion. The relationship of PP_{18} to PP_2 will then be as follows: for any given amount of promotion (A_1) the sales from PP_{18} (S_{18}) will equal half the sales on PP_2 (S_{22}) at twice the amount of pro-

FIGURE 4–3. ADVERTISING RESPONSE FUNCTIONS

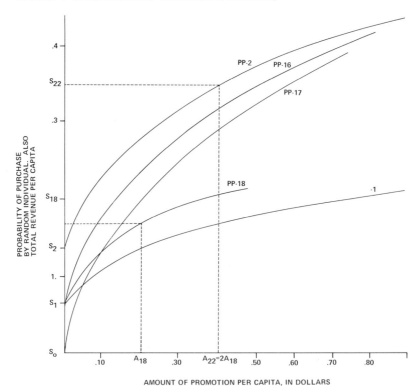

AMOUNT OF PROMOTION PER CAPITA, IN DOLLARS

motion ($2A_{18}$). This assumes that the products are identical and hence that the total "industry" sales will be the same whether a given total amount of promotion expenditure ($2A_{18}$) is spent by one monopolist or two duopolists, no matter whether the duopolists spend equal or unequal amounts. The identities of the advertisers only serve to distribute the fixed total sales produced by a given amount of promotion.

If the two firms act upon this assumption of equal expenditures the result is equivalent to complete cartel action. Each firm will then spend half as much as a monopolist would, and each will get half the sales. This solution is the *lower limit* (except for the possibility of mutual overestimation of the other's expenditures) on the amount of promotion that would follow on a change from one to two firms. Any other set of assumptions leads to *higher total* promotional expenditures.

On almost any of these sets of assumptions, however, the sum of the competitors' expenditures will be more than a monopolist's expenditures and less than twice the expenditure of a firm that thought that its competitor would not promote at all (which is the most favorable case for promotion that could face one firm). Such a state of conjecture by either firm would not be likely to last long. This latter amount, however, could be *more* than twice the monopolist's expenditure.

Explicit cartel-like action will exert a downward pressure on duopolists' expenditures, though their rational solution will never be less in total than the monopolist's. It will be obvious to each of the two competitors that explicit or implicit cooperation to restrict advertising will lead to increased profits. (Taplin found explicit mention of this in a questionnaire survey [1959, p. 232].) The more firms the more difficult is cartel action, and hence the higher the promotion expenditures. Such cartel behavior in classified telephone-book advertising is said to be very important for taxi operators in towns and small cities. (It is usually an operator from a nearby town who takes a big advertisement and thereby breaks up the cartel, I am told.)

Adding a third firm gives a result theoretically similar to the addition of a second firm. The total expenditure will be greater than for the monopoly situation, but less than three times as much as each firm would spend if others spent nothing. The solution if each of the three firms advertises the same amount indicates greater expenditures than if each of two firms advertise the same amount.

The period of the Tobacco Trust (American Tobacco Company) seems to show that a monopolist spends less for advertising than duopolists or polypolists. It was reported to Borden (1944, p. 212) that one of the important motivations in forming the trust was to reduce advertising expenses. And for 1910, prior to the 1911 dissolution of the trust, Borden calculated a total advertising expenditure for the tobacco industry of $13 million, as compared to $25 million in 1913 after the dissolution (1944, p. 216). (This increase is not explained by an increase in tobacco consumed; per capita consumption was 6.74 pounds in 1910, 6.89 pounds in 1913.)

Sherman noticed this phenomenon and described it from the vantage point of 1900:

The two combinations which have longest been prominent — the Standard Oil Company and the American Sugar Refining Company — have done practically no advertising. The latter has, however, recently taken it up as a result of the competition of independent refineries, and the former for the purpose of pushing certain of its by-products. Many of those lately formed have cut very deeply into one form of advertising — that of commercial travelers. The president of their national league testified before the Industrial Commission on June 16, 1899, that the trusts had up to that time discharged 35,000 men, and reduced the salaries of 25,000 more, entailing upon them a loss of $60,000,000 a year, which was saved to the trusts, as was also $21,000,000 railroad fare and $27,000,000 in hotel bills. He stated that there had been discharged by the tobacco combines 3000 men; by the bicycle combine 600 men; chair, 500; rubber, 300; sugar and coffee, 1000; steel rod, 300; baking powder, all but six; tin plate, nine out of every ten. Whether these figures prove to be accurate or not, economy in this form of advertising is one of the main motives and first steps of the combinations. The saving is an immense one.

Are the trusts able to make similar savings in other forms of advertising? The best opinion seems to be that, while a considerable saving can be made, it will not be as large as in the case of commercial travelers. In the first place their monopoly is not absolute. In many cases independent producers still compete with them, and in order to keep their share of the trade they must continue advertising. In other cases competition, although not actual, is at hand as a possibility whenever an opening presents itself. The trust must cover the field continuously in order to prevent such an opening. Moreover, even if the trust had a complete and safe monopoly it would generally be to its advantage to continue, and often to increase its advertising expenditure. . . .

The only mediums besides the commercial travelers to feel severely the effects of the withdrawal of advertising by the trusts have been the trade papers. The Chicago *Tribune* is authority for the statement that the failure of three or four of them is directly traceable to the formation of trusts in their industries, and the consequent cessation of advertising by the smaller concerns swallowed up [Sherman, 1900, pp. 39–40].

The only relevant disaggregated econometric evidence I could find — that relating to the cigarette industry — does not yield so clear a conclusion, however, as to whether oligopolists or polypolists spend more than would a monopolist. Basmann (1955) and Schoenberg (implicitly) (1933, pp. 15–35) found that for the cigarette industry as a whole, a 1 percent increase in promotion is associated with a .05 percent to .08 percent increase in sales in the *same year* (i.e., the promotion elasticity is .05 to .08). In 1961, for example, cigarette advertising by manufacturers was perhaps $220 million while manufacturers' sales were $2.5 billion. Considering only averages, a 1 percent drop in promotion ($2.2 million) would lead to a drop of 1/20 to 1/12 of 1 percent in net sales ($1.25 to $2 million). But now the lagged effect of the advertising must be taken into account. Telser's estimate of a decay rate of 15 to 20 percent before World War II applies to brands, and therefore it probably understates the long-run effect for the cigarette industry as a whole, but we shall nevertheless use Telser's implication that the total effect is five to eight times the effect in the first year, or (combining with the dollar estimates above) between $6.25 million and $16 million. But only the *net* revenue (net of production and selling costs) of the manufacturers should be figured, which might be 20 to 40 percent of manufacturers' sales, say between $1.25 and $6.4 million. Even if one now reduces these figures to reflect the lower efficiency of *marginal* promotion expenditures compared to *average* expenditures, the estimates of the returns to advertising probably bracket the incremental advertising expenditure itself ($2.2 million). Even if the returns are indeed at the high end, however, making the advertising actually profitable for the industry as a whole, it might still be unlikely that a monopolist would reckon in such a way, including the lagged effects of the advertising, so as to arrive at as high an advertising expenditure as the aggregated advertising by the competitive firms.

For the liquor industry now, Prest calculated its short-run promotion elasticity to be "almost negligible" (1949, pp. 33–49). Yet liquor distributors spend large amounts for promotion even though a monopolist would apparently spend little or nothing. This evidence, however, is flimsy.

At a more aggregated level, Yang (n.d.) worked with Telser's data (described in Chapter 9) on industry concentrations and average industry advertising ratios, for three-digit IRS industries. He divided the industries into three groups: industries with advertising ratios under 2 percent and under 50 percent concentration; industries with advertising ratios over 2 percent and 20 to 50 percent concentration, and industries with over 50 percent concentration. (The original logic of these groupings is not relevant here.) In the high-concentration group there was a positive correlation between a decrease in concentration — which probably may be taken as an increase in number of competitors in most cases — and an increase in the advertising ratio.[7] This jibes with the theorizing above. Yang's below–50 percent concentration groups both showed the opposite result — increases in concentration were associated with *more* advertising. If these latter results are valid (the significance levels were not uniformly high) I would interpret them this way: (1) no effect running from concentration to advertising, which is not unexpected in light of the large number of competitors involved; and (2) an effect running from more advertising to more concentration, though possibly involving a third variable. This latter effect is discussed at length in Chapter 9.

Else (1966), whose study was referred to earlier in another connection (p. 34), found that the partial coefficient for number of brands (with overall product sales held constant) was positive, suggesting that a larger number of advertisers is indeed related to more total advertising.

For retailers, Mitchell (1941) showed that for each type of retailer, holding size of store constant, the ratio of advertising to sales is larger in middle-size communities than in small communities (though in the biggest cities the ratio is lower than in middle-size cities, for reasons discussed on p. 45). This effect might be interpreted simply as a response to the larger urban environment (see Chapter 7, Section 5). But it is also consistent with an increase in promotion being related to an increase in the number of competitors.

It seems likely that the sum of competitors' spending in the above cases exceeds the monopoly expenditure because each firm takes the expenditures of its competitors as being rather fixed, an assumption which leads, as we have seen, to higher expenditure decisions by individual firms than does the assumption that all competitors will spend matching amounts. The nature of advertising makes this assumption much more reasonable than would be an assumption of the fixity of competitors' prices. And in general, conjectural promotion-response functions will not be as uncertain as conjectural price-demand schedules, for these reasons: (1) An increment of promotion by a competitor will not sweep the entire market, as can an incremental price decrease by a competitor; rather, a promotion increment by the competitor will have *less* effect than previous increments because of diminishing returns. (2) Competitors cannot alter their promotion expenditures instantaneously. (3) There is variation in the amount of promotion *within* each period by Alpha, and Beta therefore has con-

---

[7] This result was statistically significant but Yang rejected it as "not plausible" — probably because he was interested only in the effect of advertising on concentration.

siderable difficulty determining whether Alpha's expenditure level has changed. Beta's lack of good information about whether Alpha has really altered his behavior makes Beta's competitive response relatively slow and sluggish.

Evidence that it is reasonable for firms to take competitors' expenditures as fixed in the short run, and hence not to game-theorize, is provided by the relatively small amount of variation from year to year in advertising expenditures by firms in industries with relatively stable demand — which are industries in which advertising competition is likely to be greatest. The small amount of variation has been documented by Jastram (1949a) and is shown in the next chapter (p. 126), which explores the empirical variables that explain the amounts of promotion.

Jastram interpreted the lack of variation as multiple don't-rock-the-boatism. But an interpretation of mutual independence is equally compatible with the data, for the reasons given above. And a don't-rock-the-boat explanation is made less plausible by the difficulty that any firm has in detecting, quickly and surely, whether any other firm is indeed rocking the boat. This is in contrast to pricing behavior, where even secret discounts and rebates become trade knowledge very quickly.

The subject of discussion above has been small numbers of firms selling identical wares. There is no theoretical foundation for a guess about what happens as the number of firms becomes quite large — over eight, say. However, there are very great differences in other variables between towns that support, for example, one or 20 taxi services. And in the case of manufacturers, there are important limits on the number of brands of a consumer product that can obtain store distribution. Also, differences in price levels, private labels, etc., make it almost impossible to conceptualize the large-numbers situation in such a way that we can think only about the effect of numbers on promotion.

Another case is that of firms whose wares may differ physically or in some other objective manner. This case may differ from the identical-offerings case in that the *sum* of the sales created by a given promotional expenditure, half of which is spent by each of two advertisers (two motion picture theaters, say) can be much larger than the sales of a single advertiser if he spent that total for advertising. This means that the response function facing Alpha, if he assumes that Beta will match his expenditure, is far to the right of where it would be if their offerings were identical. The same is true if Alpha assumes zero promotion or any given positive level of promotion for Beta. The upper limit on the amount of promotion is not immediately obvious. However, the more different are the offerings, the less that cartel action is rational.

Some empirical evidence supports this speculation. A small study of motion picture theaters in small towns in Illinois showed that in three cases where a given town changed from two movie houses to one, the *total* promotion was indeed greater while there were two movie houses (see Table 4-1). And towns which had only an indoor theater were

Table 4-1. Column Inches of Motion Picture Theater Advertising, Total for Four Wednesdays and Four Fridays in March

City	Paris, Ill.			Streator, Ill.			Lincoln, Ill.		
Theater	Lincoln	Paris	Total	Plumb	Granada	Total	Lincoln	Vogue	Total
Date									
1954	128	60	188						
1955	137	65	202						
1956	130	xx	130						
1957									
1958									
1959									
1960							121	114	235
1961				143	84	227			
1962									
1963				132	149	281	146	33	179
1964	113		113	173	xx	173	93	xx	93

XX = Out of business

Source: Direct measurement of newspaper advertisements.

compared with towns which had one indoor theater and one outdoor theater (McHale, 1964). The total advertising expenditures for several towns are displayed in Figure 4-4. The total promotion where there is only an indoor theater is clearly lower than where there is also an outdoor theater (holding newspaper circulation constant as a proxy for population).[8]

[8] One cannot, however, postulate a *ceteris paribus* increase in promotion as the number of movie houses becomes very large, because so many things are different in a city which has 30 movie houses compared to a town that has two movie houses. One of the important differences is that all 30 movie houses are not in competition with each other as are the two in a small town; the 30 are located in different parts of the city, and the further apart any two theaters are, the less they compete with one another. We would have to go to location theory to extend our knowledge further along this line. Phillips makes a similar point with respect to price competition (1962, pp. 23–25).

In the city-wide newspapers in which all the theaters do compete with each other to some extent, my impression (which perhaps ought to be tested) is that the total linage is higher than in cities with few movie theaters. Except for the downtown movies, the theaters advertise in the form of a listing, just as do the book-finders in *Saturday Review* classified. The big ones do not squeeze out the little man with heavy advertising.

Two empirical studies are relevant here. (1) Kaldor and Silverman (1948) classified industries by the minimum number of firms that account for 80 percent of the press advertising for the industry; this is an index of industrial concentration. They then showed that the ratio of advertising to sales is related to concentration like an inverted U, with a peak at eight firms. That is, the amount of advertising is larger in indus-

FIGURE 4–4. RELATIONSHIP OF MOVIE THEATER ADVERTISING TO SIZE OF COMMUNITY

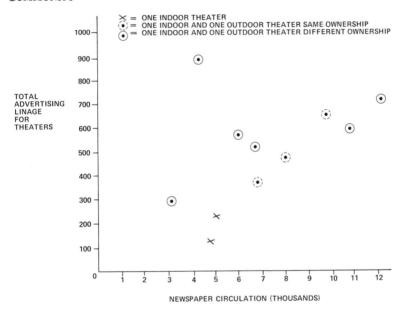

Source: McHale, 1964.

tries with eight firms accounting for 80 percent of the advertising than in industries with more and less concentration. This is consistent with the above theorizing about industries with few firms (and there is no theory about many-firm situations). (2) Telser related industrial concentration to the ratio of advertising to sales, using several different measures. He found no significant relationships at all. However, both the Kaldor-Silverman study and the Telser study suffer from the usual difficulties of cross-sectional product comparisons; also, the number of firms within some concentration limit is not necessarily a good proxy for the number of sellers. These (and some other) studies are discussed in more detail in Chapter 9.

DISCUSSION AND CONCLUSIONS

The most important conclusion is that there are no simple, general, determinate rules for what happens to promotion when there are changes in the number of firms or in the nature of the wares sold. Either an increase or a decrease in promotion might follow most types of change in the competitive market structure.

If the firms' response functions pass through the origin (e.g., mail-order firms and firms that sell products that are physically identical to competitors' products) an increase in the number of firms in the "industry" will probably lead to an increase in the sum of advertising expenditures by the firms, assuming that price remains constant. It is not the nature of the advertising mechanism that keeps the number of firms from multiplying indefinitely, but rather the nature of production costs.

A product variation that renders a firm's product less physically homogeneous with its competitors has an effect on promotion expenditures that is directionally indeterminate without further specification. On the one side, the shift of each function away from the origin and toward a flatter shape acts to diminish expenditures. On the other side, there is less reason for cartel motives and explicit or implicit limitation on expenditures as the products become less similar physically.

On most assumptions two sellers will together spend a sum for promotion greater than a monopolist even if the response function does not pass through the origin. The only exception is if each firm overestimates the amount that the other is spending for promotion — most unlikely, indeed. The bottom limit is the amount that the monopolist would spend, and this will occur only if the two competitors form a cartel and act in concert.

Some predictions about promotion expenditures are not determinate because one cannot tell from outside the firm what the shape of a firm's original or altered response function will be. However, it is quite likely that a firm itself can and does know which type of situation it is in, and hence it can better know what the effect of a change in its environmental conditions should and will be. And if the firm does not know this from prior experience, various types of empirical research can help determine the functions scientifically.

A large number of relevant parameters bear upon the direction of effect of a change in competitive environment. Some of these are cost and demand variables, discussed in the two preceding chapters. Many other variables demand knowledge of the psychology of perception, technical advertising, and other disciplines that are, if not occult, at least hard to systematize and from which it is difficult to derive objective categorizations. However, a sensible classification of products could reduce the indeterminacy. (A proposed multidimensional product classification relevant to advertising may be found in Simon (1970).

This chapter has not considered the chain of events running from a change in the competitive environment, to changes in the nature or effectiveness of the advertising of one or more firms, to changes in amounts spent for promotion. There are many curious and esoteric phenomena in advertising, too many and too strange to delve into here. But it is safe to say that every type of result may follow on some type of advertising tactic, making almost all predictions indeterminate without an inside knowledge of the situation.

5

An Empirical
Study of
Advertising-Expenditure
Decisions

The previous three chapters set forth some theory of how shifts in various variables affect the amount spent for advertising, and empirical evidence was occasionally adduced to test the theoretically deduced hypotheses. Those chapters enable us to make some statements about the direction of effects. However, they do not provide much guidance concerning the extent of effects, or the relative importance of various variables in influencing changes in firms' total expenditures. This last matter is the aim of this chapter.

The work described in this chapter began as an attempt to determine the extent of competitive interaction in advertising expenditures when the numbers of competitors are few. However, preliminary investigation showed that simple relationships between one firm's expenditures and the expenditures of its competitors, taken singly or together, would not immediately reveal the extent of competitive interaction because many other variables for a given firm are related both to the firm's advertising expenditures and to its competitors' expenditures; in such a state of affairs we cannot say what causes what, or if the cause is direct or indirect.

The study therefore was widened to include other variables that are related to advertising expenditures. This was originally a tactical decision designed to net out the effect of other influences on advertising expenditures so that the effect of competitive expenditures on the residual variation could be determined. But this alteration in approach seemed to force a widening in the purpose of the work. Unwittingly but inevitably the study became a more general empirical investigation of the determinants of the advertising-expenditure decision.

This study works with independent variables whose theoretical power is low. The variables available for empirical investigation do not correspond closely to the most important of the theoretical variables discussed in the previous three chapters. (It is interesting to note that though the study of capital-goods investment decisions is also hampered by a discrepancy between theoretical and empirical variables, the study of capital-investment decisions still has great importance.[1] But one cannot claim similar importance for a comparable study of advertising decisions, as the Postscript to Chapter 2 suggested.)

This chapter aims to aid the forecasting of advertising expenditures as well as to increase our understanding of the decision-making structure of firms, including the effect of competitors' behavior. This short statement of the chapter's objectives is annoyingly vague. Even though they will be clarified somewhat as the chapter unfolds, the severality and lack of specificity in the objectives is a major problem.

THE THEORY OF ADVERTISING-EXPENDITURE LEVELS

Under conditions of (1) certainty, (2) any given set of demand, cost, and competitive conditions, and (3) instantaneous reactions to conditions by advertisers, the advertising appropriation would be a unique function derivable by the marginal analysis, just like the optimizing price and quantity. However, it is not at all obvious how a given shift in a particular parameter will affect the optimizing appropriation; for example an increase in population may, *ceteris paribus*, lead to either an increase or a decrease in advertising expenditures, depending on other parameters.

Appropriate optimizing calculi for the firm have been given by Howard (1957), Brems (1957), Rasmussen (1952), Boulding (1951, pp. 772–779), Dorfman and Steiner (1954), and others. But these abstract models are not immediately applicable by a given firm because their parameters are not easy to estimate; the sales productivity of particular advertising campaigns and the lagged effects of advertising (i.e., continuing brand loyalty over time) are the two most important snags. These difficulties are easily surmounted in ideal situations like that of the mail-order firm. And for less ideal situations, more refined solutions have been provided by Kuehn (1961), Telser (1962), Palda (1964), Weinberg (1960a), Simon (1965a), and others.

Even if all firms did set their advertising budgets in thoroughly rational ways — and there is no evidence that rational calculi are in wide

[1] For a major example and an extensive bibliography see Meyer and Kuh (1957).

use — it would be necessary for a student of the subject to predict the future expenditures (or explain the past) with only an outsider's knowledge of the relevant parameters of the firms, and much of the relevant knowledge is not available to the outsider. Theory does not give unidirectional predictions about the effects of changes in those two sets of variables that are available for our inspection: advertising and sales data for the firm, the industry, and competitors; and indices of general economic and advertising activity. A single example to buttress this argument: the advertising for most products will probably increase as general economic activity increases; but Palda (1964) has argued convincingly and provided corroborating data that the advertising for Lydia Pinkham's remedy will decrease as disposable income increases and as medical care substitutes for patent medicines.

Though theory speaks softly about the effect of various parameter changes, we could still deduce the optimizing advertising expenditures on a period-by-period basis if we had available to us the firm's long-term advertising-response function (and its cost function). But because there is no observable magnitude that has even a flimsy correspondence to the response function, the investigation must continue in a theoretical vacuum. This absence of theory is at the root of various vexing problems of how to conduct this investigation.

There is available a handful of such theory as "Firms attempt to maintain a constant proportion of advertising to last year's sales" or ". . . to this year's sales," and other hypotheses about decision-making rules of thumb. But because these hypotheses are such weak reeds, and because they do not fit as an integral part of deductive economic theory, they are of little help except as clues about what to look at.[2]

The only previous related study was of the cigarette industry (Palmer, 1964), and it was labeled as an investigation for forecasting purposes. Palmer compared various methods of building up a forecast, using the R^2 as his test of excellence of prediction. He found that a cross section of firms gave a higher R^2 than did time-series analysis. But this is not surprising because the range of observations is much wider in

[2] The situation is much the same in the study of investment behavior, Jorgenson points out: ". . . the econometric literature on business investment consists of *ad hoc* descriptive generalizations such as the 'capacity principle,' the 'profit principle,' and the like. Given sufficient imprecision, one can rationalize any generalization of this type of an appeal to 'theory.' However, even with the aid of much ambiguity, it is impossible to reconcile the theory of the econometric literature on investment with the neoclassical theory of optimal capital accumulation" (Jorgenson, 1963, p. 247).

such a cross section than in a time series, which almost inevitably leads to a higher R^2.

Various questionnaire studies also have been made of how firms decide on their advertising allocations (see Borden, 1942, pp. 721–722; Taplin, 1959; Bullen, 1961). Typically the questionnaires have offered company-executive respondents a series of choices such as "Percentage of previous year's sales," "To achieve a particular objective," etc. The modal choices have usually been "Percentage of coming year's sales" and "of last year's sales" and "To accomplish given objective." These studies may be considered to be explorations of the structural determinants of the advertising-expenditure decision.

As to the effect of competitive behavior, the phrase "Battle of the Brands" is common in the advertising-trade literature, which gives some indication of how business executives perceive their situation. And Oxenfeldt's extensive interviews with executives of television-set manufacturing firms left him with an impression of "almost neurotic preoccupation of the individual manufacturers with the amount and uses of their competitors' advertising expenditures" (1964, p. 62). We also have some courtroom evidence showing advertising expenditures to be a sensitive competitive device for Procter & Gamble: "On or about October 14, 1957, the Purex Company began a market test in [Erie County, Penn.] by offering a new energized household liquid bleach. . . . A special advertising campaign was put on . . . Clorox . . . combined an advertising and promotion campaign to prevent the Purex entry . . ." (FTC, 1963, p. 45).

A P & G official testified that in other markets, though "we drew up a list and had ready a group of these promotions . . . in some territories, we did not meet it with a promotion, but tried to meet it with whatever increase there was in an advertising schedule" (FTC, 1963, p. 47).

On the other hand, the only available econometric evidence about competitive-expenditure effects is Telser's passing look at the correlation of residuals of his regressions of cigarette firms, an industry which we would expect to be more advertising-competitive than most other industries. Yet Telser found no competitive interaction at all. And note the last line in the following report by Nelson and Preston:

The data revealed a material association between the store's own advertising linage devoted to an item and its price. For 88 of the 254 equations showing significant results, only the store's own advertising linage proved to be a significant explanatory variable. In 31 of these cases, ad linage explained 50 percent or more of the variation in prices over the period. Sometimes the store's own advertising showed a significant relationship to price and to the prices and advertising activities of other firms. The advertising activity of competitive stores did not prove to be a significant explanatory variable [Nelson and Preston, 1966, p. 78].

There has also been a recent study by Baumol, Quandt, and Shapiro (1964, pp. 358–359) which compares the products advertised by four supermarket chains. They found that "imitation or direct differentiation of advertised items is *not* among the competitive weapons which are used consistently or systematically . . . behavior is 'more random than random.' "

Another type of relevant evidence is the variability in a given firm's expenditures. Jastram studied the changes from year to year of expenditures of firms that manufacture consumer goods. He found what he considered to be great stability, and concluded that "oligopoly advertising expenditures *tend* toward stability over time. As with prices, fluctuations are more the exception than the rule" (Jastram, 1949, p. 109).

This section does not take into account such industry variables as number of competitors (which was discussed in the previous chapter). This variable generally does not change much over the period of only a few years, and it therefore can only be studied in a cross-sectional analysis (if even that way), rather than with the time series used in this chapter to search out the dynamic effects of competitor interaction.

THE DATA

Advertising and sales data for individual brands or products are hard to come by. Consolidated data for the firm are easier to get, but except for the cases in which the firm is coextensive with a single product, firm data are not good for our purposes; heterogeneous information on different products is lumped together in the consolidated figures. Only for these few cases were the necessary data easily accessible: the California orange industry (from Nerlove and Waugh, 1961); Lydia Pinkham's remedy (from Palda, 1966); cigarettes (from Telser, 1962; Nicholls, 1951; Borden, 1942); beer (*Advertising Age*, Oct. 9, 1961; Aug. 23, 1965); liquor (Gavin-Jobson Associates, Inc., annual). These few cases do not constitute a sample of any well-defined universe. The best we can say for them is that they include very different types of situations, which provides some assurance that the study is not imprisoned by the idiosyncrasies of a single industry.

The data, and therefore the analysis, are at a somewhat unusual level of aggregation. Unlike such investment studies as that of Meyer and Kuh (1957), the data here are disaggregated far below the economy as a whole, or even sectors of the economy, which means that one cannot make any generalizations that would be immediately useful for macro-economics. But on the other hand "inside" data about one or more firms are lacking, and hence one cannot explore in depth the economic machinery and economic psychology.

Data were assembled on those variables that questionnaire surveys and/or a priori reason suggested might be important:

$A_{1,t}$ = advertising expenditures for the firm in year t

$A_{2,t}$ = advertising expenditures for the firm's largest competitor in t (where appropriate)

$A_{3,t}$ = advertising expenditures for the firm's entire industry in t (where appropriate)

$A_{4,t}$ = all–U.S. advertising expenditures in t

$S_{1,t}$ = sales of the firm in t

$S_{2,t}$ = sales of the largest competitor (where appropriate) in t

$S_{3,t}$ = sales of the firm's entire industry (where appropriate) in t

$S_{4,t}$ = final sales for the entire economy, i.e., GNP, in t

These variables are used as current values, as lagged values, and as first differences, in different parts of the investigation. There are no empirical variables to stand for whatever firms mean when they answer a questionnaire about advertising decisions: "To achieve specific objectives."

The interpretation of relationships between the dependent variable $A_{1,t}$ and other variables differs from variable to variable. Here are some examples: (1) a close association between $A_{1,t}$ and $S_{1,t-1}$ would suggest that the firm has a policy of maintaining a constant proportional relationship between advertising and sales, and that the estimate of future sales is a simple function of past sales. But a relationship between $A_{1,t}$ and $S_{1,t}$ is more complex, because to some greater or lesser extent $A_{1,t}$ causes $S_{1,t}$, and relationship between the two could not be interpreted simply as behavior by the firm to fix $A_{1,t}$ as a constant proportion of $S_{1,t}$. (2) Gross national product, $S_{4,t}$, and all–U.S. advertising, $A_{4,t}$, are intended to serve as proxies for general economic conditions and purchasing power, rather than as variables that the firm might enter directly into its decisions. (3) A positive relationship between $A_{1,t}$ and $A_{3,t}$ would suggest that the firm has a tendency to maintain a constant share of a market. But a positive relationship between $A_{1,t}$ and $S_{3,t}$ would be interpreted differently — perhaps as a response to a shift to the right in the *ceteris paribus* demand curve of all firms as the total market increases. (4) $S_{2,t}$ and $A_{2,t}$ are data for the largest firm in the industry (except when the given firm is the largest, in which case $A_{2,t}$ and $S_{2,t}$ stand for the next largest firm), for two reasons: (*a*) the largest firm is likeliest to be the industry price leader, and hence the behavior leader in general; and (*b*) including variables for all the other competitors is not feasible. (5) The special nature of the relationship between $A_{1,t}$ and $A_{1,t-1}$ will be discussed at length later.

The lengths of the time series vary greatly, as can be seen in column 2 in Table 5-1; there are 49 observations for California oranges, and only 7 for some of the brands of beer. When first-difference regressions are used they further reduce the sample size. Of course all empirical economics is at the mercy of the quality of the data. As Ferber and Verdoorn say, "careful selection and adequate processing of data is more important than acrobatics with an elaborate specification" (162, p. 92). And Morgenstern has laid bare for us the glossed-over inadequacies of so many series (1963). But the data for this study are particularly inadequate. As an example of how important are the inadequacies, the correlations for the Borden and Nicholls series for Camels and Lucky Strike show considerable differences, even when we keep the time periods the same. (Compare the Borden and Nicholls rows at the end of Table 5-1.)

I have not bothered to deflate the data to constant dollars or to make other such adjustments because they do not seem warranted by the results that follow.

THE INVESTIGATIVE PROCEDURE

This study runs unusual danger of being dragged into deep philosophical waters because, unlike most other microeconomic studies, it has little theoretical backbone. Therefore one cannot assume all the familiar conventions for the handling and interpretation of data that underlie most microeconomic studies. Nevertheless, I shall try to avoid getting bogged down in philosophy of method. A brief discussion follows in fine print, which the reader may either endure or skip over.

The choice of the variables, and the relationships between them, must depend on the purpose of the investigation. And the relationships expressed by particular equations composed of given variables can have several interpretations.

1. An equation can be interpreted as a forecast (prediction) of future events, from the point of view of a forecaster who cannot or does not affect the situation by manipulating independent variables. This interpretation asserts nothing about "structural" (causal) relationships between variables, either in substance or direction. It assumes only that the equation is a useful way to extrapolate the past into the future. This type of relationship may be thought of as having a "practical" purpose, i.e., that decisions with immediate consequences can be made using the information

it produces. In this case, such a purpose might be a firm's decisions based on expected advertising of competitors, or an advertising medium's decision to expand.[3]

2. A second interpretation is also as a prediction, but a prediction that specified changes in the dependent variable would follow changes in an independent variable if that variable were manipulated by the person making the prediction. This interpretation assumes that there is a structural (causal) relationship between the variables. If the independent-variable prediction is merely an index, or another variable affected by still a third variable, then the relationship fails for this interpretation. In this case, it matters whether a firm believes that its competitor's expenditures for advertising are influenced by the firm's expenditures, or whether both the firm and its competitor have been commonly influenced in the past by some other force.

3. An equation can also be interpreted as an embodiment of the motivational contents of decision-makers' minds. The interpretation in paragraph 2 above only asserts that given events will take place, and though the assertion may be that decision-making units act "as if" their thinking were of a given kind, it does not assert that any decision-maker really does think given thoughts. An assertion of the paragraph 2 type may only be about an aggregate, that a *distribution* may behave "as if" each unit thought in a given way, though not even one unit may do so. But this third possible interpretation asserts that particular psychological processes actually take place in the minds of some individuals. This third interpretation suggests that if the contents of some minds were altered, certain events would take place.

Perhaps the most usual approach would be to discuss the data in two separate sections corresponding to the first two interpretations above. Such a split would have the advantage of some available econometric wisdom which distinguishes practices that are appropriate for the "scientific" purpose of structural analysis, e.g., what to do about multicollinearity. But we should note that even if we chose to proceed in such a fashion, we would still have problems about how to proceed with the structural analysis; "scientific purpose" is still a remarkably broad goal, and unlike a particular forecast or policy purpose, there can be many different aims for scientific knowledge.

The chapter is not organized into separate sections on forecasting and structural analysis for two reasons. On the one hand, it is impossible in this case to keep the concepts from leaking back and forth and affecting each other. On the other hand, there are not sharp differences between the two approaches in this case, due largely to the

---

[3] This is in the spirit of Bassie's comment on sales forecasting for short periods of time: "In these circumstances the main reliance is on continuity, tempered by knowledge of special developments, many of which are of no lasting significance. The usual procedure is to project what is currently going on some distance into the future. Any method for doing this may be used, but for the analyst with judgment the simple extension of current movements from the last point of record is as good a procedure as any" (Bassie, 1958, p. 586).

Table 5-1. Simple Correlation of $A_{1,t}$ with Various Independent Variables

(* = joint median; † = median)

1	2	3	4	5	6	7	8	9	10	11	12	13	14	15	16	17	18
Advertiser	One-lag Dates	Two-lag Dates	$A_{1,t-1}$	$S_{1,t}$	$S_{1,t-1}$	$A_{3,t}$	$A_{3,t-1}$	$S_{3,t}$	$S_{3,t-1}$	$A_{2,t}$	$A_{2,t-1}$	$S_{2,t}$	$S_{2,t-1}$	$S_{4,t}$	$S_{4,t-1}$	$A_{4,t}$	$A_{4,t-1}$
Cigarettes																	
Lydia E. Pinkham–	08-60	09-60												−.13	−.07	−.09	−.07
Camels–Nicholls Data	13-39	14-39	+.82	+.84				+.82	+.80	+.69	+.67	+.72	+.67	+.55	+.59	+.35	+.42
Lucky Strike–Nicholls Data	26-39	27-39	+.59	*+.65	+.66			−.08	+.03	−.48	−.05	−.35	−.12	−.43	+.03	−.20	+.12
Chesterfield–Borden Data	30-39	31-39	+.28	+.19	+.05	+.38	+.58	+.08	−.06	+.09	+.45	+.01	+.19	−.46	−.40	−.47	−.45
California Oranges	11-59	12-59	+.94	+.87	+.89									+.94	+.94	+.90	+.89
Beers																	
Anheuser Busch	55-63	56-63	+.93	+.93	+.89	+.85	+.84	+.82	+.57	+.79	+.77	+.66	+.71	+.96	*+.16	+.97	+.97
Schlitz	56-63	56-63	+.83	+.81	+.60	+.78	+.55	+.89	+.85	+.80	+.70	+.69	+.82	+.87	−.46	+.84	+.83
Carling	56-63	57-63	+.85	+.96	+.95	+.69	+.52	+.95	+.81	+.89	+.91	+.95	+.95	+.96	+.96	+.96	+.92
Falstaff	55-63	56-63	+.87	+.91	+.89	+.78	+.64	+.64	+.93	+.73	+.87	+.95	+.95	+.93	+.92	+.90	+.89
Hamms	55-63	56-63	+.61	+.87	+.76	+.83	+.65	+.66	+.23	+.84	+.68	+.76	+.66	+.75	+.78	+.81	+.77
Coors	56-63	57-63	+.65	+.72	+.73	+.62	+.89	+.58	+.65	+.89	+.81	+.74	+.68	+.75	+.80	+.74	+.78
Liebman	55-63	56-63	+.73	−.01	+.19	−.44	−.34	−.93	−.75	−.65	−.77	−.78	−.87	−.82	−.75	−.78	−.66
Lucky Lager	55-63	56-63	+.54	−.02	+.13	+.01	−.08	−.53	−.70	−.21	−.43	−.39	−.59	−.39	−.44	−.37	−.37
Stroh	55-63	56-63	+.05	+.08	+.36	+.28	+.09	+.05	−.18	+.16	+.16	+.19	+.11	+.18	+.19	+.17	+.20
Olympia	57-63	58-63	−.43	−.27	−.25	−.15	−.30	−.21	−.32	−.17	−.36	−.21	−.21	−.19	−.34	−.17	−.40
National	56-63	57-63	+.37	−.21	−.35	−.55	+.11	−.73	−.63	−.33	−.31	−.37	−.60	−.52	−.51	−.55	−.51
Jacob Ruppert	55-63	56-63	+.45	+.35	+.27	−.21	−.01	−.41	−.70	−.12	−.12	−.06	−.31	−.26	−.27	−.21	−.26
Duquesne	57-63	58-63	+.49	−.85	−.22	†+.52	*+.52	*+.58	+.81	†+.61	+.63	+.56	+.65	*+.67	+.72	*+.60	+.77
Ballantine	55-63	56-63	+.43	+.51	+.75	+.94	+.48	*+.60	+.33	+.72	†+.50	††+.55	††+.52	††+.70	+.74	+.70	+.77
Liquors																	
Guckenheimer	53-62	54-62	+.58	+.49	+.35			+.71						−.62	−.57	−.69	−.66
Carstairs	53-62	54-62	−.16	+.15	+.20			+.14						−.27	−.15	−.28	−.21
Four Roses	53-62	54-62	−.05	+.26	+.35			+.19						+.01	−.06	−.04	−.06
Kessler	53-62	54-62	+.65	+.78	+.79			−.66						+.80	+.85	+.74	+.82

(Continued)

Table 5-1 (Continued)

(* = joint median; † = median)

1	2	3	4	5	6	7	8	9	10	11	12	13	14	15	16	17	18
Advertiser	One-lag Dates	Two-lag Dates	$A_{1,t-1}$	$S_{1,t}$	$S_{1,t-1}$	$A_{3,t}$	$A_{3,t-1}$	$S_{3,t}$	$S_{3,t-1}$	$A_{2,t}$	$A_{2,t-1}$	$S_{2,t}$	$S_{2,t-1}$	$S_{4,t}$	$S_{4,t-1}$	$A_{4,t}$	$A_{4,t-1}$
Liquors																	
Seagram's	53-62	54-62	+.78	−.77	−.80			−.72						+.84	+.86	+.78	+.79
Corby's Reserve	53-62	54-62	+.43	+.80	+.77			+.82						−.78	−.74	−.76	−.75
Imperial	53-62	54-62	+.78	+.45	−.24			−.78						+.74	+.77	+.78	+.80
Old Thompson	53-62	54-62	+.55	+.71	+.75			+.79						−.69	−.68	−.73	−.70
Echo Aprings	53-62	54-62	+.29	−.31	−.63			−.43						−.31	−.26	−.40	−.34
Ky. Gentleman	53-62	54-62	+.90	+.96	+.91			+.83						+.88	+.89	+.87	+.84
Gilbey's Gin	53-62	54-62	+.77	*+.52	*+.62			+.69						*+.62	+.62	*+.69	*+.71
Ancient Age	53-62	54-62	+.85	+.85	+.86			+.91						+.88	+.90	+.91	+.93
Gordon's Gin	53-62	54-62	+.91	−.31	+.11			+.84						+.95	+.94	+.98	+.96
Bourbon Supr.	53-62	54-62	+.76	+.73	*+.65			+.67						+.81	+.84	+.77	*+.76
Smirnoff Vodka	53-62	54-62	+.89	+.97	+.94			+.51						+.86	+.88	+.86	+.93
No. of Observations			34	34	33	15	15	32	17	17	17	17	17	34	34	34	34
Mean			+.58	+.42	+.41	+.35	+.34	+.26	+.16	+.31	+.30	+.27	+.25	+.29	+.26	+.28	+.31
Camels–Nicholls Data	30-39		−.17	+.29	−.17			+.11		−.53	−.49	−.32	−.62	+.41	+.00	+.24	−.17
Lucky Strike–Nicholls Data	30-39		+.53	+.68	+.69			−.39	−.30	−.53	−.10	−.33	−.11	−.33	+.24	+.23	−.17
Camels–Borden Data	30-39		−.00	−.10	−.39	+.45	−.27	−.13	−.18	−.24	−.30	−.52	−.35	−.05	−.46	−.25	−.17
Lucky Strike–Borden Data	30-39		+.64	+.64	+.46	+.57	−.17	−.47	−.48	−.24	−.39	−.24	−.07	−.34	+.26	+.30	+.54

(Continued)

Table 5-1 (Continued)

(* = joint median; † = median)

Advertiser	19 $S_{1,t}$	20 $S_{1,t-1}$	21 $S_{1,t-2}$	22 $A_{3,t}$	23 $A_{3,t-1}$	24 $S_{3,t}$	25 $S_{3,t-1}$	26 $A_{2,t}$	27 $A_{2,t-1}$	28 $S_{2,t}$	29 $S_{2,t-1}$	30 $S_{4,t}$	31 $S_{4,t-1}$	32 $A_{4,t}$	33 $A_{4,t-1}$
Lydia E. Pinkham	+.23	+.02	−.12									−.08		−.07	−.08
Camels–Nicholls Data	+.03	−.07	−.03			−.10	−.08	−.13	−.08	−.18	−.09	+.05	+.00	+.04	−.01
Lucky Strike–Nicholls Data	+.22	−.10	−.38			+.13	−.14	+.02	+.33	+.37	+.18	+.36	+.52	+.39	+.47
Chesterfield–Borden Data	−.00	−.34	−.35	+.58	+.29	+.13	−.33	+.64	+.24	+.66	+.05	+.01	+.30	+.42	+.35
California Oranges	+.29	+.37	+.24									+.29	+.28	+.30	+.28
Anheuser Busch	+.22	+.20	−.05	+.81	+.37	+.30	+.12	+.50	+.43	+.53	+.77	+.41	+.31	+.43	+.46
Schlitz	+.21	+.11	−.20	+.37	−.01	+.59	+.49	+.32	+.24	+.29	+.55	+.43	−.57	+.48	+.40
Carling	−.05	−.12	+.37	−.19	−.50	*+.06	−.17	−.22	−.11	+.01	†−.09	−.09	−.11	−.09	−.20
Falstaff	+.16	+.16	−.05	+.43	−.24	+.34	+.12	+.11	−.01	+.09	+.13	+.26	+.21	+.22	+.19
Hamms	*+.08	−.14	−.34	+.30	−.20	+.22	†−.09	+.04	−.14	+.04	−.07	+.06	+.02	+.09	−.09
Coors	−.00	+.11	+.26	+.43	+.14	*+.03	+.30	+.09	−.16	−.22	−.14	−.01	+.06	+.04	−.01
Liebmann	−.32	+.15	+.55	+.07	−.15	−.30	+.03	−.19	−.45	−.44	−.34	−.28	−.20	−.27	−.16
Lucky Lager	−.38	−.24	−.52	†+.17	†−.19	−.04	−.01	−.09	−.28	−.23	−.26	−.04	+.02	−.13	−.18
Stroh	+.43	*−.02	−.16	−.46	−.57	−.45	−.43	−.58	−.46	−.43	−.41	−.50	−.50	−.49	−.41
Olympia	+.10	+.08	+.16	+.06	+.05	+.06	+.02	+.17	−.00	+.10	+.07	+.17	+.01	+.11	−.05
National	−.73	−.21	−.41	−.23	−.42	−.44	−.16	−.50	−.60	−.60	−.59	−.48	−.46	−.57	−.50
Jacob Ruppert	+.39	+.16	+.04	−.12	+.02	−.31	−.28	−.13	−.18	−.19	−.38	−.19	−.23	−.27	−.29
Duquesne	−.15	−.38	+.46	−.43	−.87	−.31	−.24	−.71	−.67	−.58	−.45	−.54	−.53	−.54	−.54
Ballantine	*+.06	+.26	−.30	+.39	−.41	+.18	−.11	†−.00	−.16	†−.01	+.03	+.08	+.11	+.13	+.15
Guckenheimer	−.41	−.36				−.32						+.35	+.45	+.29	+.40
Carstairs	−.06	+.06				+.00						−.03	+.13	−.08	+.09
Four Roses	+.26	+.00				−.01						+.11	−.01	+.08	−.01
Kessler	+.15	+.14				−.07						+.13	+.20	+.09	+.20
Seagram's 7	−.26	−.16				−.20						+.15	+.27	+.09	+.25
Corby's Reserve	+.41	+.27				+.41						−.26	−.28	−.25	−.27
Imperial	+.20	−.33				+.13						−.10	−.07	−.10	−.03

(Continued)

Table 5-1 (Continued)

(* = joint median; † = median)

Advertiser	$S_{1,t}$	$S_{1,t-1}$	$S_{1,t-2}$	$A_{3,t}$	$A_{3,t-1}$	$S_{3,t}$	$S_{3,t-1}$	$A_{2,t}$	$A_{2,t-1}$	$S_{2,t}$	$S_{2,t-1}$	$S_{4,t}$	$S_{4,t-1}$	$A_{4,t}$	$A_{4,t-1}$
	19	20	21	22	23	24	25	26	27	28	29	30	31	32	33
Old Thompson	−.14	*−.06				−.01						+.10	+.16	+.17	+.19
Echo Springs	−.16	−.22				+.17						+.18	+.19	+.12	+.20
Ky. Gentleman	+.11	−.06				+.21						+.05	+.08	+.10	+.14
Gilbey's Gin	−.08	−.14				+.08						−.27	−.33	−.27	−.25
Ancient Age	−.14	−.20				−.22						−.23	−.16	−.16	−.19
Gordon's Gin	+.45	+.48				+.30						+.05	−.03	+.12	+.01
Bourbon Supreme	+.42	+.44				+.45						+.48	+.51	+.51	+.46
Smirnoff Vodka	−.08	−.22				−.14						−.19	−.18	−.24	−.13
No. of observations	34	34	19	15	15	32	17	17	17	17	17	34	33	34	34
Mean	+.043	−.01	−.04	+.15	−.18	+.03	−.06	−.04	−.12	−.05	−.06	+.02	+.01	+.02	+.02
Camels–Nicholls Data	−.21	−.27	+.11			−.36	−.16	−.26	−.01	−.29	−.21	+.10	−.04	+.07	+.02
Lucky Strike–Nicholls Data	+.55	−.02	−.36			+.26	−.07	−.07	+.33	+.37	+.16	+.37	+.52	+.62	+.53
Camels–Borden Data	−.25	−.12	+.05	+.21	−.69	−.45	−.14	+.16	−.07	−.14	−.01	−.01	+.01	+.10	+.11
Lucky Strike–Borden Data	+.58	−.27	−.69	+.42	−.74	+.18	−.23	+.04	−.31	+.47	−.14	+.50	+.55	+.81	+.55

(Continued)

Table 5-1. (Continued)

Advertiser	Simple Correlation (r) of $\triangle A_{1,t}$ with Various Independent Variables								Collinearity—Simple Correlations (r) between Various Variables			Mean Absolute % Change between Successive Years
	34	35	36	37	38	39	40	41	42	43	44	45
	$\triangle S_{1,t}$	$\triangle^2 S_{1,t}$	$\triangle A_{3,t}$	$\triangle S_{3,t}$	$\triangle A_{2,t}$	$\triangle S_{2,t}$	$\triangle S_{4,t}$	$\triangle A_{4,t}$	$A_{1,t-1} \cdot S_{1,t}$	$S_{1,t} \cdot S_{1,t-1}$	$S_{4,t} \cdot A_{4,t}$	
Lydia E. Pinkham	+.59	+.32					−.01	+.02	+.71	+.93	+.97	.15
Camels—Nicholls	+.26	−.12		−.06	−.11	−.25	+.09	+.09	+.75	+.92	+.85	.78
Lucky Strike—Nicholls	+.42	+.34		+.42	−.21	+.24	−.27	−.19	+.45	+.72	+.85	.25
Chesterfield—Borden	+.53	−.00	−.08	+.55	+.51	+.59	−.42	−.16	+.15	+.79	+.78	.17
California Oranges	−.16	+.41					+.23	+.29	+.86	+.94	+.96	.39
Anheuser Busch	+.10	−.12	+.55	+.31	+.29	+.14	−.21	−.24	+.98	+.95	+.99	.15
Schlitz	+.20	+.12	+.45	+.32	+.29	−.67	+.60	+.15	+.87	+.73	+.99	.18
Carling	+.33	+.04	+.42	+.35	−.32	+.33	+.04	+.35	+.93	+.98	+.99	.93
Falstaff	−.12	−.06	+.76	+.39	+.32	−.10	+.31	+.04	+.92	+.99	+.99	.18
Hamms	+.32	+.14	+.59	+.44	+.44	+.28	+.20	+.60	+.78	+.86	+.99	.22
Coors	−.49	−.01	+.17	−.38	+.77	−.24	−.34	−.09	+.68	+.99	+.99	.39
Liebmann	−.45	−.35	+.24	−.49	+.53	−.39	−.43	−.34	+.24	+.74	+.99	.13
Lucky Lager	−.10	+.43	+.40	−.04	+.41	+.07	−.04	+.21	+.35	+.79	+.99	.28
Stroh	+.32	+.20	+.06	−.19	−.49	−.13	−.05	−.14	−.49	+.25	+.99	.27
Olympia	+.06	+.33	+.03	+.07	+.40	+.04	+.74	+.44	−.44	+.98	+.98	.60
National	−.50	+.16	+.30	−.56	+.31	+.00	−.28	−.21	+.59	+.42	+.99	.78
Jacob Ruppert	+.59	+.27	−.17	−.15	+.08	+.54	+.24	+.17	−.06	+.96	+.99	.53
Duquesne	+.20	−.08	+.65	−.20	−.10	−.36	−.26	−.00	−.13	+.08	+.99	.79
Ballantine	−.54	+.59	+.89	+.41	+.37	−.12	−.11	−.12	+.47	+.92	+.99	.28
Guckenheimer	−.29						−.32	−.50	+.75	+.94	+.98	.52
Carstairs	−.31						−.76	−.67	+.24	+.95	+.98	.12

(Continued)

Table 5-1. (Continued)

	Simple Correlation (r) of $\triangle A_{1,t}$ with Various Independent Variables								Collinearity—Simple Correlation (r) between Various Variables			Mean Absolute % Change between Successive Years
	34	35	36	37	38	39	40	41	42	43	44	45
Advertiser	$\triangle S_{1,t}$	$\triangle^2 S_{1,t}$	$\triangle A_{3,t}$	$\triangle S_{3,t}$	$\triangle A_{2,t}$	$\triangle S_{2,t}$	$\triangle S_{4,t}$	$\triangle A_{4,t}$	$A_{1,t-1}.S_{1,t}$	$S_{1,t}.S_{1,t-1}$	$S_{4,t}.A_{4,t}$	
Four Roses	+.33						+.59	+.34	−.12	+.80	+.98	.21
Kessler	+.10						−.31	−.47	+.72	+.99	+.98	.20
Seagram's 7	−.21						−.47	−.64	−.70	+.92	+.98	.14
Corby's Reserve	+.51						+.00	+.13	+.55	+.95	+.98	.20
Imperial	+.53						−.53	+.07	+.30	+.50	+.98	.12
Old Thompson	−.20						+.23	−.10	+.80	+.96	+.98	.43
Echo Springs	+.13						−.01	−.33	−.12	+.70	+.98	.21
Ky. Gentleman	+.63						−.14	−.18	+.94	+.96	+.98	.28
Gilbey's Gin	+.09						+.18	−.02	+.52	+.73	+.98	.15
Ancient Age	+.23						−.40	+.13	+.86	+.95	+.98	.27
Gordon's Gin	−.10						+.40	+.43	−.50	+.50	+.98	.13
Bourbon Supreme	−.32						+.04	+.15	+.58	+.98	+.98	.13
Smirnoff Vodka	+.52						−.15	−.42	+.93	+.96	+.98	.31
No. of observations	34	19	15	17	17	17	34	34	34	34	34	34
Mean	+.09	+.14	+.35	+.07	+.21	+.01	−.05	−.04	+.42	+.82	+.97	.32
Camels—Nicholls Data	+.06	−.45		−.29	−.27	−.12	+.18	+.04	+.58	+.24	+.78	
Lucky Strike—Nicholls Data	+.66	+.40		+.42	−.27	+.26	−.29	−.25	+.17	+.75	+.78	
Camels—Borden Data	−.16	−.25	+.66	−.42	+.27	−.13	−.03	−.07	+.24	+.64	+.78	.69
Lucky Strike—Borden Data	+.83	+.45	+.84	+.51	+.27	+.38	−.17	−.10	+.18	+.49	+.78	.26

lack of strong theory. So for better or for worse, the investigation and discussion will proceed all at once, with discussions of the various purposes branching out at various times. This choice avoids much redundancy, though it may lose in clarity.

The considerable amount of discussion about each of the technical choices may seem tedious to the reader, and cause him to feel that, given the degree of importance of the findings, I am laboring mightily to bring forth a mouse. The justification for the methodological discussion is twofold: (1) The conclusion would not be tenable without the discussion to support it,[4] and (2) one hopes the discussion itself has value as being a very explicit argument about some issues in empirical studies that are usually glossed over or ignored, sometimes to the detriment of the empirical work.

THE EMPIRICAL INVESTIGATION

The original focus of this chapter was on the influence of competitive-advertising expenditures, but that focus broadened to include the effects of other variables. One must first ask, however, influence on what? More specifically, one must decide whether one wants to study the amount of the advertising expenditure, or the *changes* in it. The distinction is not trivial; one might want to explain the size of a quantity even though it remains constant.

The extent of changes in advertising expenditures can be best measured with the mean percentage change from year to year,

$$\frac{\sum\limits_{t=1}^{n} \dfrac{A_{1,t-1} - A_{1,t}}{A_{1,t-1}}}{n}.$$

This is a more appropriate measure than is the variance, because the variance would be very large for a long series that had only small changes from period to period but a long-term trend.

The mean percentage change yearly is shown for each firm in column 45 of Table 5-1. The median of these means is 25.5 percent, which, for our purposes, is reasonably low, leaving "low" undefined for now except to note that it is lower than a similar measure of capital investment changes. The mean change would be even lower if adjusted for all-economy secular trends. In order to get a wider sam-

---

[4] In this connection this statement of Theil's is relevant: "Since every econometric analysis is an essay in persuasion — just as is true for any other branch of science — the line of thought leading to the finally accepted result must be expounded" (Theil, quoted in Palda, 1964, p. 83).

ple of experience in this regard, the mean percentage change yearly for the six-year period 1957–62 was also computed for those 63 firms that were among the 100 largest advertisers in all six years. The mean of the firms' means was 15.4 percent, which certainly indicates remarkably slight variability from year to year. And the variability would be considerably smaller if adjusted for secular trend.

Jastram's study agrees with this finding. Of his 42 "dominant" manufacturers of consumer goods, 26 "had a relative dispersion of less than 10 percent in their ratios of advertising outlay to sales revenue over [1935 to 1940]." Jastram's use of the advertising ratio, as well as his more accurate data (obtained directly from the firms), make it reasonable that he would find greater stability than that found in the calculations here.

A "low" amount of yearly change suggests two things: (1) $A_{1,t-1}$ is a good predictor of the absolute size of $A_{1,t}$; and (2) attention should be directed to the changes in $A_{1,t}$ rather than to its absolute size.

Meyer and Kuh described in detail how they gradually penetrated the thicket of variables involved in the capital-investment decision, and how they chose variables to retain in the analysis. Like theirs, this analysis begins with an examination of the matrix of simple correlation coefficients for the dependent variable with the various independent variables.

Looking now at column 4 in Table 5-1, it is obvious that the correlation coefficient $r_{A_{1,t} \cdot A_{1,t-1}}$ is quite high for most firms. Its mean correlation is higher and its median correlations are almost as high as for any other variable with $A_{1,t}$, and even more important, it is positive in more cases than any other variable. Taken together, this suggests that $bA_{1,t-1}$ is a better predictor of the absolute size of $A_{1,t}$ than is any other single variable under consideration.[5]

Notice that the strength of $r_{A_{1,t} \cdot A_{1,t-1}}$ is not directly related to the stability of $A_{1,t}$; if the changes in $A_{1,t}$ were tiny but random, this correlation would be zero. This correlation tells us, then, that a type of linear time trend (starting anew with each $A_{1,t-1}$ observation, but each with a common slope, as shown in Figure 5-1) explains some of the variation that does occur in $A_{1,t}$.

$A_{1,t-1}$ is not a very pure kind of economic variable and its accepta-

[5] It is not at all clear which central-value measure is appropriate for comparing sets of correlation coefficients. The mean R^2 is not useful because high negative correlations produce a high mean R^2, leading to absurd results in the case of S_4, $_t$, for example. Taking the mean of correlation coefficients seems peculiar though there is no logical reason for not doing so. The median is perhaps least objectionable. But a conclusion based on several measures of central value is most sensible, I think.

bility for either forecasting or structural explanation requires justification. This matter will be discussed later in this section and then at length in the last section of the chapter. Assuming for now that $A_{1,t-1}$ will be used as a variable, one must consider how to proceed further. More specifically, one must consider (1) in what kind of an estimating equation to use $A_{1,t-1}$, and (2) which other variables to include, if any, and how. These two matters are interrelated, of course.

FIGURE 5–1. SHORT-RUN AND LONG-RUN VARIATION IN THE ADVERTISING EXPENDITURE

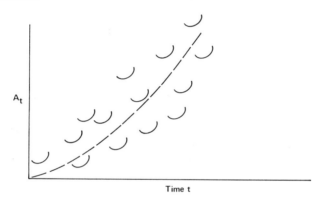

As to the form of the equation in which to use $A_{1,t-1}$, the customary (linear) single-variable equation, whether for forecasting [6] or for structural investigation, would be $y = a + bx$, which gives a better fit (a higher r^2) than any other linear form. But one must think twice about using such an equation, even for forecasting, because several of the time series are sufficiently skimpy that it seems to make sense to pay relatively much attention to "theoretical" ideas about the function compared to the brute force of the data alone. In Bayesian language the a priori distribution seems relatively reliable compared to the observed distribution.

If one estimates $A_{1,t} = a + bA_{1,t-1}$, a structural interpretation of a is that it is a sum that the firm considers its floor advertising expenditure, a kind of threshold. However, no such floor is likely to remain

---

[6] The objectives of a possible forecast should also be specified further. We shall consider the type of forecast that might suit the needs of a firm or of an economic analyst trying to build up a prediction about a particular industry. However, the type of forecast discussed would not be of use to a prospective purchaser or investor in the firm; the information of interest to him would be a forecast of the sales response to advertising.

the same over a long period of time, which means that the estimate of *a* is sensitive to the length of the data series, and this means that a is really a variable rather than a real parameter. So even if such a floor has a meaning — which I doubt — it has a major flaw for the purposes here, even for forecasting.

The interpretation of b is that it is an estimate of some "trend." If one allows b to take values other than one, it implies that the entire frequency series must have a common trend, and more specifically, a

FIGURE 5–2. CUMULATIVE GROWTH OF LINEARLY INCREASED ADVERTISING EXPENDITURE

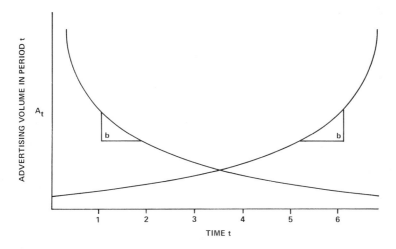

geometric trend, whether $b > 1$ or $b < 1$. If the relationship were perfectly determinate, then $A_{1,t} = bA_{1,t-1}$ would be the same as a geometric time-constant of the form $A_{1,t} = b^t A_{1,t=0}$, and would follow one of the two curves in Figure 5-2. However, if the relationship is not perfectly determinate, the relationship $A_{1,t} = bA_{1,t-1}$ differs from the time-variable relationship in looking like Figure 5-1 (ignoring a possible $b = 1$).

Another approach is to set $b = 1$, and to forecast changes from $A_{1,t-1}$ to $A_{1,t}$ on the basis of other variables. This approach has the advantage of being more responsive to possible cycles in the series or to any other fluctuations, up to the limit that each year is independent of each other year. It seems to me that a forecaster would prefer to estimate long-term trends separately, and to inject them into his forecast in a more explicit fashion than by the device of a coefficient for $A_{1,t-1}$.

There are also other types of trends that might be introduced automatically into the forecast. For a single example, an arithmetic trend might be included, as in $A_{1,t} = bA_{1,t-1} + gt$. However, such variables will not be included for the reasons above and because trend variables use information from the particular past of the particular firm. The poor quality of most of the data, as well as the arbitrary length of the series, calls into question how the past is related to the future of the firm. This is a philosophic issue, of course, but I think it is generally acceptable that one should not include automatic trends until one has used subject-matter variables as fully as possible. By analogy, one prefers a national-income forecast that takes into account various sectoral analyses to a simple trend extrapolation of the past.

If one constrains $b = 1$, and $A_{1,t} = bA_{1,t-1} + x_1 + x_2 + \ldots + x_n$, then $A_{1,t} - A_{1,t-1} = x_1 + x_2 + \ldots + x_n$. This has some similarity to a difference-equation approach, in that other variables will be used to explain $(A_{1,t} - A_{1,t-1})$. But the other explanatory variables need not be first differences themselves, though they may be.

If one's interest is less in making forecasts and more in the direction of "understanding" the workings of economic units and the economic system, then one must inquire into the nature of $A_{1,t-1}$ in a somewhat different fashion.[7] Because $A_{1,t-1}$ can "account for" so much of the variance in $A_{1,t}$, it seems reasonable to ask whether it is sensible to say that $A_{1,t}$ "explains" much of the variance in $A_{1,t}$. A variable may be legitimate for a forecasting equation without having to shoulder the heavier burden that accompanies "explanation" and "causality" — the latter a concept that cannot be avoided easily in a discussion of motivation such as is undertaken in this section.

It is not unlikely that in a discussion of an advertising appropriation the decision-makers might actually utter such words as: "Let's increase last year's budget by about 8 percent because our sales increased last year" or "because this is going to be a good year." If such conversations really precede and influence a given firm's decision, then one can reasonably consider that last year's expenditure is a "true" structural (behavioral) variable, and not a "mere" proxy for other variables, or "mere autocorrelation."

If b is a "true" structural parameter, it must stand for words like "Let's try to increase the budget by 5 percent every year from now

---

[7] A structural investigation in this case is an investigation into the *motivations* of businessmen, and it is therefore an exercise in economic psychology in the behaviorist tradition. (We shall often use the word "structural" as a substitute for "motivational" in the context of this book.) Analogously, Meyer and Kuh claimed to study the motivational determinants of the investment decision.

on," or "Let's hike it up a million every year as we keep making money." But unfortunately it is impossible to determine from outside whether this is a true description, or whether b (and *a*, too) only sums up the general tendencies of many other small variables.

The model of a firm beginning its budget decision with last year's budget, and then modifying it with reference to structural variables, has at least the virtue of greater simplicity than a model in which $a \neq 0$ and $b \neq 1$. Therefore such a model plus refinements will be the basis of an attempt to explain the variation of $A_{1,t}$ from period to period. As a first approximation, then, the expenditure in t is here said to be equal to the expenditure in t-1. The reasoning is simply that, based on the simple correlation coefficients, a point estimate based on $A_{1,t-1}$ will be more accurate than a point estimate calculated as a multiplicative function of any other variable such as, for example, "a constant percentage of last year's sales."

Before concluding this discussion of $A_{1,t-1}$, one might note that neither $S_{1,t}$ nor $S_{1,t-1}$ would be much better grounded theoretically than $A_{1,t-1}$. One frequently hears such statements as "Budgets are set as a constant percentage of sales," but that really only assumes that firms will repeat behavior that was apparently profitable in the past — which is exactly what can be said about continuing the same budget from one year to the next.

Now other variables may be added. In conventional fashion the first tactic was to run step-wise multiple regressions of the form $A_{1,t} = a + b A_{1,t-1} + \ldots$, including all the other variables discussed above. But this fishing expedition came to a bad end. There was no observable regularity from firm to firm as to which variables came into the regression in which order (except for $A_{1,t-1}$), or in the relative importance of variables in the final regression step that included all the variables. Partly this may be due to real differences among the firms. But more likely the source of the trouble is the high multicollinearity of the variables, especially between such pairs as $S_{1,t}$ and $S_{1,t-1}$, or $S_{4,t}$ and $A_{4,t}$. Multicollinearity is expected to continue in the future. But in a situation like this one, in which the short time series give little basis to predict whether or not the multicollinearity will indeed continue, one cannot continue to add variables with gay abandon even for the restricted purpose of forecasting. One reason is that when the number of observations in the various time series is small, it would seem sensible to insist on a sizable increase in the R^2 before including new variables, to compensate for the loss of degrees of freedom.

Multicollinearity also works to make it very difficult to choose among the candidate variables in the long time series. In such cases as Lydia Pinkham, California oranges, and Lucky Strike (all of whose time series are long), if one were to use $A_{1,t-1}$ in a forecasting equation, so much of the variance in the dependent variables is thereby accounted for that it would not be sensible to include any other variables. To include a variable with high multicollinearity may increase the R^2 somewhat, but at a cost to increased variation in all the regression coefficients. But if one thinks in terms of difference equations, then other variables may come out from under the multicollinearity umbrella.

There is at least one important difference between outside forecasting and an explanation model. Contemporaneously-dated variables such as $S_{1,t}$, etc., cannot be used for forecasting. The inside adviser might forecast $S_{1,t}$ on the basis of inside knowledge about decisions concerning other marketing changes such as personal selling or product change. But the outside forecaster does not have information about these other decisions, and hence he cannot make an independent forecast of $S_{1,t}$, or use $S_{1,t}$ in his forecast of $A_{1,t}$.

This study explores the advertising-expenditure behavior of not just one firm, or just one industry, but many firms in several industries, which reduces our ability and willingness to employ variables specific to particular industries. Instead, pooled evidence is used to select variables.

The highest (by far) median correlations with $\triangle A_{1,t}$ are for $\triangle A_{3,t}$ and $\triangle A_{2,t}$. The number of positive-correlation observations for these variables is sufficiently large that they are very unlikely to be specious hunt-and-pick variables. Some of the variables are handicapped because of lack of data. But $\triangle A_{3,t}$ correlates consistently higher with $\triangle A_{1,t}$ than any other variable for those firms for which we have data.

At first thought the lack of correlation of $\triangle S_{1,t}$ and $\triangle S_{1,t-1}$ with $\triangle A_{1,t}$ is surprising. But it is less surprising when we remember that $S_{1,t}$ and $S_{1,t-1}$ are highly correlated with $A_{1,t-1}$. Once $A_{1,t-1}$ has entered into the accounting, $S_{1,t}$ and $S_{1,t-1}$ and their first differences have indirectly been allowed for already.

That $\triangle A_{3,t}$ does better than $\triangle A_{2,t}$ is neither surprising nor very meaningful, probably. Most of the data are for beer brands, and many breweries are regional. This makes it much less likely that there will be a single advertising leader (analogous to a price leader). Furthermore, the competitor in the data is simply the largest advertiser nationally, not always a good sign of a leader. And last but not least, $\triangle A_{3,t}$ includes $\triangle A_{2,t}$.

The data, then, suggest that there is an important competitive influence on advertising expenditures. However, $\triangle A_{3,t}$ suggests that a given firm reacts to the industry trend as a whole, and the reaction will therefore be glacial rather than a volatile week-to-week reaction of head-to-head competition. Again it must be emphasized that this refers only to firms that sell in well-defined industries.

One might also note that $\triangle A_{3,t}$ is not likely to be a summary proxy for the influence of such variables as $S_{1,t}$, $S_{1,t-1}$, $A_{4,t}$, $S_{4,t}$, and their first differences, because the mean correlation of none of these other variables with $\triangle A_{1,t}$ is very different from zero.

Next one must consider how to use $A_{1,t-1}$ in combination with $\triangle A_{3,t}$, for a forecast perhaps. The usual way of doing so would be to include the second variable in a regression equation

$$A_{1,t} = a + b\, A_{1,t-1} + c(A_{3,t} - A_{3,t-1}).$$

Or if a constant $a \neq 0$ or a "trend" $b \neq 1$ is not acceptable, the appropriate regression has this general form:

$$A_{1,t} = A_{1,t-1} + c(A_{3,t} - A_{3,t-1}) \text{ or}$$
$$A_{1,t} - A_{1,t-1} = c(A_{3,t} - A_{3,t-1}).$$

This latter form allows one to discuss c in more general terms, because c can be estimated unconditionally rather than conditionally upon particular values of b.

Whether an estimating equation for $A_{1,t}$ should use a constant determined from the single time series or a pooled industry coefficient (it is perfectly obvious that no estimate of c that pools *different industries* makes any sense) cannot be answered in a general way, but must be decided upon by the forecaster with reference to the facts of the series he wishes to forecast. A forecaster with a long time series available might even substitute another variable that is relevant to his particular industry.

One might also consider adding dummy variables for growth, or a general-economic-conditions variable such as $S_{4,t-1}$. This might be particularly appropriate if the forecaster wished to make a forecast for two or more time periods in the future. But if he is just forecasting one period ahead, an ad hoc adjustment would probably be as good as any dummy variable. Also, if a decision-maker does keep his eye on general economic conditions, it is only because of how he expects his own sales to be affected, in which case it makes more sense to forecast his own sales directly. Furthermore, there are some firms whose sales are inversely related to general economic conditions; Lydia Pinkham is an example.

CONCLUSIONS

For the representative general advertiser, expenditures do not change much from period to period, perhaps 10 to 25 percent on the average. This is much less period-to-period change than in capital investments, and agrees with the more aggregated data (Chapter 2, Postscript) in suggesting that advertising is not a crucial exogenous variable for macroeconomic models.

$A_{1,t-1}$ is a strong predictor of $A_{1,t}$, whether one chooses to think of it as a "real" psychological variable or as a portmanteau summary of the effect of many other variables. The prediction of $A_{1,t}$ can be improved for a given firm by adjusting $A_{1,t-1}$ with a multiplier of some sort, but this multiplier is probably best estimated from independent evidence rather than from a regression of $A_{1,t}$ on $A_{1,t-1}$.

The familiar hypothesis that advertising expenditures are fixed as a function of sales in the prior or current period is inferior to $A_{1,t-1}$ in accounting for variations in $A_{1,t}$, and once one has allowed for the effect of $A_{1,t-1}$, neither $S_{1,t}$ nor $S_{1,t-1}$ nor their first-difference forms is helpful in explaining $A_{1,t-1}$.

Looking now at the *changes* from year to year in advertising expenditures, $\triangle A_{1,t}$, the first-difference competitive-advertising variables show the greatest amount of influence. The median correlation of $\triangle A_{3,t}$ with $\triangle A_{1,t}$ is .40, and for $\triangle A_{2,t}$, $r = .31$. These correlations are not spectacularly high, but given the big differences in size between these and the correlations for the other variables, it is reasonable to conclude that competitive advertising has *some* measurable effect on a firm's advertising expenditures.

It is probably not sensible to compare the effect of the industry's expenditures ($\triangle A_{3,t}$) and the leading competitor's expenditures ($\triangle A_{2,t}$) in an attempt to infer who or what the firm thinks of as the competition when the firm sets its budget. First of all, $A_{3,t}$ includes $A_{2,t}$. Furthermore, the firm represented by $A_{2,t}$ was here chosen arbitrarily by magnitude of expenditure, and a true leader — if there is one — need not be the largest advertiser, especially among regional breweries who comprise a large part of the study sample. Therefore it is probably wiser, though less valorous, simply to conclude that a firm's advertising expenditures seem to be affected by the advertising expenditures of one or more other firms in the same industry, in addition to general economic and advertising trends.

Though one may say that the "representative firm" acts "as if" described by these statistical results, there probably is great variation in the actual decision-making process from firm to firm. The data for breweries even suggest that some firms follow cyclical patterns and other follow countercyclical patterns. This is pure speculation, of course.

The inaccuracy in the available data probably results in a lower measure of association than is "really" the case (i.e., measurement error). Advertising data for a given firm may contain major errors, but the errors are likely to be very highly correlated from year to year. There is much less reason to think that there will be high correlation in errors considered cross-sectionally among firms. This inaccuracy operates especially strongly against the measures of association of $A_{1,t}$ with the competitive variables.

The inability of firms to estimate their competitors' advertising expenditures with high precision may act to lessen competitive interaction. Changes in competitors' price policies can usually be known quickly, but changes in advertising-expenditure policy cannot. Furthermore, a competitor's price change affects *all* of a firm's market relationships, whereas a change in a competitor's advertising affects a firm only at the margin.

Postscript: Is "Continuation" ($A_{1, t-1}$) A Legitimate Variable?

The economic purist may object to using $A_{1,t-1}$ as a variable (except perhaps in forecasting), even if it does enter directly into the thinking and behavior of decision-makers. He might argue that if one constructs a profit-maximizing equation for a firm for any given year in the best marginalist tradition, $A_{1,t-1}$ would not enter into the equation at all. The equation would only include terms for costs and revenues in the current period, plus costs and revenues that occur in later periods but that are attributable to the present period. Terms for past periods could only enter if they stand for delayed effects attributable to past periods that must be deducted in order to observe the net effect of the current variable.[8] A marginalist point of view assumes that the rational economic man has no habits and recalculates his profit-maximizing behavior *ab initio* every year (or perhaps each hour). $A_{1,t-1}$ does not fit into any of these categories because it only expresses a habit, or a tendency for the past to continue into the future.[9]

Some other commonly used economic variables that have much the

[8] A paradigm for doing so is described in Simon (1965a).

[9] Ashby, in his *Introduction to Cybernetics* (1963), points out that whether a given variable is interpreted as a continuation from the past in the form of "memory," or as a force that exists in the present as a physical "trace" of what happened in a prior period, depends only on the information available about the system being discussed. This strikes me as a very wise and useful observation.

same nature as $A_{1,t-1}$ in the sense of being "continuation" variables include "sticky prices" and "brand loyalty" ("transition purchase probability").[10] These examples seem to obey what Boulding calls "the first revised law of economic behavior," to wit, "we will do today what we did yesterday unless there are very good reasons for doing otherwise" (Boulding, 1963, p. 86).

But Boulding's "law" leaves one feeling uneasy. One wants to delve further and ask if there are rational *economic* reasons for the behavior that follows this law, even if the reasons have no obvious place in the marginal analysis. Boulding suggests that uncertainty about the future, and imperfect knowledge about the current market, make it reasonable to repeat yesterday's behavior. In the case of advertising expenditures, the firm can certainly make a more certain estimate about the effect (in profit terms) of an $A_{1,t}$ which is equal to $A_{1,t-1}$ than of a much larger or much smaller $A_{1,t}$. If the firm is willing to pay to avoid risk, the likelihood is therefore increased that an $A_{1,t}$ equal to $A_{1,t-1}$ will maximize the firm's utility. Similarly, the effect of small changes between $A_{1,t-1}$ and $A_{1,t}$ may not seem very uncertain, and hence they have a higher utility than if one calculates the firm's utility without taking account of its prior experience.

But there may also be important internal reasons for setting $A_{1,t}$ equal to $A_{1,t-1}$. A first reason is trivial: to alter anything costs money. The second reason, however, is more weighty: the given fixed scale of the firm's plant and organization makes one level of sales, in the intermediate run, cheaper per unit of sale (counting in all costs except advertising) than any other sales level. If $A_{1,t-1}$ was properly adjusted to obtain that optimum level of sales, then setting $A_{1,t}$ equal to $A_{1,t-1}$ makes good sense. The same argument explains the relative constancy of the labor force from year to year. (This is why Holdren treats supermarket labor as a fixed cost in the short and intermediate run, giving a persuasive justification for doing so [1959].)

Figure 5-3 illustrates this point. The crucial curve in the graph is Total Production Cost.[11] It differs from the usual Total Variable Cost curve because it purports to represent the firm's cost function *as perceived by the firm*. It takes into account the firm's assumption that if it produces no units it can sell off the plant and fire all personnel, but if it is to produce at all it must keep the (indivisible) plant and main-

---

[10] Note that to the extent that we translate "brand loyalty" into a distributed-lag concept, it is not a continuation variable; the cause of the purchase behavior in the present is selling activity in the past, and not just a "repetition" or "continuation" of past purchasing behavior.

[11] The monotonically diminishing advertising-response function is also important here. Evidence for this is presented in Chapter 1.

tain the work force. This latter assumption by the firm includes the assumption that it will then also produce in future years.

The cost curve drawn from the point of view of a prospective *entrant* to the field would be nowhere as flat as between inflection points K and L in Figure 5-3, because a new entrant could choose many sizes of plant and work force. But the flatness of the established firm's cost function sharply reduces the range of advertising expenditures that could be profitable. This is why there is much less variation within a firm's expenditures than there is cross-sectionally among firms in

FIGURE 5–3. THE PERCEIVED COST FUNCTION

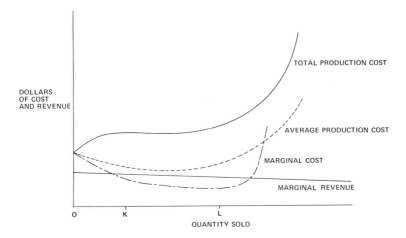

the same industry. This entire argument is closely related to Chapter 3, which discusses the influences of cost upon advertising expenditures.

It is not possible to estimate the production function of Figure 5-3 for a firm — or many firms together — from outside the firm. Hence one cannot easily test the argument given above. But at least the arguments show that there is no *necessary* disjuncture between marginalist theory and the use of $A_{1,t-1}$ as an explanatory variable.

It may be instructive to consider why Meyer and Kuh (1957) did not use a habit variable in their investigation of capital-goods investment decisions, even though they used other variables that are not commonly found in a marginalist investigation. Their volatility from period to period indicates that capital-goods investment decisions are largely one-time decisions, or are thought of in that fashion. Some firms may indeed have policies for constant investment. But if Meyer and Kuh are right, the amount of "residual funds" is important in influencing investment decision, and that residual is likely to be one of the most variable quantities in the firm's accounts. The difference in accounting treatment of advertising and investment is also illuminating. Advertising is treated as "current expense," while investment is not. This points up the relatively routine aspect of advertising, which is why a habit variable is more appropriate here than in the study of capital-investment decisions.

6

Three Studies
in Advertising's
Industrial Organization

Section A of this chapter deals with a phenomenon that has been very much present recently in the world of advertising agencies — mergers. Advertising-agency mergers are not typical of industrial mergers. Yet their analysis may tell something about mergers in general as well as about mergers of agencies.

Sections B and C both deal with the advertising rate structure. The cost of advertising — both the absolute level and the rate structure — affects the total amount of advertising and the amounts spent for advertising by different classes of advertisers. This is why advertising rates are important in the study of advertising. (Advertising rates may also be interesting for what they teach about the behavior of prices generally [e.g., Simon, 1969] but that is not within the purview of this book.)

Neither Section B nor Section C is a general descriptive or analytic study of the advertising-rate structure. (Nor does such exist; the best partial discussions are by Blake and Blum (1965) and Peterman (1965) on television [1] and by Ferguson (1963) and Borden et al. (1956) on newspapers.) Rather, two empirical studies of special topics in this area are presented here.

A. The Success of Mergers: of Advertising Agencies [2]

There are at least three reasons why the effect of mergers upon profitability is of interest (The term "merger" will be used in this chapter to refer to all types of combinations of firms.):

---

[1] See also *Columbia Law Review* (1965) for discussion focused more on the legal aspects of quantity discounts, and *U.S., Senate* (1967) for a full legislative airing of the matter, including many interesting facts.

[2] By Harold W. Johnson and Julian L. Simon.

1. Whether or not mergers are profitable influences our assessment of the efficiency of larger firms as compared to smaller firms.

2. If mergers are not profitable and efficient they are less of a long-run threat to competition, because smaller competitors can then be counted upon to gain on the merged firms.

3. Classical economic logic holds out the hope that *if* mergers are unprofitable, businessmen will eventually learn that fact and fewer mergers will occur.

Previous studies have generally concluded that larger firms are not on balance more profitable than small firms (Blair, 1965; Stigler, 1952), which implies that merged firms are not more profitable than their smaller predecessors. However, the previous work has been at a very high level of aggregation, treating samples of firms in many industries, and the firms themselves have often spanned several industries. The variability in the profitability results has been high, and the conclusions therefore have not been definite.

Mergers among advertising agencies have several useful properties for the study of mergers: (1) The firms in the sample are homogeneous. (2) The firms are not conglomerate; their product is strictly the making of advertisements. (3) The mergers in the sample take place within a short time span, thereby avoiding secular changes in conditions. (4) No advertising agency has more than a small share of the market. This means that the scale effects of the merger can be assessed without the appearance of a monopoly effect, which can help us understand the mechanism of mergers. This is often not the case in other industries.

There is also an important peculiarity of mergers among advertising agencies which may lessen the generality of the results. Many advertiser-clients do not wish to have their agency work on another brand of the same product. And a fairly small number of products account for important chunks of advertising-agency business: autos, cigarettes, beers, etc. This would seem to be a built-in force against profitable mergers. Yet mergers do occur anyway, and we shall therefore try to assess their effects.

Between 1955 and 1961 there were mergers of seven pairs of advertising agencies whose combined billings exceeded $10 million, and which did not engage in other mergers within four years. To assess the effect of the mergers we compared the post-merger performance of the merged agencies against two control-group standards: (1) For each merged unit, pairs of two agencies whose pre-merger-date billings totalled within ± 15 per cent of the merged units were designated as matches for each merged agency. There were two such matched pairs for each merged agency, except agency V. (2) For each merged agency, single agency matches were found whose pre–merger-date billings were within 15 per cent of the *combined* billings of the merged agencies. For each merged agency there were two or more matches, a total of 16 for the seven mergers. The means of its matches in each category were used for each merged agency's comparisons. All agencies in the universe were used in control groups (1) and (2) with the exception of those that were dropped for incomplete data and related reasons. No agency was used in more than one match.

The reader will note that the dependent variable is not profits but rather size of agency's gross revenue. For most sorts of businesses, revenue would only be a good proxy for profit if profits were a constant proportion of revenue. And if the latter were true, one might then consider that firms of all sizes had the same profitability.

Revenues are, however, a good proxy for profits in advertising agencies. First of all, at least until recently (and throughout most of the period of the study) the prices charged by almost all advertising agencies were the same, i.e., 15 per cent of the price paid to the media. Second, agencies usually proceed by hiring people to staff accounts they have already gained, and personnel are hired on a rule-of-thumb fixed basis, usually five people per million dollars of billings, in such manner as to provide an anticipated (and easily anticipatable) profit margin. Third, new accounts are usually gained on the basis of the agency's supposed success with its existing accounts. Fourth, occasional surveys in *Advertising Age* indicate that the ratio of profit to billings shows no trend among various size agencies. There is no doubt among advertising men that the test of an agency's own success is the number of new accounts it gains (less the ones it loses). For the aforegoing four reasons, each increment of billings can be considered as an increment of profit, and as a function of performance on existing accounts. That is, if two agencies A and B have billings of x in year t, and billings in t + 1 are x and x + K in t + 1 respectively, and given an equal proportion of profit, the agency B earns more profit and has "done better" over the period in question.

RESULTS

Merged agencies were compared with their matches for five years before and four years after the merger. For comparison purposes the billings were standardized to a base of 100 in the year before the merger. The standardized results appear in Figure 6-1 (Graphs I–VII). The adjusted and unadjusted data are shown in Tables 6-1 and 6-2.

FIGURE 6–1. PERCENTAGE CHANGES IN TOTAL ANNUAL BILLINGS OF ALL AGENCIES FOR FIVE YEARS BEFORE AND FOUR YEARS AFTER MERGER

GRAPHS I-VII

———— REPRESENTS THE COMBINATION GROUP
– – – – REPRESENTS CONTROL GROUP 1, THE NON-COMBINED PAIRS
············ REPRESENTS CONTROL GROUP 2, THE NON-COMBINED SINGLES

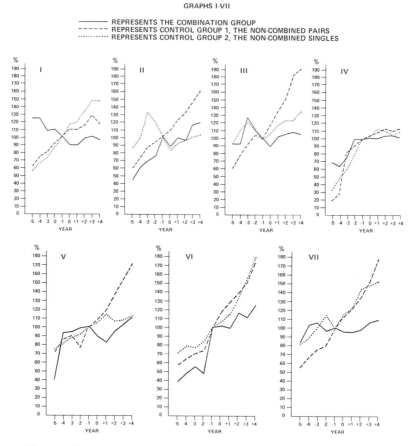

The graphs make clear that the merged agencies did poorly after their mergers. Of the 14 comparisons — seven against pairs and seven against single agencies — the merged agencies did *worse* on 13; one merged agency (II) did better than one single-agency match. This is despite the fact that the merged agencies were *not* doing worse *before* their mergers. The year immediately following the merger was especially poor for the merged agencies.

DISCUSSION

The most interesting outcome of this study is that mergers do take place even though they are ill-fated. And the fate is particularly clearly written in the advertising business, both because of the account-conflict problem and because the results of previous mergers are relatively easy to assess. Certainly this result gives the lie to the frequently-heard argument that "Mergers *must* be profitable or they would not take place."

The most important possible weakness of this study is that the fact of a merger may itself be a signal that the merging agencies' futures are relatively not good. Support for this possibility may be found in this quote by the president of a merging agency: "Because mergers tend to be looked upon as ways of overcoming weaknesses, and because ours is a business in which assumptions and suppositions are given the widest circulation, I want to emphasize that this merger represents the coming together of two strong and financially sound companies." (Weir, 1968, p. 8).

Table 6-1. Total Annual Billings of Agencies in Merger Groups and Control Groups for Five Years before and Five Years after Merger [a]

| Agency | | Total Annual Billings | | | | | | | | | | |
| | | Years Before | | | | | Merger | | | Years After | | |
Sets	Grps.	−5	−4	−3	−2	−1	0	+1	+2	+3	+4	+5
I		1952	1953	1954	1955	1956	1957	1958	1959	1960	1961	1962
	MG	75.0	75.0	65.3	66.5	61.0	54.0	54.1	59.5	60.4	58.0	58.5
	C1	43.9	52.5	57.3	65.3	72.0	78.4	77.7	81.5	92.3	83.5	85.8
	C2	36.5	41.6	46.3	54.3	63.6	73.3	75.3	84.0	92.9	92.7	96.5
II		1953	1954	1955	1956	1957	1958	1959	1960	1961	1962	1963
	MG	19.5	26.6	30.1	32.8	43.5	38.0	42.7	41.3	50.0	51.0	64.5
	C1	29.3	32.4	38.4	41.1	44.0	47.7	53.4	57.3	63.5	69.7	75.2
	C2	33.0	42.2	50.6	45.7	38.5	31.5	35.2	36.7	38.2	39.3	42.7
III		1953	1954	1955	1956	1957	1958	1959	1960	1961	1962	1963
	MG	27.0	27.0	37.2	32.6	29.2	26.3	29.8	31.0	31.4	30.9	a
	C1	16.9	21.3	25.5	28.8	27.7	32.8	37.5	43.3	50.5	52.5	
	C2	25.3	29.9	33.0	30.0	27.3	29.1	32.0	33.5	33.5	36.7	
IV		1954	1955	1956	1957	1958	1959	1960	1961	1962	1963	1964
	MG	16.1	15.1	17.9	23.4	23.4	23.9	23.5	24.3	24.5	24.0	26.0
	C1	4.5	6.5	19.1	21.2	23.2	24.4	25.2	26.5	25.8	26.5	27.4
	C2	7.4	10.8	13.4	17.4	22.0	22.9	24.8	24.4	23.2	24.1	26.9
V		1954	1955	1956	1957	1958	1959	1960	1961	1962	1963	1964
	MG	5.0	11.4	11.5	12.1	12.2	11.0	10.2	11.7	12.5	13.5	15.1
	C1	9.5	11.4	11.9	10.2	13.2	14.3	15.7	18.3	20.5	22.8	26.7
	C2	9.4	10.3	11.1	11.5	12.5	13.3	13.0	13.4	13.5	14.0	14.1
VI		1954	1955	1956	1957	1958	1959	1960	1961	1962	1963	1964
	MG	4.0	4.8	5.6	4.8	10.2	10.3	10.1	11.8	11.3	12.7	14.3
	C1	6.3	7.1	7.7	8.1	11.0	12.9	14.1	15.2	16.5	19.1	21.7
	C2	6.4	7.1	7.0	7.6	9.0	9.6	10.3	12.2	13.8	16.1	19.7
VII		1951	1952	1953	1954	1955	1956	1957	1958	1959	1960	1961
	MG	38.4	47.7	48.9	44.5	46.3	44.4	44.1	45.4	49.0	50.0	53.6
	C1	24.7	29.3	33.5	39.4	44.3	49.7	53.2	59.3	69.0	78.2	90.3
	C2	36.0	39.9	44.6	52.4	45.5	51.2	53.7	63.6	67.2	67.7	68.3

[a] Except for Agency Set III, which has billings for five years before and four years after merger.
MG=Merger Group, consists of merging agencies.
C1 =Control Group 1, consists of average of non-merging *paired* agencies.
C2 =Control Group 2, consists of average of non-merging *single* agencies.

The only rebuttal to this is our data on the performance of merged agencies prior to merger, which give no sign that the merging agencies were in fact in worse shape than nonmerging agencies. But, of course, such data cannot show the effect of such events as the death of an important principal in an agency.

Table 6-2. Indices of Total Annual Billings of All Agencies for
Five Years before and Four Years after Merger [a]

| Agency | | Index of Total Annual Billings | | | | | | | | | |
| | | Years Before | | | | | Merger | | | Years After | |
Sets	Grps.	−5	−4	−3	−2	−1	0	+1	+2	+3	+4
I	MG	123.0	123.0	107.0	109.0	100	88.5	88.51	97.5	98.75	95.0
	C1	60.75	73.0	79.5	90.5	100	108.9	108.0	113.5	127.5	116.0
	C2	55.7	65.5	72.5	85.3	100	115.0	132.0	132.0	145.5	145.0
II	MG	44.9	61.1	69.5	75.0	100	87.5	98.2	95.0	115.0	117.0
	C1	59.7	73.5	87.5	93.5	100	108.0	121.0	130.0	144.0	158.0
	C2	85.7	109.5	131.5	119.0	100	82.0	91.5	95.5	99.0	102.0
III	MG	92.5	92.5	127.5	111.5	100	90.0	102.0	106.0	107.5	105.0
	C1	61.0	78.0	92.0	104.0	100	118.5	135.0	151.0	182.0	189.0
	C2	92.7	109.5	121.0	110.0	100	106.5	117.0	122.5	122.5	134.5
IV	MG	68.9	64.5	75.1	100.0	100	102.0	100.5	104.0	104.5	102.5
	C1	19.4	28.0	82.5	91.5	100	105.0	108.5	114.0	111.0	114.0
	C2	33.6	49.1	61.0	79.0	100	104.0	112.5	111.0	105.5	109.5
V	MG	41.0	93.5	94.25	99.0	100	90.0	83.75	95.0	102.5	110.5
	C1	72.0	86.5	90.0	77.25	100	108.0	119.0	138.5	155.0	171.0
	C2	75.0	82.5	89.0	92.0	100	106.5	114.5	107.0	108.0	112.0
VI	MG	38.8	48.0	55.0	48.0	100	101.0	99.0	116.0	111.0	125.0
	C1	57.4	64.5	70.0	73.5	100	117.5	128.0	138.0	150.0	173.5
	C2	71.0	79.0	77.75	84.5	100	106.5	114.5	135.5	153.2	179.0
VII	MG	83.0	103.0	105.5	96.25	100	96.0	95.5	98.0	106.0	108.0
	C1	55.8	66.25	75.75	89.0	100	112.5	120.25	134.0	151.0	177.0
	C2	81.0	89.5	100.1	115.0	100	115.0	120.75	143.0	151.0	152.0

[a] Base: Total Annual Billings of Each Group in Year − 1, Found in Table 6-1.

B. The Cause of the Newspaper-Rate Differential: A Subjective-Demand-Curve Analysis

With very few exceptions, American newspapers charge "national" advertisers a higher rate than "retail" advertisers.[3] The differential is substantial and is larger than any possible cost difference. In 1956 the average differential was 34 percent for papers with circulation under 50,000, and ranged upward to an average of 72 percent for papers with circulation over 300,500 (Ferguson, 1963, p. 3; see *Advertising Age*,

[3] The definitions of "national" and "retail" differ among newspapers. The trade-association definition of retail advertising is "advertising offering to sell to the public through one or more local retail stores owned, controlled, and operated entirely by an advertiser whose signature and/or address appears in the advertisement" (Ferguson, 1963, p. 1).

April 26, 1965, p. 52, for similar 1965 data). The variation among papers is great, from no differential to well over 200 percent (Borden et al., 1946, p. 437). And the differential increased steadily over the 30 years prior to 1960.[4] (However, a decline occurred from 1963 to 1965 [*Advertising Age*, May 3, 1965, p. 95].)

The explanation of newspaper-rate-setting behavior is the subject of this section. But though this question is entwined with the question of the price elasticities of demand for advertising space, this is not an investigation of the elasticities themselves; it is rather an investigation of what decision-makers in the newspaper business consider the comparative elasticities of demand for retail and national advertising to be.

Ferguson reasoned a priori that the national demand should be more elastic and the national rate consequently lower. (His reasons are given below.) He found that supply conditions could not explain the lower retail rate. He then offered this ingenious hypothesis: (1) an increase in retail linage causes an increase in newspaper circulation; (2) an incremental sale of retail space, therefore, brings indirect revenue through circulation-building as well as direct sales revenue; (3) if this effect is important, it provides a rationale for a lower retail rate even if the retail-demand elasticity is not less than the national elasticity.

Ferguson called this the "joint-product hypothesis." He tested the hypothesis with multiple regressions in which changes in retail advertising linage and other variables were used to explain changes in circulation. Ferguson did find a "positive relationship between retail advertising and circulation" (1963, p. 45), which is consistent with his hypothesis. His finding is also consistent, however, with causality running in the other direction, that is, increases in circulation causing increases in retail linage sales.

The alternative hypothesis is simply that the higher observed rate for national advertisers is due to a lower elasticity of national demand.[5] And elasticity of demand alone should be the governing factor rather than cost, because the supply of advertising space is unlimited, with a constant (and low) marginal cost.

Kolens examined retail and national lineages before and after national and retail rate changes (1964). The study was on a very inadequate scale, with data on only 15 newspaper-rate changes available for analysis, and these data were crude and badly flawed for many reasons. Nevertheless, the data are worth mentioning: in 12 out of 15 cases, the

[4] See Borden et al. and Ferguson for a complete description. Note that quantitative statements about the differential are imprecise because a variety of discount rates are offered to local advertisers.

[5] A proof of this well-known proposition may be found in Boulding (1941, p. 611).

retail demand was more price-elastic than the national demand, in contradiction to Ferguson's assumption.

Ferguson was impressed by national advertisers' opportunities to substitute other media for newspapers. He showed that newspaper advertising was only 13.3 percent of all national advertising in 1956, whereas newspaper advertising was 61.5 percent of all retail advertising. And he found no off-setting strong reasons why the demand for retail advertising should be more elastic. He therefore concluded that "in view of the alternatives open to the two groups of advertisers, a larger number of more attractive alternatives being available to national advertisers, it can be said that national advertisers have a more elastic demand for space in daily newspapers than retailers" (Ferguson, 1963, p. 27).

There are also a priori reasons for believing in a greater retail elasticity, however, including:

1. A single given newspaper gets a much smaller proportion of a national firm's advertising budget than of a retailer's budget.

2. Space in many newspapers is often bought as a block by national advertisers.

3. Perhaps most important, retailers can measure the sales produced by particular advertisements run in particular media more accurately than can national advertisers. It seems obvious that the better the ability of a buyer to estimate profitability, the more sensitive will be the buyer to a change in price. A similar situation, with similar results, occurs in magazines. Mail-order advertisers have an almost perfect measure of the effect of their advertising, and they receive sharp discounts below the rates paid by general advertisers who have the same alternative opportunities as do the mail-order firms. For example, the one-time, one-page, black-and-white rates for *Bride's Magazine* were in 1965: "general" advertisers, $3,600; mail-order advertisers, $1,250; hotels, $1,700; retail stores in New York, $1,250; retail stores outside of New York, $1,100 (from the rate card).

4. Large newspapers, whose rate differential is greatest among all newspapers, also have different rates for many other classes of local advertisers — political advertising, food advertising, entertainment advertising, restaurant advertising, etc. (The *New York Times'* 1968 rates are shown in Figure 6–2.) These diverse rates seem explicable on no basis other than as estimates of what the various markets will bear.

Since there is reason on both sides of the argument, one cannot arrive at a unidirectional and compelling theoretical deduction about the relative elasticities; it is necessary to appeal to the empirical facts. The relevant empirical data are the contents of the decision-makers' minds. As Machlup says: "All the relevant magnitudes involved — cost, revenue, profit — are subjective — that is, perceived or fancied by men whose decisions or actions are to be explained (the business men) — rather than 'objective.' . . . Marginal analysis of the firm should not be understood to imply anything but subjective estimates, guesses and hunches" (Machlup, 1963, pp. 150–151).

For this study, questionnaires were mailed to 100 percent of the daily newspapers in several states surrounding Illinois, making a total of 300 mailed questionnaires in the basic sample. The questionnaires were addressed to publishers, national-advertising managers, and retail-advertising managers, alternately down the list of papers. Three questions were asked:

1. If your paper's national and retail advertising rates last year had been 10 percent higher than they actually were, how much lower (in percent) would you guess your national and retail advertising linage would have been? Naturally this can be only your estimate.
   Retail linage_____percent less than actual
   National linage_____percent less than actual
2. If your national advertising linage had been 20 percent higher than it was, but your editorial content had been the same, what effect would this have had on circulation, in your opinion?
   Circulation_____   _____percent
             up   down
3. If your retail advertising linage had been 20 percent higher, what effect would this have had on circulation?
   Circulation_____   _____percent
             up   down

The wording of question 1 is important. It was phrased to avoid "theorizing" on the part of the respondent, and it attempted to elicit the respondent's estimates of magnitudes with which he was likely to be familiar, without asking him about his mental processes or his abstract ideas. It is this specificity that saves this technique from Friedman's pronouncement that "questionnaire studies of businessmen's . . . beliefs about the forces affecting their behavior . . . seem to be almost entirely useless as a means of *testing* the validity of economic hypotheses" (Friedman, 1953, p. 31).[6]

Table 6-3 shows the joint distribution of individual estimates. To illustrate, read that nine respondents estimated that retail and national linage would each have been 5 percent less if rates had been 10 percent higher.

[6] A pioneer attempt to use a similar technique was that of Gilboy (1931–32). Shaffer (1959) is the only other study I know of that has used this potentially valuable device.

FIGURE 6–2. *New York Times* ADVERTISING RATES (EXTRACTS)

ADVERTISING RATES
Effective August 1, 1968. (Card No. 75.)
Received May 27, 1968.

5. LINE RATE

	Daily	Sun.
Open, per line	3.10	3.75

General Contract Brackets within 1 yr: Per agate line

2,500 lines	2.93	3.59
5,000 lines	2.90	3.56
10,000 lines	2.89	3.55
15,000 lines	2.88	3.53
25,000 lines	2.87	3.52
50,000 lines	2.85	3.49
75,000 lines	2.83	3.47
100,000 lines	2.80	3.43

Separate magazine sections Sunday only (rotogravure, min. 16 pages), may be purchased by one or group of advertisers—contact publisher.

ANNUAL BLANKET CONTRACTS
Full run general contract advertisers may apply magazine linage, color and monotone, to fullfillment of their black and white contracts. The rate for such linage is same as though amount of space used were equivalent to that specified in black and white space contract.

6. COMBINATION RATES
General ads repeated in Saturday edition (within 7 days) 1.45 per line.

8. CLASSIFICATION AND OTHER RATES
These rates are for ads ordered and accepted under designated classifications. Ads ordered elsewhere are charged general advertising rates, unless classification is higher. Position charges extra. Box charge .75; mailed 1.25.
Display ads of bonafide agencies promoting service of own agency, 20% from card rates, less contract discounts. No agency commission.

	Daily	Sun.
†Amusements, per agate line	3.15	3.80

(†) Ticket Agencies and ads with admission charge. Min. 1 col. 6 lines; double col. 28 lines deep. Sports pages .35 extra per line; minimum 14 lines. Ordered R.O.P., Amusement rates apply.

Per agate line

Within 1 year:	Daily	Sun.
2,500 lines	2.98	3.65
5,000 lines	2.92	3.55
10,000 lines	2.87	3.50
15,000 lines	2.82	3.48
25,000 lines	2.76	3.44
35,000 lines	2.72	3.34
50,000 lines	2.69	3.30
75,000 lines	2.66	3.27
100,000 lines	2.58	3.22
125,000 lines	2.57	3.21
150,000 lines	2.55	3.19

Neighborhood Theatres	2.17	2.71
2,500 lines	2.10	2.67
5,000 lines	2.06	2.46
10,000 lines	1.96	2.33
15,000 lines	1.92	2.26
25,000 lines	1.81	2.18
35,000 lines	1.73	2.05
50,000 lines	1.67	1.94

Effective August 1, 1968. (Card No. 77C.):

Decorations, Art Auctions	2.10	2.95
13 days in 1 year	1.95	2.70
20 days in 1 year	1.85	2.60
30 days in 1 year	1.75	2.55

Min. 14 lines. Special combination rates available.
Automobiles—general rates apply.

Boats on Boat pages, 1 day	......	2.55
13 days or 1,000 lines in 1 year	......	2.25
26 days or 2,000 lines in 1 year	......	2.15
3,000 lines in 1 year	......	2.05
5,000 lines in 1 year	......	1.95
7,500 lines in 1 year	......	1.85
10,000 lines in 1 year	......	1.80

Classified min. 3 lines; Display min. 14 lines.

Effective August 1, 1968. (Card No. 75.):

Per agate line

	Daily	Sun.
Books on Book Page	2.55	*

Within 1 year:		
2,500 lines	2.45	......
5,000 lines	2.44	......
10,000 lines	2.43	......
15,000 lines	2.42	......
25,000 lines	2.41	......
30,000 lines	2.40	......
40,000 lines	2.39	......
50,000 lines	2.38	......
75,000 lines	2.37	......

Book ads repeated in Saturday edition (within 7 days) 1.45 per line. Minimum 14 lines.
General advertising rates apply on book ads ordered R.O.P. If position ordered, add position charges to R.O.P. contract rates.
(*) See Sunday Book Review rates in Newspaper Distributed Magazine Section.

Per agate line

	Daily	Sun.
Business pages, open	3.10	3.85
2,500 lines	2.93	3.69
5,000 lines	2.90	3.66
10,000 lines	2.89	3.65
15,000 lines	2.88	3.63
25,000 lines	2.87	3.62
50,000 lines	2.85	3.59
75,000 lines	2.83	3.57
100,000 lines	2.80	3.53

Min. 14 lines.

Effective August 1, 1968. (Card No. 75)
Charity (when application for rate has been approved by Times) general rates less 20%; no agency commission. Minimum 14 lines.

Per agate line

Co-Partnership or Dissolution:	Daily	Sun.
Display (min. 14 lines)	3.10	3.85
Classified	2.65	3.20
Election Notices	2.55	3.10
Financial (min. 14 lines)	3.20	4.05
Once a week for 1 year	3.05	3.80
Twice a week for 1 year	3.00	3.75
3 or more times a week for 1 year	2.95	3.70
When ordered R.O.P.	3.20	4.05

R.O.P. discounts apply on R.O.P. contracts. Insertions ordered R.O.P. applied on time contracts.
Financial ads repeated in Saturday edition (within 7 days), 1.50 per line.

Main Financial News Page	3.70	......
Once a week for 1 year	3.55	......
2 times a week for 1 year	3.45	......
3 times a week for 1 year	3.40	......

Stock table page or other designated pages, add .35 per line.

Financial Notices, Dividends, Redemptions, Corporate Meetings and other Notices addressed to securities holders	2.25	2.72
Mortgage Loans	3.25	4.05
Gardens, Home Improvement & Maintenance (min. 14 lines)	......	2.26
7 consecutive Sundays	......	2.11

Per agate line

Within 1 year:	Daily	Sun.
13 Sundays or 1,000 lines	......	1.97
26 Sundays or 2,500 lines	......	1.95
40 Sundays or 5,000 lines	......	1.93
10,000 lines	......	1.87
20,000 lines	......	1.85
30,000 lines	......	1.83
50,000 lines	......	1.79

Weekday insertions charged Sunday rates if classified Gardens. Sunday Garden ads repeated on Wednesday or Friday (within 7 days) 1.45 per line.
Deadline: Monday night.

Effective August 1, 1968. (Card No. 77C.):

Per agate line

	Daily	Sun.
Restaurants ("Going Out Directory")	2.15	2.45

Within 1 year:		
13 days or 1,000 lines	2.02	2.32
26 days or 2,500 lines	1.98	2.30
52 days or 5,000 lines	1.95	2.26
156 days or 10,000 lines	1.94	2.25

Min. 14 lines. Special combination rates available.

Effective August 1, 1968. (Card No. 75.):

Per agate line

	Daily	Sun.
Legal Notices, Public Notices and Proposals (Display) not on Financial pages	3.10	3.75
Classified	2.60	2.97

Statutory Legal rates do not apply. Financial rates apply if ordered on Financial Pages. Minimum 14 lines.

Political (no contract discount)	3.10	3.75
Real Estate (Display)	2.25	2.43

Within 1 year:		
2,500 lines	2.04	2.20
5,000 lines	1.99	2.15
10,000 lines	1.97	2.08
25,000 lines	1.88	2.03

Sunday Real Estate ads repeated on Wednesday or Friday (within 7 days) 1.45 per line.
Real Estate Mortgage Loans (Real Estate

Display pages only)	2.25	2.43

Minimum 14 lines.

Resorts—Travel	2.30	2.90
10 consecutive Sundays		2.77
2,500 lines	2.20	2.77
5,000 lines	2.15	2.75
10,000 lines	2.13	2.72
25,000 lines	2.10	2.69
50,000 lines	2.05	2.64
75,000 lines	2.03	2.62

Sunday Resort and Travel Agent ads repeated on Tuesday or Thursday (within 7 days), 1.45 per line. Min. 7 lines.

Transportation—general rates apply for weekday ads.

	Per agate line	
	Daily	Sun.
Savings Banks & Savings & Loan Associations (R.O.P.)	2.80	3.32
2,500 lines in 1 year	2.63	3.16
5,000 lines in 1 year	2.60	3.13
10,000 lines in 1 year	2.59	3.12
Savings & Loan Assn. Statements	2.90	3.45

Effective August 1, 1968. (Card No. 77C.):

Shopping Guide (Display)		2.60
4 Sundays in 1 year		2.40
13 Sundays in 1 year		2.25
26 Sundays in 1 year		2.20
52 consecutive Sundays		2.15

Minimum 14 lines. Special combination rates available. 3 business references required.

POSITION CHARGES

Position and designated page charges which are added to general transient or contract rates.
Medical ads not accepted on pages 1-5 weekdays o. in Main News Section Sundays. For top of ads (min. depth 42 lines), add .75 per agate line to specified page rate; top of ad and next to reading, or following and next reading, at Times' option, (min. depth 42 lines), add .85 per agate line to specified page rate. Page opposite Editorial not sold.

WEEKDAY EDITIONS

	Specified	Next to
		Pages Reading
Specified Position, per line		.35
Page 2 or 3 (at publisher's option)	1.00	1.50
Page 4 or 5 (at publisher's option)	.65	1.00
Society News Page	.30	.65
Last Page, second section	.40	.75
Page 6 to 13 (publisher's option) or		
other specified pages	.35	.70

SUNDAY EDITIONS

	Specified	Next to
		Pages Reading
Specified position in R.O.P. sections		.35
Page 2 or 3 (publisher's option) Main News Section	1.30	1.95
Page 4 to 25 and Society Pages, Main News Section	.50	.85
Main News Section	.30	.65
Page 2 or 3, Sport Section	.20	.65
Other specified pages in R.O.P. sections	.20	.55

10. CLASSIFIED AD RATES

15% agency; 15th following month; cash with order unless credit established.
Real Estate and Classified (Employment Advertising) Sections. Sundays, included in all copies in New York Metropolitan area and adjacent territory.

Effective June 1, 1968. (Card No. 77C.):

	Per agate line	
	Daily	Sun.
Auction Notices	1.15	1.40
5 or more days in 1 year	.95	1.20
Minimum 7 lines.		
Automobile Exchange	1.95	2.45
Ads signed by single dealer:		
3 or more days a week	1.85	2.35
30 consecutive days	1.70	2.25
156 days (3 or more days a week for 52 consecutive weeks)	1.65	2.20
365 consecutive days	1.60	2.15
Ads signed by more than 1 dealer	2.10	2.60
Classified min. 3 lines; Display min. 14 lines.		
Boats and Accessories	1.65	1.95
3 or more days a week	1.40	1.85
4 consecutive Sundays		1.80
13 or more days in 1 year	1.30	1.77
26 or more days in 1 year	1.25	1.75

52 or more days in 1 year	1.20	1.70

Special combination rates available.

Business Directory	1.90	3.30

Effective June 1, 1968. (Card No. 77C.):

Business Opportunities	2.10	3.30
3 or more days a week	1.80	2.75
52 consecutive Sundays		2.65
156 days (3 or more days a week for 52 consecutive weeks)	1.65	2.30

Minimum 3 lines. Special combination rates available. 3 business references required.

Cameras, Services		2.65
7 consecutive Sundays		2.36
13 Sundays in 1 year		2.28

	Per agate line	
	Daily	Sun.
26 Sundays in 1 year		2.25
40 Sundays in 1 year		2.23
Employment Agencies	1.14	1.27
3 or more days a week	1.04	1.17
52 consecutive Sundays		1.02
3 or more days a week for 4 consecutive weeks, or 2 days a week for 52 consecutive weeks	.94	1.02
156 days (3 or more days a week for 52 consecutive weeks)	.83	.96
365 consecutive days	.81	.94

Note: Ads in regular Help Wanted columns charged .30 extra per line (if on contract) to be paid on fulfillment of insertion contracts:

	Specified Next to	
	Pages Reading	
1,000- 1,999 lines in 1 year, per line		.04
5,000 -9,999 lines in 1 year, per line		.05
10,000-14,999 lines in 1 year, per line		.06
15,000 lines and over in 1 year, per line		.07

	Per agate line	
	Daily	Sun.
Help Wanted	3.20	3.35
3 or more days a week	3.05	3.25
7 consecutive days	3.00	3.20
30 consecutive days	2.88	3.08
156 days (3 or more days a week for 52 consecutive weeks)	2.72	2.90
Instruction (Classified)	1.60	1.85
3 or more days a week	1.50	1.75
30 days (3 or more days a week for 10 consecutive weeks) or 30 consecutive days	1.40	1.65
52 consecutive Sundays		1.70
156 days (3 or more days a week for 52 consecutive weeks)	1.35	1.60
365 consecutive days	1.25	1.50

Minimum 3 lines. 3 business references required.

Mortgage Loans	2.25	2.75
3 or more days a week	2.00	2.45
7 consecutive days	1.97	2.42

Minimum 3 lines. 3 business references required.

Real Estate	1.93	2.60
3 or more days a week	1.63	2.30
7 consecutive days	1.53	2.20
52 consecutive Sundays		2.25
30 consecutive days	1.28	1.90
156 days (3 or more days a week for 52 consecutive weeks)	1.33	2.00
365 consecutive days	1.23	1.85

Minimum 3 lines. Special combination rates available.

	Daily	Sun.
Schools and Colleges (Display)	1.90	2.50
13 Sundays in 1 year	*1.85	2.45
26 Sundays in 1 year	*1.75	2.35
30 days (3 or more days a week for 10 consecutive weeks) or 52 consecutive Sundays	*1.70	2.30
156 days (3 or more days a week for 52 consecutive weeks)	1.60	2.15

Minimum 7 lines.
(*) Additional weekdays.

	Daily	Sun.
Shopping Suggestions	1.75	
4 consecutive days	1.70	
13 days in 1 year	1.65	
26 days in 1 year	1.60	
52 days in 1 year	1.40	
104 days in 1 year	1.20	

Minimum 4 lines. Published every Tuesday and Friday.

Stamps and Coins:		
Classified (min. 3 lines)		1.95
26 Sundays in 1 year		1.78
52 consecutive Sundays		1.73
Display (min. 14 lines)		2.10
26 Sundays in 1 year		1.93
52 consecutive Sundays		1.88

First line set in agate boldface type. Count 4 words per line (caps); 5 words per line (small letters). Box charge .75. Mailed 1.25.

Source: *Newspaper rates and data*, Standard Rate and Data Service, Inc., April 12, 1969, pp. 404–406.

Of the 176 respondents, 101 estimated the demand for retail linage to be more elastic than the demand for national linage, 22 respondents estimated retail demand to be less elastic, and 53 (including 38 who estimated no change for either, i.e., zero elasticities) estimated equal elasticities of demand for national and retail lineage. I will not report mean-elasticity estimates, because they might be misleading. Even if one disregarded no-change estimates — which would not be justifiable — I believe that the mean-elasticity estimates are far below objective reality, on the basis of the body of objective-demand studies of other commodities. Perhaps more important, the estimates are also too low because they are not in accord with pricing practices. Never-

Table 6-3. Executives' Subjective Estimates of
Newspaper Advertising Demand Function

Estimated Change in National Linage for a 10 Percent Rate Increase	Estimated Change in Retail Linage for a 10 Percent Rate Increase (Number of Respondents Choosing Particular Range Shown in Each Cell)											Sum
	0	−1	−2	−3	−4	−5	−6	−7	−8	−9,−10	<10	
+												0
0	38	3	15	3	6	29	2		2	3	2	103
−1	1	2	3	2		2			1		1	12
−2			2		2	8	1					13
−3					1	2		1				4
−4				1	1			1				3
−5	3	1	2	3	1	9			4	2	2	27
−6										1		1
−7						2						2
−8			1			1		1				3
−9, −10	1		1			1	1				1	5
<10				1		2						3
Sum	43	6	24	10	11	56	2	3	8	7	6	176

theless, the data allow us to compare subjective elasticities, and the results are consistent with a price-discrimination explanation of the rate differential.

An earlier mailing, as well as a mailing to a control sample at the time of the main sample, asked a question phrased in the future tense: "If your paper were to raise its retail and national advertising rates by 10 percent each, by what percentage would you expect retail and national linage to fall? Make an estimate for the year following the rate change, as compared to the year preceding the rate changes. Assume that if there had been no rate changes, linage would have been the same for the two-year period." The distribution of responses was almost identical to the main mailing except for the occurrence of some positive-elasticity estimates.

To check whether nonresponders were different from responders, a 100 percent response was obtained from a group of 34 Illinois small-town newspaper executives to whom the questionnaire was given in person. Their responses agreed with the other response distributions.

Ferguson's joint-product hypothesis received some support from the answers to questions 2 and 3 in that more newspaper executives believe that retail advertising has a positive rather than a negative effect on circulation. Half of them believe, however, that an increase in retail advertising has either no effect or a negative effect on circulation.

In sum, unless there is reason to think that the questionnaire responses of rate-setters do not reveal what the rate-setters believe, or that their actions are not consistent with their beliefs, the data force acceptance of the discrimination hypothesis, at least as a partial explanation, rather than Ferguson's hypothesis. That is, retail rates seem to be lower because the national-advertising market will bear a higher rate, due to the lesser sensitivity to price changes of national advertisers.

C. The Effect of Geographic Monopoly on the Price of Newspaper Advertising [7]

There exist theoretical reasons why monopoly might result in both higher and lower prices compared to several competitive enterprises operating in the same-size market. On the one hand, competition may be expected to squeeze out monopoly profits and to bring price down to the competitive level; this is the point emphasized by price theory. On the other hand, a monopolist might enjoy substantial economies of scale, and his lower cost curve might lead to a profit-optimizing price lower than the competitive price of several firms with smaller output. This is the point emphasized by Schumpeter.

As to the available empirical evidence, Leibenstein recently surveyed the evidence on the welfare effect of monopoly (and other misallocations) and found a consensus that the effect is small (1966, pp. 392-394). (1) Particularly relevant is Schwartzman's finding that "monopoly" does not much affect prices when one compares the United States and Canada. Schwartzman estimated that the mean differences in price between concentrated versus less concentrated industries is only 8.3 percent of average variable cost (1959, p. 359). It is worth noting of Schwartzman's work, however, that it is not a comparison of monopolists with overwhelming shares of markets versus much smaller concen-

[7] By Ian Bowers and Julian L. Simon.

trations, and that the existence of suppliers across the border in the United States places a limit on a Canadian industry's market power. (2) Bain (1951) throws indirect light on the matter with his estimate that the average profit rate was 12.1 percent for highly concentrated industries (four firms with over 70 percent share of markets) compared to 6.9 percent for less concentrated industries. While this difference in profit rates is not inconsiderable, however, a price difference of perhaps 5 to 10 percent could account for all of it, which is not enormous to most buyers of products.

The newspaper industry permits a microscopic examination of the effect of monopoly on price. The commodity sold — newspaper advertising space — is quite homogeneous and there are enough comparable markets to make up a sample of reasonable size. Furthermore, a monopolist newspaper owner has a strong monopoly. Newspapers in other cities usually offer little competition. Radio, television, and other media offer some competition but are poor substitutes for most advertisers, as retail-store experience during newspaper strikes indicates. Against these advantages of empirical tractability is the disadvantage that newspapers are but one industry, and not necessarily a representative one.

We took a sample which included four types of market structures: (1) single evening newspapers; (2) one evening and one morning newspaper separately owned; (3) one evening and one morning paper jointly owned and offering an "optional combination" rate as well as separate rates; and (4) one evening and one morning newspaper jointly owned and in which the advertiser must purchase space in both papers together as a "forced combination" (tied rate.) [8] The 161 sampled papers are those which are large enough to be included in the statistics gathered by trade sources. Together with the even bigger papers in cities with more than two papers, a very large proportion of the total U.S. circulation is accounted for in this sample.

One cannot simply compare the mean rates for papers in these four market structures, for two reasons: (1) It is well established (Borden et al., 1946; Ferguson, 1963) that, *ceteris paribus*, the larger the circulation of the paper, the lower the milline rate (i.e., the cost of a line of advertising per million readers); and since market structure is associated with city size, simple means would be badly misleading. (2) There are two mean rates possible — the mean rate if an advertiser wants to advertise in both papers in a two-paper city, and the mean rate if he wishes to advertise in only one paper. Therefore several comparisons must be made separately.

---

[8] "Optional combination" and "forced combination" are trade terms.

Advertising in One Newspaper in a City

Assume that an advertiser wishes to purchase space in just one paper, say the evening newspaper. Will he have to pay a higher price if a given city has one or another type of market structure?

First compare separate-ownership ("competitive") markets (morning and evening papers owned separately) versus single-ownership optional-combination markets. (The separate-ownership price is obviously lower than and not really comparable to the forced-combination rate because the advertiser cannot purchase the evening-paper space alone; the optional-combination comparison with the separate-ownership papers is therefore more interesting.) One would like to compare rates in towns of the same population. But to take out the circulation effect is even more important, so we shall compare evening papers of the same circulation; the effective comparisons are, however, much the same as for same-population situations. (In fact, all comparisons in this chapter are of newspapers of equal circulation, or of pairs of newspapers with the same total circulation when we compare pairs of newspapers.)

Columns 2 and 3 in Table 6-4 extracted from the basic data in Table 6-8 show national rates [9] in those circulation categories in which both optional combination and separate-ownership market structures exist.[10] Columns 4 and 5 combine the data in columns 2 and 3 to show that it is clearly more expensive to buy space if the publisher also owns the other newspaper in town. It would not be prudent to average the differences for evening or morning papers across circulation categories because of the downward trend with larger circulations, at least for evening papers. But it seems fair to say that the difference is of the order of 20 to 30 percent for the observed range of national advertisers.[11]

[9] The national advertising rates were chosen as data rather than the retail rates simply because more retail rates were unavailable. To work the analysis with both sets of rates would be redundant.

[10] If there is no optional-combination paper in the same category, the next higher or lower category is used, but never further than 5,000 circulation away. Where there are two or more observations in a cell, the mean rate is used, shown in brackets.

[11] We also tried comparing the two market structures by fitting curves (both freehand and semilog least-squares regressions) to the observations for each structure and then examining the differences in intercepts and slopes. But on reconsideration this approach is neither very practical nor does it have much solid rationale. On the former, the ranges of the data are different for the different structures. On the latter, we are interested only in the individual comparisons at particular given circulations, rather than in the form of the best functions for either market structure or for a comparison of them. Therefore this pooled-data approach of curve-fitting was abandoned.

The reason for the lower price charged by separately owned newspapers seems clear to us. It is the logic of tie-in sales. Publishers who own both morning and evening papers set prices so as to maximize the profit from both morning and evening papers together. And given that the publisher's marginal cost of advertising space is low, and given that the marginal sales response to the "additional" paper is not so relatively low, the publisher of two papers who chooses to offer an optional combination is wise to price a single paper dear relative to the combination. (The forced-combination price scheme is simply the ultimate extension of this pricing logic, and on the face of it must be inferior to a rationally figured set of optional-combination rates.)

The difference of 20 to 30 percent between separate- and single-ownership papers may be considered to understate the difference rela-

Table 6-4. National Rates for Newspapers in Separate-Ownership and Optional-Combination Market Structures

1	2	3	4	5
Circulation	Separate-Ownership Rate	Optional-Combination Rate	Difference: (3 − 2)	Ratio of Difference to Competitive Rate (4 ÷ 2)
A. Evening Papers				
60,000	$5.35;	$5.69;	$ + .34	+ .06
75,000	3.85; 4.31 [4.08]	5.52	+ 1.44	+ .38
85,000	3.43	5.00	+ 1.57	+ .46
130,000	2.98	8.30; 4.84; 4.28; 3.38; 4.33 [5.03]	+ 2.05	+ .69
170,000	3.24	4.18; 3.99 [4.09]	+ .85	+ .26
200,000	2.88	3.99	+ 1.11	+ .38
225,000	3.04; 3.13 [3.09]	2.65	− .44	− .14
340,000	2.97; 2.93 [2.95]	2.75	− .20	− .07
360,000	2.55	3.07	+ .52	+ .20
B. Morning Papers				
30,000	$6.55	$11.50; 8.92; 5.20; 8.21 [8.47]	$ + 1.92	+ .29
35,000	7.03	8.52	+ 1.49	+ .21
40,000	5.71	7.43	+ 1.72	+ .30
55,000	4.58	4.81; 5.10; 6.29; 7.96 [6.04]	+ 1.46	+ .32
95,000	3.45	4.29; 5.64 [4.96]	+ 1.51	+ .44
130,000	2.64	3.43	+ .79	+ .30
160,000	2.74; 3.67 [3.20]	3.96	+ .76	+ .24
170,000	2.33; 2.61 [2.47]	3.57	+ 1.10	+ .45
195,000	3.26	3.92	+ .66	+ .20
225,000	3.16; 2.62 [2.89]	3.25	+ .36	+ .12

Source: Table 6-6.

tive to their costs. This is because the single-ownership papers must have lower long-run costs than separately owned papers, due to economies of printing and other overhead. This suggests that if the separate-ownership price is considered as a "competitive" base, the "markup" (however figured) must be more than 20 to 30 percent higher for the single-ownership than for the separate-ownership papers.

Table 6-5. National Rates for Newspapers in One-Newspaper and Two-Separately-Owned-Newspaper Cities

1 Circulation	2 Single Evening Paper	3 Evening	4 Separate Ownership Morning	5 Difference	6 Ratio of Difference to Single Paper Rate (5 ÷ 2)
45,000	$5.91		5.71	$ − .20	− .03
55,000	4.59; [4.86] 5.14		4.58	− .28	− .06
60,000	5.45; 4.37 [4.91]	5.35		+ .44	+ .09
75,000	4.49	3.85; 4.31 [4.08]		− .41	− .09
90,000	4.38; [4.13] 3.87	3.43		− .70	− .17
100,000	3.09; 3.70 [3.39]		3.45	+ .06	+ .02
125,000	3.12	2.98		− .14	− .04
170,000	2.84	3.24		+ .40	+ .14

Source: Table 6-6.

It is also interesting to compare the same-circulation evening-paper rates (for example) in cities where there is only one newspaper compared to cities with two newspapers (separately owned evening and morning papers) as in Table 6-5. In this case the insufficiency of point-to-point estimates requires that three morning-newspaper rates must also be pressed into service. Columns 5 and 6 show a lack of consistent direction in, and small size of, differences.

The lack of difference between the two sets of prices (for single newspapers, and for two newspapers separately owned) can be explained in either of two ways. First, it is possible that the cross-elasticity of substitution between morning and evening papers (where two papers exist in a city) is not very large, in which case the single paper in a one-paper town is in much the same position as either of the papers in a town where there are two separately owned papers. The other possibility is that competitive prices tend to reduce rates in the two-newspaper town, but that circulation per thousand is worth less in small cities (where the single paper is usually located, compared to a newspaper of the same circulation in a larger two-newspaper town); these two forces might balance each other.

Advertising in Both Newspapers in a City

Now consider the fate of the national advertiser when he wants to buy space in both the evening and morning papers in a given town. The appropriate comparison is then between the milline rates for both morning and evening newspapers together, holding total circulation constant.

Table 6-6, extracted from the basic data in Table 6-9, shows the relationship among separate-ownership (column 2), forced-combination (column 3), and optional-combination (column 6) markets, where observations at the same circulation are available. The difference in rates between separate-ownership and joint-ownership situations is considerable indeed, as columns 4, 5, and 8 show. But the advertiser does much *better* under monopoly. Again, it is wise to refrain from calculating a simple average because of trend, but the difference is of the order of 20 percent for both forced- and optional-combination markets.

Table 6-6. National Rates for Morning and Evening Newspapers Taken in Competitive, Forced-Combination and Optional-Combination Structures

1	2	3	4	5	6	7	8
	"Competitive"	Forced-Combination	Difference	Col. 4 ÷	Optional-Combination	Difference	
Circulation	Rate	Rate	(3 − 2)	Col. 2	Rate	(6 − 2)	(7 ÷ 2)
90,000	6.19	4.00; 3.50 3.80; 4.90 [4.05]	−2.14	−.346	3.49	−2.70	−.446
105,000	5.20	4.42; 3.96 [4.19]	−1.01	−.194	4.54	− .66	−.126
115,000	5.01	3.57; 4.00 [3.79]	−1.22	−.243	3.21; 4.41 [3.81]	−1.20	−.239
180,000	3.44	2.72	−0.72	−.209	3.18	−0.26	−.075
225,000	3.91	3.91	−0.00	−.000	2.86; 3.26 3.28 [3.20]	−0.71	−.181
230,000	3.59	2.60	−0.99	−.275	2.88	−0.71	−.198
295,000	4.10	−	−	−	3.06; 2.97 [3.01]	−1.09	−.266

Source: Table 6-7.

What explains this disadvantage of the separate-ownership markets? Part of the explanation may be economies of scale in production: single printing plant, overhead, and perhaps some editorial economies. But the more likely source is not technological but rather promotional. The owner of two papers offers a deal of "two for almost the price of one" that the single paper cannot. Because the marginal cost of advertising space is so low, the two-paper owner has strong motivation to offer such a deal. Hence the advertiser who wishes to buy both evening and morning papers benefits from the two-paper owner's profit-maximizing option. The outcome for the advertiser who would not automatically prefer to advertise both in the morning and evening newspapers is not clear; whether he is better or worse off with joint ownership depends upon his advertising-response functions.

Now let us consider the rates in cities with equal populations, but with one versus two newspapers. (The circulation will not be the same in this comparison, of course.) This is the relevant issue when an advertiser considers what might happen to rates if a given city goes from one to two newspapers or the reverse. Notice that the comparisons are to evening newspapers where there are both morning and evening papers, because where there is just one paper it is almost always an evening paper (and data for the two exceptions are omitted).

First let us make the comparison between a single evening newspaper, and the evening-newspaper price where there is joint ownership of morning and evening newspapers. Column 11 of Table 6-7 shows clearly that the advertiser would have to pay *much* more per evening-newspaper circulation under joint ownership. If, however, he wishes to advertise in both the morning and evening newspapers, it is not clear whether the joint situation will give him a cheaper rate per thousand. (The results in column 7 are mixed.)

There are unfortunately too few cases with two (morning and evening) separately owned newspapers to allow a comparison.

CONCLUSIONS (STUDY C)

The results offer something for both the critics and the apologists of monopoly and bigness.

The advertiser who wishes to buy space in only the morning or evening newspaper does better under separate ownership ("competition") than under point ownership ("monopoly"). But if the advertiser wants to advertise in both morning and evening papers he clearly does better under joint ownership than under separate ownership, because of the joint-maximizing pricing policy open to the owner of two papers, perhaps in combination with the production economies of scale available to him. Furthermore, even if the advertiser was initially inclined to advertise in only one paper he might do better with advertising in both the jointly owned papers than if he could advertise in only one at the separate-ownership rate; the outcome depends upon his advertising-sales response functions.

Looked at either way, however, the effect of monopolistic ownership is large, in contradiction to recent suggestions that monopoly has little effect on price. There seems no simple way to compare these two effects to arrive at an overall welfare judgment.

Table 6-7. Comparison of Rates in Cities of Equal Size and Differing Market Structures

1	2	3	4	5	6	7
City Zone Population	Single Evening Newspaper	Two Newspapers, Forced Combination Rate	Difference (3 − 2)	Ratio of Difference to Single Paper Rate (4 ÷ 2)	Optional-Combination Join Rate	Difference (6 − 2)
70,000	5.84	4.54; 5.32; 5.23 [5.03]	−0.81	−0.138	4.225 [80,000]	−1.615
100,000	5.72	4.72; 3.35 [4.035]	−1.685	−0.294	—	—
110,000	4.70; 4.64 [4.67]	4.03; 4.56; 4.66 [4.61]	−0.06	−0.012	4.80 [120,000]	+0.13
130,000	4.59; 4.12 [4.35]	4.81; 3.64 [4.225]	−0.130	−0.029	3.12	−1.235
140,000	4.37	4.37; 4.42; 4.66 [4.438]	+0.068	+0.155	4.385	+0.015
170,000	4.76; 4.52 [4.64]	4.00; 4.15 [4.075]	−0.565	−0.121	5.05	+0.04
190,000	4.50; 3.77 [4.13]	3.93; 5.69; 6.99 [5.54]	+1.41	+0.339	3.90	−0.235
210,000	3.04	—	—	—	—	—
220,000	3.87	—	—	—	3.347	−0.523
230,000	3.09	—	—	—	3.99	+0.90
240,000	4.30; 5.04 [4.67]	4.15	−0.52	−0.111	3.96	−0.71
260,000	5.44	3.57	−1.87	−0.343	—	—
270,000	4.38	3.49	−0.89	−0.203	3.76	−0.62
290,000	3.12	—	—	—	4.08	+0.96
300,000	3.70	—	—	—	3.18 [310,000]	−0.52
460,000	2.84	2.88	+0.04	+0.014	3.16 [470,000]	+0.32
850,000	5.91	—	—	—	—	—

Table 6-7. (Continued)

City Zone Population	8 Ratio of Difference to Single Paper Rate (7÷2)	9 Optional-Combination Evening Newspaper	10 Difference (9 − 2)	11 (10÷2)	12 Two Separately-owned Newspapers, Evening Rate	13 Difference (12 − 2)	14 (13÷2)
70,000	−0.276	7.175 [80,000]	+1.335	+0.228	—	—	—
100,000	—	—	—	—	—	—	—
110,000	+0.027	9.11 [120,000]	+4.44	+0.948	—	—	—
130,000	−0.283	6.33	+1.975	+0.453	—	—	—
140,000	+0.003	6.875	+2.505	+0.573	5.35	+0.98	+0.224
170,000	+0.008	6.85	+2.21	+0.476	3.85 [160,000]	−0.79	−0.170
190,000	−0.056	7.24	+3.105	+0.750	—	—	—
210,000	—	—	—	—	—	—	—
220,000	−0.135	8.727	+4.857	+1.255	4.31	+0.22	+0.071
230,000	+0.291	5.974	+2.884	+0.933	3.43	−1.24	−0.265
240,000	−0.152	12.10	+7.43	+1.591	—	—	—
260,000	—	—	—	—	—	—	—
270,000	−0.141	5.89	+1.51	+0.342	—	—	—
290,000	+0.307	8.83	+5.71	+1.830	—	—	—
300,000	−0.140	6.96 [310,000]	+3.26	+0.881	2.98 [310,000]	−0.72	−0.191
460,000	+0.112	3.57 [470,000]	+0.73	+0.257	—	—	—
850,000	—	—	—	—	3.04 [840,000]	−2.87	−0.487

Table 6-8. National Milline Rates for Space in Newspapers Bought Individually (i.e., Space in Only an Evening or a Morning Newspaper)

Net Circulation	Evening Editions			Morning Editions		
	One Newspaper in City	Optional Combination	Separate Ownership	One Newspaper in City	Optional Combination	Separate Ownership
20,000		$ 9.22				
		12.10				
25,000		11.36			$11.14	
		5.69			9.39	
30,000		8.43			11.50	$6.55
		10.82			8.92	
		10.29			5.20	
		6.86			8.21	
		6.88				
35,000		15.35			8.52	7.03
		6.33				
		9.74				
		7.55				
40,000		5.83			7.43	5.71
45,000	$5.91	10.19			4.29	
		6.24			7.86	
		8.06				
		5.92				
		6.55				
		6.87				
		5.59				
		5.34				
50,000	5.72; 5.84	8.04			6.55	
	4.50; 4.20					
55,000	4.59	5.62		$5.14	4.81	4.58
		8.03			5.10	
		5.98			6.29	
		6.85			7.96	
60,000	5.45	5.69	5.35		6.46	
		5.77			5.07	
65,000	5.04				4.75	
	4.52				4.06	
	4.12				5.09	
					7.08	
70,000	4.76	6.54			6.79	
	4.64	6.63			4.83	
	3.77				4.87	
					3.75	
75,000	4.49	5.52	3.85			
			4.31			
80,000		6.96				
85,000		5.00	3.43			
90,000	4.38	4.80			3.62	
	3.87				5.26	
					3.32	

(Continued)

Table 6-8. (Continued)

Net Circulation	One Newspaper in City	Evening Editions		Morning Editions	
		Optional Combination	Separate Ownership	Optional Combination	Separate Ownership
95,000	3.09	589		429	345
	3.70			564	
100,000				453	
105,000	4.30	423		515	
		503		401	
				478	
110,000		347		345	
115,000	3.04				
120,000				452	
125,000	3.12	830		466	
		484		404	
		428			
130,000			298		264
135,000		338		343	
		433			
140,000		428		372	
				367	
145,000				479	
150,000			349	397	
155,000				416	
160,000					274
					367
165,000		418		396	
170,000	2.84		324		
175,000					
180,000		357			
185,000				357	
190,000					223
					261
195,000					326
200,000			288		
205,000				392	
210,000					
215,000					
220,000		265			
225,000			304	341	316
			313	325	
230,000					262
235,000					
240,000					
245,000					
250,000			223		
255,000			262		
260,000					
265,000					
270,000					
275,000					

(Continued)

Table 6-8. (Continued)

Net Circulation	One Newspaper in City	Evening Editions		Morning Editions	
		Optional Combination	Separate Ownership	Optional Combination	Separate Ownership
280,000					
285,000		278			
290,000					295
295,000					
300,000					
305,000					
310,000					
315,000					
320,000					
325,000					
330,000					259
335,000					
340,000	277	297			
345,000		293			
350,000					259
355,000					
360,000		255			
365,000					
370,000					
375,000					
380,000					
385,000					
390,000					

Sources: *Newspaper Circulation and Rate Trends*, 1964; *Newspaper Rate Differentials*, 1964.

Table 6-9. National Milline Rates for Both the
Morning and Evening Newspapers Together (Where Both Exist)

Net Circulation	Combination Rates			Net Circulation	Combination Rates		
	Forced	Optional	Separate Owner		Forced	Optional	Separate Owner
45000		565		135000		310	
50000	484	428		140000	364		
	542			145000	340		
	567				323		
55000	523	496		150000		376	
	532			155000		396	
60000	454			160000		329	
	466					389	
	491					410	
	505			165000			
	520			170000		299	
	527			175000		318	
	550			180000	272		344
	569			185000			
	437			190000			

(Continued)

Table 6-9. (Continued)

Combination Rates				Combination Rates			
Net Circulation	Forced	Optional	Separate Owner	Net Circulation	Forced	Optional	Separate Owner
65000	437	444		195000	292		
	472			200000		370	
	512			205000		329	
70000	481	418				384	
	403	419		210000	312	316	
	464			215000			
75000	466	414		220000			
	490			225000	391	286	391
80000	420	505				326	
	462					328	
	524			230000	260		359
	456			235000		288	
	452			240000			
	364			245000			
85000	450	372		250000	288		
	446	390			270		
	393	459		255000			
	390			260000			281
90000	490	349	610	265000		242	
	380			270000			
	400			275000			
	350			280000			
95000	323	385		285000		288	
		395		290000		306	
100000	415	408		295000			410
		324		300000		297	
		379		305000			
		364		310000			
105000	442	454	520	315000			
	396			320000		248	
110000		313		325000			
115000	357	321	501	330000			
	400	441		335000			
120000	699	425		340000			
	349	367		345000			
125000		406		350000			
		398		355000			
		312		360000			
130000				365000			

Source: Same as Table 6-8.

PART TWO:

Advertising in the Economy and Society

7

The Economic
Development
of Advertising

There is a strong relationship between the extent of advertising in an economy and the level of development of the economy. In the manner of Colin Clark (1940), Figure 7-1 plots per capita income against advertising as a proportion of gross national product, based on data in Table 7-1. The association is obvious and strong.

This not to say that the association between advertising level and development level is invariable; there exist countries which deviate from the pattern, such as Spain, South Africa, Finland, and France. For some of these countries ad hoc explanations spring to mind — the unequal distribution of income in South Africa, for example — but the explanations for other deviants do not come so readily. (The advertising data are atrocious, of course, which may account for some of the deviation.) The overriding fact, however, is that the richer a country is, the larger the proportion of its income is spent for advertising.

The question asked in this chapter is why this should be so. What is there in the nature of advertising that accounts for its appearance in larger quantity when per capita income is high? The answer to this question also tells us much about the nature of advertising and its relationship to an economy.[1]

Though the focus of this chapter is upon amounts spent for advertising, it is worth a note in passing that choices of media and styles of advertising content also vary from country to country. And these differences in manner of advertising apparently are deeply rooted. In 1900 Sherman noted: "The bright, incisive, clean-cut style of our commercial paragraphers is wanting. Instead the Englishman says 'use so

[1] For another treatment of the subject of this chapter, though mostly in the context of North America, see Borden (1942, Chapter II).

Table 7-1. Advertising and National Population, 1962-64

Country	1 Population in 1964 (Millions)	2 Gross National Product in 1964 ($ Millions)	3 GNP ÷capita 2÷1	4 1962-64 Advertising ÷GNP (IAE estimate)	5 1964 Advertising less promotion ÷GNP (IAE estimate adjusted)	6 1964 Advertising ÷GNP (Advertising Age estimate)	7 1964 Advertising ÷GNP (Advertising Age estimate) modified for comparability with IAE estimates Col. 6 x 1.27
1. Argentina	21.3	11,160	523	.97	.97	.60	
2. Australia	11.2	21,100	1,884	1.7 [1961]	1.7	1.23	
3. Austria	7.2	8,450	1,171	1.1 [1960]	1.1	1.28	
4. Belgium	9.4	15,360	1,638	.97	.82	.78	
5. Brazil	79.7	14,100	177	1.41	1.37	.88	
6. Canada	19.2	43,440	2,258	2.05	2.05	1.48	
7. Chile	8.3	3,920	471				
8. Colombia	16.5	5,065	306	.92 [1961]	.92		
9. Curacao					1.16		
10. Denmark	4.8	8,920	1,861	1.4 [1958]	1.4		
11. Ecuador	4.8	1,032	215	.65 [1960]	.57		
12. Egypt							
13. Finland	4.6	6,550	1,430	2.2	1.47		
14. France	48.4	87,480	1,807	.77	.77	.59	
15. Germany	58.3	103,350	1,773			1.28	1.63
16. Greece	8.5	5,000	588	.07	.07	.30	
17. Iran	22.9	5,038	220				
18. Rep. of Ireland	2.8	2,590	909	.95	.84	.11	
19. Israel	2.5	3,111	1,257	.61	.53	.48	

Table 7-1. (Continued)

	1	2	3	4	5	6	7
Country	Population in 1964 (Millions)	Gross National Product in 1964 ($ Millions)	GNP ÷ capita 2 ÷ 1	1962-64 Advertising ÷GNP (IAE estimate)	1964 Advertising less promotion ÷GNP (IAE estimate adjusted)	1964 Advertising ÷GNP (Advertising Age estimate)	1964 Advertising ÷GNP (Advertising Age estimate) modified for comparability with IAE estimates Col. 6 x 1.27
20. Italy	51.1	49,520	969	.81 [1961]	.81	.72	
21. Jamaica	1.8	785	438	.44 [1959]	.44		
22. Japan	96.9	69,400	716	1.56	1.56	1.39	
23. Lebanon	2.4	950	392			.56	.71
24. The Netherlands	12.1	16,790	1,385	1.67 [1960]	1.52	1.25	
25. Norway	3.7	6,250	1,691	1.6 [1960]		.51	
26. Pakistan	109.6	9,020	82	.19		.52	.66
27. Rep. of the Philippines	31.3	4,795	153				
28. Peru	11.3	3,166	280	1.18 [1960]			
29. Portugal	9.1	3,320	365	1.5 [1961]		1.05	
30. Rep. of S. Africa	19.6	10,326	527			1.45	1.85
31. Spain	31.3	17,720	565	.02		.36	
32. Sweden	7.7	17,480	2,282	1.6 [1959]		(.68)	.66
33. Switzerland	5.9	12,920	2,200	1.6		1.31	
34. Thailand	30.5	3,445	113	.25 [1960]			
35. Turkey	30.3	7,425	245	.34	1.37	.05	
36. United Kingdom	54.2	92,160	1,700	2.0		1.60	
37. U.S.A.	192.1	628,700	3,272	2.74	.31	2.30	
(38. Mexico)	39.6	17,970	454		1.72	.82	1.04

Sources:
Columns 1 and 2: Agency for International Development, in *Advertising Age*, May 9, 1966, p. 110.
Columns 4 and 5: *International Advertising Expenditures*, 1963.
Column 6: 1964 Advertising expenditure data from *Advertising Age*, May 9, 1966, pp. 89-117, divided by Column 1.
Occasional data from scattered other issues and sources.

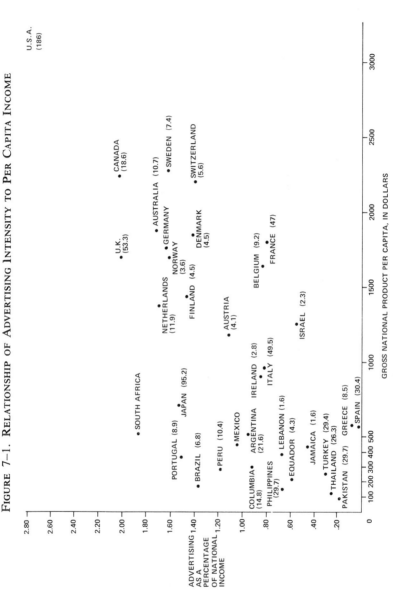

FIGURE 7-1. RELATIONSHIP OF ADVERTISING INTENSITY TO PER CAPITA INCOME

Notes: Population figures for each country are in brackets. Advertising excludes exhibitions, point-of-sale displays, and promotional schemes. Estimates of Advertising/GNP are from column 4, Table 5–1, except where no estimates exist. In that case, estimates come from column 7.

Source: Table 5–1.

and so,' 'wear so and so,' 'eat so and so,' 'they are the best'; and that exhausts his descriptive and persuasive powers" (Sherman, 1900, p. 32). The same description probably applied in 1938, and perhaps also a bit in 1968, mitigated perhaps by the American advertising agencies now operating in Great Britain.

If advertising were merely a consumption item and an interesting part of our culture, there would be little reason to discuss its origins. But advertising is itself a part of the economic development mechanism. Schumpeter (1934, p. 66) says that "development in our sense is then defined by the carrying out of new combinations." As one of his cases of development he includes "a new way of handling a commodity commercially." The beginning of advertising for a particular commodity, then, is very much a developmental change in Schumpeter's sense.

This chapter discusses the conditions and causes of there coming to be advertising and promotion where there was before no promotion for a commodity. The effect of advertising upon the general course of economic development is not discussed except for a brief section at the end. Rather, the chapter seeks to understand the social and economic infra-structure of advertising itself, i.e., when and why advertising appears in an economy. This inquiry may be seen as a continuation of the topic discussed in Chapters 2 to 4, the conditions under which there is more or less promotion, though the approach here is deeper and more general.

It is not surprising that Quesnay's *Tableau Economique* operates without promotion or that Marshall's conception of the economy had small place for promotion, because promotion was indeed a minor aspect of earlier economies for reasons we shall explore. Unlike such economic activities as production, exchange, consumption, investment, and even research and development, promotion is a relative newcomer. In the very widest sense it is true that promotion has always been with us; sellers have always exerted pressure upon potential buyers, and goods have always been displayed to increase the rate of sales. But even the personal selling that took place in medieval and earlier years in Western civilization was not promotion as we know it. It was either trading between merchants, which was largely a matter of higgling and settling terms, or it was passive selling like that done today by clerks in retail stores, most of whose work is best not classified as promotion. In earlier years there was little of what is now called, in the pretentious but not meaningless phrase of today's businessman, "creative selling." It is only a few centuries in the West now since there has been any appreciable amount of activity that self-consciously, systematically, and actively reaches out afar for new customers.[2] It is this quality that is the hall-mark of promotion.[3]

But promotion has no place in most modern analytic schemes of the economy, either. Commodities move from sector to sector in an input-output table in an apparently automatic way. Promotion is excluded as an influential factor just as is transportation. The widest possible way of looking at our economy, the Parsons-Smelser (1956) view of the economy as a subsystem of the entire society, also ignores the role of promotion. Transactions take place across the boundaries of sectors and subsectors in a frictionless fashion and without motivation except for the constant needs of the various sectors.

In discussions about the "function" and "role" and "place" of promotion in developed economies, the very terms "function" and "role" are themselves symptoms of the undeveloped state of the discourse; such terms are not necessary for, and are seldom found in, formal analysis. The best that one can do formally is to specify conditions under which there will be more or less promotion; that is the closest possible formal representation of "advertising serves to . . ." or "advertising is necessary when. . . ." The task of this chapter is to specify some of the more basic conditions for the appearance of promotion.

It is interesting to consider why, if promotion has size and possible importance, it has been left out of economic schema. The reason is, I think, that promotion requires *exchange*. Advertising can speed and increase exchange of a good, but it cannot begin the process of exchange. Exchange can exist without any promotion, as illustrated by the famous anthropological phenomenon of "silent trade" in many primitive settings, in which the trading parties leave their goods, then retire and wait for the other tribe to leave other goods in exchange or to refuse to trade. But promotion cannot exist without exchange. Because promotion is therefore not causal in the crudest sense, and because promotion has not been important historically, it has been reasonable to neglect promotion when considering the structure of development of economies.

---

[2] Historians of advertising begin their accounts with the symbols marked over the various shops in ancient Rome and elsewhere. The bush, of which good wine supposedly had no need, is a famous example. But these symbols were hardly promotion. Rather, they seem to say, "If you are looking to buy wine, here is where you can get it," not a very aggressive act of reaching out to create customers who would not otherwise purchase.

There were surely isolated examples of true promotion in early times. Presbrey mentions a sign at the outskirts of one Roman town praying of the traveler that he patronize a tavern in another town (1929, p. 9). This is much more like contemporary promotion in that it reaches afar to create customers, in the manner of Burma Shave or Stuckey's roadside shops.

[3] For a working definition of promotion see Chapter 2, p. 25.

It is only when one focuses on the finer detail of economic development, as does Schumpeter, that one sees that promotion might be important just as are other changes in commercial practice, because it is such "discontinuous" changes in the structure itself, each of which may be small but which bulk large in the aggregate, which effect economic growth.

The following explanation of the appearance of the phenomenon of promotion in various situations is different from Schumpeter's explanation of economic development, however. Schumpeter gives mainly psychological explanations of developmental acts (1934, Chapter 2), which he therefore considers "spontaneous." The present chapter tries to classify various conditions which are necessary for promotion to occur; all of these conditions are economic in the broad sense, and some of them are also economic in the narrower sense of being elements of standard price theory.

The central question of this chapter may be phrased as "Why is there promotion at some times and in some places for some commodities, and why is there not promotion at other times and in other places for the same commodities?" Unlike the matter of the *amount* of promotion, this question cannot be treated with the sort of static analysis used in Chapters 2 to 4. The discontinuous question about yes-or-no promotion is a question about economic and social *structure*, which is why, as Schumpeter (1934, p. 63) explains, we must "turn aside from traditional theory" for a study of this kind.[4]

Because exchange must precede promotion, inquiry into the necessary and sufficient conditions for promotion must deal with the preconditions of exchange. We shall see, however, that almost every precondition of exchange also has a special relationship to promotion, in the sense that promotion is not simply a proportional function of exchange as exchange is affected by variations in the condition.

This chapter, then, tries to distinguish and classify the most important social and economic conditions that must be present before promotion can become an important activity in an economy and society. It is the inevitable fate of such a discussion that the forces it discusses seem obvious to the reader.[5] And the discussion takes the uninspiring form of

[4] The arguments about development being discontinuous, and about changes in social structure, are given by Schumpeter (1934, Chapter 2, especially p. 81n), though they are still not quite satisfactory, I think.

[5] Some of these same forces have been adduced to explain other phenomena, notably the rise of industrialization. Max Weber covers a lot of the ground in one paragraph:

"An economic prerequisite for the appearance and existence of a factory in this sense is mass demand, and also steady demand, that is, a certain organia laundry list rather than the flowing stream of a reasoned argument. The usefulness of such classifications as this becomes apparent, however, when one tries to study further in the field.

Table 7-2. **Manufacturers' Expenditure on Advertising as a Percentage of Manufacturers' Net Sales of Selected Consumers' Goods in the United Kingdom and the United States, 1935**

	United Kingdom	United States
Flour	1.8	0.4
Canned and bottled foods	2.2	2.3
Coffee, tea, cocoa, beef extracts, etc.	3.3	3.2
Cereals, biscuits and preserves	4.3	6.5
Sweets and toffee	3.6	5.3
Beer	1.8	4.7
Soft drinks	3.6	15
Tobacco	9.3	8.2
Soaps, cleansers, polishes and disinfectants	13	13
Heating and refrigerating equipment	4.9	5.7
Domestic electrical equipment	5.4	4.5
Radios and accessories	8.6	5.3
Boots and shoes	0.9	4.0
Hosiery and knitted underwear	1.5	4.2
Toilet goods	25	28
Proprietary medicines	37	34
Motor cars, motor cycles and accessories	4.2	4.0
Petrol and motor oil	8.7	6.4†

† This includes a proportion for wholesalers' advertising given on p. 65 of Borden, 1942.

Source: Kaldor-Silverman, 1948, p. 31. British figures estimated by Kaldor and Silverman from Census of Production, Statistical Review, and other sources. See Kaldor-Silverman, Chapter III, for method. The American figures were obtained from three surveys, two undertaken by the Association of National Advertisers (1931 and 1934 to 1935), and one by the Harvard Business School into the Marketing Expenses of Grocery Manufacturers for 1927. The number of firms included in each commodity appears to have been small (from 3 to 41 in the 1934 to 1935 enquiry). The United Kingdom ratios relate to manufacturers' sales exclusive of duty and the American figures are comparable.

zation of the market. An irregular market is fatal to the entrepreneur because the conjuncture risk rests on his shoulders. For example, if the loom belongs to him he must take it into account before he can discharge the weaver when conditions are unfavorable. The market on which it reckons must be both sufficiently large and also relatively constant; hence a certain mass of pecuniary purchasing power is necessary, and the development of money economy must have reached the corresponding stage, so that a certain demand can be depended upon. A further requisite is a relatively inexpensive technical production process. This requirement is implied in the fact of a fixed capital which requires the entrepreneur to keep his establishment going even when conditions are unfavorable; if he utilizes hired labor only, the danger is shifted to the worker, if the loom, for example, is left idle. In order to find a steady market, again he must produce more cheaply than under the traditional technique of house industry and the putting-out system" (1961, p. 129).

It is interesting to note that Weber developed a very simple chain of events: existing military and luxury demand leads to industrialization which leads to mass demand. He neither tried to explain the presence of promotion, nor used promotion to help explain demand or industrialization. Weber also gave price competition part of the credit for what he called "mass market demand."

The approach of this chapter assumes that the course of the development of advertising is determined (at least in part) by the stage of development of the economy and society. Support is lent to this approach if one shows that two economies at the same stage of development show a similar picture of the (quantitative) development of advertising. Therefore it is interesting to examine Table 7-2 (from Kaldor and Silverman) which shows the high correspondence between the proportions of manufacturers' net sales spent for advertising in England and the United States in 1935; the correlation between the two countries' columns is .93 (Kaldor and Silverman, p. 30). The point of showing these data in this context is that a given product will be advertised to much the same degree in heavily industrialized countries, but certainly to relatively different degrees in less developed countries.[6]

1. Division of Labor

As long as each person, or each household, produces the same goods and services to satisfy the same needs, there will be no exchange, except perhaps as Americans take turns buying each other a cup of coffee.[7] If there is no exchange, and no felt need to exchange, there will obviously be no promotion.

After labor has been divided, buyer and seller begin to encounter difficulty in finding and reaching each other. This is especially true when labor is divided geographically, as when different towns and regions specialize in different products. As noted before, the trade among the specialized producers may at first get along without promotion, as demonstrated by silent trade and also by arrangements such as this Trobriand Island case discussed by Malinowski (1964, p. 22): "[there are] . . . standing arrangement[s] between two village communities. The inland village supplies the fishermen with vegetables: the coastal community repays with fish." But as division of labor continues further,

[6] The high intercountry correspondence is of general interest, too, as Telser has noted (1961; 1968, p. 3). Telser also found that the "Canadian figures giving advertising as a percentage of sales by product category are roughly the same as the U.S. figures" (1968, p. 3).

[7] "In original form, the economic life of the indigenous communities in Central Africa was carried on in closed and largely self-sufficient units. Trade in goods, with but a few exceptions, was negligible. Part of the explanation for the lack of organization exchange lay in the general poverty of the area. . . . The absence of any sizeable exchange was also partially accounted for by the relatively uniform resource endowment of the African interior and the physical barriers to the movement of goods. The former limited the opportunities for advantageous exchange, and the latter, for isolated communities, recommended self-sufficiency as the least hazardous objective of economic activity" (Barber, 1961, p. 44).

and as the difficulty of buyers and sellers finding each other increases in a much-faster-than-linear fashion, more efficient search mechanisms (i.e., promotion) become crucial.

As an illustration of the relationship between geographical specialization, international trade, and promotion, much early advertising, in the eighteenth and nineteenth centuries, announced that the advertised commodity was a "New Importation." (Later the natural extension of this point will be discussed under the heading "Transportation.")

2. Existence of Wealth above the Subsistence Level

This condition is the commonest explanation given for the rise of promotion (viz. Galbraith, 1952, Chapter VIII; and Potter, 1954, Chapter VIII).

The concept of a surplus has been attacked by Pearson under the provocative title "The Economy Has no Surplus" (Polanyi et al., 1957, Chapter XVI). Pearson's point is that the needs of any community, no matter how underdeveloped, have some subjective basis, and hence we cannot determine objectively what the subsistence level is. However, the concept of a surplus can be rehabilitated with somewhat more rigorous phrasing, to wit: as per capita income rises in a society, the individual will purchase a greater variety of goods. This can be deduced immediately from indifference-curve analysis; as the individual moves up his budget line the marginal utilities of previously purchased goods fall as he buys more of them, and hence he will at some point begin to add other goods as their marginal utilities are exceeded. (This also explains an increasing tendency for income to be paid in money rather than in kind as income increases.)

To return to loose usage, the potential buyer, or the community of potential buyers, must have the wherewithal to finance purchases from the seller. There is not much reason for a traveling jewelry salesman to take his sample case to a settlement where all human energy is devoted to raising enough corn and sweet potatoes to support life. But when income increases people will buy a wider variety of products and those products will naturally be advertised: ". . . the range of goods now advertised in the African press will be found remarkable by those who still think in terms of 'Kaffir truck' and is clearly indicative of the expansion in the range of goods desired. Advertising of bicycles and bicycle accessories probably takes pride of place, closely followed by patent medicines, toilet preparations, and cosmetics. Other goods which are widely advertised are musical instruments, gramophones and records, cameras and films, foodstuffs and non-alcoholic drinks" (Rhodesian-Nyasaland Board of Trade report of 1965, quoted by Bauer and Yamey, 1957, p. 86.).

But wealth does more than make payment possible by creating discretionary income. Wealth also creates new needs, and hence new scope for advertising. For example, Warren's Shoe Blacking was one of the earliest nationally advertised brands in Great Britain, at the beginning of the nineteenth century. In an earlier time when few people owned shoes no one would have wanted or needed shoe polish even if they could have paid for it.

3. Ability to Manufacture Goods on a Large Scale

The section above notes that a community must be able to produce more than it needs to sustain life, as one condition for promotion. But goods must also be produced on a scale large enough for the producer to seek buyers far away from him. A shoemaker working with crude implements can sell all the shoes he can make to people who live close to his shop. It is not until he mechanizes his production of shoes or garments or what-have-you that he must promote and sell to customers who do not already know of his existence by simple proximity and who are not bound to him by local monopoly. And so, until processing facilities have reached a high level of productivity, a necessary condition for promotion does not exist.

One mark of processing or manufacturing is that the production-worker's labor, together with the special processes and capital goods, must produce a quantity of goods that is much greater than any householder can produce in the same length of time. Such an increase in labor productivity can result from a simple division of labor, by one man becoming a bootmaker and another a pinmaker. But the more important sources of this higher productivity are: (1) organization of production, for example the organization of the pinmaking process as described by Adam Smith; (2) capital investment; (3) the introduction of machinery; and (4) together with (1)–(3), the development of a pool of skills and knowledge. (A second important mark of a factory, as Weber [1961] emphasizes, is that in a workshop workers can be shifted to other work when demand decreases, but not in a factory. Nor can a specialized pinmaking machine be shifted to other uses. Such immovability means low marginal cost during some periods, which is conducive to advertising.)

A nice illustration of how early manufacturing went hand in hand with early promotion is the fact that the very pins (and similar notions) cited as a production example by Smith were a staple of the Yankee and not-so-Yankee peddlers who roamed the United States selling from farmhouse to farmhouse in the nineteenth century.

The rapid proliferation of drummers in the years from 1870 to 1900 accompanied the rise in manufactured products (Brink and Kelley,

1963, p. 38). And the rise of the drummers had a return effect by providing profitable outlets and hence stimulating more investment in manufacturing. It would be an interesting test to correlate the time-series data on output and number of salesmen, industry by industry. The relationship should not be linear.

Patent medicine makes an interesting example for this argument. The recorded history of patent-medicine advertising goes back to 1591 (Presbrey, 1929, p. 289). One important condition for patent-medicine promotion was (and is) the incredible ease of "manufacturing" a potion which the purchaser is nevertheless unable to produce for himself since he does not know the "formula" of what he is buying.

Patent-medicine "manufacturing" made promotion possible, even though little or no capital investment was required. But in other industries the technological opportunity for cost reduction through capital investment not only makes large-scale production and promotion possible, but it also makes it necessary. The reason is the lower marginal cost made possible by the fixed capital investment, and the bigger margin between price and marginal *production* cost. If the producer does not take advantage of his production capacity he will lose money in the long run. This matter was explored earlier, in Chapter 3, Section 4, along with the illustration of the promotion done by the snow-shoveling entrepreneur after he acquired a mechanical shoveling device.

4. Geographical Distance between Sellers and Potential Buyers, and Transportation to Surmount It

Section 3 of Chapter 4 analyzed in comparative-static terms the effect of a change in transportation cost upon promotion for a particular product. This section treats a similar issue but in a more historical and structural context, and it considers the effects on all goods rather than on individual products.

Nineteenth-century drummers would not have proliferated as fast as they did if railroads had not existed. But important as transportation is in carrying salesmen and advertising, its existence as a carrier of goods is even more important. There is no point in making sales unless you can deliver the goods, and without excessively high delivery costs. Marco Polo traveled vast distances, of course, but his role was primarily that of buyer of goods, rather than seller. As a promoter and seller he would have been much hampered by the absence of a dependable means of transportation with which he could fill orders that he obtained, especially on a regularized, repeat basis.

Adam Smith compared the costs of shipping goods overland and by sea, pointing out how the high cost of transportation made it difficult to do business at a distance even in the same small country. As the cost of transportation falls, it becomes more profitable to sell in faraway places. Promotion is then needed to develop those faraway sales. In the United States, the Erie Canal reduced to one-tenth the previous cost of transporting goods along its route. The railroads had a similar effect on costs. These transportation improvements were an important precondition for advertising and traveling salesmen to be profitable in the United States.

Mail-order selling is a particularly clear example of the importance of a system for transporting goods. Sears Roebuck, Montgomery Ward, and other mail-order firms were utterly dependent upon the express companies for delivery of goods in their early days. Pending legislation to provide parcel-post service got enormous support from the mail-order houses because they anticipated the great benefits that parcel post would bring to them. Their anticipations were correct. Parcel post did do wonders for the mail-order business.

And it was not accidental that Richard Sears got his start as a railroad telegrapher. His first sales, of watches, were via other railroad telegraphers and agents.

Transportation as a commodity is self-satisfying in the requirement for transportation. It makes sense, then, that transportation was one of the early commodities to be advertised heavily in England and the United States. "The first stage coach notices in England appeared in the year 1658" (Sherman, 1900, p. 12). (The low marginal cost compared to total cost is also an important reason for promotion of ship runs and other scheduled transportation, as noted earlier.)

Improvements in packaging have an effect similar to improvements in transportation. Preservation of foods by freezing, and speedy transportation of them by airplane, are substitutes for each other. For an earlier example, it was an improvement in packaging that made possible the wide sale of canned tomatoes in the 1890s.

5. Urbanization

For the purpose of this argument, a large town is a place (1) within which a merchant can deliver his goods easily, but (2) many of whose inhabitants are not likely to know of the existence of each merchant, and the quality of his merchandise, purely by firsthand experience and back-fence chatting. Urbanization diminishes the effectiveness and comprehensiveness of personal contact. In a community of 20 people one can easily ask after a lost dog, or sell the pups. But in a large town, one must resort to a classified advertisement. It is not surprising, then, that Presbrey (1929, p. 18) found that "one explanation of the increase in advertisements . . . (ca. 1800–25) is found in the growth of towns and their environments . . . ."

Promotional practices in the British Cooperative Movement illustrate the point: "It was originally maintained that cooperative retailing had no need of advertisement and that the saving obtained in this way was a legitimate cooperative economy. . . . In the small village societies of about 250 to 500 members, publicity in the ordinary sense is practically unknown, except for the display of a few bills in the shops. There is no need to advertise the stores, which are well known to all. . . . In the larger societies the scope of advertising and sales promotion is considerably wider . . ." (Carr-Saunders et al., 1942, revised edition, p. 123).

The department store is a creature of advertising. Without advertising to attract customers from all over a large town or city (and without rapid transportation to get people back and forth to the store), the department store would not be possible.[8] It is one of the first institutional changes in our economy and society which one can say was caused by advertising.

Mitchell's data shown earlier (Chapter 2, Table 2-8) on the proportion of sales spent for advertising by stores in different sizes of communities is a cross-sectional view of a process similar to that discussed in this section. In general, bigger communities have more advertising as a proportion of sales.

Traveling amusements such as circuses and theater groups are examples that help one understand the dynamics of urbanization and promotion. Traveling amusements differ from established retailers primarily in that they cannot depend upon the gradual accretion of custom from the townspeople who become informed about the retailer over a period of time. Instead, the traveling amusement requires the forced-draft effect that only advertising can provide. This explains why traveling amusements became important advertisers long before retailers did.

6. Monetization

Promotion follows (and is followed by) an expanded scale of enterprises. A barter system is a great hindrance in the development of any large-scale enterprise; hence monetization must be a precondition of promotion. Promotion also causes, allows, and permits increased rou-

---

[8] The 1966 transit strike in New York City nicely illustrates the interrelationship of transportation, advertising, and department stores. The absence of subway and bus transportation caused "one of the worst business days I [David Yunich, president of Macy's] can remember. . . ." Also, department-store advertising was reduced sharply. " 'We decided to hold back ads' a spokesman for Macy's said" (*New York Times*, January 4, 1966, pp. 1, 14).

tinization of transactions. (Branding of goods is allied with promotion in doing so.) Advertised brands are purchased repeatedly and habitually, and salesmen develop trade channels. But large-scale and routinized transactions are possible only in societies where prices are not renegotiated with each transaction. And a money system is indispensable in making fixed prices possible.

Also, promotion acts to create sales at long distances from the producer. This means, first of all, that seller and buyer cannot meet face to face to settle terms of barter. Also, back-hauling and reselling goods taken in barter would raise the seller's cost very greatly. These are additional reasons why a society must be very largely monetized before promotion can become very important.

7. Printing and Literacy

Advertising symbols were in existence before there was printing, and many soft-drink companies in many countries of the world still use advertising symbols that are well known to illiterate people. However, a written advertisement can do a selling job that is, for many products and selling situations, enormously more powerful than only a visual symbol, or even a radio or television message. And in those many situations in which a personal solicitation is impossible, any other promotion might also be impossible without printing and literacy — the print advertising of many industrial products, for example, could not be substituted for by other promotional techniques such as radio or television. Printing and literacy are indeed important preconditions for the emergence and growth of advertising.

8. Individualism and the Individualization of Property

The vesting in individuals of title to worldly goods affects people in their roles as producer-sellers, as well as in their roles as consumer-buyers. On the consumer side, the person who buys for the possession of only himself and his family is likely to be more attentive to the purchasing process than is a person who belongs to a consumer cooperative, or to a tribe that owns everything in common. Hence, the individual owner is a better target for promotion, because he will be more interested in it.

The more attentive the audience is, the more fruitful the advertising; and the more fruitful the results of promotion, the more promotion there will be.

To make the above argument in a different fashion, we begin by noting that individualization of property implies decentralization of purchase decisions, and therefore more decision-makers. The greater the number of decision-makers for a given quantity of goods, the more promotion there will be. This casual observation is backed by the empirical evidence of the lower promotion expenditures (relative to sales) for industrial sales of a product as compared to consumer sales of the same product (Lewis, 1954). I would guess that this is so because the amount of information that the decision-maker will absorb does not rise as fast as the size of the sum the decision-maker will spend, though the number of decision-makers decreases inversely with the size of each decision-maker's expenditure. And in general, the amount of promotion is proportionally less for larger units of sale. The selling cost for a single house is only 5 to 6 percent and for industrial property even less. The selling cost of no low-unit-sale consumer product comes close to being that low.

Individualization of production property, together with a private profit system, is an important related condition. Promotion is a tool of competitive, aggressive commerce (though it may also be used by socialized enterprises as we see more and more in USSR, Yugoslavia, and other socialist countries). As producers become more rational on their own behalf, and more acquisitive, they turn to promotion as a device for realizing the earning ambitions that only individualization of production property makes possible.

9. Differentiation of Wants [9]

The emphasis till now has been primarily on economic and physical conditions. Now we turn to conditions that are rooted deeper in the social and psychological nature of people in society.

As in the history of a society there come to be differences among people in vocations, wealth, power, and beliefs, so people also come to want different kinds of goods. Also, there arise differences in their ability to afford different types of goods; the rich buy caviar, and the poor buy salmon roe.

The differentiation of wants goes hand in glove with the division of labor to increase the number of transactions that are necessary for goods to end up in the hands of people who are willing and able to have them. Together these two influences also decrease the probability that any random person will want to trade goods with another random person or even only sell goods to or buy goods from the other. As this process continues, there is more and more need for promotion. To illustrate: if half the men in a community catch fish and half raise corn, any particular fisherman has a 50-50 chance that the first man he meets will be a trade partner. But if, instead, a man is the only fisher for shad in

---

[9] Professor James W. Carey suggested to me that differentiation of wants is an important precondition for promotion.

the village, and if there are only ten people in the village who like shad, the man needs to do more searching (that is, promotion) to find customers.

A society like that of the United States develops enormous differentiation of wants. Every time an American changes jobs and/or social position, he finds that a different set of purchases is appropriate. This means that new information about the goods and services is sought, and is responded to. Each time a person (or household) changes his place in society, he must acquire new information about commodities and services. This rapid turnover of people's stocks of information is favorable to the growth of promotion. American society may or may not be more mobile than England's, say, but compared to a primitive society, the amount of mobility and the consequent differentiation of wants is very great.[10]

The more heterogeneous a society is, the more differentiation of wants there will be. To the extent that the United States retains its melting-pot characteristics, promotion is increased. For example, the variety of ethnic foods offers scope for a greater amount of promotion than if all Americans had an identical food heritage; and the promotion for ethnic foods is aimed at both the particular ethnic groups and to other Americans as well, viz. pizza, Kosher pickles, French bread, Polish ham, halvah, and so on.

10. Impersonalization

In non-Western, nonindustrialized societies most economic relationships are with friends and relatives. For example, in a Mexican village in which each of the three major kinship families trades only at the store maintained by a member of that family, the need for and value of promotion is less than if all buyers would patronize all stores (Redfield, 1950, Chapter III). And Malinowski describes the Trobriand Island Kula ring in which promotion is superfluous: "Between the two communities the exchanges are not carried out haphazard, any two individuals trading at random. On the contrary, every man has his permanent partner in the exchange, and the two have to deal with each other" (1964, p. 25). Many immigrants to the United States, even those who came from sophisticated societies, had a very strong tendency to trade and work in this country only with their landsmen and kin. Such a limitation of trade to prescribed channels reduces the use that can be made of the wide-ranging information that promotion might bring. The employment of columns of a daily general newspaper were of little value to

---

[10] De Grazia puts it this way: ". . . people landed in his [the advertiser's] net because they were groping for a station in life . . ." (1962, p. 235).

a Ukrainian in the United States who was only willing to work with other Ukrainians.

In the contemporary United States such limited preferences have largely broken down and trade takes place much more impersonally, in the sense that a transaction may be undertaken with a complete stranger almost as readily as with someone you know.[11] This expands the size of the market and increases competition between outlets and brands, both of which are favorable for the growth of promotion.

How an impersonal point of view resulted in advertising by an Egyptian bank in the nineteenth century is made clear by Landes (1958, pp. 144–145):

The private bank was of its essence particularistic: its clientele was restricted to friends and friends of friends . . . ; its operations were secret; its whole procedure, as confidential as possible. Among such firms there existed a certain understanding, a sort of gentlemen's agreement that restricted competition and made high finance a well-bred game. . . . Beyond this dignified sphere lay the impersonal, universalistic corporation — the Ottoman Banks — dealing with anything and anybody so long as the risk was good, publicizing its operations, and even advertising for clients. . . .

11. Rationalization and the Retreat from Custom, Superstition, Animism, and Fatalism

This section refers to the sources of information people use, and the kind of authority they credit, in the process of making purchasing decisions. To the extent that goods are bought because they have always been bought in the past, or because a particular household god has commanded it, the prospective purchaser will not be interested in or affected by promotion. But to the extent that a person believes that facts and reason should be the basis for decision, promotion can, literally, get its foot in the door. The closed mind is closed to most important forms of promotion.

The fatalistic view that what will be will be and there is no sense trying to control the future is also inimical to promotion (partly because the argument to foresight and making provision for the future is one of the most powerful appeals in a promoter's kit).

Fatalism is diminished by the obvious demonstrations of power to control and predict nature that are so evident in materially advanced cultures.

[11] One should not discount the importance and strength of time-deepened relationships among industrial firms. But curiously, the participants in such relationships usually rationalize them — perhaps correctly — in terms of increased economic efficiency springing from such established relationships.

12. Promotional Know-How, and a Desire to Promote

All students of economic development now agree that a reservoir of "modern" knowledge and skills is crucial for economic development, and a reservoir of capital and capital goods is not sufficient. Just so is promotional skill a prerequisite to large amounts of promotion.

The ability to promote is not an ability that any fast-talking story-teller can develop in jig time. Successful promotion demands the study of promotion. Over time there is an accretion of skill in a country. There is little doubt that selling and advertising were done less skillfully 75 years ago in the United States than now; an inspection of old advertisements is persuasive in this regard. Probably the same is true of personal selling.

Perhaps even more basic than skill in promoting are the desire to promote, and a conception of business as reaching out for customers. (This may be related psychologically to a way of thinking about business as a process that creates additional product by the organization of production and the expansion of markets, rather than as simply a process for distributing fixed quantities of product and money among consumers and sellers. The former view is one which someone suggested appeared for the first time with the Industrial Revolution.) Geertz describes the point of view of the trader in the *pasar* of Modjokuto, an Indonesian town:

Traders often say quite explicitly that finding prospective customers is not a problem in their minds: they either come or they do not, the market is either crowded or it is not; and whatever the causes may be of the flurries and dead spots which so mark *pasar* trading, they are not within the control of the trader . . . the ideal is not so much to create or stimulate a market for whatever you have to sell; rather it is to be present when a chance to sell appears, and most especially, to be capable of making the most of it. . . . [A trader tends not] to regard his primary task as one of creating or stimulating buyers, through advertising, aggressive salesmanship . . . [Geertz, 1963, p. 35].

J. B. Say long ago noted manufacturers' complaints that they could not dispose of the goods they made.[12] Perhaps slumps were a cause, but lack of selling skill and lack of distribution channels were surely also causes. The manufacturers in Say's time suffered from focusing only on the problem of production; they had never even recognized the necessity for promotion.

The amount of promotion done is particularly sensitive to the quality

[12] "It is common to hear adventurers in the different channels of industry assert that their difficulty lies, not in the production, but in the disposal of commodities; that produce would always be abundant, if there were but a ready demand, or vent" (1821; in Kapp, 1949, p. 170).

of execution of the promotion, because the difference in revenues produced by good and poor promotion may be of the magnitude of ten or
more. Poor promotion is demonstrably unprofitable, and must quickly
lead to decreased promotion.

DISCUSSION

The aforementioned necessary and sufficient conditions for the appearance of promotion are several and varied. They include economic conditions as well as conditions that are usually referred to as noneconomic. All of these are conditions that we assume will be increasingly
prevalent as a country is modernized. It is reasonable to assume, therefore, that in the absence of governmental prohibition, the appearance of
promotion generally will be a concomitant of economic development,
as the cross-national data show in Table 7-1.

But though the process in general may seem automatic, the appearance of advertising in any specific market situation where previously
there had been no advertising is a discontinuous leap which has the nature of a spontaneous Schumpeterian new combination. It is safe to say,
then, that though the appearance of promotion in the aggregate is
rather inevitable, the speed and pervasiveness of its appearance depends on characteristics of the entrepreneur himself, characteristics
which vary within and among developing economies.

The effect of promotion on the rate of economic development has not
been discussed above. On this issue there is neither empirical evidence
nor sound theory to go on, other than Schumpeter's assertions that new
commercial combinations have a prima facie positive effect on
development.[13] However, it is worth mentioning in passing that promotion surely has a stimulating effect on the development of new consum-

[13] Kindleberger notes the importance of promotion as a part of market communication:

"Too little attention is generally paid in these accounts [of economic de-
velopment] to the spread of communication needed to link markets. Face-to-
face trading in which the producer or his agent must deal directly with the
buyer or his agent imposes a considerable limitation on the extent of the
market. The peddler is an inefficient marketer compared with the traveling
salesman who follows up leads derived from direct mail advertising, telephone
canvas, or records of previous sales. Provision must be made especially for
communication of price information so that the village trader can tell whether
and when he chooses to take his plums to which city. In modern markets there
has grown up a paraphernalia of market quotations in the general and specialized press, telephonic and telegraph communication, including ticker tapes,
avalanches of discussion by mail of specifications, price, and delivery dates.
Along with transport, or rather some distance in advance of capacity to transport, there must be a network of communication which is vital to market operation" [Kindleberger, 1958, p. 98].

er-durable industries. Without promotion the inventor and entrepreneur could not count on rapidly expanding the market for the color television set, the bicycle (advertising for which accounted for almost 10 percent of national advertising in the 1890s), the auto, the washing machine, etc. The possibility of selling a lot of goods in a hurry is a potent stimulus to entrepreneurs, and hence the possibility of advertising must speed the development of these markets. Indeed, the volume of advertising for these durables is greater during the introductory years than it is later when the products are known and established, as was seen in Chapter 2.

Postscript: The Future Growth of Advertising in Industrial Societies

It is a natural extension of this chapter — and especially of the material in Table 7-1 — to ask what is likely to happen as per capita income increases even beyond the present income in the presently richest country, the United States. Will the amount spent for advertising and promotion continue to rise?

One thing does seem to be clear: the absolute amount of advertising will probably continue to rise as national income increases; the amount of advertising has not ceased to rise in the past, except temporarily when business conditions were bad. But when one looks at the *proportion* of national product spent for advertising,[14] the picture is not so clear. The extrapolation of the past into the future depends upon which numbers you look at, and the period of time at which you look, e.g., the decade of the Thirties was a traumatic period for business, and the Forties included war and recovery from it. Over the very longest period the proportion of national product and income used for advertising obviously has risen (see column 8 in Table 7-3). But this seems less important than whether the proportion has continued to rise in recent years. And if one looks at the ratio of the *Printer's Ink* expenditure estimate to GNP (column 8), there seems to have been no increase in the past decade or so. The same is true if one uses PCE or DPI as a denominator (columns 12 and 16); the period centered on 1956 was the high-water mark.[15]

---

[14] Here as elsewhere in the book the working definition of advertising refers to messages, and excludes such aspects of promotion as premiums, trading stamps, etc. The major continuing sources of total-advertising data — McCann-Erickson (*Printers' Ink*), and more lately Yang (*Advertising Age*) — use a definition like this one.

[15] This statement accepts as correct Blank's argument (1962) that the

If one looks at column 9, the Internal Revenue statistics (and the Yang–*Advertising Age* statistics, column 10, which are largely based on IRS data), the picture is different, however. There one sees that over the period in which the *Printers' Ink* data suggest a plateau, the IRS data (as a ratio to GNP or PCE or DPI) show a steady increase. The increase is not great, to be sure, from 1.09 percent in 1954 to 1.18 percent in 1964 (*Advertising Age*, January 13, 1958, and September 18, 1967). But the increase is steady and is enough to keep us from concluding that the process has leveled off.

To better ground a forecast of the future one wants to go deeper than a mechanical extrapolation of the past history of the aggregate, however. One source of pertinent information is the behavior of the parts of the aggregate. There has been a good-sized increase over the 11 years from 1954 to 1964 in the advertising ratio of such products as: soft drinks, from 5.06 percent of sales to 6.39 percent; liquor, from 1.94 percent to 2.72 percent; tobacco, from 4.03 percent to 6.06 percent; drugs, from 8.54 percent to 11.05 percent; and soap, from 9.12 percent to 10.68 percent. These products are especially worth looking at for two reasons: (1) they are not new products (except some prescription drugs), and therefore would be expected to have already reached a plateau if any products would; and (2) they are products which are heavily advertised (as a ratio of advertising to the cost of production).

The continued past increase in the advertising ratio of the above products suggests to me that the advertising ratio for many classes of products will continue to rise in the future. A major reason for my holding this view is that I believe that the most important reason for the rise during the last 10 or 20 years in the industries named above is that oligopolists gradually inch up their advertising expenditures as they try to steal marches on their competitors, and as they find that such increases are not unprofitable. They often say something like this, I think: "We made money last year spending 5 percent of sales for advertising. Let's budget 6 percent this year." The proportions of sales spent for advertising started off at low bases not too many years ago, and were increased only gradually because of lack of understanding by advertisers as to how profitable or unprofitable the expenditures were, and also because of each industry's common interest in holding down the industry's advertising expenditures. But advertisers also understood that there are advantages, both to the firm and to the industry, in "attacking" competitors with advertising rather than price. One important reason is that an advertising attack is not met immediately, as a price change is likely to

---

Printers' Ink figures for the 1920s were too high, and that Blank's estimate for 1929 (column 7) is better.

Table 7-3.

	1	2	3	4	5	6	7	8
	Gross National Product (GNP) in billions of dollars	Personal Consumption Expenditures (PCE) in billions of dollars	Disposable Personal Income (DPI) in billions of dollars	McCann-Erickson Printers' Ink Advertising Expenditure Series (PI) in millions of dollars	Internal Revenue Service Advertising Expenditure Series (IRS) in millions of dollars	Yang-Advertising Age Advertising Expenditure Series (YAA) in millions of dollars	Blank Estimates of Advertising Expenditures (BLK) in billions of dollars	PI ÷ GNP (4 ÷ 1)
1931	76.3	61.3	63.8	2282				0.030
1932	58.5	49.3	48.7	1627				0.028
1933	56.0	46.4	45.7	1302				0.023
1934	65.0	51.9	52.0	1627				0.025
1935	72.5	56.3	58.3	1690			1.7	0.023
1936	82.7	62.6	66.2	1902				0.023
1937	90.8	67.3	71.0	2071				0.023
1938	85.2	64.6	65.7	1904				0.022
1939	91.1	67.6	70.4	1980				0.022
1940	100.6	71.9	76.1	2088			2.1	0.021
1941	125.8	81.9	93.0	2236				0.018
1942	159.1	89.7	117.5	2156				0.013
1943	192.5	100.5	113.5	2496				0.013
1944	211.4	109.8	146.8	2724				0.013
1945	213.6	121.7	150.4	2874	1923			0.013
1946	210.7	147.1	160.6	3364	2408		3.4	0.016
1947	234.3	165.4	170.1	4260	3032	4241		0.018
1948	259.4	178.3	189.3	4864	3466	4907		0.019
1949	258.1	181.2	189.7	5202	3773	5331		0.020
1950	284.6	195.0	207.7	5710	4097	5864	5.7	0.020
1951	329.0	209.8	227.5	6426	4553	6497		0.019
1952	347.0	219.8	238.7	7156	5027	7161		0.021
1953	365.4	232.6	252.5	7755	5481	7784		0.021
1954	363.1	238.0	256.9	8164	5770	8080		0.022
1955	397.5	256.9	274.4	9194	6602	8997	9.2	0.023
1956	419.2	269.4	290.5	9904	7062	9674		0.024
1957	440.3	284.4	305.1	10311	7666	10313		0.023
1958	444.5	290.1		10302	7875	10414		0.023
1959	482.7			11117	8747	11358		0.023
1960	502.6	325.2	350.0	11932	9291	11900	11.9	0.024
1961	518.2		364.4	11845	9563	12048	11.8	0.023
1962	560.3		385.3	12381	10391	12919		0.022
1963	590.5	375.0	403.8	13051		13639		0.022
1964	631.7	401.4	438.5	14155		14571		0.022
1965	681.2	431.5	469.1	16255		15570		0.024
1966	739.6	464.9	505.3	16545		16810		0.022
1967						17330		
1968						18350		

Sources: Col. 1 Up to 1957: *Historical Statistics of the U. S.*, 1957, p. 139. After 1957: *Statistical Abstract*, 1967, p. 319.
Col. 2 *Historical Statistics of the U. S.*, 1957, p. 142. *Statistical Abstract*, 1967, p. 321.
Col. 3 1902-1957: *Historical Statistics of the U. S.*, p. 139. 1958-1966: *Statistical Abstract*, 1964 and 1967, p. 326.
Col. 4 Up to 1957: *Historical Statistics of the U. S.*, 1957, p. 52. After 1957: *Statistical Abstract*, 1967, p. 806.

9	10	11	12	13	14	15	16	17	18	19
IRS ÷ GNP (5÷1)	YAA ÷ GNP (6÷1)	BLK ÷ GNP (7÷1)	PI ÷ PCE (4÷2)	IRS ÷ PCE (5÷2)	YAA ÷ PCE (6÷2)	BLK ÷ PCE (7÷2)	PI ÷ DPI (4÷3)	IRS ÷ DPI (5÷3)	YAA ÷ DPI (6÷3)	BLK ÷ DPI (7÷3)
							0.041			
							0.038			
							0.041			
							0.036			
							0.041			
							0.038			
							0.043			
							0.042			
							0.041			
							0.042			
							0.042			
							0.042			
							0.042			
		0.02-0.023	0.043			0.027-0.03	0.041			0.025-0.029
							0.035			

Table 7-3. National Product (Inco

	1	2	3	4	5	6	7	8
				McCann-Erickson *Printers' Ink* Advertising Expenditure Series (PI) in millions of dollars	Internal Revenue Service Advertising Expenditure Series (IRS) in millions of dollars	Yang-*Advertising Age* Advertising Expenditure Series (YAA) in millions of dollars	Blank Estimates of Advertising Expenditures (BLK) in billions of dollars	
	Gross National Product (GNP) in billions of dollars	Personal Consumption Expenditures (PCE) in billions of dollars	Disposable Personal Income (DPI) in billions of dollars					PI ÷ GNP (4 ÷ 1)
1867	6.71			50				0.007
1880	9.18			200				0.022
1890	12.3			360				0.029
1900	17.3		14.1	542				0.031
1904	24.2		20.0	821				0.034
1905				885 *				
1906				949				
1907				1014				
1908	35.9			1077				0.030
1909	36.8			1142				0.031
1910	37.1			1174 *				0.032
1911	38.8			1206				0.031
1912	41.3			1238				0.030
1913	112.4			1270				0.030
1914	43.6			1302				0.030
1915	49.0			1302				0.027
1916	58.2			1468				0.025
1917	67.2			1627				0.024
1918	75.9			1468				0.019
1919	78.9		63.3	2282				0.029
1920	88.9		71.5	2935				0.033
1921	74.0		60.2	2282				0.030
1922	74.0		60.3	2607				0.035
1923	86.1		69.7	2935				0.034
1924	87.6		71.4	2935				0.033
1925	91.3		73.0	3099				0.034
1926	97.7		77.4	3262				0.033
1927	96.3		77.4	3262				0.034
1928	98.2		77.5	3262				0.033
1929	104.4	79.0	83.1	3426			2.1-2.4	0.033
1930	91.1	71.0	74.4	2607				0.029

* = interpolation

(Continued)

9	10	11	12	13	14	15	16	17	18	19
IRS÷ GNP (5÷1)	YAA÷ GNP (6÷1)	BLK÷ GNP (7÷1)	PI÷ PCE (4÷2)	IRS÷ PCE (5÷2)	YAA÷ PCE (6÷2)	BLK÷ PCE (7÷2)	PI÷ DPI (4÷3)	IRS÷ DPI (5÷3)	YAA÷ DPI (6÷3)	BLK÷ DPI (7÷3)
			0.037				0.036			
			0.033				0.033			
			0.028				0.028			
			0.031				0.031			
		0.023	0.030			0.030	0.029			0.029
			0.030				0.029			
			0.031				0.029			
			0.029				0.029			
			0.029				0.028			
		0.021	0.029			0.029	0.027			0.028
			0.027				0.024			
			0.024				0.018			
			0.025				0.022			
			0.025				0.019			
0.009			0.024	0.016			0.019	0.013		
0.011		0.016	0.023	0.016		0.023	0.021	0.015		0.021
0.012	0.018		0.026	0.018	0.026		0.025	0.018	0.025	
0.013	0.019		0.027	0.019	0.028		0.026	0.018	0.026	
0.015	0.021		0.029	0.021	0.029		0.027	0.020	0.028	
0.014	0.021	0.020	0.029	0.021	0.030	0.029	0.027	0.020	0.028	0.027
0.014	0.020		0.031	0.022	0.031		0.028	0.020	0.029	
0.014	0.021		0.033	0.023	0.033		0.030	0.021	0.030	
0.015	0.021		0.033	0.024	0.033		0.031	0.022	0.031	
0.016	0.022		0.034	0.024	0.034		0.032	0.022	0.031	
0.017	0.023	0.023	0.036	0.026	0.035	0.036	0.033	0.024	0.033	0.034
0.017	0.023		0.037	0.026	0.036		0.034	0.024	0.033	
0.017	0.023		0.036	0.027	0.036		0.034	0.025	0.034	
0.018	0.023		0.036	0.027	0.036					
0.018	0.023									
0.018	0.024	0.024	0.037	0.029	0.037	0.03659	0.034	0.027	0.034	0.034
0.018	0.023	0.023					0.033	0.026	0.033	0.032
0.019	0.023		0.035				0.032	0.027	0.034	
			0.035				0.032			
			0.038				0.032			
			0.036				0.035			
							0.033			

Col. 5 Backman, 1968, p. 18.
Col. 6 *Advertising Age*, April 8, 1968, p. 56; March 3, 1969, p. 45.
Col. 7 Blank, 1963, pp. 33-38.

be, because of the lags in competitive response.[16] (Lack of exact and immediate data on competitive advertising is an especially important reason.) Furthermore, an advertising-expenditure increase can be reversed more easily than can a price cut, because customers do not complain. But as long as advertising increases do not bring the oligopolists to the point of losing money — as they did not in the industries listed above, because the firms started out advertising so much less than equilibrium amounts — the budgets keep inching up. And these budgets seem to be on a ratchet; there is no force to drive them down again except realization by consumers that there are no differences among the products, or agreement among the competitors, which seems to be particularly complicated to achieve with advertising.[17]

The process described above is not only relevant to the increase in advertising ratios in homogeneous-package-goods industries; eventually the level of advertising must stop at some levels in those industries, and it might be soon. Rather, I think, the same process will catch fire in other (oligopolistic) industries, one after the other, though these late-coming industries are probably not so "advertisable," for assorted reasons.

Another contributing cause of the aggregate increase in advertising may be the increase in the number of brands being advertised within product classes.[18] For the one set of product classes for which data are easily available, drugstore products, consider these increases from 1961 to 1967: "Drugs and Other Health Aids," from 359 brands to 439; "Toiletries and Cosmetics," from 574 to 1,078 (*Drug Trade News,* June 24, 1963, p. 8; July 1, 1968, p. 52). The number within almost every one of the subclasses (e.g., "Cough and Cold Products") increased also. The theory in Chapter 4 suggests that such an increase in the number of advertisers is likely to lead to increased promotion.

Other writers lay more stress on other factors as causes of a continuing long-run increase in advertising, e.g., Blank:

Most of the factors generally assigned to the recent rise in relative importance of advertising are of fairly long duration. These include the rise in importance of national brands and the decline in the personal sales function; the growth of supermarkets, discount houses, vending machines and self-service operation in general; the proliferation of new products

---

[16] Brems emphasizes and develops this point (1958). And it was discussed in Chapter 4, pp. 106–7.

[17] The aforegoing is the sort of process that seems to have occurred in both the liquor industry and the ethical-drug industry, the two industries I know best.

[18] There has also been an increase over time in the number of product classes being advertised and sold. This fact obviously implies a larger absolute amount of advertising, but I see no reason why it should imply a rise in the proportion of GNP spent for advertising.

which require larger than average amounts of advertising at their birth. All of these factors tend to impose a continuously greater need on the part of manufacturers for direct selling of customers and, indeed, of dealers. Since the trend in retailing is increasingly in this direction, we probably can expect a further rise in the relative importance of advertising in the future" [Blank, 1963, p. 38].

But I would guess that the trend in retailing is near its end, at least for many products. Beer, cigarettes, most packaged foods, gasoline, liquor, and other similar products are already sold without any in-store personal selling. The end of this trend may be indicated by the leveling off

Table 7-4. Proportions of National and Retail Advertising in Total Advertising in the United States

1	2	3	4
	Total Advertising Expenditure	National Advertising Expenditure	National as a Percentage of Total Advertising
Year	(in $ Millions)	(in $ Millions)	(Col. 3 ÷ 2)
1935	$ 1,690	$ 859	50.82%
1936	1,902	1,003	52.73
1937	2,072	1,103	53.23
1938	1,904	1,031	53.20
1939	1,980	1,086	54.84
1940	2,088	1,163	57.91
1941	2,236	1,259	56.21
1942	2,156	1,212	56.21
1943	2,496	1,452	58.17
1944	2,724	1,669	61.27
1945	2,875	1,775	61.73
1946	3,364	1,963	58.35
1947	4,260	2,487	58.38
1948	4,864	2,776	57.07
1949	5,202	2,965	56.99
1950	5,710	3,257	57.04
1951	6,426	3,701	57.59
1952	7,156	4,096	57.23
1953	7,755	4,521	58.29
1954	8,164	4,812	58.94
1955	9,194	5,407	58.81
1956	9,905	5,926	59.82
1957	10,311	6,253	60.64
1958	10,302	6,331	61.45
1959	11,255	6,835	60.72
1960	11,932	7,296	61.14
1961	11,845	7,253	61.23
1962	12,381	7,661	61.87
1963	13,107	8,124	61.98
1964	14,155	8,713	61.68
1965	15,255	9,365	61.38
1966 (prel.)	16,545	10,075	60.89

Source: U.S., *Statistical Abstract,* 1967, p. 806.

of the proportions of national and local advertising. As Table 7-4 shows, if there has been any continuing shift since 1957 toward a larger proportion of national advertising, the trend is glacial.

Furthermore, if there were still a continuing trend to more "automatic" selling and less personal selling one would expect retailers to be increasing their advertising. But advertising as a proportion of sales does not seem to be rising much among retailers — it was 1.52 percent in 1954, and 1.58 percent in 1964. (Some of the subcategories rose, others fell.)

A disaggregated look also reveals a contrary force acting. Blank (1962) drew our attention to the shift in the proportion of spending, as income increases, from goods to services (and especially government services) which tend to be advertised less than goods. If such a shift were pronounced enough, the aggregate proportion spent for advertising could decrease even if the proportion spent for each individual category increased. My guess is, however, that this effect will not be great enough to bring to a halt, at least for quite a while, the increase in the aggregate advertising ratio.

One wants to know more than the direction of an expected effect, however; one wants to know its expected magnitude. If one extrapolates the trend of the IRS data one would estimate that the proportion of advertising will double in about 90 years. Such a doubling would not be insignificant, representing another 2½ percent of national production. But it is not unlikely that some or much of this increase would come out of a decrease in other forms of promotion, e.g., personal selling. A historical study of the cross relations among the various forms of promotion would be useful in this regard (and might well be worth doing).

The future magnitude of advertising has different meanings to different classes of people, some of which we might review briefly. (1) For people in the *advertising-agency* business, aggregate changes are not crucial. This is so because so much of the change in volume of individual agencies comes from account shifts among agencies. (2) For *advertising media* the relevant trends are the trends in their own media. For some media the future is bright, but some other media may not have glamorous futures as "growth industries," e.g., newspapers. (3) For *economists*, that part of advertising that may truly be regarded as "waste" (see Chapter 11), may increase somewhat. But the absolute magnitude of the increase in the next 45 or 90 years, say, is trivial relative to national product. (4) For *citizens as sentient individuals*, the growth in number of exposures per person will be less than the aggregate growth, because the growth of advertising will be accompanied by further proliferation of media, e.g., new business magazines and new television networks. Individuals will still be exposed to media for about the same total time per person (or at least I think so, McLuhan to the contrary).

So, one may or may not applaud the future trend of advertising. But I think that all will agree that even if this is bad, we will be lucky indeed if no worse disaster befalls our society in the next 45 or 90 years. Hence I am not much disposed to worry much about whether this future growth of the advertising ratio is too large or too small.

8

The Effect
of Advertising
upon the
Propensity
to Consume

Thirty-five years ago the topic of this chapter would have been literally inconceivable; nobody would have asked the questions which this chapter asks except some contemporary economic quacks and some long-ago economists such as Malthus. But since Keynes (or at least until recently) perhaps the most important single issue to government economic planners in the United States and some other industrialized countries has been aggregate demand, and the forces that influence demand. This chapter considers the extent to which advertising may be an important force in influencing aggregate demand by way of influencing the individual propensity to consume.

Much importance has been attached to the subject, and the conclusions drawn about it:

. . . business men and economists have few doubts that advertising increases consumption for the economy as a whole. In fact, the opinion of our profession seems almost unanimous. K. S. Rothschild is most categorical in his assertion: "I think it hopeless to try a quantitative estimate of the effects of total advertising on total consumption. All we can say is that the habit of advertising must be responsible for a considerable increase in the propensity to consume." Lawrence Klein is also sure: "The advertising industry has certainly had a bad influence on many aspects of our lives . . . but it has also served to maintain consumption at a higher level than it otherwise would have been. Advertising is not the best way to get a high-consumption, low-savings economy, but it is *a* way." Fellner is more cautious: "The historical behavior of the [consumption] function could be interpreted as being produced in the passage of time by continuous upward shifts of the household budget function. The trendlike upward shift suggested by this hypothesis might be the result of technological innovations which place *new products* on the market, or of other impacts producing a continuous decline in thriftiness. . . . It is conceivable that technological change and the increasing sales effort on the part of producers and retailers tend to produce an upward shift of the consumption function" [Brems, 1951, pp. 85–86].

Even if advertising can (and does) affect aggregate demand, however, this does not (by itself) make advertising indispensable. As of 1969 many industrialized countries, perhaps including the United States, have apparently learned how to manipulate their economies so as to be able to stay tolerably near full employment. That is, governments probably have available to them tools for influencing aggregate demand that are at least as productive (from a social point of view) as advertising is. Hence even if advertising increases aggregate demand, this alone would not be a sufficient justification of advertising. Nevertheless, it is interesting to speculate on the extent to which advertising does have such an effect.

On first thought, of course, advertising and other sales promotion seem sure to increase consumption and the propensity to consume. Advertising makes someone purchase a brand of cigarettes he has never smoked, take a trip to a country he has never seen, and splurge on a new type of movie projector that is now a bargain at a local discount store. The evidence that advertising can affect people's behavior is immediate and overwhelming, both from introspection of our own experience and from the fact that advertisers spend hard cash to pay for advertising. This type of evidence is the basis for the advertising industry's self-justification that advertising is a positive force in maintaining a booming economy. The same type of evidence also persuades some economists, Ackley for example (1961, p. 268), that promotion does affect the propensity to consume, though this argument risks the fallacy of composition.[1]

The only possible counterbalance to an increase in advertising, it would seem, would be an increase in advertising for savings institutions that may induce people to save some monies that they might otherwise spend immediately (cf. Norris, 1960). But the quantity of advertising for savings institutions is tiny relative to all other advertising.

On second thought, however, there is both empirical evidence and theory to call the matter into question. The empirical evidence is the

[1] Yang takes this position especially strongly and explicitly, as the following quote from a news story indicates: " '$1 in Ads Generates $16 in Income: . . . The economic significance of advertising can best be appreciated if we evaluate the consequence of stable or slowly changing consumer taste, which would be inevitable in the absence of advertising.' He said the promotional elasticity is about 0.1 . . ." (*Advertising Age*, Dec. 20, 1965, pp. 1, 39).

relative stability over a period of many years of the long-run average propensity to consume, despite a great increase in the absolute and relative amounts of advertising in the society. As for theory, the permanent-income consumption-function theory invented by Modigliani (e.g., Modigliani and Brumberg, 1954) and Friedman (1957) seems to imply (though more clearly in the case of Modigliani than Friedman) that the amount spent for consumption will not be affected by advertising, because consumption is a function only of the spending unit's long-run expected income.[2]

There is, then, a possible theoretical alternative to the hypothesis that advertising affects saving, to wit, that advertising merely affects how people distribute their expenditures in any given year, and does not affect the sum of them. One may call this the "spread-it-around" hypothesis. This hypothesis implies that some constant proportion of income is "taken off the top" for saving, and what is left is spent according to the prevailing tastes of the spending unit.[3] This is not a novel hypothesis; Bain (1957, p. 389), for example, states it. And most students of the consumption function write as if advertising does not have an important effect on aggregate spending; advertising is not included in their discussions and their models. Ferber's survey of work in this field may serve as an example (1962).

The life-cycle view of the consumption function of Modigliani et al. (Modigliani and Brumberg, 1954; Ando and Modigliani 1963; Modigliani, 1966) provides a formal framework for this point of view. Its basic premise is that individuals intend to allocate all their income over their lifetimes, inheritance being too minor to matter. Of course if advertising induced people to concentrate their spending more heavily during their early years, it would therefore diminish aggregate savings.

The purpose of this chapter is to consider some of the evidence for the relative plausibility of this spread-it-around hypothesis and of the hypothesis that aggregate advertising affects aggregate spending.

Psychological Evidence

The customary psychological arguments do not aid us much. The fact that promotion causes an increase in desire for (or purchase of) par-

---

[2] Friedman does assume that consumption is a function of tastes. But in practice Friedman compares the expenditures of homogeneous groups, a practice which would make no sense unless he assumed that the differences among the groups are not due to tastes. We shall proceed as if this wider interpretation of his theory governs.

[3] Of course one must recognize that saving is not simply nonspending; to a greater or lesser extent saving is spending later rather than spending now. But people may hold money for reasons other than straightening out their income streams, e.g., bequeathing it to children.

ticular commodities or brands is not inconsistent with the spread-it-around hypothesis as long as people have unsurfeited wants. As long as an increase in income would lead a person to spend more (i.e., as long as he has unsatisfied desires) then it is not necessarily true that an increase in wants would lead to more spending out of a fixed income. Promotion is sure to lead to increased spending out of a fixed income only if the person would have no unsatisfied desires without the promotion, i.e., if he would spend no more even if his income increased (and if the promotion succeeds in creating new wants, of course). If this were the case, then promotion might well lead to an increase in spending, because an increase in wants could be translated into an increase in purchasing without opposition from a budget restraint.

But it seems contrary to fact to regard the wants of a community as being satiated at a point in time. In his survey of economic anthropology Herskovits tells us that "wants are capable of a degree of expansion the end of which has not been reached by any known society. . . . The nature of the available goods and of the wants they are to satisfy is likewise restricted . . ." (Herskovits, 1952, pp. 5, 7).

It is reasonable to think of wants as unsatiated if we consider that the desire for puchases is based on human desires in general, and that purchasing is a way of satisfying basic desires. Few if any men have all the comfort, love, approval, time, etc., that they want. And even those few who might not buy anything more for themselves if their incomes were increased would not be likely to turn down an offer of increased purchasing power to give to others. In other words, almost everyone can be thought of as feeling the pinch of some desires that might be satisfied by expenditures. Given this state of affairs, a spread-it-around theory is not psychologically unreasonable. And hence, psychological evidence does not help us discriminate between the two hypotheses.

Quasi-Experimental Evidence from Newspaper Strikes

The best test of the hypothesis that aggregate advertising affects aggregate expenditures would be an experiment in which some randomly selected groups of people would receive more promotion than do others, and the expenditures would then be monitored. This is not an easy experiment to carry out, though it might be done in such situations as the *Milwaukee Journal* "laboratory," in which the newspaper and television advertising inputs to a panel of people are varied systematically by "blacking out" selected advertisements and television commercials. The closest thing to such a controlled experiment is a newspaper strike, during which a substantial portion of the normal advertising flow is cut off.

During newspaper strikes one does indeed find that those indices of sales that can be measured, especially department-store sales, do fall off (Mindak et al., 1963; Starch, 1963). However, this evidence certainly does not show conclusively that there is a drop in aggregate expenditures, because all or some of the apparently lost expenditures might merely be transferred to other outlets, e.g., auto purchases, entertainment purchases, purchases in stores other than downtown department stores, etc. Furthermore, the apparently lost expenditures might be shifted forward in time, though one of the strike studies did claim to have found no evidence of such an expenditure buildup and subsequent release after the strike was over (Starch, 1963).

Though the evidence from newspaper strikes is shaky and is not easily quantifiable in terms of the total effect on expenditures, one should also note that even if no effect had shown up it would not prove that advertising does not affect expenditures, because newspaper advertising is not as likely a candidate, dollar for dollar, as magazine and television advertising as a stimulator of aggregate expenditures. The content of newspaper advertising is heavily informative about what is available and at what prices, and this would not seem to be as instrumental in affecting wants as advertising which gives people reasons why they should want commodities — for example, auto and travel advertising. Furthermore, it might be that the influence of promotion on expenditures is very gradual and long run, in which case such a small part of the effect would show up over the ten weeks or so of a newspaper strike as to be practically unmeasureable. Again, however, it is not retail advertising in newspapers whose effect will be strongly lagged as compared to say, travel or cigarette advertising.

The best measure of the effect of newspaper strikes on aggregate expenditures would be savings rather than expenditures. A savings measurement would avoid the possibility of expenditures being shifted away from the observed stores into unobserved outlets. However, Federal Reserve figures on deposits in savings banks are either unavailable or, where they are available, too gross to give any indication. Certainly the effect on savings is not so great as to show up visibly against the long-run pattern of savings deposits. For example, Table 8-1 shows the savings and time-deposit data for the periods before, during, and after the Cleveland newspaper strike of November 29, 1962, to April 4, 1963. The data for the prior year are also included for comparison as to seasonal variation.

Time-Series Evidence

It is obvious that time-series analysis of aggregates of promotion and spending is fraught with unusual difficulties. One problem is that it can be misleading to look at expenditures in terms of a propensity to con-

Table 8-1. Savings and Time Deposits of Individuals, Partnerships,
and Corporations in Reporting Banks in Cleveland, Ohio
(In Thousands of Dollars)

		Savings Deposits	Other Time Deposits			Savings Deposits	Other Time Deposits
1961				**1962**			
Aug.	2	1,256,404	156,373	July	4	1,391,574	269,008
	9	1,256,952	159,608		11	1,403,852	269,357
	16	1,256,332	160,495		18	1,404,593	266,427
	23	1,255,724	160,508		25	1,405,548	265,478
	30	1,255,597	162,370	Aug.	1	1,407,006	268,770
Sep.	6	1,255,845	162,058		8	1,409,343	270,546
	13	1,255,607	162,076		15	1,411,143	272,347
	20	1,255,115	161,862		22	1,412,474	276,384
	27	1,256,028	160,801		29	1,412,921	275,284
Oct.	4	1,255,545	164,998	Sep.	5	1,415,140	276,098
	11	1,257,159	163,914		12	1,416,671	277,222
	18	1,258,241	163,182		19	1,419,261	278,184
	25	1,258,237	168,076		26	1,421,588	278,977
Nov.	1	1,258,582	165,261	Oct.	3	1,424,005	273,153
	8	1,260,882	165,597		10	1,429,762	274,982
	15	1,260,133	164,167		17	1,430,872	275,524
	22	1,261,571	163,032		24	1,431,269	281,131
	29	1,261,652	166,353		31	1,433,012	267,954
Dec.	6	1,263,129	165,581	Nov.	7	1,435,980	272,212
	13	1,264,210	158,657		14	1,437,245	271,953
	20	1,266,491	157,157		21	1,439,867	277,611
	27	1,270,181	156,828		28	1,440,914	278,878 .
				Dec.	5	1,444,006	280,083 .
1962					12	1,446,200	281,656 .
Jan.	3	1,289,097	166,364		19	1,449,248	277,299 .
	10	1,310,853	169,428		26	1,453,793	283,931 .
	17	1,314,246	172,706				
	24	1,316,326	185,147	**1963**			
	31	1,317,583	194,391	Jan.	2	1,483,045	294,228 .
Feb.	7	1,321,093	210,902		9	1,484,093	303,035 .
	14	1,323,391	217,674		16	1,484,139	310,677 .
	21	1,325,949	222,099		23	1,484,041	307,443 .
	28	1,328,531	228,672		30	1,483,665	311,592 .
Mar.	7	1,332,618	234,333	Feb.	6	1,485,028	306,379 .
	14	1,336,223	242,380		13	1,485,476	308,414 .
	21	1,339,758	247,901		20	1,486,130	318,503 .
	28	1,342,117	254,292		27	1,487,045	317,554 .
Apr.	4	1,344,071	257,685	Mar.	6	1,490,108	337,086 .
	11	1,351,638	256,377		13	1,492,614	336,005 .
	18	1,350,553	257,613		20	1,495,069	341,210 .
	25	1,351,359	257,247		27	1,497,068	351,167 .
May	2	1,352,932	259,870	Apr.	3	1,496,478	356,939 .
	9	1,355,654	262,047		10	1,504,010	360,394
	16	1,357,298	263,155		17	1,500,719	360,211
	23	1,358,734	263,166		24	1,500,621	355,422
	30	1,359,404	266,791	May	1	1,500,836	357,575
June	6	1,361,066	271,893		8	1,502,158	362,051
	13	1,363,108	269,584		15	1,502,895	360,802
	20	1,365,061	271,952		22	1,503,898	362,226
	27	1,369,067	270,371		29	1,504,015	361,105

Period of Strike (bracketed from 1962 Nov. 28 through 1963 Apr. 3)

(Continued)

Table 8-1. (Continued)

		Savings Deposits	Other Time Deposits
1963			
June	5	1,505,333	364,837
	12	1,506,601	366,138
	19	1,508,340	372,623
	26	1,511,145	372,131
July	3	1,534,455	365,964
	10	1,540,991	364,323
	17	1,541,079	362,438
	24	1,540,864	362,914
	31	1,541,241	374,302

Source: Research Department, Federal Reserve Bank of Chicago.

sume, because the ratio of advertising to sales might remain the same even if promotion actually stimulated more want and more spending. This apparent paradox could occur if the chain of causation were: promotion ⟶ increased wants ⟶ moonlighting in order to have more income to satisfy the wants ⟶ spending of a proportion of the moonlighting income equal to the average propensity to consume.[4] This is how advertising could have an important effect on spending without a visible change in the consumption function, or even with an apparent decrease in the proportion spent. Education's effect may be similar; even if education increases the knowledge of and desire for the things that money can buy, education also leads to higher income.[5]

Another major difficulty is the time-diffused effect of advertising alluded to before. If promotion increases wants and spending, it could manifest its effects in several ways other than an immediate increase in purchasing:

1. The effect of advertising can be a repeated series of purchases, e.g., the lifetime stream of cigarette purchases by a person induced to start smoking by advertising. Such effects are not easily shown up by time-series analysis because the purchase level in subsequent periods does not drop even if the promotion drops. This is like an experiment in which the dependent variable is always positive after the first trial with

[4] This notion remains the same no matter which is the appropriate concept of income — e.g., permanent, lifetime wealth, etc. — though the longer the income time-horizon the harder it is to detect an effect of advertising with time series.

[5] Hicks actually considers advertising as a form of adult education (1962). This may be useful conceptually, but it surely does stretch the meaning of the term "education."

a positive independent variable. It is impossible, then, to gain any information from subsequent trials with a negative independent variable.

2. Promotion at time t can stimulate purchases at time t + T, either because the message is remembered and acted upon later or because the message is transmitted through other people (the famous two-step flow of influence, which takes some time). Therefore, purchases which we say are a result of "a standard of living" may (or may not) actually be the result of delayed impact of promotion filtered through a network of other people and accepted by the entire culture. In other words, salesmen or advertising may have been responsible for the first sales of inside-the-house bathtubs; nowadays one buys bathtubs whether or not there is advertising, "because it is part of our standard of living," though in some important sense the early promotion may have been a necessary condition for the entire process to get started.

3. Advertising could actually result in a short-run decrease in spending and an increase in savings if it causes a desire for durables which can only be purchased after one has acquired a sum for a down payment or for the total price.

All these difficulties blur any short-run point-to-point relationships between advertising and expenditure. And the lack of short-run variation in the consumption data (Friedman, 1957, p. 204) is an extremely uncongenial circumstance for time-series analysis to be effective, especially because education and general cultural changes operate to obscure long-run trends.

These difficulties are sufficiently acute for Kaldor to assert that an investigation of the relation of advertising to expenditures is impossible in principle, but he does not provide much basis for the assertion (Kaldor, 1949–50, p. 9). There has been one time-series attempt to estimate the relationship, by Yancey (1957), which was mostly an exercise to compare the results from various estimation techniques. Yancey was further hampered by the inadequacy of the sales and advertising data available. Despite the obstacles, Yancey's work did show that "the application of selling effort and product quality, as represented by advertising, appears to have raised the level of consumption" (Yancey, 1957, pp. 6, 7). It is worth noting that all the major difficulties to estimating this relationship are of such nature as tend to obscure the effect of advertising, and to bias the estimated effect downward rather than upward. It becomes more noteworthy, then, that Yancey was able to find some positive effect.

Yang says that he has

found that changes in consumers' tastes have been largely responsible for this continuing upward shift [in the consumption function]; and that there is substantial evidence showing that advertising has played an important role. . . .

The magnitude of an increase in income that an extra amount of advertising expenditures can create depends on the promotional elasticity of advertising with respect to consumption, the acceleration coefficient and the multiplier. I have found this promotional elasticity to be about 0.1. That is, an additional increase of 1% in advertising expenditures beyond and above the rate of increase in Gross National Product can generate one-tenth of one percent increase in consumption. In absolute figures, an additional amount of $150 million in advertising expenditures can bring about an increase of about $400 million in consumption. This increase in consumption requires an additional investment of $800 million, using Professor Hansen's acceleration coefficient of 2. The increased investment of $800 million will lead to an increase of $2.4 billion in income, applying the multiplier of 3 obtained from data for the period 1950–1963. Thus, each additional dollar of advertising investment can create $16 of additional income [Yang, 1966, pp. 1–2].

But I have not been able to ascertain the method by which Yang arrived at this estimate.

Evidence from Surveys of Expenditures

One can ask whether there are some homogeneous groups of people within the larger society who differ from other groups in how much promotion they are exposed to, and one can then compare the saving and spending of the groups. However, this type of evidence could only throw doubt on a spread-it-around hypothesis, rather than provide positive evidence for the effect of promotion. To illustrate why, it may be that the Amish spend a smaller (or larger) proportion of their income than do families with similar incomes, income expectations, ages, etc., who live in the same-size communities. The Amish receive less promotion because they do not have television sets, radios, or autos with auto radios. Hence if there is a difference in spending between the Amish and similar groups the difference might be attributed to promotion. On the other hand, the difference might also be attributed to basic tastes that have root in the Amish religious beliefs and cultural values. Or the differences might stem from the lesser exposure to the nonadvertising aspects of radio and television, which may have a powerful effect in making people want goods and/or income. So if we were to find differences between Amish and non-Amish spending the most that we could say is that a pure spread-it-around theory does not hold, in that *something* is able to result in a propensity to consume that is different for one group than for another group.[6]

---

[6] The existence of such cross-sectional differences is probably not compatible with Friedman's version of the permanent-income theory, either. I say "probably" because, as noted earlier, though Friedman's symbolic formulation indi-

Expenditures of different-size families are relevant evidence. If we could assume that two groups of families were alike in all respects except the number of children, then a spread-it-around hypothesis would imply the same ratio of savings to income for each family. The expenditures required for pure physical subsistence are very small relative to the income of most families; someone once reckoned that an American could live healthfully on less than $100 worth of soybeans a year; anything over that (except for some expenditure for shelter) must be regarded as above "subsistence." Also, as Baran points out, the argument can go either way: "It could be argued that larger spending on the support of big families would reduce personal saving; it could be held equally strongly that the responsibility for the upbringing of larger families would call for larger reserves and for reduced current spending" (Baran, 1957). Hence, no matter how big a family, we can assume that there is no *necessary* reason why the larger family should spend more except its "standard of living."

The evidence is that larger families do spend more than smaller families (Morgan, 1954). Of course the comparison of size-group is imperfect because size of family is not a completely random variable relative to the family's power; i.e., size of family may be related to differences in income expectations and differences in other characteristics that do not show up in the present income data. But to the extent that the various size-groups may be compared, the evidence does suggest that there is a "standard-of-living" notion held by both sets of families that leads the larger family to spend more to maintain the same standard of living as the smaller family. This means that the proportion saved is not an automatic and all-pervasive constant; rather, it depends upon the mental state of the spending unit, in this case the standard-of-living notion. Such mental states as a standard of living can be altered, which makes it seem possible in principle, at least, that promotion might alter the amount of spending and saving, directly or indirectly.

Evidence on the spending of people in communities of various sizes is also relevant. We exclude farmers because it is difficult to distinguish between their consumption and their investment. The best comparisons seem to show that saving is inversely related to size of community (Morgan, 1954). Not only is this finding not consistent with a spread-it-around hypothesis, but there is also a correlation with intensity of advertising, because less promotion comes into smaller communities.

cates that the propensity to consume of a group may depend upon its tastes, Friedman uses cross-sectional comparisons among various groups to show that the propensity to consume is the same when permanent income and its influences are held constant.

(The newspapers in smaller communities are smaller and carry less advertising, perhaps largely because the cost per thousand readers is higher than in larger communities. The same is true of television.) But this finding is also consistent with other explanations, such as that more active people with more active wants may choose to live in larger cities rather than in smaller towns.[7] It might be possible to make a better comparison of this sort if we really could hold all things constant except present community residence as, for example, in a comparison of armed-forces families with matched backgrounds that happen to be sent to bases near large cities or far out in the country. If any differences in their spending and saving do appear, one could then assume that they are due to differences in amount of promotion exposure and retail outlets nearby, rather than to self-selection in the sample.

Historical Consumption-Function Evidence

If one views the consumption function as Keynes originally did, as linear and not passing through zero consumption at zero income, i.e., diminishing propensity to consume as income increases, then one must explain why the average propensity to consume has remained roughly constant over many decades in the United States. One explanation is that advertising (along with other forces) has shifted the consumption function upward over time.[8] But Modigliani (e.g., Modigliani and Brumberg, 1954) and Friedman (1957) have offered another explanation, that the propensity to consume does not diminish with income (or at least does not diminish as sharply as one-period cross-sectional evidence speciously suggests). If so there is nothing for advertising to account for.

Evidence from the Distribution of Advertising Expenditures

A priori, some advertising expenditures are more likely than others to stimulate total spending and to diminish saving. Most especially, it is advertising for innovations that is claimed, on an intuitive basis, to be effective in increasing aggregate spending. But advertising for innovations is a very small part of all advertising. To illustrate this point, retail advertising accounts for more than half of all advertising; another quar-

---

[7] Morgan (1954, p. 186) notes that "we cannot say whether it is differences in cost or in standards of life which make people save less when they live closer together." Kuznets (1953, p. 168) makes the same point about upper-income families in communities of various sizes. But neither of these possibilities is consistent with a spread-it-around hypothesis in which the proportion of savings is determined independently of the rest of the individual's demand functions.

[8] See the lines from Fellner quoted earlier in the chapter, from Brems.

ter of all advertising is done by manufacturers of "package goods" such as cigarettes, soap, and beer, the demand for all of which is surely not very advertising-elastic. The amount spent in any year for what are at that time genuine innovations — such as television in the early 1950s, color television in the 1960s, and autos before World War I — is very small relative to the sum of all advertising (see data in Chapter 11).

On the other hand, one should not completely write off the effect of advertising for even those goods that are apparently well-established and stable commodities. Consider as an example the situation of cigarettes in the present decade. A given advertising expenditure for a given brand has a much greater proportional effect on the brand's sales than on the industry's sales, and a greater effect on the industry's sales than on total spending, i.e., the brand's promotion elasticity is greater than the industry's promotion elasticity which is greater than aggregate spending's elasticity of demand with respect to cigarette advertising, because a shift from one brand to another washes out when we look at the effect of the advertising on the industry, and a shift to cigarettes from other forms of tobacco or other forms of entertainment or spending washes out with respect to total consumption.[9] Nevertheless, the industry elasticity of demand with respect to cigarette advertising for particular brands was calculated to be between .05 and .08 before World War II (Basmann, 1955; Schoenberg, 1933), and the effect is not as small as the elasticity may suggest; it translates into a change of $1 million in cigarette advertising leading to a drop of almost that much in expenditure for cigarettes. (Of course some of the drop in spending would certainly be shifted into other spending for other forms of tobacco or other commodities, but we have no idea how much.)

This type of evidence is provocative but almost totally uninformative because good relevant data do not exist.

Evidence from Advertising Intended to Increase Saving

One might ask whether advertising *might* affect total consumption as well as whether it *does* affect consumption. It is therefore relevant to consider attempts to decrease consumption with advertising. And wartime campaigns to increase purchases of bonds may well decrease consumption. Even if the final result is just to postpone consumption, there might be a long-run effect on a nation's capital stock. Hence this would suggest that perhaps advertising can indeed affect total consumption.

It is worth remembering, however, that wartime advertising to save is quite different from peacetime advertising to buy particular commodi-

---

[9] Brems (1959, pp. 84–85) developed a line of argument of this sort.

ties. Perhaps an advertising campaign to spend more money for the sake of the country might affect consumption whereas product advertising would not.

CONCLUSIONS

Two antagonistic hypotheses are logically possible: that advertising does affect aggregate spending, and that advertising does no more than affect how people "spread around" the sum they make available for spending.

Advertising might affect consumption even if the propensity to consume remains constant, if advertising leads to more moonlighting.

The considerable stability in the average propensity to consume over many decades is consistent with a spread-it-around hypothesis. But Yancey did find some slight indication in his time-series study that advertising is related to consumption.

Evidence from newspaper strikes suggests that spending does decrease during a strike, but there are many leaks in the conceptual and empirical framework.

Data on consumption by families of different sizes, and by families in different-size communities, is consistent with the existence of different spending propensities among different groups, and is evidence against a strict automatic-and-constant-savings-ratio theory. And the fact that spending is less in smaller communities is consistent with the view that more advertising (in the larger communities) leads to more spending.

Even if advertising does affect the long-run propensity to consume by affecting tastes just as education affects tastes, it is doubtful that such an effect could occur quickly enough to affect spending over the business cycle. On the other hand, advertising might affect the short-run propensity to consume by informing consumers of bargains during recession.

There are great difficulties in relating promotion to spending, namely the repetition of purchases of many commodities; the intertwining of the effect of promotion with the effects of education, the mass media, and other cultural forces; the existence of the group values we call "the standard of living"; the possibility of moonlighting as a response to promotion; and temporary saving to buy durables.

Ratio data showing consumption/income are not very useful for studies of this type because advertising (like education) may cause an increase in income as well as in consumption.

Even if advertising increases aggregate demand, this by itself is not a sufficient social justification for advertising. Other devices that are at least as socially productive as advertising are available for manipulating aggregate demand, and industrialized countries seem to have learned to use these other devices successfully.

Postscript: Can Advertising Change Seasonal Demand? The Case of the January White Sale

It is clear that advertising can affect consumers' choices among brands; the billions of dollars spent for brand advertising by firms is conclusive proof. But this may not mean a net effect on consumer demand.

Advertising may also increase generic demand for such commodities as oranges (Nerlove and Waugh, 1961) and cigarettes (Basmann, 1955; Schoenberg, 1933), though the case for even the latter is not ironclad; Tennant (1950) argues that the rise of the cigarette in the twentieth century was caused by urbanization. But even if advertising does increase generic demand, the effect might be only a shift among commodities leading to no macroeconomic effect, as was discussed earlier in the chapter.

It would be more interesting if advertising really aids in performing Knight's fifth function of an economy, allocating resources in the short run. And indeed, classified employment and retail advertising are certainly examples of advertising that helps adjust supply and demand in the short run, as does advertising for perishables like fruit and vegetables. Advertising for clearance sales is another example, as is shown clearly by the Soviet use of advertising to call attention to overstocks being sold at a "discount." The Soviets have an ideological bias against advertising, and in those instances in which they use advertising anyway, one can be sure it is ruble-profitable (Goldman, 1960).

This postscript shows in some historical detail a case in which advertising has come to help adjust demand over time so that facilities can be used in keeping with their *ceteris paribus* marginal cost. To the extent that advertising accomplishes this it is analogous to the use of price in such demand-adjusting schemes as Vickrey's variable-subway-fare scheme, and public-utility peak-load pricing.

Department stores have several capacity-utilization cycles — within the day and the week, and within the year. For example, the peaks of all capacity-utilization cycles coincide and the store is jammed during an evening when the store is open late before Christmas. The yearly cycle shows at least two periods when physical facilities and personnel are particularly underutilized — right after Christmas, and during the summer. If demand for some class of goods is increased in these slack peri-

Table 8-2. Department Store Advertising and Sales Patterns

1	Percentage of Yearly Advertising for Towels in Each Month				Yearly Index for Household Textiles (excluding piece goods)			No. of Pages of "White Sale" Advertising in *New York Times*		Total Yearly Dept. Store Linage in Chicago 1,000s of lines
1	2	3	4	5	6	7	8	9	10	11
	Jan.	July	Aug.	Dec.	Jan.	Aug.	Dec.	Jan.	Aug.	
1936	16.3	11.5	7.8	3.8						
1937	17.1	10.4	7.9	3.4						
1938	16.6	10.3	7.9	4.7						14,276
1939	20.7	11.4	8.7	4.2						13,592
1940	17.4	10.4	8.5	4.2				6.2	1.50	13,013
1941										12,877
1942										12,884
1943										13,303
1944										13,680
1945										14,820
1946										18,036
1947	12.0	8.0	9.3	8.6	111	92	141			19,158
1948	12.8	8.0	10.2	8.2	100	100	100			19,926
1949	14.4	8.4	7.3	9.1	159	107	134			19,000
1950	14.5	7.4*	7.7*	10.9	153	141	152	20.5	9.87	19,868
1951	13.5*	9.9	9.3	10.1	216	115	137			
1952	15.6	8.4	9.3	8.6	168±	112	150±			
1953	15.7	9.2	11.1	9.2	163	125	147			
1954	17.0	8.5	13.2	8.9	163	128	144			
1955	19.2	11.0	10.8	7.8	165	143	154			
1956	20.3	10.6	12.2	7.5	181	152	158			
1957	21.0	10.5	12.0	7.7	189	158	157			
1958	20.5	10.6	12.4	9.1	189	151	165			
1959	19.5	9.4	14.9	8.5	183±	162±	166±	48.0	27.5	25,969
1960	21.7	12.1	13.5	6.6						
1961	21.9	12.7	12.0	8.6						
1962	19.0	12.3	13.3	8.6						
1963	19.2	11.6	13.6	8.4						
1964										
1965										

* These reversals in trend are probably explainable by the Korean war. (Continued)

± The rises in these indices from 1947-49 are the highest (to the dates marked) of any departments with the department store data.

ods, the marginal cost of the goods is less than at other times (excluding for the moment the cost of shifting the demand by price reduction or promotion. Household textiles such as towels and linens ("white goods") are an ideal possibility for this role because their use is "neutral" throughout the year. The question is whether advertising can alter demand seasonally to take advantage of the situation.

These are the historical facts. In 1900 two New York City depart-

Table 8-2. (Continued)

Percentage of Yearly Sales of Household Textiles in Each Month,
7th Federal Reserve District

1	12 Jan.	13 Feb.	14 Mar.	15 Apr.	16 May	17 June	18 July	19 Aug.	20 Sept.	21 Oct.	22 Nov.	23 Dec.
1936												
1937												
1938												
1939												
1940												
1941												
1942												
1943												
1944												
1945												
1946												
1947	9.2	6.8	6.8	7.2	8.2	8.3	7.2	7.6	8.8	8.9	9.1	11.8
1948	11.8	5.6	5.9	7.2	7.9	8.5	7.3	8.8	8.6	8.4	9.0	11.1
1949	13.7	6.0	6.4	6.5	7.7	7.7	6.6	9.3	8.7	7.7	8.5	11.2
1950							10.7					11.5
1951							7.1					10.5
1952												
1953												
1954												
1955												
1956												
1957												
1958												
1959												
1960												
1961	13.9	5.0	5.0	6.4	7.5	6.8	8.1	12.4	7.1	7.2	8.5	12.1
1962												
1963	14.0	5.1	5.1	5.7	7.5	6.7	6.6	12.8	6.6	7.3	8.0	12.6
1964												
1965	13.7	4.9	5.2	5.8	6.7	6.7	8.2	13.3	7.3	7.3	8.4	12.5

(Continued)

ment stores ran *New York Times* advertisements in the month of January headlining "White Goods Sale," [10] constituting a total of 1 7/8 pages of advertising.[11] By 1910 there were 6 1/2 pages of white sale advertising. There was little further growth in January white sale advertising until after World War II (6 1/8 pages in 1940). Then in 1950 there were 20 1/2 pages of advertising and 48 pages in 1959. Now the phenomenon of the January white sale is found in most cities in the nation. (This postwar growth is not accounted for by a rise in total depart-

[10] These data on *New York Times* advertising, as well as some of the other data shown below, were collected by Miss Suzanne Brown for an undergraduate reading course.

[11] Prior to this time there had been "January Clearance Sales," but the concentration on household textiles was not so heavy or so self-conscious.

Table 8-2. (Continued)

Percentage of Total Store Sales Accounted for by Household Textiles
7th Federal Reserve District

1	24 Annual	25 Jan.	26 Feb.	27 Mar.	28 Apr.	29 May	30 June	31 July	32 Aug.	33 Sept.	34 Oct.	35 Nov.	36 Dec.
1936													
1937													
1938													
1939													
1940													
1941													
1942													
1943													
1944													
1945													
1946													
1947	3.2	4.6	3.4	2.7	2.9	3.1	3.3	3.5	3.6	3.3	3.1	2.8	2.6
1948	3.2	5.5	2.8	2.3	2.8	3.1	3.2	3.5	4.0	3.3	2.9	2.8	2.6
1949													
1950													
1951													
1952	3.0	6.0	2.5	2.4	2.2	3.0	2.7	3.6	3.8	2.9	2.6	2.6	2.5
1953	3.0	5.8	2.6	2.2	2.7	2.9	2.8	3.7	4.2	2.8	2.7	2.6	2.4
1954	3.0	5.8	2.8	2.4	2.2	3.0	2.6	3.5	4.2	2.9	2.6	2.5	2.4
1955	3.0	6.0	2.7	2.4	2.3	2.9	2.8	3.4	4.5	2.7	2.6	2.5	2.4
1956	3.0	6.4	2.6	2.0	2.6	2.9	2.6	3.8	4.3	2.6	2.6	2.5	2.4
1957	3.0	6.5	2.7	2.4	2.1	2.9	2.7	3.7	4.3	2.6	2.5	2.4	2.4
1958	3.0	6.5	2.6	2.1	2.4	2.7	2.8	3.7	4.4	2.5	2.5	2.4	2.4
1959	2.9	6.5	2.3	1.9	2.5	2.6	2.7	3.8	4.7	2.6	2.5	2.4	2.3
1960	2.7	6.8	2.5	2.3	2.1	2.9	2.7	3.7	4.7	2.5	2.5	2.4	2.4
1961	3.0	6.8	2.6	1.9	2.6	2.7	2.5	3.8	4.7	2.5	2.4	2.4	2.3
1962	2.9	6.4	2.8	2.1	2.1	2.5	2.6	3.9	4.7	2.5	2.5	2.4	2.3
1963	3.0	6.9	2.7	2.0	2.2	2.7	2.5	3.9	4.6	2.5	2.5	2.4	2.3
1964	3.0	6.9	2.6	2.0	2.5	2.5	2.6	4.0	4.7	2.5	2.4	2.4	2.3
1965	3.0	7.0	2.6	2.3	2.2	2.6	2.7	3.7	5.2	2.6	2.5	2.4	2.3

(Continued)

ment-store advertising; Chicago department-store advertising merely increased from 13 million lines in 1940 to 26 million in 1959.) [12]

Because of the January white sale, advertising for white goods is high in January compared to the rest of the year. (See Table 8-2 for many of the following data.) In 1947 and 1948, 12.0 percent and 12.8 percent of all yearly towel and sheet advertising, respectively, was done in January, compared to, say, 8.6 percent and 8.2 percent for December and 6.0 percent and 5.7 percent for February, for towels in 1947 and 1948 [13] respectively. And January household textile sales show the effect of the heavy advertising. Household textiles accounted for slightly over 3 percent of annual sales of all types in 1947 and 1948, and almost

[12] *Chicago Tribune* promotional release (April, 1964, p. 2).
[13] Neustadt (annual).

Table 8-2. (Continued)

Percentage of Yearly Sales of Towels (including linens) in Each Month
7th Federal Reserve District

1	37 Annual	38 Jan.	39 Feb.	40 Mar.	41 Apr.	43 May	44 June	45 July	46 Aug.	47 Sept.	48 Oct.	49 Nov.	50 Dec.
1936													
1937													
1938													
1939													
1940													
1941													
1942													
1943													
1944													
1945	100	8.8	7.0	7.3	6.8	7.6	7.7	7.3	7.1	7.2	8.2	10.8	14.0
1946	100	6.7	6.9	6.8	7.0	8.5	7.9	7.4	9.0	8.1	8.7	10.3	12.7
1947	100	8.2	6.4	6.5	7.3	8.2	8.4	7.4	7.8	8.0	8.5	8.9	14.4
1948	100	10.1	5.6	5.9	7.0	7.8	8.4	7.2	8.2	7.7	8.0	10.2	14.0
1949													
1950													
1951													
1952													
1953													
1954													
1955													
1956													
1957													
1958													
1959													
1960													
1961													
1962													
1963													
1964													
1965													

(Continued)

exactly 3 percent each year from 1952 to 1965 (1949–51 data are missing). But January household textiles accounted for 4.63 percent and 5.54 percent of all-store sales in 1947 and 1948 respectively, far above the annual average (Federal Reserve Bank of Chicago annual), a phenomenon for which there is no apparent reason except advertising. The white sale advertising evidently created an otherwise-unexplained sales hump for household textiles in January, whereas low-advertising February is a very poor sales month for household textiles.

But more. By 1964 January advertising rose to 19.2 percent of the entire year's advertising for towels, and 24.2 percent for sheets. And in January of 1964 household textiles accounted for 6.9 percent of all sales made in the period (compared to the all-year average of 3.0 percent). An even heavier concentration of advertising had created an even bigger sales hump in the month than in early postwar years.

Table 8-2 (Continued)

Percentage of Total Store Sales Accounted for by Towels (including linens)
7th Federal Reserve District

1	51 Annual	52 Jan.	53 Feb.	54 Mar.	55 Apr.	56 May	57 June	58 July	59 Aug.	60 Sept.	61 Oct.	62 Nov.	63 Dec.
1936													
1937													
1938													
1939													
1940													
1941													
1942													
1943													
1944													
1945	1.3	1.7	1.4	1.1	1.3	1.4	1.3	1.5	1.3	1.2	1.1	1.3	1.4
1946	1.5	1.7	1.6	1.3	1.2	1.6	1.5	1.7	1.6	1.4	1.4	1.5	1.4
1947	1.3	1.6	1.3	1.0	1.2	1.3	1.4	1.4	1.5	1.2	1.2	1.3	1.3
1948	1.3	1.9	1.1	0.9	1.1	1.2	1.3	1.4	1.5	1.2	1.1	1.3	1.3
1949													
1950													
1951													
1952													
1953													
1954													
1955													
1956													
1957													
1958													
1959													
1960													
1961													
1962													
1963													
1964													
1965													

Sources:
Columns 2-5: Neustadt, annual
Columns 6-8: Federal Reserve Bank of Chicago, "Departmental Sales at Apparel and Department Stores," an annual publication.
Columns 9-10: Compiled by Suzanne Brown for term paper, University of Illinois, 1962
Column 11: *Chicago Tribune* promotional release, April, 1964. Data originally from Media Records.
Columns 12-23: Federal Reserve Bank of Chicago, "Departmental Sales at Apparel and Department Stores," an annual publication.
Also Burton, 1959, p. 52.

Further corroboration is given by the August experience. In 1940 there were only 1 1/2 pages of August white sale advertising, but there was a sudden postwar rise to 9 1/2 pages in 1950, and 27 1/2 pages in 1959. The August white sale obviously is a post–World War II phenomenon. And in August of 1947 household textiles accounted for only 3.57 percent of all-store sales, only slightly more than the all-1947 amount, 3.17 percent. Towel advertising in August was 9.3 percent of the yearly total in 1947, and August sheet advertising in 1948 was 12.4 percent of the yearly total. By 1963 the towel and sheet advertising fig-

Table 8-3. Seasonal Department Store Sales Patterns

Percentage of Year's Total Sales Done Each Month in 1961

	Jan.	Feb.	Mar.	Apr.	May	June	July	Aug.	Sept.	Oct.	Nov.	Dec.
INFANTS' & CHILDREN'S WEAR–TOTAL	3.8	4.6	9.2	5.5	5.9	6.3	5.4	9.4	8.3	8.0	12.9	20.7
Infants' Wear (Incl. Infants' Furniture)	5.3	5.6	9.5	6.5	6.3	6.2	5.7	8.4	9.0	9.5	11.8	16.2
Children's Shoes	4.5	5.5	12.6	6.3	7.1	7.4	5.7	12.0	10.8	7.4	8.6	12.1
Girls' Wear	3.6	4.6	10.9	5.5	6.2	6.0	5.6	11.6	8.8	8.9	11.6	16.7
Boys' Wear	4.0	4.8	9.5	6.0	6.4	6.7	5.2	10.6	8.8	8.4	11.3	18.3
Toys & Games	1.5	2.4	3.6	3.0	3.5	5.5	4.7	4.4	4.1	5.6	21.3	40.4
Untrimmed Cloth Coats	8.8	8.5	15.1	11.1	4.4	1.6	1.9	4.8	9.5	13.5	13.2	7.6
Wash and Play Dresses	7.0	5.7	7.5	16.4	18.6	15.6	10.1	5.7	3.5	3.2	3.2	3.5
Fur Coats	11.6	6.9	7.8	6.4	3.2	2.3	4.4	11.6	8.1	14.0	12.8	10.9
Blouses	4.6	6.7	11.1	10.4	10.5	7.0	4.8	6.9	8.6	7.1	10.2	12.1
Slips	5.3	6.1	10.2	9.6	11.2	7.7	4.5	5.0	7.4	7.6	11.1	14.3
Junior Misses' Dresses	5.4	6.1	10.1	11.4	12.0	9.2	4.5	8.7	9.3	7.7	8.4	7.2
Foundation Garments	5.7	5.4	11.4	10.7	9.5	7.4	5.0	7.7	9.6	11.5	8.7	7.4
Brassieres and Bandeaux	5.1	5.9	10.6	7.7	10.2	10.9	5.7	6.4	9.0	11.0	10.3	7.2
Gowns and Pajamas	5.5	5.9	5.5	9.1	11.1	6.9	5.2	6.4	6.0	8.7	14.8	14.9
Handbags	4.7	5.8	13.3	7.4	10.0	5.4	3.7	5.8	9.3	9.8	10.3	14.5
Robes and Negligees	4.7	5.9	6.3	7.4	11.0	5.1	3.4	4.2	5.6	8.2	16.0	22.2
Skirts	6.7	6.1	5.9	9.9	7.3	6.2	5.2	11.5	12.6	11.8	10.1	6.7
Sweaters	5.8	4.9	3.4	4.4	5.1	3.7	4.6	12.1	11.8	10.5	14.9	18.8
Fur Trimmed Cloth Coats	13.9	6.4	1.5	0.4	0.5	2.0	4.6	13.3	9.7	20.0	17.2	10.5
Costume Jewelry	6.0	6.2	10.6	7.6	8.8	4.8	4.0	4.9	8.1	10.0	12.6	16.4
Cloth Coats (Junior Misses')	5.4	6.3	15.4	6.7	1.7	1.1	3.2	12.0	12.3	17.0	12.3	6.6
Fabric Gloves	5.3	7.1	15.3	6.9	10.2	4.6	3.3	5.2	9.2	9.1	10.7	13.1
Bathing Suits	–	–	–	–	30.1	41.2	22.8	5.9	–	–	–	–
Slacks and Shorts	5.6	4.4	4.8	12.4	14.3	12.7	6.7	6.3	7.5	9.4	8.9	7.0
Sportswear (Junior Misses')	4.9	5.2	6.6	10.7	7.4	5.8	7.1	14.3	9.2	10.2	9.4	9.2
Junior Misses' Suits	3.8	16.4	26.7	13.1	5.5	2.3	2.2	12.9	8.0	4.7	2.4	2.0
Jackets	4.6	4.9	9.6	13.0	10.9	5.8	4.7	11.1	8.8	9.5	9.1	8.0
Leather Gloves	2.9	3.3	8.8	1.9	2.3	0.5	0.2	3.7	10.3	22.3	21.9	21.9

(Continued)

Table 8-3. (Continued)

Percentage of Year's Total Sales Done Each Month in 1961

	Jan.	Feb.	Mar.	Apr.	May	June	July	Aug.	Sept.	Oct.	Nov.	Dec.
PIECE GOODS & DOMESTICS—TOTAL	12.1	6.2	6.9	6.8	7.7	6.9	7.9	10.3	7.5	8.2	8.8	10.7
PIECE GOODS	7.6	8.8	11.0	8.6	8.2	6.6	5.9	7.9	8.9	9.8	9.2	7.5
Silks, Velvets & Synthetics	7.8	9.3	12.0	9.1	8.0	5.9	5.4	7.0	8.0	9.6	10.2	7.7
Woolen Yard Goods	8.5	7.8	7.3	2.0	1.6	1.6	4.3	10.8	15.0	16.2	14.2	10.7
Cotton Yard Goods (Incl. Linings)	7.1	8.8	11.8	11.6	11.4	10.2	8.3	7.6	6.3	6.0	5.7	5.2
HOUSEHOLD TEXTILES	13.9	5.2	5.2	6.2	7.4	7.0	8.7	11.2	7.0	7.6	8.5	12.1
Linens & Towels	11.7	5.0	5.5	6.2	7.2	7.1	8.5	10.2	6.4	7.3	9.7	15.2
Domestics—Muslins, Sheetings	17.8	5.6	4.8	6.1	7.8	6.9	10.4	13.5	6.8	6.3	6.0	8.0
Blankets, Comforters & Spreads	11.8	4.9	5.3	6.4	7.5	6.8	7.5	9.7	8.0	9.0	9.8	12.4
HOME FURNISHINGS—TOTAL	6.8	6.6	7.3	7.4	8.2	7.9	7.5	8.1	8.4	9.1	10.5	12.2
Furniture & Bedding	7.9	7.7	7.4	7.6	8.3	8.2	8.4	9.4	8.5	9.2	9.5	7.9
Mattresses, Springs & Studio Beds	8.7	7.8	7.4	7.7	8.4	8.5	9.5	10.6	9.1	9.3	7.8	5.2
Upholstered & Other Furniture	7.3	7.9	7.4	7.6	8.2	8.3	8.1	8.9	8.2	9.1	10.3	8.7
Domestic Floor Coverings	8.2	7.4	7.9	7.4	7.8	6.5	6.7	8.0	9.1	11.3	11.7	8.0
Rugs & Carpets	7.8	7.7	7.7	7.3	7.6	6.9	6.8	8.4	8.5	11.2	12.5	7.6
Linoleum	8.4	6.7	9.3	9.7	10.3	7.0	8.5	7.5	8.0	9.5	9.0	6.2
Draperies, Curtains, Upholstery & Awnings	5.9	6.1	8.1	8.4	9.3	8.5	6.6	7.2	7.9	10.5	11.5	10.0
Lamps & Shades	7.2	6.5	7.1	7.5	7.5	6.4	5.9	6.9	7.8	9.9	12.4	14.9
China & Glassware	6.4	6.3	7.0	6.6	7.5	6.8	6.1	7.5	7.4	8.2	11.8	18.4
Major Household Appliances	6.8	6.0	7.1	7.4	8.6	10.3	11.0	10.1	9.6	8.2	7.7	7.2
Housewares (Incl. Small Appliances)	5.5	5.8	7.3	7.7	9.1	8.9	7.4	7.4	8.3	7.9	9.5	15.2
Gift Shop	4.5	4.9	5.7	6.0	7.0	6.6	5.6	6.7	6.1	7.8	13.5	25.6
Radios, Phonos, TV, Records & Instruments	6.8	6.4	6.8	5.9	5.8	5.9	5.7	6.5	8.6	8.9	12.6	20.1
Radios, Phonos, & TV	7.3	5.4	5.9	5.2	6.4	4.8	5.4	6.4	9.4	9.7	14.3	19.8
Pianos, Records, Sheet Music, Instruments	4.9	7.7	7.4	6.7	6.1	6.3	6.0	5.9	4.9	7.6	12.1	24.4

Source: ANPA, 1962.

Table 8-4. Seasonal Department Store Advertising Patterns

Percentage of Year's Total Linage Used Each Month in 1961

	Jan.	Feb.	Mar.	Apr.	May	June	July	Aug.	Sept.	Oct.	Nov.	Dec.
Toddlers & Tots	4.3	5.7	13.7	7.3	6.9	6.3	5.6	12.6	8.5	10.4	10.9	7.8
Boys' Furnishings	4.3	4.3	7.4	7.8	6.7	6.9	5.0	16.6	9.9	9.3	10.2	11.6
Girls' Sportswear	4.0	3.4	3.9	8.7	10.3	9.7	5.9	17.5	8.8	8.2	9.9	9.7
Boys' Outer Apparel	5.5	5.8	11.6	6.5	4.8	4.6	4.0	14.3	10.1	13.1	12.0	7.7
Girls' Coats & Suits	4.5	7.1	21.2	2.9	0.5	0.3	2.8	9.7	12.2	17.3	14.3	7.2
Girls' Dresses	3.2	6.4	14.2	7.2	4.8	4.4	5.9	24.7	7.6	4.2	8.8	8.6
Boys' & Prep Clothing	1.8	8.6	45.0	2.6	4.0	1.7	0.9	7.5	8.0	7.5	6.5	5.9
Teen & Pre-Teen Coats & Suits	7.2	9.9	21.9	4.2	0.9	0.4	3.6	9.5	11.1	14.7	11.5	5.1
Teen & Pre-Teen Dresses	3.7	6.0	14.1	9.4	10.3	7.7	4.8	14.8	9.1	4.7	9.1	6.3
Students' Clothing	4.7	5.9	20.7	4.2	7.4	3.7	3.3	14.7	15.4	6.7	8.2	5.1
Wool Suits	9.9	8.6	16.3	6.8	0.7	0.3	0.5	4.4	13.8	16.0	14.0	8.7
Sportswear	6.7	4.7	6.1	7.7	5.4	7.4	3.1	4.1	9.0	13.9	15.9	16.0
Shoes	6.5	4.5	13.2	7.9	8.9	9.1	5.5	5.9	10.8	10.5	9.4	7.8
Summer Suits	0.1	0.6	2.0	16.0	31.3	26.2	18.1	5.5	0.2	—	—	—
Sport Shirts	5.7	4.3	3.5	6.4	8.2	17.2	8.5	5.5	5.1	8.2	11.3	16.1
Outer Coats	17.8	9.5	6.1	2.0	0.4	0.1	1.1	5.2	4.8	16.7	23.2	13.1
Dress Shirts	5.8	5.2	8.4	6.6	8.1	11.0	5.5	4.8	8.5	9.5	11.6	15.0
Sport Coats	6.9	6.7	9.8	11.1	12.1	9.8	6.5	5.9	8.3	8.3	6.7	7.9
Hosiery	6.1	6.7	7.1	7.4	7.8	9.7	5.2	6.1	8.2	9.7	12.0	14.0
Neckwear	5.5	6.1	9.9	4.4	3.9	12.8	4.1	3.3	5.8	8.1	14.2	21.9
Hats	3.8	4.2	12.9	5.9	11.2	7.6	1.9	1.3	11.1	15.6	12.2	12.3
Slacks	5.4	5.9	6.3	8.9	13.3	15.0	8.5	6.9	8.6	7.7	7.1	6.4
Sheets	24.5	3.9	3.1	8.8	7.4	4.4	12.1	14.3	3.6	5.7	3.3	8.9
Bedspreads	11.4	4.9	6.1	10.0	8.4	5.9	7.7	9.7	7.7	10.5	9.4	8.3
Linen Dept. Items	15.2	4.5	5.9	7.9	6.9	5.3	8.5	8.4	5.2	7.7	13.4	11.1
Blankets	11.7	4.2	3.4	4.1	4.3	3.4	8.0	7.5	8.6	15.2	16.7	12.9
Silk & Synthetic Piece Goods	10.5	11.8	13.2	12.1	6.2	5.8	4.9	4.7	9.6	9.3	8.8	3.1
Cotton & Linen Piece Goods	10.8	10.6	7.7	14.2	10.8	10.3	7.7	7.8	6.7	7.0	4.0	2.7

(Continued)

Table 8-4. (Continued)

Percentage of Year's Total Linage Used Each Month in 1961

	Jan.	Feb.	Mar.	Apr.	May	June	July	Aug.	Sept.	Oct.	Nov.	Dec.
Towels	21.9	4.2	3.2	8.3	6.9	6.3	12.7	12.0	4.8	6.4	4.7	8.6
Comforters	15.1	5.5	5.6	6.3	5.9	4.1	7.4	8.3	8.5	10.6	12.2	10.5
Television Sets	7.0	9.3	8.4	7.7	6.7	5.6	5.1	5.8	8.8	11.9	12.0	11.7
Refrigerators	5.1	5.7	6.5	7.7	9.3	13.4	16.3	10.7	8.2	7.6	5.5	4.0
Bedroom Suites	8.8	9.7	7.3	9.1	8.6	7.6	9.7	10.8	7.8	9.3	7.3	4.0
*Housewares	4.3	5.9	8.4	12.0	12.1	9.1	5.9	7.2	11.9	10.0	8.9	4.3
Broadloom Carpeting	8.1	8.4	8.0	10.4	8.1	6.3	6.1	7.9	9.1	12.5	10.8	4.3
Occasional Living Room Chairs	7.5	8.0	6.5	8.4	7.8	8.4	7.6	7.7	7.1	9.4	12.6	9.0
Studio Couches & Sofa Beds	8.7	8.8	7.4	8.9	8.8	8.6	8.0	9.5	8.4	9.8	8.8	4.3
Living Room Suites	7.5	7.5	7.8	9.1	8.8	7.1	8.7	8.6	8.9	11.5	9.2	5.3
Mattresses	10.0	9.5	6.9	9.2	8.2	8.6	8.8	9.3	8.7	9.9	7.4	3.5
Curtains	6.3	6.8	7.5	13.0	8.6	6.9	4.1	6.0	9.0	14.4	11.0	6.4
Sofas	8.4	9.3	8.0	9.0	8.6	6.6	8.5	9.9	7.7	11.0	8.7	4.3
Radios	4.6	5.8	6.3	7.3	7.9	7.9	5.4	5.2	7.7	10.5	14.1	17.8
Dinette Sets	8.9	9.0	8.2	8.9	8.0	7.9	7.4	8.0	9.3	10.5	9.1	4.8
Occasional Living Room Tables	7.5	7.7	6.8	7.3	7.0	6.8	8.1	8.9	6.0	10.6	12.6	10.7
Slip Covers	6.9	8.0	8.9	11.1	9.7	8.1	6.6	6.2	7.9	11.3	9.9	5.4
Gas Ranges	7.4	6.8	6.8	8.7	8.9	8.2	6.0	6.1	7.1	16.5	12.6	4.9
Luggage	6.6	5.5	4.7	8.0	12.3	15.5	10.5	7.7	4.6	3.7	8.5	12.4
Dinner Sets	6.9	6.9	8.0	10.9	8.8	7.9	4.8	5.1	9.1	10.6	13.4	7.6
Made-up Drapes	6.1	6.6	7.6	10.4	7.8	5.8	4.5	5.5	10.7	15.7	13.6	5.7
Dining Room & Junior Dining Sets	7.3	10.1	6.6	7.1	6.9	6.3	8.9	10.2	7.2	12.0	13.2	4.2

*Housewares Include: Cooking Utensils, Kitchen Furniture, Household Sundries, Unpainted Furniture, Bathroom Equipment and Paints.

Source: ANPA, 1962.

ures were 13.6 percent and 15.6 percent respectively, and August household textiles accounted for 4.6 percent of all-store sales, compared to the all-1963 amount, 3.0 percent. Furthermore, a big leap to above 4 percent (textile sales as a percent of all-store sales in August) occurred in 1953, the year in which the month's advertising share rose from 9.3 percent to 11.1 percent of the year's advertising for textiles.

As additional evidence, the various categories of white goods all had January and August sales index rises between 1947–49 (the base year) and 1965 far greater than any other categories of goods in the store — even though their yearly shares remained the same or declined slightly.

The data on advertising and sales distributions throughout the year for various categories of department-store merchandise are shown in Tables 8-3 and 8-4, for the reader who wishes to examine for other related points of interest. (The sales data differ slightly from those in Table 8-2 because the latter are only for the Seventh Federal Reserve District.)

There is not much question about the interpretation of the relationships. There is little reason to believe that higher sales cause higher advertising in these cases, nor is there reason to attribute the movements in both sales and advertising to some third factor. It seems safe to conclude that exogenous changes in the advertising pattern affected the pattern of seasonal sales of household textiles.

On another matter now. A shift in sales to low-capacity months makes a prima facie case for the social usefulness of white sale advertising. But also relevant to welfare judgments is the price of white goods in department stores, and the possible effect of advertising cost on the price to consumers. One wants to know whether the transaction price of household textiles would be less *on the average for the entire year* if there were no white sale advertising. But the interacting alternatives are sufficiently complex so that I cannot deduce an answer. For example, white sale prices are lower than prices for the rest of the year, a fact which superficially suggests a relationship between white sale advertising and lower prices. But it is possible that if there were no advertising, prices during the white sales would be lower still, as an alternative method of increasing demand. On the other hand, if the store could not advertise the white sales it might not conduct the sales for lack of store traffic, and might not even carry the merchandise, in which case customers might buy at higher-priced (or lower-priced) stores. And so on, adding complexity to the point that the effect of advertising for household textiles cannot be assessed without assessing the effect on price of *all* department-store advertising — and the historical foundation of the central-city department store was newspaper advertising, as discussed in Chapter 7.

To sum up, the January white sale — whose history runs back to 1900 — has altered yearly department-store demand for household textiles. Heavy sales now occur in those months in which marginal cost (excluding advertising) is low because of otherwise low utilization of facilities. This fact, together with lower prices during the sales, makes a prima facie case for believing that white sale advertising is a good thing, though unanalyzed and complex price relationships could conceivably reverse the appraisal.

9

Advertising
and
Market Power

The common economic meaning of market power is that one or several firms in an industry are able to gain profits higher than the average in the economy for reasons other than unusual competence of the owners and managers. Such market power is commonly regarded as undesirable because (1) the profits come out of high prices, (2) having market power may reduce the firm's motivation to innovate and manage efficiently, and (3) such market power may result in disproportionate social power to affect government decisions and individual lives.

The topic of this chapter is the relationship of advertising to market power. It is mostly a critical review of work done by others, more of which has been done on this topic than on other topics treated in this book.

Let us distinguish three ways in which advertising might be implicated in firms having more market power than they would have otherwise. Each of these will be discussed in separate sections of this chapter. Here is a preview list of them:

A. Advertising might be a proximate cause of greater market concentration, which then might well lead to market power. This is the case in which concentration would not be expected to occur if the instrument of advertising were not available to the firm, or in which concentration might be greater than if advertising were not available.

B. Another possibility is that advertising might increase the market power of firms in industries which would be highly concentrated even if advertising were not an available business instrument.

C. A third possibility is that some types of goods are more "advertisable" [1] than others, and the heavier advertising for them pro-

---

[1] This term is used by Kaldor (1949–50), Comanor and Wilson (1967), and others.

duces higher profits even if increased concentration is not a causal intermediate between advertising and market power.

To clarify the general question that we seek to answer, it is useful to ask what kind of an experiment one would run to answer the question if such an experiment were possible. There are several plausible experiments, however. One experiment might be to construct two countries that are identical to what the United States (or Great Britain) was like in 1880 (or what some other country of interest was like before consumer advertising was of great importance), and then permit advertising to take place in country A just as in the United States, but prohibit consumer advertising (or raise its cost sharply) in identical country B in perhaps every second mass-consumption industry.[2] Ninety years later one would compare the rates of profit (and also the price and the concentration ratios) in the advertising-ban industries in country B versus the same industries in country A.[3]

A second conceivable experiment might be to construct two economies like the United States of *today*. Then prohibit (or sharply raise the cost of) advertising in half the mass-consumer industries in country D, but make country C identical to the United States as it really is now. Then one would examine the two countries at perhaps ten-year intervals.

A major conceptual difference between these two experimental models is that the second refers to the effects of a change in the environment upon an existing equilibrium, whereas the first refers to structural development. The second of these experiments is clearly more relevant for social decisions made by United States courts and legislators. But it is the first which is clearly the model for some important work on this subject (e.g. Kaldor, 1949), and it is not clear which experimental model other work refers to. The first model may be more appropriate for some developing countries today, e.g., Israel, Taiwan, India. And it is certainly not sure that the results of these two experiments would be the same.

Nature has not been bountiful with relevant evidence. As we shall see, the data that are cast up by natural forces are in crucial ways not

[2] Only mass-consumption goods are included because most a priori speculation focuses on them. The purpose of allowing advertising in just half the industries in country B is so that one could afterward compare the allowed-advertising industries with the same industries in country A to see whether the former are affected by the ban on advertising in the other half of the industries in country B. This would allow us to learn something about whether the advertising ban works in each industry separately, or rather through the economy as a whole. (If the experiment were cheap one would certainly also run a third economy with no advertising at all.)

[3] One would also like to look at overall economic indicators in the two countries, of course, but that is not relevant here.

like those that would be provided by a complete experiment, which makes it particularly difficult to arrive at satisfactory conclusions to the questions we seek to answer.

Before launching into the substance of the issue, it is necessary to digress briefly to discuss the notion of economies of scale, which is an important intermediate concept between advertising and market concentration. Stated in a loose way, one wants to find out if a larger firm has an advantage over a smaller firm in a given industry. The definition of "larger" is not immediately obvious, however. One firm might be considered larger if its advertising expenditure is larger but all else is the same. This case was discussed in Chapter 1 as the study of marginal returns. A firm will also be larger than another if it employs more of two or more factors of production (and presumably, less of no factor). A special case is that in which the proportions in which the factors are used are the same for the smaller and larger firm. This is the only context in which economists inquire about what are known as "returns to scale" — the case when all inputs are increased in a given proportion (Stigler, 1966, p. 146). But a larger firm need not, and usually does not, employ factors in the same proportions as the smaller firm. Therefore, empirically it is customary (and necessary) to consider the results achieved by firms of different *total* size, measuring the total by assets or sales or similar measures. Such an investigation is commonly referred to as a study of "economies of scale" (e.g., Stigler, 1958), though it would be clearer to talk of "economies of size."

For such a situation, that in which the factors used may not be in the same proportion, it would seem appropriate to evaluate the effect of different sizes of firms in one of several ways. One possibility is to study the rate of profit at various plant sizes. A related tactic is to determine whether the ratio of the value of the output to the value of the input is greater at some firm sizes than at others. Both of these methods suffer from a difficulty of obtaining data. Still another possibility is to study which size classes of firms grow most and "survive" best (Stigler, 1958). What is most important here is that none of these measures corresponds to the theoretical notion of economies of scale.

Now on to the first way in which advertising might lead to more market power.

A. ADVERTISING AS A PROXIMATE CAUSE OF INDUSTRIAL CONCENTRATION

This section considers the possibility that advertising actually causes concentration, i.e., it asks whether advertising leads to concentration where concentration would not occur if advertising were not possible.

To repeat, the next section considers the possibility that advertising increases market power in some industries where there is no concentration. And the last section treats the possibility in which advertising is not a proximate cause of concentration but where advertising may help firms increase the profits and market power that flow to them in an industry which would be concentrated even without advertising.

Industrial concentration in general is a subject of considerable contemporary discussion, both by economists and by governmental policymakers. For a long time the issue was the global question of whether or not concentration is increasing in the economy as a whole. More recently the discussion has shifted to inquiry about the forces that increase, decrease, and maintain concentration in particular industries. These forces include diversification, absolute size of industries, and overall growth or decline of industries, as well as production efficiencies. And as Nelson observed in the 1964 concentration hearings: "The contributions of administration, marketing, finance and research are probably more difficult to measure than the contribution of plant economies. . . . However . . . it is here that further research is most likely to produce significant additions to our understanding of industrial concentration" (Nelson, 1964, p. 272).

Advertising has been charged with being an important promoter of concentration. Kaldor put it most strongly: "The economic effects of advertising must be judged therefore in terms of the advantages of the manufacturer's oligopoly (as against the polypoly under wholesalers' domination) which it helped to create and maintain . . . after advertising has been generally adopted . . . sales will have been concentrated among a smaller number of firms, and the size of the representative firm will have increased" (1949, p. 13).

This section begins by surveying the relevant theory about advertising's role in industrial concentration, and then considers the existing empirical work. Some new data are then presented pertaining to the importance of the issue. It is well to remember that this section deals only with the case that may be diagrammed as Advertising $\rightarrow$ Concentration $\rightarrow$ Market Power. This is the case in which advertising causes concentration, rather than just being just a cooperating element in industries that are concentrated for other reasons.

We can subclassify the ways in which advertising might cause concentration as those (1) in which there are increasing returns to advertising, independent of the workings of other industrial forces; and (2) situations in which advertising interacts with other forces to produce economies of scale that lead to market concentration. These will now be considered separately.

Any conclusion about advertising causing concentration must depend at least somewhat upon one's assumptions about the initial state of an industry. Advertising could not presently reduce concentration among wheat farmers; neither could it presently increase concentration in the telephone industry. This makes any analysis somewhat messy. I think it is sensible to limit the discussion to those consumer-goods markets where half the sales are concentrated among one to ten firms, and ask whether such markets would be more or less concentrated if the firms could not advertise.

1. Increasing Returns to Advertising as a Cause of Market Concentration

According to the loose practice in which empirical research in the matter is necessarily conducted, we wish to inquire in this section whether increasing returns are ever present, and hence whether there are any economies of scale due to advertising along. This is what I interpret to be the mainspring of Kaldor's argument about advertising on concentration:

> The reason for this [increase in concentration] is that the shift of the demand curve resulting from advertising cannot be assumed to be strictly proportionate to the amount spent on advertising — the "pulling power" of the larger expenditure must overshadow that of smaller ones with the consequence (a) that the larger firms are bound to gain at the expense of the smaller ones; (b) if at the start, firms are more or less of equal size, those that forge ahead are bound to increase their lead, as the additional sales enable them to increase their outlay still further. Hence, after advertising has been generally adopted, and the trade settles down again to some sort of equilibrium, the pattern of the industry will have changed; sales will have been concentrated among a smaller number of firms, and the size of "representative firm" will have increased [1949, p. 13].

The mechanism under discussion is this: because the larger advertiser has an advantage over the smaller advertiser, the larger advertiser(s) will drive out the smaller and there will eventually be only a few large firms or one large one. (The final number of firms depends, by this line of thought, on whether at some point well below the total size of the industry the marginal returns cease to increase.)

At the *corporate* level, advertising sometimes has led to increased concentration by diversification because of multiproduct volume discounts on advertising time and space. For example, the FTC record revealed that Procter & Gamble could buy television time for 25 percent less than could the Clorox Company and this was an admitted motivation in P & G's purchase (Federal Trade Commission, 1963). Blake and Blum (1965) have compiled the relevant data on these volume discounts and provide compelling analysis to show that they must have been an important reason for firms that advertise heavily to seek mergers and reduce the cost of advertising.

This effect is illustrated by a recent trade-paper story:

The proposed Cadbury-Schweppes merger, which sees economies in advertising and overseas expansion as its chief benefits, will create (if the Board of Trade permits) the United Kingdom's fourth largest food group, with estimated sales of $600,000,000.

Savings would come from the group buying of television time, which accounts for at least 75% of the companies' joint budget in that medium. In 1968, the two companies put out $13,650,000 for advertising, the second largest budget in the country . . . [*Advertising Age*, March 3, 1969, p. 26].

(Recently, however, the television networks in the United States have altered their rate structures in ways that may reduce or remove altogether the strength of this force toward concentration [Blank, 1968]).

From here on, the discussion refers to *brand* advertising, and asks whether the existence of advertising as a business tool makes it more likely that there will be fewer competing brands in a market than if advertising did not exist. This level of discussion is appropriate because it is the brand that is advertised, and if advertising is to have an effect on the firm or on the industry or on the economy, it must be because it helps one or more brands to increase their market shares disproportionately. If concentration occurs by way of one firm maintaining several brands in a market (e.g., the severality of liquor brands sold by Schenley listed in Chapter 1) the consequent concentration cannot be laid at advertising's door; just the opposite.

We must conclude, however, that advertising does not cause concentration by way of increasing returns. From a speculative point of view, Kaldor is certainly wrong that the larger expenditure *must* overshadow the smaller; there is a congeries of psychological and economic reasons on both sides of the question that make such an a priori conclusion quite untenable. So theory must defer to evidence. And there is practically no evidence of increasing returns at any level of advertising, but rather almost all of the evidence shows *monotonically diminishing returns* as Chapter 1 showed. This includes the effects of volume discounts (except multiproduct discounts).

The lack of increasing returns also constitutes a strong technical argument against the likelihood of predatory advertising. In a duopoly situation, one firm can overadvertise and thereby reduce the efficiency of the other firm's advertising by simply raising the "noise" level. But the greater the imbalance between the firms' advertising expenditure, the less efficient (relatively) is the advertising by the larger advertiser because of the diminishing-returns effect. This means that predatory advertising is a less effective weapon than predatory pricing, because the losses are relatively the same to each firm when pricing is below cost. And there is also little danger of predatory advertising when there are many competitors, because the effect of one firm's advertising on any one or all of its competitors will be relatively small.

2. Market Concentration Caused by Advertising in Conjunction with Other Forces

This is the possible case in which advertising works in conjunction with other forces to produce economies of scale, which then lead to the larger firm(s) surviving the smaller ones. The clearest example of this phenomenon would be a new patented product which could not easily be exploited without advertising, but which could be exploited readily with the aid of advertising. Another example is the conjunction of advertising and the department-store concept, as discussed in Chapters 3 and 7.

An advertising-created barrier to entry is another theoretical reason that has been advanced for advertising causing increased concentration. There are two subarguments: (*a*) advertising by existing firms raises the ante to get into the game; and (*b*) heavy advertising lowers profits for existing firms and therefore makes entry less attractive, the same argument that has been made about oligopolists' pricing. Let us consider these subarguments separately.

a) The importance of the size of the capital requirement as a barrier to entry is weakened by the possibility of entry into markets by large firms that have positions in other markets. The barrier argument may be somewhat stronger for advertising than for capital for producer goods, however, because lenders cannot easily take a lien on and repossess advertising investments.

b) The barrier of lowered profitability by increased advertising might conceivably operate to keep out some entrants. But to demonstrate that such a barrier actually operates, one would have to show that profits are lower in the industry than they would otherwise be. There is no reason to believe that industry price levels are independent of whether or not firms in the industry advertise. And there are certainly many devices besides advertising — especially price — to hold profits at any desired level below the maximum attainable. Advertising seems to have no unusual properties as a profit-reducer except one: in industries in which customer loyalty can be made high from year to year, advertising that enhances brand loyalties (if any does so, which has not been shown) would make the payout period much longer for a potential entrant. That is, his own advertising expenditures would be just as efficient as those of his competitors once he was in the industry — but in the first and subsequent years his profits would appear to be less because his competitors would still be getting returns from advertising in prior years. If the potential entrant does not clearly understand the lagged nature of advertising's effect, his ignorance might act as a barrier to his entry.

A last possible way that advertising could conceivably affect concentration is that the larger advertiser may take advantage of relative production economies, i.e., advertising may permit him to operate on a lower point of his cost curve. But no one thinks that this is an important possibility, nor does it worry anyone. The bogey is, instead, the possibility of advertising leading firms up the total cost curve.

A digression at this point on advertising and retail stores is useful both as an analogy to manufacturer advertising and because more than half of all advertising is done by nonmanufacturing firms (see Chapter 11). The nature of advertising is force at a distance, as was discussed in Chapter 7. It makes sense, then, that retail advertising tends to reduce geographic monopoly. A famous example is the rise of mail-order firms such as Sears Roebuck and Montgomery Ward at the end of the nineteenth century, a rise which was opposed by boycott and physical violence from small-town merchants whose monopolies were being weakened. Similarly, the downtown department store which was actually created by advertising and its power to transcend distance between buyer and seller, generated new competition for neighborhood stores. And in middle-size communities, with larger numbers of competitors than in small communities, there are higher ratios of advertising to sales, holding size of store constant. (See Mitchell's data in Table 2-8, noting that this effect does not continue to the largest communities).

In retail trade, then, there is no theoretical reason to believe that there is less competition in a society that has advertising than in a society that does not. Just the opposite. And the data in Chapter 4 showed that if one holds size of community constant, where there are larger numbers of competitors there is more total advertising. For example, if there are two moving-picture theaters in a town of 7,000 people, there will be a much larger total amount spent for theater advertising than if there is only one theater, or after one theater goes out of business. The same is true for taxi firms.

Because there is more advertising where there are more retail competitors does not imply that the availability of advertising causes there to be more competitors. On the other hand, however, this finding is not consistent with the hypothesis that the possibility of advertising causes there to be *fewer* retail competitors.

Empirical Relationships Relevant to Advertising as a Cause of Industrial Concentration

In classifications 1 and 2 of Section A we have considered the theory and the indirect empirical evidence concerning advertising as a cause of industrial concentration. Now we shall consider the direct empirical evidence on the matter.

Kaldor and Silverman (1948) classified industries by the number of firms accounting for 80 percent of an industry's advertising,[4] and then calculated the mean ratio of advertising to sales for each concentration category. They found the highest ratio (which they interpret as the "most" advertising) in the eight-firm group, and lesser ratios progressively as one moves toward monopoly and toward many-firm competition, e.g., an inverted U-curve. These data are consistent neither with the idea that advertising is a pressure toward monopoly nor with the idea that monopolists advertise heavily as a barrier to entry. But these data are not inconsistent with the hypothesis that advertising reduces classical competition in favor of oligopoly, and that oligopolists advertise more than "the many." This evidence alone does not tell us much about the causal significance of advertising in industrial concentration, however.

Telser (1964) tackled the problem in two ways, the first of which is conceptually similar to Kaldor-Silverman. But Telser examined the linear relation between advertising ratios and concentration of sales among the four leading firms in 42 three-digit consumer industries. Telser expressed the result of this test as a correlation coefficient (actually he put it in terms of the variance, from which it is here transformed), $r = +.16$ ($R^2 = .03$) (pp. 542–544) suggesting to him that "concentration and advertising intensity are virtually independent" (p. 558).

But re-analysis of much of the same data used in Telser's first-mentioned test shows that in 1954 nine of the ten industries with the lowest concentrations among the 44 industries had advertising ratios below the median of the 44 industries, a finding which suggests that low-concentration industries do advertise less (measured by the advertising ratio) than higher-concentration industries. This observation agrees with at least half of the Kaldor-Silverman data, i.e., that firms in fragmented industries advertise less than do firms with higher degrees of concentration.

As mentioned earlier (Chapter 4), Yang (1966) subjected Telser's

[4] Later I shall argue that that is indeed a useful measure of concentration.

data to another sort of re-analysis. He divided the observations into three groups. Both in the group with under 2 percent advertising ratios and under 50 percent concentration, and in the group with over 2 percent advertising ratios and under 50 percent concentration, an increase in concentration over time was associated with an increase in advertising.[5] This finding jibes with Kaldor-Silverman. (Concerning the negative correlation in the high-concentration group see Chapter 4.)

Still another study is that of Mann, Henning, and Meehan (1967). They also used a linear model, regressing concentration in 14 consumer industries on the average advertising ratio of the few largest advertisers in each industry. Their advertising data were less subject to definitional error than were Telser's, being (like the data of Kaldor and Silverman) derived from commercial services that check and count each firm's advertising in major media. But the sample of Mann et al. was not only limited to the largest advertisers; it also was built up using as criteria that "the firms did not produce in regulated industries, employed advertising as the principal means of sales promotion, and were not highly diversified" (page 35, fn). Mann et al. found that the advertising ratio was positively related to concentration. (The simple correlation coefficients ranged from .41 to .72 among their several regressions [pp. 37–38]).

I will not attempt to assess the empirical methods used by the three studies mentioned above or try to reconcile them, but rather I will focus on issues common to all of them which I consider more important here. As I see it, the question is, what do the various observed results imply about the causal effect of advertising in industrial concentration? This is what we are interested in, as a step in studying the causal effect of advertising on market power. The following discussion might be tedious, but I hope the reader will follow it through because much of it pertains not only to the studies already mentioned above but also to others that will be described later in this chapter. And this discussion calls into question the importance of all of these tests.

There are only two possible sets of conditions under which any of the already-mentioned empirical observations could suggest causality running from advertising to concentration. One possibility is if advertising is a disequilibrating force in an industry, and an injection of advertising by one firm (which makes its budget larger than other firms' budgets) permanently disadvantages the other firms. One could then imagine that for random historical reasons there were sizable initial disequili-

---

[5] I assume that if these two groups were not separated the overall result would be the same. Yang's logic for separating the group does not seem to me to be relevant here.

brating injections in some industries and not in others, roughly as at the start of conceptual experiment one, described early in this chapter. If one further assumed that once the disadvantage occurred competitors could never catch up, even without continued advertising by the initial advertiser, it would then follow that the existence of industries where advertising is low and monopoly high (as in the very-high-concentration segment of the Kaldor-Silverman data) is consistent with advertising causing monopoly. Or, if one assumed that continued high advertising is required to maintain the advantage, this would then allow a causal interpretation to be placed on the observation that there is less advertising where firms are many than where they are few (as in my re-interpretation of the low-concentration range of Telser's data, and as in the data of Mann et al.).

This set of assumptions about the disequilibrating force of initial advertising seems to me rather unlikely for most industries. And if Telser's interpretation of his data is correct, it would at least show that the observed pattern is not determined by historical injections of advertising, either initially or at some later time. That is, Telser's interpretation of his data suggests two related things: (1) the initial injections of advertising in an industry are not decisive; and (2) it is not the case that in some industries, but not in others, at some time a given firm takes a major initiative with advertising which gives him a monopoly which then persists. Rather, Telser's interpretation of his data suggests that industries tend toward equilibria without being determined by historical advertising events.

That a decision by one advertiser in an industry to greatly jump up his advertising does not forever determine the future of advertising (and hence concentration) in an industry is also shown by the high similarity of relative advertising intensities in American and British industries (see Table 7-2) and for Canadian industries as well. This similarity suggests that the structural features of an industry rather than decisions by single firms determine the intensity of advertising in the industry.

To leap ahead for a moment, there is one other possible set of conditions which would allow interpretation of the data of Kaldor-Silverman, Telser (my re-analysis), and Mann et al. as showing causality. It might be that some products are more "advertisable" than others. One could give content to this vague idea by saying that one product is more advertisable than another if the former's advertising-sales response function is more elastic than the latter's, i.e., Figure 9-1a rather than Figure 9-1b. One might assume that a sample of industries differs only in this respect, at least at the outset; or rather, one might assume that no other industry characteristics related to concentration are also systematically related to advertisability. If one assumes further that the amount of advertising done by an industry is a function of only advertisability, one then might reasonably treat advertisability as an exogenous independent variable which is like the prohibition of advertising in conceptual experiment one. The correlations found by Kaldor-Silverman, Telser, and Mann et al. could then be interpreted as measures of the causal effect of advertising on concentration; more about this later.

FIGURE 9–1. ADVERTISING RESPONSE FUNCTIONS

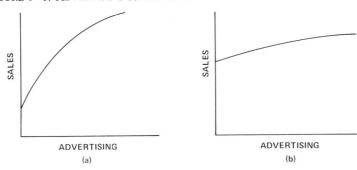

Unfortunately for this line of thought, however, the basic assumption is not met. At least one other variable, capital requirements in the industry, is related to both the amount of advertising and the extent of concentration within industries. Since capital requirements would seem to be quite exogenous, being based on technical-production conditions, it would seem that a line of causality flows from capital requirements to advertising, perhaps through market structure (concentration). (The Kaldor-Silverman data and the theory given in Chapter 4 above fit together to give support to this line of thought.) If so, this sort of test does not well represent either experiment one or experiment two.

So far I have suggested that an observed positive relationship between advertising and concentration should not be interpreted as causal. But one must also consider the meaning of Telser's conclusion of a lack of association between the variables, if his conclusion is correct. This conclusion suggests that industries reach their equilibrium states of advertising and concentration without being determined by the previous advertising history in the industry, as noted before. It also suggests that an equilibrium situation with high concentration need not also have high advertising. But Telser's conclusion does not say anything about what kind of an equilibrium would be reached if advertising were prohibited or were much more costly; his data do not suggest that

such an equilibrium might not contain more (or fewer) firms in industries, on the average. And it certainly is reasonable to think that if one
important element in such an equilibrium is changed, others would be
different too. But we have no evidence as to whether the resulting difference would be in the direction of more or less concentration. So even
if Telser's conclusion is empirically sound it does not suggest that without advertising there would be less (or more) concentration.

Telser also carried out another ingenious sort of test. He examined
the stability over time of brand shares in food products, compared to
the stability in soaps-waxes-polishes, compared to the stability in toiletries and cosmetics. Telser's reasoning was that "If advertising is a
source of monopoly, the more heavily advertised class should also contain the products with the more stable shares." This test also indicated
practically no correlation at all between concentration and the ratio of
advertising to sales.[6] (Such a lack of relationship might flow from either
a lack of underlying relationship or from large measurement and definition error, of course, but as above we shall consider only the logical
aspects of the test.) On the face of it this test certainly suggests that advertising does not cause monopoly. But again we must ask why advertising is low or high in an industry. Capital requirements (or some such
other variable) might be at least a partial cause, directly or indirectly,
and might also be the cause of brand-share stability, especially because
firms are bound to be less willing to vary their output greatly if fixed
production costs are high. So again advertising does not seem to be exogenous, and there does not seem to be a good correspondence between
this test and either experiment we might like to run.

Perhaps Backman's recent book (1967) should be mentioned here.
Backman concluded that the volatility of a brand's market-share behavior does not suggest that advertising reduces competition. But Backman's widely reported conclusion seems to be based only on an impres-
sionistic examination of market-share data.

All the above discussion adds up to the idea that none of the tests yet

[6] Notice, however, that one might interpret Telser's conclusion as implying
a positive relationship between concentration and absolute advertising expenditure per firm, by the following reasoning: *ceteris paribus*, firms will be bigger
where industries are more concentrated, simply because there are fewer to di-
vide up a given volume of business. If the advertising-sales ratio is the same in
concentrated and unconcentrated industries, expenditures per firm must be
higher where concentration is greater. (It would be better to test this empirically, as could be done easily with Comanor and Wilson's data). And if absolute expenditures per firm, like capital requirements, constitute a barrier to
entry in some cases (as will be discussed later), then a causal connection between advertising and market power (profits) is reasonable, not by causing
concentration but by cooperating with it. More about this in the next section.

performed is an adequate measure of the effect of advertising on concentration; none of them is a satisfactory representation of the experiments that one would like to run to measure the causal influence. Nor does it seem likely that good tests will arise soon, because the variable we want to make independent — advertising — is importantly or completely determined endogenously.[7] Case studies, perhaps a survey of existing case studies, might allow satisfactory inferences to be drawn. It is crucial, however, that the sample of case studies cover the whole range of industry, because the effects of advertising on concentration must surely differ from industry to industry. For example, I would guess that if advertising were not possible, concentration in the cigarette industry would be less; but I would also guess that the possibility of advertising does not affect the extent of concentration in automobiles or electric utilities. Nor do I think that the structure of medical practice would change if doctors were allowed to advertise.

The Trend in Absolute Concentration of Advertising Expenditures among Firms

If one cannot determine advertising's role in concentration, then it may be useful to study further the importance of the phenomenon of concentration. If concentration itself were found to be relatively unimportant, or if it were found to be declining, then one would not worry about advertising's effect on concentration. And while at first thought this seems to be heavily worked-over ground, it turns out that the facts about concentration relevant to advertising are not so well known.

As a trial run, let us first work with the usual unit of analysis in the study of concentration, business firms, partly to insure that the method to be used shortly on brands gives results similar to those of other methods.

A positive relationship between advertising and sales is demonstrated both by logic and by the observed stability of the advertising-sales ratio within industries and firms. Therefore, if one observes that advertising is more concentrated in the industry or economy at time $t + 1$ than at time t, it is reasonable to infer that sales are more concentrated at time $t + 1$, or vice versa. Such data would not of themselves

---

[7] One useful test might be to search out products for which advertising is legally prevented in some places but not in others, and then compare the resulting market structures. For example, cigarette advertising is allowed in the United States, banned now in Italy, and partially banned (from television) in England. And dentists in this country may advertise in some states but not in others. Another useful test may become possible when business games are sufficiently realistic so that players can behave like real oligopolists with respect to advertising. One could then examine resulting industry structure and behavior when advertising is prohibited or its price raised sharply in the game.

tell anything about advertising as a cause of concentration; for example, a merger causes an increase in both advertising concentration and sales concentration. But the advertising concentration is of interest as an index of industrial concentration, in the same spirit as sales and asset indices of concentration.

A first sort of relevant data is the proportion of expenditures in each advertising medium, and in all media together, accounted for by perhaps the top advertiser, the top 10 advertisers, the top 50, and the top 100. The published data are voluminous. But unfortunately, the data are also shot through with incomparability. For example, the number of newspapers and magazines included in the samples shifts from year to year. And the cutoff expenditure level below which a firm is excluded varies, sometimes being $10,000, sometimes $30,000. The published total data do not include the same media from year to year, e.g., sometimes including and sometimes excluding radio. I have attempted to develop concentration indices anyway. A rise in advertising concentration is what one would expect if asset and sales concentration has risen, and I have the impression that firm concentration has generally risen since 1948, or at least not decreased, though year-to-year variablity is great. But the data are so bad and potentially so misleading that I do not wish to have them enter the literature.

Concentration within Markets

It has been a difficulty in studies of industrial concentration that "Neither uncorrected-census product or census industry data offer a very good approximation to economic markets" (Mason, 1964, p. 42). An important advantage of advertising-concentration data is that unlike census data on product sales these data do refer to markets that are very well defined. The trade compilers of the advertising statistics categorize brands and firms for the convenience of advertisers who want to keep an eye on what their competitors are doing. Therefore, the brands included in each category are those that the advertisers themselves think should be included in share-of-the market calculations. The category titles indicate the sharpness of definition, e.g., "hair preparations," "frozen foods," "pet foods." And the "auto" categories do not include trucks, as does the SIC category.

A disadvantage of these data, however, is that they cover only consumer goods plus those few producer goods such as business machines that are advertised in consumer magazines. But the likelihood that advertising affects concentration is much less in industrial markets than in consumer markets, because the absolute amount of industrial advertising is relatively small. Therefore this latter limitation of the data is not disabling.

These data will be considered in two ways, first by examination of the numbers of competitors, and then by examination of the concentration of advertising expenditures in the various markets.

1. *Number of competitors.* Excellent data are available on advertising expenditures of all classes of products sold in drugstores.[8] These include both those classes of products sold primarily in drugstores (e.g., vitamins and tonics) as well as products sold in other types of outlets also (e.g., soft drinks, cigarettes). From 1961 to 1965 the number of brands advertised increased in 20 of the primarily-drugstore product classes and decreased in 6 (one tie). For non-primarily-drugstore products, the number of brands increased in 8 product classes and decreased in 1.[9]

Data on number of brands advertised are also available from a series of 1964–65 *Printers' Ink* articles titled "Battle of the Brands." Mostly the data are for *brands* for 1958, 1962, and 1963, but in some markets such as cereals, autos, and insurance, the data refer to *firms*.[10] All the markets covered are particularly advertising-competitive, but these are the very markets in which advertising's role is greatest. The number of brands advertised (more than the cutoff expenditure) increased in six of six markets from 1958 to 1963. (The number of firms, however, increased in two markets, decreased in three, and remained the same in two.)

Comprehensive British advertising data are available since 1935; a commercial compiler, *Statistical Review of Press Advertising*, has done a thorough job and has had fewer media to cover than in the United States. In the 73 markets considered,[11] the number of advertised brands increased in 60 categories and decreased in 10 (three ties) from 1935

[8] Annual compilations appear in *Drug Trade News* from 1955 on. The data for later years are better summarized than in earlier years. However, the categories have been changed from time to time, which accounts for the years chosen for the various comparisons that follow.

[9] The underlying data differ slightly in media included (e.g., outdoor) and lower cutoff point of expenditures, but the biases are trivial.

[10] In some markets the data were unusable because some firms advertise many brands together whereas others advertise brands singly. And all the data include only brands (firms) above such arbitrary cutoffs as $10,000 or $100,000 of advertising. Also, some bias is introduced because the cutoff is dollar-constant over the six years, whereas the price level has risen and total advertising has increased.

[11] Retailers and a few other categories were omitted for such reasons as noncomparability between measurement periods and noncomparability of the product classes over time (e.g., television). The data are for print advertising only, for the January–March quarter in each year.

to 1964. Considering only postwar and post–paper-rationing data, the number of brands increased in 43 categories and decreased in 27 (one tie) from 1958 to 1964.

Taken together, these data on the number of brands advertised suggest an increase in competition and a decrease in concentration.[12] (But note that the firm data do not go in the same direction. Also note that these data do not show that advertising caused the increase in competition.)

2. *Concentration of expenditures.* A more direct approach to studying concentration within markets is to measure changes in concentration of the advertising expenditures:

a) For the drugstore data first (which includes products other than drugs), of the 16 categories that were comparable in 1956 and 1965, the share accounted for by the largest advertiser increased in 6 categories and decreased in 10. For the 29 categories that were comparable from 1959 to 1965 (including the categories used in the 1956 to 1965 test), the share accounted for by the largest advertiser increased in 13 categories and decreased in 16.

b) From 1958 to 1963, top-firm concentration increased in two of the six *Printers' Ink* product classes, and decreased in four.

c) From 1935 to 1964 in Great Britain top-firm concentration increased in 30 categories and decreased in 43.[13]

Taken all together, the United Kingdom and United States data suggest that at the level at which advertising works — the level of the brand, rather than of the firm, because advertising sells brands — concentration is not increasing, and surely it is not increasing faster than is firm concentration measured in assets or sales. This conclusion follows both from the observation that top-firm and top-two-firms advertising concentration is decreasing in a majority of markets, and from the observation of an increasing number of brands that are in the advertising competition.

Two exemplary products offer insights into the relationship of advertising to asset or sales concentration:

i) In the auto industry concentration is very high. Is this because the Big Three's advertising makes it impossible or uneconomic for others to advertise and sell, and hence uneconomic for others to build capacity?

---

[12] Backman (1967, pp. 63–81, esp. p. 68) drew the same conclusion from the numbers of brands sold in various sets of industries.

[13] Concentration decreased in a majority of markets in subperiods 1938–63, 1935–38, 1938–51, 1951–64, and 1955–58, 1958–64. However, it increased in a majority of markets (40 to 32) from 1955–64 despite the opposite result in the two constituent periods 1955–58 and 1958–64. I am inclined to consider this reversal an anomaly and disregard it.

Not so. The number of firms advertising increased from 21 to 25 over 1958–63, and the number of brands from 37 to 52. The Big Three's share of advertising dropped from 88 percent to 84 percent over that period. Particularly interesting is the growth of the foreign-car advertising share; the data for foreign-car manufacturers allow us to examine the effects of advertising competition apart from other possible barriers to entry such as high capital requirements, and they also allow us to consider the marketing decision separate from the production decision. The observed auto-advertising data suggest that the existence of advertising as a business tool does not operate differentially in favor of the Big Three. (This is a kind of survivor test, *à la* Stigler 1958.)

ii) The liquor industry was for a long time a prize example of increasing concentration. The number of distilling firms declined from 144 in 1947 to 88 in 1958 (Wattell, 1954, p. 7), though this trend may have reversed recently (Ferguson, 1965, p. 3). And distilling plants declined continuously from 311 in 1937 to 170 in 1962 (Wattell, 1953, p. 7). But the number of advertised brands has increased, from perhaps 200 to more than 350 over the period 1950–62.[14] This is consistent with the notion that there are concentration-creating economies of scale in production and other facets of the business but the opposite in advertising — or else why would a firm advertise multiple brands of the same type of liquor, as all the big firms do?

In sum, the above evidence on concentration among brands, which is where advertising might have an effect, suggests that concentration is decreasing, or at least is not increasing. This suggests that whether or not advertising has an important role in increasing concentration is itself not too important a question.

B. MARKET POWER CAUSED DIRECTLY BY ADVERTISING OF "ADVERTISABLE" PRODUCTS

All of the previous parts of this chapter, both theoretical and empirical, dealt with the possibility that advertising might cause market power by causing economies of scale (including increasing returns to advertising), the economies of scale in turn causing concentration. That is, we have been concerned with the causal chain

Advertising →Economies of Scale→Concentration→Market power.

In the rest of this chapter we shall be concerned with possibilities in which advertising might lead to market power even if it does not cause concentration. That is, in the third section we will be interested in the

---

[14] In newspapers, 192 advertised brands in 1950, 348 in 1962; in magazines, 165 and 187 in 1950 and 1962 respectively (*Liquor Handbook*, annual).

case in which advertising cooperates with concentration. In this section we will consider the case in which advertising leads to market power even in the absence of concentration. In both of these sections the theory and the empirical work available will be discussed together.

Where there are above-average profits one might reasonably assume that there is market power, unless one has reason to believe that the industry's businessmen are unusually aggressive and efficient. And if one finds that where there are above-average profits there is also an above-average intensity of advertising, one is bound to inquire into the meaning of the relationship between advertising and profits.

And indeed, such a simple relationship has been observed to hold. Comanor and Wilson (1967) found a simple correlation of .42 between the average advertising-sales ratio and the profit rates in their sample of "minor industries" (like three-digit SIC groups), and a correlation of .43 between advertising-per-firm (for the firms accounting for the top 50 percent of the output of each industry) and profit rates. (The correlations between profit rates and the logarithms of the advertising variables were .27 and .50 respectively [p. 430].)

Backman used an entirely different technique. He worked with a sample composed of most of the 125 firms which spent the most for advertising in the United States in 1964 and 1965, and he found correlations of .345 and .315 respectively between the advertising-sales ratio and profit rates (1967, pp. 150–151).

The methods of both Comanor-Wilson and Backman have their drawbacks, of course. In both methods the denominator in the profit-rate computation is invested capital, which (as Backman notes) is very sensitive to accounting policies. And the limiting of Backman's sample to the largest advertisers would seem to make his sample much more homogeneous with respect to the advertising-sales ratio than the entire universe of American firms, which would seem to bias his observed correlation coefficient downward. That the same sort of finding nevertheless emerges from these two very different studies strengthens the finding.

Now we must ask whether a greater intensity of advertising [15] causes a higher rate of profit; unless it does so we are not really very interested in the observed relationship. Another part of the work by Comanor and Wilson bears upon this question. They regressed profit rates upon sev-

---

[15] Here as elsewhere in the book I am satisfied to let total dollars spent for advertising be a basic measure of advertising intensity, rather than number of messages or some other physical or psychological measurement. (For an opposite view see Telser [1964, section IV].) I am much less happy with the advertising-sales ratio as a measure of advertising intensity, for reasons given in Appendix B.

eral other relevant variables (including capital requirements, growth of demand, concentration, and economies of scale), as well as on the advertising-sales ratio and advertising per firm. And from their entire series of multiple regressions they concluded that advertising really does play a causal role: "On the basis of these empirical findings, it is evident that for industries where products are differentiable, investment in advertising is a highly profitable activity. Industries with high advertising outlays earn, on average, at a profit rate which exceeds that of other industries by nearly four percentage points" (p. 437).

I am less convinced about this causal relationship than are Comanor and Wilson, however. First of all, a crucial clause in their conclusion, "where products are differentiable," is without meaning, as argued in Appendix A.[16] Second, as Comanor and Wilson note, there is collinearity (in the expected directions) between the advertising-sales ratio and the other important independent ("structural") variables — with the log of economies of scale, 0.27; with the log of capital requirements, 0.21; and with the log of growth of demand. 0.40 (p. 433, fn.). If their measure of the importance of the variables (the t ratio; the standardized regression coefficients might also have been very informative but are not given) appeared to be invariably higher for advertising than for the other variables, one might nevertheless be satisfied on statistical grounds that advertising really is causal. But this is not so; in at least some of their regressions another variable has a much higher t ratio (e.g., log of capital requirements, equation 1, table 9, p. 436 in the Comanor and Wilson article).

Just as one must resort to empirical data when theory speaks in conflicting voices, one is forced back on to theory (or at least onto a priori speculation) when the empirical data do not provide a clear answer. In this case one is forced to speculate about the roots of above-average profits. In the present context it seems to me that above-average profits arise from either (1) monopoly power and barriers to entry at a point in time (excluding advertising as a barrier to entry); or (2) being ahead of the competition technologically or promotionally.[17] The role of advertising is different in these two cases. In the latter case, as we have seen earlier in Chapter 2, advertising is higher when products are new than after their introduction and early growth in demand; this is

[16] What Comanor and Wilson may intend is simply to compare industries with firm demand curves that are elastic with those where they are unelastic, a notion identical to their "advertisable" notion mentioned earlier in this chapter. But even this interpretation does not strengthen their sentence.

[17] Bain (1959, pp. 374–376) also mentions risk and windfall increase in demand (p. 374) as sources of above-average profits, but both of these tend to be short-run and random, and are therefore not relevant here.

consistent with the simple correlation of 0.40 between growth of demand and the advertising-sales ratio found by Comanor-Wilson (p. 433, fn.). (Windfall increases in demand may also be part of this relationship.) This role of advertising is outside our definition of market power and is certainly not socially undesirable.

Earlier in this chapter it was noted that one possible way advertising could cause higher profit without causing concentration (and even without assuming that the industry is already concentrated) is if some products are more "advertisable" than others. This seems to be the line of reasoning of Comanor and Wilson. They identify advertisability with "product differentiation," but for reasons given in Appendix A I find that meaningless. And if advertisability is as defined earlier in the chapter (i.e., an elastic advertising-response function) then there would have to be increasing returns in advertising to prevent new entrants from coming in. But Chapter 1 argues that there is no reason to believe that such increasing returns exist, assuming no structural differences (an appropriate assumption if the industry is not concentrated for other reasons, and if there are no other barriers to entry). Furthermore, one would expect firms to enter industries where profits are above average, and to thereby reduce them to normal profits. There seems to be nothing in the mere fact of advertising being important in an industry that prevents such a movement. For example, products sold only by mail order are certainly among the most "advertisable" of products, and advertising is of the highest importance to sellers in such markets. But there are plenty of new entries, strong competition, and no evidence of higher-than-normal profits in mail-order industries. So "advertisability" by itself does not seem to explain any of the relationship between advertising and profits.

C. MARKET POWER CAUSED BY ADVERTISING IN COOPERATION WITH CONCENTRATION

Now we must consider a third possibility, that high advertising in conjunction with concentration and monopoly power (caused by other forces) results in above-average profits.[18] One important subclass is that of industries with high capital requirements which discourage large numbers of potential competitors.[19] We notice first that the simple cor-

[18] This does not assume that where there is high concentration there is also high advertising; that may or may not be the case, as discussed in the first section (though none of the data there refers to the question of the relationship between concentration and high absolute advertising expenditures).

[19] One may argue that *no* capital requirement for physical capital or advertising capital is a strong barrier, on the grounds that capital may be borrowed, and existing firms in other industries have liquid assets to invest. But anyone

relation coefficient of capital requirements with profit rates is as high or higher (in both natural units and logs) than the correlation of profit rates with any of the other structural variables, including advertising (Comanor and Wilson, 1967, p. 430). And clearly this correlation is not due to collinearity with another variable, because capital requirements are determined exogenously by technological factors. (This statement is consistent with the significant coefficient for capital requirements in almost every one of the Comanor-Wilson regressions). However, even if an industry's high profits come from monopoly power (e.g., from capital requirements), advertising could still be involved in the mechanism. It might be that oligopolists wish to compete for larger shares of the pie but recognize that price competition is less desirable to them than advertising competition (e.g., the cigarette industry). If so, the opportunity to advertise might result in higher profits than if it were not possible to advertise. If this is really the case in an industry, one may choose to say that it is advertising that causes the higher profits, or one can say that it is the monopoly power that causes the higher profits. But there are also other reasons why firms with high capital requirements do relatively much advertising. First, they are absolutely large firms; absolutely large advertising expenditures are therefore to be expected on the most naive of grounds. Furthermore, as Chapter 3 suggested, larger fixed costs cause higher advertising because of the lower marginal cost of incremental units of product when production is below capacity. And it is very clear that advertising for either of these latter reasons cannot sensibly be regarded as a cause of market power and above-average profits.

Another sort of market structure in which advertising and concentration may be found together is that where retailers stock a limited number of brands. In such cases there is indeed a very real advertising-expenditure threshold for the potential manufacturer-entrant; he must advertise enough to displace one of the existing brands or he will make no sales at all. In turn, the smallest brands must advertise enough to be sure to keep their places. This in turn may trigger strong advertising competition among all the existing brands.

The above two examples of market structures where high advertising may be found in conjunction with concentration and high profits [20] are

who has considered going into business for himself knows introspectively that the likelihood of his entry into an industry is affected by the amount of initial investment he thinks he needs. Those who have been in on the investment decisions of large companies know that the same is true there.

[20] Comanor and Wilson's positive finding for the effect on profits of "advertising requirements" (in addition to the effects of concentration, capital requirements, and the advertising ratio) offers statistical support for advertising as a barrier to entry.

not intended to be exhaustive. There are certainly others, including the situation where production economies of scale lead to fewness of firms. In all these cases, however, one cannot say a priori whether profits would be higher or lower if advertising were prohibited or taxed. In cases such as that of limited store distribution, the entrenched competitors might be more sheltered from competition and hence make even higher profits if advertising were prohibited. In other cases firms might turn to price competition if they could not advertise. Without an experiment that actually separates the effect of concentration from the effect of the advertising that may (or may not) accompany it, one just cannot tell what would happen in the aggregate. I think that close case study of a particular industry might make such a judgment possible, but it is not unlikely that the judgment would be very different for different industries.

It should also be noted that, as is the case whenever the changes in a situation are structural, it is difficult to forecast the welfare effect of the final outcome. For example, I would guess that if advertising for cigarettes or cake mixes were abolished, it would then be easier for a new brand to challenge existing brands by means of low prices, a situation which would be good for the consumer. A related reaction would probably be a rise in private-label sales, which at first also seems to benefit the consumer. But a further effect might be a disadvantaging of small stores because of the relatively high fixed cost of private labels. (This further effect also would have made it more difficult for "discount" stores, which were based on selling only branded merchandise, to rise after World War II.) Once more one can trace these structural changes with confidence only if one studies the nature of a particular industry; comparative statics here breaks down completely as does aggregate statistical analysis.

There is no way of telling for sure whether the above categories account for all the observed relationship between advertising and profit rates. It might also be that industries where promotion is important are especially hospitable to above-average managerial competence; but if this is so it is not market power that causes the above-average profits. The same is true of the category "growth in demand" which Comanor and Wilson show to have a strong relationship to profit rates (only .17 in natural units, but .42 in the logarithm [1967, p. 430]).

SUMMARY AND CONCLUSIONS

It is doubtful that advertising causes concentration, in the sense of there being more concentration than if firms could not advertise. The main warrant for this conclusion is theoretical; most important is that such a causal process requires increasing returns in advertising, which do not seem to exist in fact.

The empirical data, and the interpretations of them, conflict about whether or not there is even a correlation between advertising and concentration. And in any case the existing data are not well suited to a test of causality from advertising to concentration because it is not very reasonable to think of advertising as exogenous. A sample of case studies might help us draw a sound conclusion. But the crucial experiment that would really give a satisfactory answer is not feasible.

The combination of advertising (measured both as a ratio of advertising to sales, and as an absolute amount per firm), and concentration stemming from heavy capital requirements or limited places in the distribution channels, produces above-average profits.

The available data give absolutely no clue as to whether, if advertising were prohibited or made more costly, there would be more or less concentration in the aggregate, higher or lower profits for firms in concentrated industries, or more or less market power. Every sort of effect would probably appear in some industry. The aggregate effect can probably only be learned from the accumulated findings of a wide range of industry studies.

The largest advertisers may be increasing their share of all advertising; i.e., concentration in advertising may be increasing at the firm level. But even if this is so it may well be the result of mergers and acquisitions. And at the level of aggregation at which advertising exerts its force — the brand rather than the firm — there is apparently a decrease in the biggest brands' shares of total advertising in a majority of product classes, as well as an increase in the number of competitors who advertise. This should reduce worry about the possible effect of advertising on market power.

10

**Cigarette Advertising
and the
Nation's Welfare:
A Case Study
in Welfare Economics**

This chapter was originally written as an article in 1964, in the midst of
Federal Trade Commission debates about whether cigarette companies
should be required to post a "danger to health" warning on packs of
cigarettes and in advertisements. Those hearings were an outgrowth of
the Surgeon General's report on the health hazards of cigarette smoking
(*Smoking and Health*, 1964). A lot of political words have been spo-
ken since then, and a law requiring a warning on the pack has gone into
effect. But the situation with respect to cigarette advertising has not
changed radically up until now (1969). Therefore I have not thought it
necessary or sensible to update the material, but rather to leave it much
as it appeared then except for a small amount of newer data.

Many individuals and groups favor a warning requirement. Some
want cigarette advertising prohibited completely. However, no responsible person has suggested outlawing the manufacture or sale of cigarettes themselves, mostly because of the sorts of dangers that arose during liquor prohibition in the 1920s.

People who oppose the warning and the ban on advertising base their
opposition on grounds of legality as well as of economics. This chapter
considers only the economics of a warning requirement or a ban. It
does not consider other economic alternatives such as an increase in
cigarette taxes. (In the latter connection see Lyon and Simon, 1968.)
The chapter discusses the possible effects on cigarette use, and the consequent economic impacts, of these two proposals on the groups within
the economy and society that have a stake in what happens. Mostly it
refers to the abolition of all cigarette advertising, rather than the effect

of a warning, because the effect of advertising abolition is better understood. The effect of a warning requirement would probably be much less than that of an advertising ban, but of the same general nature.

Effect on Cigarette-Consumption Rate

Opponents of a warning or ban say that forbidding cigarette advertising, or requiring a danger warning, would have "practically no effect" on consumption. Supporters argue, however, that advertising has a "substantial" effect in influencing people to start smoking, and in keeping them smoking. Where is the truth?

It is perfectly clear that advertising has the power to influence the purchase of particular brands of cigarettes; the $200 million [1] spent annually for cigarette advertising as of 1963 (perhaps $260 million in 1967) is positive proof of that. But we are not interested in the power of advertising to shift smokers from one brand to another. We want to know how cigarette advertising as a whole starts people smoking or keeps them smoking.

Borden (1942) examined the role of cigarette advertising in the astounding growth of cigarette smoking starting about 1900, when the annual consumption of cigarettes per person over the age of 15 was 49. By 1962 the yearly rate had risen to 3,598 cigarettes per capita (U.S., F.T.C., Bureau of Economics, n.d., p. 3; 4,280 cigarettes per person over the age of 18 in 1967: *Statistical Abstract*, 1968, p. 737). Borden did not say that advertising caused the rise in cigarette consumption. He argued that if the public had not been ready to take up cigarette smoking, advertising could never have caused such a large increase in consumption. Nevertheless, Borden concluded that advertising was an important factor in the size and speed of increase in cigarette smoking.

Basmann (1955) studied the rise and fall in cigarette advertising from year to year in the United States, and its apparent effect on cigarette consumption, using sophisticated regression techniques. He found

---

[1] Almost all of the statistics mentioned in the chapter apply to the year 1963. Some of the estimates are extrapolations because only earlier data were available when the paper was written in 1964. Other estimates are my own compromise judgments resulting from several conflicting estimates. In many cases all the sources for the estimates of cigarette advertising will not be cited individually because there were so many of them and because the available data were extrapolated and adjusted by the author. Sources from which data were taken include various issues of *Broadcasting, Advertising Age, Printers' Ink*, and the *Statistical Abstract*. In many places I have cited only the source of the raw data which I then fiddled with. In the case of the footnoted estimates above, the most important sources are estimates in *Advertising Age* (August 31, 1964, pp. 36–37) of $252 million and $207 million for the expenditures in total and in measured media, respectively, of the six biggest cigarette manufacturers.

that for each 1 percent change in total cigarette advertising, the number of cigarettes smoked changed 1/20 of 1 percent. In an earlier study Schoenberg (1933) arrived at a similar estimate, between 1/20 and 1/12 of 1 percent. In other words, the consumption of cigarettes is affected by the amount of advertising, but it takes a big change in the amount of advertising to make much of a difference in consumption. This is typical of an industry once it has become well established, but it may also result from the degree to which the smoking habit takes hold of people and the fact that nothing else is a good substitute for smoking.

What would happen if all cigarette advertising were cut off? An extension of the Schoenberg-Basmann finding (using Basmann's estimate) suggests that if there had been no cigarette advertising in any past year, consumption would have been about 5 percent less than it was. If the ban on advertising continued, one might expect further decrease in the amount of consumption each year, but the absolute decrease would be less each year. These predictions are subject to many technical reservations, and they go far beyond the data. But they are the best that one can do at this time.

A required danger warning in the advertisements would be a type of negative advertising.[2] One cannot estimate how much the warning would cut smoking, but certainly the effect would not be as drastic as a ban on advertising, or else no firm would continue to advertise. Our inability to come up with any better prediction is testimony to how little scientific knowledge we have about the effect of different forms of advertising copy. But it should certainly be possible to pretest advertisements that contain warnings, just as other advertisements are pretested, in order to obtain an estimate of the effect of a warning.

Effect on Life Expectancy

Now let us estimate the health effect of an advertising ban and its resulting reduction in cigarette consumption.

1. People who are kept from starting to smoke will live, on the average, four to five years longer than if they had started smoking. For each cigarette smoked, someone's life is shortened by five to nine minutes. We shall figure seven minutes per cigarette (Simon, 1968a; 1968b).

---

[2] By now we seem to have solid evidence that negative advertising can reduce smoking: ". . . a mounting barrage of negative publicity . . . has been taking its toll. This year [1968], for the first time since 1964, producers sold fewer smokes than they did the year before . . . a decline in the total number of smokers and a decrease in consumption per capita, plus signs that fewer young people are taking up the habit. . . . One of the strongest influences in the antismoking campaign is the profusion of new TV spots by health groups" (*Business Week*, December 21, 1968, pp. 68–70).

This assumes that all of the relationship between smoking and life expectancy is causal.

2. About 500 billion cigarettes were smoked in 1963 (U.S., F.T.C., Bureau of Economics, n.d., p. 3; 527 billion in 1967: *Business Week*, Dec. 21, 1968, p. 69). A decrease of 5 percent in consumption for just one year would therefore mean an increase of human life in the United States of about 180 billion minutes, or 340,000 years of life. Remember, this is the amount of lifetime increased by a decrease of 5 percent in smoking for just one year.

Effect on Employment and Local Economies

An estimated 225,000 people make a substantial part of their living in tobacco agriculture (*Statistical Abstract*, 1963, p. 617). Cash receipts were $1.3 billion (Bureau of Economics, n.d., p. 13), providing earnings of approximately $600 million last year (ibid, p. 634), of which about $450 million came from cigarettes (USDA, 1963, p. 112). Some 31,000 factory workers earned $150 million from cigarette manufacture in 1963 (*Statistical Abstract*, 1963; estimates jibe closely with those of Hill and Knowlton, 1964, and are much the same for 1967). In total, then, cigarette purchases put about $600 million into the pockets of workers and farmers. How would a ban or a warning affect them?

A drop in consumption would have no immediate effect on farm earnings, because of the government subsidy program. Unless the government removed the subsidy, the taxpayers at large rather than the farm population would take the loss. But assume that the subsidy were cut. If so, the effect of a loss in earnings would probably be worse than the figures show, because the effect would be concentrated in a few states that are already economically backward. Many tobacco farmers are already poor and would find it hard to find new jobs. For example, North Carolina is an agricultural state and almost half of its farm income comes from tobacco.

Using the estimates above, employment and earnings would be cut by 5 percent *at most* during the first year of an advertising ban. In subsequent years, the further cut in jobs and/or dollars would be less. I say "5 percent at most" because there is good reason to believe that an important proportion of smokers who quit smoking cigarettes, or young people who never start, would use other forms of tobacco instead. Table 10-1 shows that cigarettes largely replaced other forms of tobacco and did not create much new demand for tobacco. To the extent that smokers switch to pipe tobacco, cigars, chewing tobacco, and snuff, the damage to tobacco farming would be reduced, even though cigarette tobacco is a more expensive product than other types of tobacco.

Furthermore, some or many tobacco workers who are thrown out of work would get other jobs, so one overestimates greatly when one assumes that the equivalent of lost cigarette-industry wages would be lost to the economy as a whole. But the worst (or close to it) is assumed for the sake of argument. Later we shall look at the potential effects on employment again, when the overall picture is considered.

Table 10-1. Consumption of Tobacco Products, Selected Years, 1900 to 1960 (Per person Aged 15 years and Over in the United States)

Year	All tobacco (pounds)	Cigarettes (number)	Cigars (number)	Pipe tobacco (pounds)	Chewing tobacco (pounds)	Snuff (pounds)
1900	7.42	49	111	1.63	4.10	0.32
1910	8.59	138	113	2.58	3.99	.50
1920	8.66	611	117	1.96	3.06	.50
1930	8.88	1,365	72	1.87	1.90	.46
1940	8.91	1,828	56	2.05	1.00	.38
1950	11.59	3,322	50	.94	.78	.36
1960	10.97	3,888	57	.59	.51	.29

Source: U.S. Department of Agriculture, Economic Research Service, as shown in *Smoking and Health*, 1964, p. 45.

Effect on Cigarette Companies

To understand the effect of a ban or a warning requirement on the cigarette companies, one must first understand the nature of advertising as a business investment. When a firm spends a dollar in advertising a brand of cigarettes this year, the advertising bought with that dollar increases cigarette sales this year. But it also increases cigarette sales next year, and the year after, and in subsequent years. Customers get into the habit of buying a given brand, a habit that may continue for many years. To say it another way, a dollar of advertising may create some good will or brand loyalty that persists long into the future, though each year the effect of that single dollar of advertising is less than the year before. Cigarette advertising is really an investment, just like an investment in a new machine that will produce for many years after it is bought. (Fuller statements of the "distributed-lag" property of advertising may be found in Jastram, 1955; Telser, 1962b; and Palda, 1964.)

Telser studied the pre–World War II cigarette market in considerable detail (1962). He found that only 15 to 20 percent of the advertising investment is used up in the year in which the advertisements appear. This means that for each $1 of sales created in the advertising year, much more than $3 of sales will be created in subsequent years. (However, because of the chaos in the postwar cigarette market, investment is probably used up faster now than Telser's estimate.)

Therefore, even if all cigarette advertising were stopped tomorrow, the established cigarette brands would continue to sell well for many years, though at continually diminishing rates. During that time the cigarette companies would be recouping the investments they had already made. Furthermore, since all the firms would have to stop advertising, the investments already made would not be used up as fast, a situation which would give the cigarette companies a better return on their invested dollars than they expected to earn when they made the investments.

The total effect, then, would be that in future years the sales of any brand would gradually decrease. But the gross profits from a brand would be at a very high rate for a while, because the firm would not be making any further investment in advertising. The cigarette companies would have a fine opportunity to "milk" their brands for profit.

The cigarette companies already know how to milk a brand after they cease advertising it. For example, substantial quantities of non-filter Old Golds have been sold in the last couple of years despite the fact that Lorillard has practically stopped advertising them.

If advertising were stopped, the cigarette companies would generate large amounts of cash each year, which they could either liquidate to stockholders or use to diversify. The former is not likely because of our tax structure and because no executive likes to liquidate himself out of a job. In the latter case (a process which had already begun in earnest by 1969), much of the capital would go to create new jobs in other industries.

Either way, I would guess that a cigarette stock would have a very solid value if advertising were banned. The same type of predictions would apply to a warning, but the effects would not be as sweeping.

Effect on Advertising Media [3]

As of 1964, the advertising media had already been hit by the Surgeon General's report. Some radio and television stations voluntarily restricted cigarette advertising to certain hours of the day, while others cut it off completely. Some magazines and papers have always refused to accept tobacco advertising, notably the *Reader's Digest*. And the cigarette advertisers set up an authority to regulate copy and media.

[3] Estimates in this section are from data contained in the *Statistical Abstract* 1963, p. 847; 1968, pp. 783–785, and *The World of Advertising* (Chicago: Advertising Age, January 15, 1963, p. 29). One may make rough estimates for 1967 by multiplying each 1963 figure by 1.5.

A warning requirement would not hit the media as hard as a ban, of course. But a warning that really affected consumption would make advertising less profitable for the cigarette firms, and the firms would therefore advertise less.

Television would lose more than $120 million in advertising revenue ($220 million in 1967), about 7 percent of its total revenue in 1963. But that would not represent a dead loss to television stations and networks. Television time is limited, especially on networks, and the available time is therefore rationed among potential advertisers. If cigarette advertising were banned, the television time could be sold to other advertisers, though at a somewhat lower price.

Television stations are charged with the public interest to a greater extent than are other communications media, because they are given a free franchise for a channel. This franchise gives them some monopoly power. Therefore, the television people should be particularly slow to complain about the loss of cigarette advertising revenue if it is in the public interest.

Radio would lose an estimated $20 million in cigarette-advertising revenue as of 1963. Other advertisers would not replace this revenue, because unlike television there are never more advertisers who wish to buy time than there is time available at current rates. But radio stations also have a franchise granted free by the public.

The $34 million loss (very slightly more in 1967) to general and farm magazines would be a complete loss, about 7 percent of their total revenue, and costs remain almost the same no matter how much advertising they carry, which makes the loss even more serious. The magazines would not find other advertisers to replace cigarettes, and some magazines would feel a considerable strain. But since it would hit them all, they could all be expected to reduce their editorial cost somewhat, without fear of losing advertisers or circulation to competition. This might cushion the impact somewhat.

The $18 million lost to newspapers (less in 1967) would be only 1/2 of 1 percent of their advertising revenue.

Effect on Advertising Agencies

The advertising-agency business would take a beating if cigarette advertising were banned. Agencies would also be hurt if a warning in the advertisements were required, because in that case total cigarette advertising would decrease. Madison Avenue–type agencies would lose approximately $200 million billing ($266 billion in 1967; *Advertising Age*, June 17, 1968, p. 8) of their total of perhaps $4 billion (more in

1967), about 5 percent of their total.[4] (Actually, only 15 percent of the $200 million — $30 million — stays with the agencies. The rest goes to the media.) Perhaps a thousand copywriters, account executives, and other agency people would be scurrying about looking for jobs, and the job market for advertising men would be glutted for a while.

It is interesting to note that after the Surgeon General's report came out, some major advertising agencies said that they would refuse to handle cigarette advertising because they considered it immoral. None of those agencies had a cigarette account at the time. Their statements do mean something, nevertheless.

Effect on the Economy as a Whole

The total cigarette market was about $6.8 billion in 1963 (*Advertising Age*, August 30, 1965, p. 259), and $8.9 billion in 1967 (*Business Week*, April 28, 1969, p. 82). Excluding taxes, the industry accounts for $3.6 billion ($5.2 billion in 1967), much less than 1 percent of the Gross National Product.

In the long run Americans tend to spend a fairly constant percentage of their total yearly income, year after year. This suggests that a decrease in cigarette sales would lead to a compensating increase in other spending. If so, the effect on the economy as a whole would be lessened. Exactly how much the first impact would be, we cannot say. It would be somewhere between no effect and $180 million (i.e., 5 percent of $3.6 billion).

On the other side of the ledger, the "multiplier effect" would magnify the ill effects of whatever decrease in spending does take place, by a factor of two or three. This effect is due to the spending of money again and again by people in the business chain. In other words, if people saved half of the $180 million drop in cigarette sales, the drop in national income would then be between $180 million and $270 million.

1. The effect on the advertising media will not be profound. There should be no effect on television programming, and slight effect on the station stockholders. Newspapers will not be affected much. Some magazines and radio stations might be hurt painfully, but they are not likely to be forced out of business.

2. The economy's progress and overall vitality would hardly be affected. There would be a disturbance in tax revenues at federal, state, and municipal levels, but it would cost no more in the long run to levy other taxes.

3. A clutch of advertising agencies would be hit hard. But the over-

---

[4] Estimates by the author for 1963 based on yearly *Advertising Age* statistics on total big-agency billing, and earlier-cited estimates of cigarette advertising.

all magnitude of the effect would be infinitesimal — maybe a thousand jobs and about $33 million net revenue lost.

In sum, then, we must balance the expected effect on health against the expected effect on employment and earnings.

4. The above estimate of the decrease in consumption was in terms of number of cigarettes, and not in number of smokers. We have no idea whether a 5 percent decrease in cigarette consumption would mean 5 percent fewer smokers or 10 percent fewer smokers or zero percent fewer smokers. We predict only that the number of cigarettes smoked will decrease by 5 percent.

5. Using the data from the Surgeon General's report, we estimated that for each cigarette smoked, someone's life expectancy is decreased by seven minutes. Putting together the previous estimates, one can say that it takes a reduction of 880 cigarettes to produce a drop of $1 in a tobacco-worker's earnings. And a drop of that many cigarettes means that someone's life expectancy goes up by 880 x 7 minutes = 104 hours. The drop in both consumption and earnings would be less in subsequent years. But they would stay in step with each other, so the same type of dollars-for-hours-of-life relationship would hold.

In any case, a small yearly decrease in cigarette sales and cigarette advertising, made even smaller by a shift to other forms of tobacco, would not be even a drop in the bucket for the economy as a whole. (The aforegoing discussion is best read in the light of Chapter 8.)

Cigarette smoking affects the federal economy and the economies of the states and some cities, too, by way of taxes paid on cigarettes. Federal excise taxes amount to $2 billion, state taxes are above $1 billion, and municipal taxes are $40 million (Bureau of Economics, n.d., p. 12; *Statistical Abstract*, 1963; *Statistical Abstract*, 1968, p. 409). These taxes are important to the tax-collecting bodies. But at first the loss would be 5 percent of taxes that represent 2 percent of total government revenues. Furthermore, if taxes are not collected one way they can be collected another way, at the same total cost to the public.

On the other hand, cigarettes may cost the economy far more than they contribute. Louis Dublin estimated that cigarettes cost the nation $10 billion annually in lost services and earnings of men killed prematurely by cigarettes (personal correspondence). My own estimate is a loss of more than $3.6 billion, based on a year of life lost by the average smoker before the age of 65 (Simon, 1963, p. 117), half of the men in the United States being smokers, and an annual payroll of $322 million. Furthermore, deaths caused by smoking decrease consumption spending. In the hundred or so hours lost by each dollar of cigarette-industry earnings, a live person would spend more than $20. This consumption spending may be important to the economy.[5] (Harry Skornia pointed out to me that fire losses due to cigarette smoking must be very large — including burned buildings and furniture, and forests.)

AN OVERVIEW

One must balance the expected effects on health against the expected effects on employment and earnings. These are the relevant considerations, as I see them:

When one considers the $4 billion to $10 billion in earnings lost each year by men killed prematurely by cigarettes, it is clear that the country will gain more in live men's earning power than it will lose in direct revenue. And the gain in earning power for people kept alive by not smoking would be 10 to 20 times the loss in earning power of tobacco-industry workers.

This, then, is the decision that will eventually be made, if the above assumptions are correct. Should the nation decrease employment temporarily to gain perhaps a hundred hours of life per dollar of earnings lost? Should the nation reduce tobacco-industry revenue, gaining $2 in earnings from live men for each $1 decrease in tobacco-industry reve-

---

[5] A. James Heins chided me for mentioning only the benefits of people living longer and not mentioning that if people live longer beyond the time they stop working they consume what otherwise would be consumed by others. To get a rounded answer about the net effect on the economy of reduced cigarette consumption and increased life expectancy one would need to construct a complete model of the economy and run it with two sets of parameters, one set appropriate for continued cigarette consumption and the other for reduced consumption. Crucial inputs would include the extent to which men (who are more important in production than women) die relatively earlier than women on account of smoking; the amount of work people do after the nominal retirement age; the amount that older people spend for consumption; the amount of social services they use; what would happen to their savings if they did not consume them before dying; and the amount of time people lose from work before 65 because they are sick from smoking-induced diseases. Furthermore the answer must depend greatly on whether one assumes an economy with full employment or less than full employment.

Perhaps most important is to recognize that for the most part the community as a whole has little if anything to gain by any given old person, even if totally unproductive, dying earlier than otherwise. The gain would only be to the immediate family, which would either gain an inheritance or cease to support the old person. Therefore the issue comes down to whether one would prefer that one's own mother and father die earlier or later. If most people prefer the utility of their parents living longer to the utility of the money they would differentially have if their parents died earlier, then one cannot say that the community has anything to lose by people living longer — and on the other side, there are surely gains to the community as a whole from people living longer as a result of not smoking.

nue, and also gaining $10 to $20 in earnings of men kept alive for each dollar of a tobacco-worker's earnings lost?

There are two technical postscripts to the discussion. First, the statistics in this chapter are rough and ready. Some of them, such as estimates of effects of an advertising ban on consumption and life expectancy, could be off so much as to be half or double the real figures, though most of them are fairly accurate. However, the argument would be exactly the same in any case, because it is the general magnitude of the estimates that will affect the conclusion. Does it matter much whether it is 100 hours or 50 hours or 200 hours that are being traded for $1 in earnings? I think not. Perhaps it would make no difference even if it were only one hour per dollar, and the data could not possibly be that far off.

Second, if a nation wishes to decrease cigarette consumption, raising the tax on cigarettes is an obvious alternative or additional measure that might be taken. Fewer cigarettes will be bought if the price is higher (cf. Lyon and Simon, 1968, and references therein). However, if the price of cigarettes goes up, people will smoke the butts closer to the end, and the more of a cigarette that is smoked, the more dangerous it rapidly becomes. So an increase in taxation may not be a good alternative solution.

And now a personal postscript, which many will feel has no place in a scientific work. Up until now, I have been speaking as an economist with some special knowledge of advertising. Now I would like to say a couple of things as a layman who has no special knowledge of morals or values. These are one man's opinions:

1. Some people say, "If you advocate a ban on advertising, wouldn't it be consistent to advocate a prohibition on cigarettes?" Others say, in the same vein, "It is an American principle that if a product is acceptable for sale, it is acceptable for advertising."

I reject both the logic and the Americanism of these two positions. I think it is most American, and most logical, to treat each proposal pragmatically on its own merits, without being hamstrung by precedent. My personal chain of reasoning goes like this: (*a*) advertising can be banned without prohibiting smoking; (*b*) a ban on advertising will bring about no boomerang noneconomic ill-effects; (*c*) a prohibition of cigarette sales could have harsh repercussions, as with the prohibition of alcohol in the Twenties, and therefore is not sound policy; (*d*) there are other commodities (e.g., contraceptives, medical services, liquor on radio and television, stocks and bonds, and many others) that are sold but cannot be advertised freely, so this would be no new precedent; and (*e*) therefore, let's ban cigarette advertising.

2. I am distressed at the venality, duplicity, and general lack of morals of those who testify in government hearings against the cigarette-advertising ban or a warning requirement. Since the authoritative Surgeon General's report was issued, those who testify can hardly fail to know that smoking kills people. Perhaps they have managed to lie to themselves until they have come to believe that cigarettes really are not harmful. Perhaps they are merely men of zero integrity. Perhaps they themselves are only going through the motions and hope they lose their battle, in which case they are guilty of terrible hypocrisy. Perhaps — the most hopeful possibility — they really see themselves as advocates, so caught up in the "game" that they have forgotten that human lives are at stake.

3. I think that the decision to cut out cigarette advertising is astonishingly clear-cut. There is much to gain, little to lose by stopping the advertising of cigarettes.

11

A Disaggregated Appraisal of Advertising in Society[1]

This concluding chapter takes a broad view of the social and economic effects of advertising, drawing upon the material in the previous chapters though not summing it up. The chapter's purpose is primarily to appraise the economic effects of advertising in the various parts of the economy in which advertising is important. Therefore the first step must be to draw boundary lines to mark off homogeneous sectors of the economy within which advertising's effects are not likely to be both positive and negative on particular dimensions of evaluation.

Though the appraisal is primarily economic, this chapter will also venture occasionally into the muddy waters of social appraisal. I do so because a total judgment of the welfare effect of advertising in a particular sector surely demands examination of the balances and trade-offs of economic and noneconomic pluses and minuses. However, I shall attempt to offer only those social evaluations of a particular sector of advertising that are either documented or are not very arguable (e.g., that laxative advertising on television is usually not pleasant), or I shall indicate the chief point at issue (e.g., whether or not auto advertising has a deleterious effect on many people by making them more materialistic). In either case I shall try to avoid rendering arguable social evaluations.

Let us begin by listing the major positive and negative effects that a given sector's advertising might have. These are the positive effects that have been claimed for some or all advertising: (1) lowers prices; (2)

[1] The literature appraising advertising's effects is enormous. To name only a few of the widest-ranging pieces: Vaile (1927), Moriarty (1923), Borden (1942), Kaldor (1950), Telser (1968), Preston (1968).

provides product information for efficient consumer choice and for efficient business operation; (3) supports communication media; (4) disperses economic power by aiding aggressive competitors; (5) increases consumption, with consequent benefit to the economy; (6) increases enjoyment of life by increasing people's wants; [2] (7) substitutes for coercion as a method of social control, and hence supports pluralistic society.

These are the negative effects that have been attributed to some or all advertising: (1) raises prices; (2) obfuscates consumer choice by misinforming; (3) concentrates economic power in a few hands by reducing competition; (4) wastes economic resources; (5) accentuates the business cycle; (6) induces harmful or foolish purchases; (7) offends taste; (8) corrupts character and warps personal values; (9) tells lies, makes false promises, and in general cheats.

Succeeding sections examine how each of these positive and negative effects applies to each industry and trade channel, though in each case only those issues will be mentioned that seem important.

The reason for the disaggregated approach taken in this chapter is that one can easily arrive at wrong conclusions if one evaluates all types of advertising together. This is because most of advertising's effects, e.g., the effects of advertising on prices and on output, can go in either direction, and in fact opposite effects may be found in different sectors.[3]

[2] Knight emphasizes that it is too few wants rather than too many that impoverishes the spirit (1936). See also Taplin (1960, Chapter 1) on this general subject. But Rottenberg emphasized the complexity of this issue:

"Any public policy which is calculated to sharpen the aspirations of backward peoples for goods, to make income-earning a more powerful lever, to introduce the competitive spirit, and to make them over in our puritan image, so that they, too, will look upon the leisurely as social pariahs, is fraught with danger. The backward peoples may very well be socially more stable as they are. To make a revolution among them, destroying value-systems which are ancient and rooted, may do enormous harm. But this is the risk to be run and, possibly, the price to be paid for economic development. In the backward areas, now, people live badly; they are malnourished, badly housed, ill and diseased. To improve their conditions of life, either more of them must work, they must work more hours, and they must produce more in each hour of work; or they must be a charge on the people of the developed areas. Our traditions must become theirs, or they must remain poverty-stricken, or the world's well-to-do must move a never ending flow of gifts to them. There is no other way out" (Rottenberg, 1952, p. 531).

[3] Samuelson provides a theoretical reason why a single effect should not be expected to appear in all sectors:

"Thus, the direction of change of output depends upon the direction of shift of the marginal-revenue schedule (upwards or downwards) as advertising changes. Now there is nothing in the formulation of the problem which requires that this shift be of any particular direction. Hence, short of quantitative empirical investigation of sales responses to advertising no presumption is pos-

We begin with those sectors of advertising — classified advertising, for example — that are least controversial and whose effects are easiest to appraise. We then move on through other sectors of advertising, examining various types of advertising (e.g., mail order) as well as var-

Table 11-1.   1966 National and Local Advertising Expenditures by Media
(in millions of dollars)

Local Retail Advertising		
Newspaper classified		$1,400 million
Newspaper display		2,520
Radio		642
Television		461
Direct mail, fliers, etc.		613
Outdoor		62
Transit		16
Miscellaneous		<u>1,334</u>
	Subtotal, local retail advertising	$7,048 million
National Advertising		
Newspapers		$ 956
Radio, network		65
Radio, spot		294
Television, network		1,373
Television, spot		931
Magazine, consumer		1,295
Farm papers		34
Business papers		712
Outdoor		119
Transit		18
Direct mail		1,841
Miscellaneous		<u>1,859</u>
	Subtotal, national advertising	$9,497 million
	Grand Total	$16,545 million

Sources:

Classified newspaper advertising: This was estimated by *Advertising Age* at $800 million in 1961, compared to the $3.6 billion estimated by the same source as the total for newspapers in 1961 *(World of Advertising,* 1963, p. 56). The table estimate is 22.2% of the $4,876 million total newspaper expenditure for 1966 *Statistical Abstract,* 1967, p. 807). This proportion jibes fairly well with the proportion of retail linage to total linage in 52 cities (e.g., 27.5% for 1966; *Statistical Abstract,* 1967, p. 808), taking into account that rates differ for linage in various categories.

Local newspaper display: Local newspaper expenditures ($3,920 million) *(Statistical Abstract,* 1967, p. 807) minus estimated classified newspaper advertising.

Local direct mail: First, total direct mail was estimated to be $2,454 million *(Statistical Abstract,* 1967, p. 807). Then it was noted that food stores, department stores, and home furnishing stores together accounted for 11.1% of bulk third class mail, but accounted for 11.1/41.9 = 26.5% of the bulk third class included in a *World of Advertising* table p. 137; data originally from 1959 Department of Commerce Survey. With this data and my householder's intuition I estimate that ¼ of direct mail advertising is local.

Other media figures in the table come directly from *Statistical Abstract,* 1967 (p. 807).

sible. Moreover, since there is ambiguity as to the instantaneous rate of direction of quantity response to a change in advertising expense, there is *a fortiori* ambiguity as to the effect of a finite change in advertising expense. It is not possible, therefore to state whether output will be larger or smaller under positive advertising expenditures as compared to no advertising expenditure. It may be pointed out that the effect of advertising upon price is also incapable of unambiguous inference, as one should intuitively expect from the arguments which have been presented on both sides of the case" (Samuelson, 1947, p. 42).

ious industries (e.g., autos). We shall end this section with the most controversial and difficult group, which I call "homogeneous package goods," or "HPG" for short, e.g., cigarettes and beer.

Before proceeding it is suggested that the reader refer to Table 11-1, which indicates the orders of magnitude of expenditures in the various sectors of advertising.

Classified Advertising

Classified advertising is not insignificantly small in the economy. Classified represented about $1.4 billion in 1966, which was more than 8 percent of the 1966 total of $16.5 billion spent for advertising. (For sources of these and other data, see tables and source notes.)

Table 11-2. 1966 Advertising Expenditure in Some Important Product Classes
(in $ millions)

Auto manufacturers (excluding accessories)	$ 330 million
Other auto advertising, including local	225
Food manufacturers	1,417
Other food, including wholesale and retail	678
Homogeneous package goods (see breakdown in Table 11-3.)	2,519

Warning

No figure in this table should be quoted except perhaps the total. All figures in the table are crude and are subject to *large* error because of the different (and inconsistent) sources used, the different definitions of advertising by various sources, and the various adjustments made by the author of this book specifically for the special purposes of this chapter. To do a really good job on this and the following table would be a work of months or even years. (See Appendix E.)

In every case the estimation began with the IRS statistics for industries. The advertising/sales ratio for 1964-65 was reported in *Advertising Age* (September 18, 1967), and the business receipts were taken from Statistics of Income (1963-64 pp. 54-59). The result was multiplied by 1.2 to scale it up to 1966, on the basis of the growth from 1963-64 to 1966 in the Yang and PI series.

Further modifications were made for the following classes of advertising:

Auto manufacturers: IRS figures were ignored because recorded media expenditures were higher, and there is the chance that the latter are too high. The estimate includes $299 million for American makers *(Advertising Age,* November 6, 1967), plus 10% for foreign makers *(Printers' Ink,* July 9, 1965, p. 12. See Chapter 2 of this book for the data.)

Other auto: Including gasoline, this category was $300 million in 1960 and $396 in 1964, by IRS statistics *(Statistical Abstract,* 1967, p. 809). Examination of television and other media expenditures suggests that perhaps half is for gasoline, and half for local auto sellers. I extrapolate $450 million for both together in 1966. hence $225 for each one.

Food manufacturers: Estimates for malt liquors (unreduced), wines and brandy, soft drinks, and liquor, subtracted from overall IRS estimate.

Other Food: Includes IRS categories of wholesale groceries and retail food stores.

Homogeneous Package Goods: See Table 11-3.

Classified advertising fulfills an important function in bringing together buyers and sellers. Job seekers find opportunities and employers find employees through classified. Homes are bought and sold with a small fraction of the energy and money outlay that would be necessary if only personal sales contacts were possible. The bigger and more mobile that society becomes, the more useful is the search mechanism and information disseminator that classified advertising is. The cost to society is clearly less than the value of the benefits.

Such evils as exist in classified advertising seem to be the evils of personal immorality rather than a defect in the institution of advertising. The individual who sells his car by advertising his lemon as a creampuff is the individual who tells the same lie in person.

Local Advertising Other than Classified

Retail and local advertising is a very substantial portion of all advertising. Retail display advertising in newspapers accounted for $2.5 billion in 1966. And 64 percent of radio's $1 billion advertising (1966) is retail. Retail advertising on television is about $461 million. Other local advertising, of which direct-mail and classified are a large part, account for another $2 billion. The total is $7 billion, about 42 percent of total U.S. advertising in 1966. (See Table 7-4 for the trend of national and retail advertising proportions since 1935. That table estimates on a slightly different basis than here.)

Few men and even fewer women would deny the direct benefits of retail advertising. Shopping is the woman's family business, and retail advertising helps her execute that business efficiently and enjoyably. Women surveyed during a major newspaper strike claimed they missed the advertising more than any other part of the paper. And think how misdirected our lives would be without the guidance of movie theater ads.

Retail advertising disseminates information that keeps the overall retail market fluid. As noted in the Postscript to Chapter 8, even the Soviets — whose ideology is opposed to advertising (Goldman, 1963, pp. 2–4) — find it necessary to advertise retail merchandise to tell customers what is available, and to prevent wasteful stocks of goods from building up (Goldman, 1963, pp. 79, 195, 199–200). In this way advertising helps the economy perform one of Knight's five functions of an economic organization, efficient allocation of available resources in the short run, after goods have been produced. The Soviets do not believe they need to increase overall consumption "artificially," and they do not calculate any indirect multiplier benefits of advertising. Nevertheless, on the direct-benefit reckoning alone, the Soviets are apparently convinced that retail advertising conserves rather than wastes the resources of their economy by facilitating the workings of their retail markets.

There are abuses in retail advertising, certainly. Some merchants resort to age-old techniques of bait-and-switch, phony pricing, mislabeling, and out-and-out misrepresentation. Records of Better Business Bureaus, the Federal Trade Commission, district attorneys, and other policing agencies show that both large and small stores are guilty of cheating practices from time to time. But shoppers have a powerful sanction: loss of patronage. The fear of this sanction is one of the forces that keeps stores in line, although it may not affect fast-buck, one-time-sale outfits that cater mostly to transients.

I do not think that other possible effects of advertising are sufficiently germane to retail advertising to consider them here. For example, retail advertising would not seem to be instrumental in inducing materialistic values and stimulating total consumption. There is generally a qualitative difference between retail and national advertising for the same article. Consider automobiles: the manufacturer's national advertising says that its car is more beautiful and efficient than its competitors', and it tries to show that one's life will be better if he buys it, appeals that could conceivably affect the values of individuals; but retail auto advertising just hammers away at prices, an appeal which is not likely to affect value structures at all. Nor can retail advertising be an important cause of higher retail prices. Retail advertising runs about 1 1/2 percent of retail sales (IRS data in *Advertising Age*, September 18, 1967, p. 77), so that even if all advertising costs were "returned" to the shopper in some way, prices could not be made much lower.[4]

Mail-Order Advertising

The total volume of mail-order advertising is not large — less than $1 billion in 1966, I estimate. But mail-order advertising affects people out of proportion to its dollar volume,[5] and it has been responsible for much of the theory and practice of other advertising, so it deserves some discussion here.

Mail order is many things. It is Montgomery Ward, Sears Roebuck, and three or four other general-merchandise catalog merchants who

[4] Advertising expenditures for department stores that sell lower-priced merchandise constitute a larger proportion of sales than do advertising expenditures by department stores that sell higher-priced merchandise (Edwards and Howard, 1943, pp. 98, 158–159). Furthermore, the lower-priced stores concentrate more advertising on cut-price merchandise rather than on their regular price lines, as compared to higher-price stores; in normal pre–World War II times 38 percent of the advertising budget of "medium to low price" stores went for "special promotions" compared to 21 percent for "medium to high price" stores, and the percentages were respectively 49 percent and 63 percent for "regular price lines" (Edwards and Howard, 1943, p. 171). These data are not consistent with the notion that advertising causes higher prices. But I most emphatically would not interpret these data as suggesting that advertising causes lower prices. Rather, higher advertising and low prices are joint characteristics of one type of store.

[5] Big-city retail advertising can exert an analogous effect on small-town prices. For example, Chicago auto dealers' price advertisements are read in Chicago papers by people in Champaign-Urbana, 130 miles from Chicago, who then know that there is a good alternative open to them if the local price is more than $50 or $75 higher than the Chicago price.

differ from department stores only in that they do business by mail rather than over the counter. Catalog houses played a valuable role in the development of America and its rural areas, and most of their history as well as all of their present practice is clearly beneficial. The "wish books" exerted a powerful educational force in bringing the tastes and products of the wide society to many drab rural areas. And the mail-order houses had a beneficial effect on prices paid by rural consumers by offering an alternative to local monopolists; this was the cause of the violent resistance of local retailers to the mail-order houses in their early days.[6] In their infancy, however, the practices of even the largest firms were sometimes dubious and occasionally sheer fraud (Emmett and Jeuck, 1950, p. 69; Simon, 1965b, pp. 33–35).

Magazine publishers are in the mail-order business very heavily. The sale of magazine subscriptions by mail accounts for almost 10 percent of all third-class mail in the United States. Almost no magazine could exist without direct-mail subscription efforts. Even *Consumer Reports* — which states as a reason for its existence the protection of the consumer from advertising — finds it necessary to spend a large part of its total budget in direct-mail and display-space mail-order advertising in order to get enough subscription revenue to stay alive.

Other consumer mail-order advertising varies widely in its practices and effects. Gift and specialty houses are not very consequential to society or to the economy but they bring small pleasures to consumers, and the firms are outlets for creative free enterprise. Mail-order stamp firms help many people have a serene hobby in a world of tension and strife. Mail-order book advertising helps publishers spread education and culture, and provides royalties to authors. Some firms, however, specialize in the shady and the near-fraudulent. Their diabolically clever advertising panders to unattainable dreams of beauty, health, and riches. These are out-and-out crimes that mobilize the Post Office Department and the Federal Trade Commission, which sometimes succeed in exacting punishment. Advertising makes these crimes of robbery and fraud peculiarly possible, and the customer has few weapons on his side. The fraudulent mail-order merchant is not subject to loss of

[6] "The hostility took many forms. In some small towns merchants were able to exert sufficient community pressure to compel townfolk to burn their mail-order catalogues in the public square in a grand but ineffective auto-da-fé. In some instances local storekeepers offered prizes to those bringing in the greatest number of catalogues for destruction; in others, a straight ten cents per book was paid to provide fuel for the bonfire. Another device was to admit free to a moving-picture theater every child who brought a mail-order catalogue for destruction. A candidate for mayor of Warsaw, Iowa, declared he would discharge any city employee found purchasing from a mail-order company" (Emmett and Jeuck, 1950, p. 151).

patronage or even loss of reputation with people who know him personally. The institution of advertising must be held accountable for these mail-order crimes. But because they are clearly evil, and are legally punishable already, we need not consider further what society should do about them, or what judgments it should make.[7]

Many people resent receiving mail-order solicitations by "junk mail." Objectors feel an invasion of their privacy, and perhaps they resent the effort required to open the mail before identifying it and throwing it away. It is not possible to guess at the social cost of this annoyance. "Junk mail" is a term for direct mail [8] used largely by newspapers and mailmen. Newspapers fear third-class mail as an important competitor for advertising, for Congressional favor for mailing privileges, and as a promotional tool of magazines. Mailmen have a simple point of view; they resent extra loads on their backs. Taking a longer view, however, the letter carriers' association is a strong supporter of third-class mail in Washington, because it provides jobs for postmen. Increased postal employment is an example of the indirect effect of advertising.

Critics of direct-mail advertising claim that no one reads it. But mail-order firms are the only firms that have perfect accounting control over their advertising results, and their continued use of direct mail is absolutely conclusive evidence that enough of the audience reads and buys to produce sales in better than break-even quantities.

Advertising is a relatively high proportion of mail-order sales expense, perhaps 10 percent. But advertising replaces all other selling expenses. And it is quite clear that if there were no advertising, there would be no mail-order sales at all, which can hardly be an economic improvement.

Industrial Advertising

This category includes all advertising to firms and professions. Or to put it another way, industrial advertising is advertising for producer goods rather than for consumer goods that are used by individuals for personal gratification.

Industrial advertising was $1.8 billion, more than 10 percent of all advertising, in 1966 (*Advertising Age*, June 20, 1966, p. 84). Good data tell us that $712 million was in business publications and trade papers (Table 11-1). Perhaps an equal amount was in industrial direct mail, and other amounts were in miscellaneous media.

[7] For a fuller discussion of these matters see Simon, 1965b, Chapter 5.

[8] Not all direct-mail is mail-order advertising, and much mail-order advertising is not done by direct mail, of course.

No one criticizes most types of industrial advertising. Purchasing agents rely on industrial advertising to supply knowledge of product improvements and new applications, and they maintain files of ads. Executives learn of new sources of supply from industrial advertising. Farmers, small tradesmen, and retailers read trade advertising avidly. The advertising content of the trade press is an important component of its total value to its paying subscribers.

Industrial advertising and salesmen are partial substitutes for each other. If advertising did not exist, more personal selling would be required, at a higher cost and therefore higher final selling price.

Industrial advertising may well be responsible for lowering some prices by increasing the sizes of markets and hence making possible lower production costs. And industrial advertising is not likely to cause artificially high prices, because industrial purchasers are relatively price-sensitive. Furthermore, the cost of industrial advertising is far less than 1 percent of industrial sales.

Keen and rational buying by commercial purchasers is a powerful bulwark against deceptive advertising and other abuses. Sellers cannot afford to lose the confidence of purchasers. But for some types of industrial advertising there is vociferous criticism. "Ethical" (prescription) drug advertising to doctors is an example worth examining at some length, and it accounts for the substantial sum of $225–275 million per year.[9] There are two major criticisms of prescription-drug advertising: that it causes higher prices, and that it misleads doctors. We shall consider them separately and at some length, partly because this example can be well isolated and partly because the Kefauver committee hearings (U. S. Senate, 1961–62) developed a lot of publicly available information.

The argument that ethical-drug advertising raises prices is really an argument about brand-name marketing, of which advertising is a crucial element. If the doctor would prescribe by generic name rather than by brand name, the customer would ask for the cheapest brands of the

---

[9] The total for drugs in 1966 was $595 million, figured as 120 percent of the total estimated for 1963–64 in *Internal Revenue Statistics*. (See source notes in Tables 9-2 and 9-3 for procedure.) Subtracting the $317 million for patent-drug advertising (see Table 9-3) yields $278 million. Another line of estimation is that the 22 biggest drug companies spent $580 million for all promotion in 1958, of which $330 was for detail men (Telser, 1964, p. 553, fn.). A large proportion of the balance must have gone for advertising, which almost squares with my own industry estimate of one-third of promotion for advertising. Then HEW estimated $600 million for promotion (*Advertising Age*, September 16, 1968, p. 2), probably based on 1964 data. A blowup of the 1958 and 1964 estimates raises them somewhat. On the other hand, only $75 million was reported in medical-journal advertising in 1965 (*Advertising Age*, May 2, 1966, p. 108), a sum which should represent almost half of the year's total.

product at the drugstore, and price competition and lower prices would result. This battle was fought out bitterly at the Kefauver committee hearings, and the law now requires generic (chemical-name) labeling on packages. (If the seller holds a patent on the drug, the argument about brand-name effects on price does not apply unless the patent-owner has licensed the drug to other firms without an agreement about retail price. It is another question, and an open one, whether the public would benefit from a system of less-protected patents, as compared to the present system that offers great financial incentives for new drug discovery.)

The second charge — that drug advertising misleads doctors — is more serious, I think. Puffing and exaggeration may be annoying but tolerable in most commodities. But if an advertisement exaggerates a drug's benefits and minimizes or ignores its side effects the drug can be dangerous to patients.

The therapeutic merits of a drug are hard for any single person to judge. Unlike the taste of a wine or the style of a dress or the functioning of a lawn mower, the virtues and defects of a drug are not obvious upon inspection, even to an expert. It often takes months or years of controlled scientific testing to determine the effects of a drug. Therefore, it is specious for a drug advertiser to claim that a doctor cannot be taken in by exaggeration and hyperbole. *Caveat emptor* is not sound doctrine for drugs. (Doctors do test drugs informally, and they share their knowledge with colleagues. A misadvertised drug will not be misused for very long. But in the short run the results can be tragic, as the Thalidomide case showed.)

The drug companies argue that their advertising "educates" doctors about new drugs. They point to sociological studies showing that doctors get much of their post–medical school drug knowledge from advertisements. But the Kefauver hearings gave frightening evidence of at least occasional deceit in drug advertising (Kefauver, 1965).[10]

From firsthand knowledge, I know that there are significant abuses in the prescription-drug advertising business. With considerable shame I remember writing strong copy about the merits of a tranquilizer, a carload of which I don't think would tranquilize a tabbycat. And I remember shouting in print about a "new" drug that was a combination of two common ingredients, each well known for over 50 years. Yes, firms are limited by their desire to retain the confidence of doctors; but they also tell some whoppers.

[10] May (1963) is a very useful and readable discussion of the issues from the point of view of both society and the physician. It also contains much useful information.

On balance, is drug advertising a beneficial force in the United States? [11] If drug advertising did not exist, there would have to be some other method — governmental, commercial, or nonprofit — of communicating new drug information to doctors. It is enlightening to compare the situation in the Soviet Union, where state institutions are responsible for all drug communication. Information about new drugs is disseminated very slowly in the U.S.S.R., say Bauer and Field (1962), to the detriment of the treatment of patients. Commercial advertising in the United States does not prevent impartial and noncommercial drug communication. The American Medical Association is certainly strong enough and rich enough to finance any information bulletins that are necessary. One would expect that if the noncommercial bulletins really did the job promptly and fully, commercial advertising would then carry no information to doctors and would wither from lack of effectiveness. It is curious that a situation that is so much complained of, and apparently so easy to remedy, continues to exist unchanged — which suggests that there may be very real benefits from the present system that may outweigh its drawbacks.

Travel and Tourism Advertising

States and countries advertise themselves to increase the number of people who come to vacation (or invest) there. A large proportion of the advertising for airlines, steamships, and even railroads has the same

[11] This chapter and book are about commercial advertising. But it is interesting to note the results of a noncommercial health campaign (cited in this section only because no place in the book is more appropriate):

"The campaign to secure the immunisation of children against diphtheria, directed by the Ministry of Health and the Department of Health for Scotland, is possibly the most demonstrably successful of all recent official publicity campaigns. In the ten years from 1931 to 1940, there were on the average about 2,800 deaths annually from diphtheria in England and Wales. In 1940 itself there were 2,480 and in 1941 there were 2,641. It was in that year, 1941, that the publicity campaign opened. The number of deaths since then has followed this sensational course:

1942 —	1,827	1946 —	472
1943 —	1,371	1947 —	244
1944 —	934	1948 —	156
1945 —	722	1949 —	85

"(In Scotland deaths fell from 518 in 1941 to 14 in 1949.) In the same period the number of original uncorrected notifications of diphtheria has steadily fallen from about 55,000 a year to 5,000. It would have been impossible to achieve such results unless publicity had brought home the need and made known the opportunities for immunisation. Indeed, about half the mothers who had immunised children under the age of five said in the course of a survey that they had been caused to do so by publicity." (Annual Report of the Central Office of Information, 1949–50; quoted in advertisements for Garland Advertising, *World's Press News*, July 6, 1951, p. 62.)

object, as does the advertising for hotels. The aggregate does not represent a very large proportion of total advertising — less than $175 million in 1966.[12] On the face of it, this advertising seems like an unalloyed social good, giving people information about places to enjoy their vacations better. Puffing might be excessive in some cases, and some people might be fooled, but I doubt that anyone would criticize this sort of advertising for those reasons.

Yet even travel advertising cannot now be shown to be a good thing with economic logic alone. From the point of view of the advertisers it is plausible that travel advertising is almost a zero sum game — what one advertiser gains in volume another loses, and if the propensity to save is unaffected by advertising (as Chapter 8 suggests may be the case), and if people do not go out and earn extra money to pay for extra advertising-induced vacations, then even if the travel industry gains as a whole, other industries lose the same amount. And from the viewpoint of the consumer one cannot make for travel advertising the usual consumer-sovereignty justification of a commodity — that it is actually purchased — because the advertising is offered jointly with the product (Kaldor, 1950; Telser, 1964).

In sum, the usual economist's logic about allocation of resources fails to establish the worth of travel advertising. To judge its value one must ask such questions as (1) whether he himself is willing to pay a slightly higher price for his travel (if indeed the price is thereby made higher), (2) whether a world that contains travel advertising (including travel posters) is more interesting and exciting than a world without — taking into account whatever it does to people's wants and their motivation to work to satisfy those wants, and (3) whether the possibility of advertising and the consequent competition energizes the travel industry to provide better services to the traveler.[13]

[12] The sum of transportation and hotels-and-resorts categories in newspapers and magazines was $144 million in 1966 (*Statistical Abstract*, 1967, pp. 807–808). And in 1963, 17 percent of total travel expenditures were in television (Travel Research International, 1964).

[13] Despite the inability of allocation logic to show advantages for promotion, I doubt whether many economists would be in favor of a system in which universities were forbidden to promote their wares to attract professors from "competing" institutions. Considering the system as a whole, there is little or no reason to think that more research or better teaching would be done even if economists were randomly assigned to universities. Of course salaries would be lower than under a system in which universities compete by promoting their wares, but perhaps that would benefit the consumer without loss to anyone except professors. Is it just self-interest that leads professors to be for university competition? Or do professors believe that the whole system is more vigorous when universities can compete vigorously for professors, with sales

The classes of products and the types of advertising mentioned so far in this chapter are not the most controversial. The discussion was intended to convey these two points which are necessary for perspective on the advertising industry: (1) the advertising industry includes many types of advertising activity that critics generally ignore; (2) this "forgotten" advertising accounts for a substantial proportion of total advertising expenditures.

The types of advertising discussed up till now — as well as some other types yet to be discussed — are relatively informative advertising, containing considerably more facts and arguments than do other types of advertising that will now be discussed, although the distinction between "informative" and "persuasive" [14] is difficult to make. We now turn to branded consumer goods.

Advertising and branding are interlocked practices, because advertising has no value if the advertiser's merchandise cannot be advertised and identified for sale by brand. In those industries in which branding has little or no effect — fresh fruits and vegetables, for instance — advertising must advertise the entire industry or not at all. Branded consumer-goods advertising often is "combative" advertising, using relatively little fact and argument. It is this type of advertising that is most criticized as wasting resources, being obnoxious, and corrupting values. Branded consumer-goods advertising will now be examined in some detail.

Auto Advertising

Auto manufacturers spent $330 million in 1966 to advertise new cars. Large sums were also spent locally to advertise sales, service, and accessories. This sum divides out to something less than 2 percent of the cost of the average new car sold.

The main charges against auto advertising are that it induces overly materialistic values in Americans, and that it raises prices. "Artificial obsolescence" is said to work hand in glove with advertising to cause these evils. Defenders of auto advertising rely on the counterclaim that auto advertising helps the economy sell more cars than would be sold otherwise, which they say benefits the economy.

Let us examine the aid-the-economy issue first. Unfortunately, no one has systematically studied the effect of advertising on total auto

---

pitches as well as with salaries? The same questions exist about sales pitches (i.e., catalogs and notices) designed to bring students to the university.

[14] Marshall (1919, pp. 304–307) distinguished between "combative" advertising and "constructive" advertising, the latter roughly equivalent to "informative" advertising.

sales. This may be because demand studies have been quite successful in explaining much of the variation in auto sales with only income and price and stock of cars on the road, apparently leaving little variation for advertising to explain. However, advertising may be highly correlated with the other variables, and hence may be a "real" causal variable.

Even if auto advertising does increase auto sales, one must also estimate the effect on the overall economy of whatever "extra" sales advertising does induce, because people may simply purchase cars instead of other goods. Car purchases are only important if people spend money on cars that they would otherwise save, thereby changing the consumption function, or if they work more to earn the price of a new car. And to estimate the effect of advertising for a single commodity on aggregate demand, one must also be able to estimate the effect of aggregate advertising on aggregate demand, and this one cannot now do sensibly, as Chapter 8 discussed.

The effect of auto advertising on the business cycle is another matter for inquiry, both the direct effect as an autonomous expenditure and the possible effect in stimulating consumption. As was shown in the Postscript to Chapter 2, advertising in general is nowhere near as volatile as is investment; the amplitude of all advertising's peaks and troughs is about the same as that of industrial production. However, auto advertising (and advertising of other durables) is considerably more volatile than most other advertising (see Figure 2-14b, Chapter 2). Furthermore, the timing of the auto-advertising cycle is such as to aggravate rather than to damp the overall business cycle. But there seems to be no basis for estimating the magnitude of the effect on the business cycle. (The entire problem is discussed in greater detail in the Postscript to Chapter 2.)

Does auto advertising cause higher prices? The advertising expenditure is about $20 per car for the lowest-priced Big Three cars, and up to $60 per car for the high-priced makes. Unless advertising also exerts some downward pressure on prices one can hardly avoid the conclusion that advertising raises prices. At this advanced stage in the development of the auto industry, it is unlikely that advertising makes possible larger-scale and lower-cost production of cars. If the auto makers were forced to stop advertising, they might compete harder by offering somewhat lower prices. How the quality and rate of innovation in cars would be affected is anybody's guess. (Advertising may increase the innovation rate by making innovations profitable more quickly.) Innovations aside, it is probably true that the net effect of auto advertising is to raise prices, and this conclusion is almost certainly true for the marginal advertising expenditures. But the magnitude of the largest possible net effect — $20 to $60 per car — is, in my judgment, too small to warrant either great concern or much further analysis into what is certainly a very complex issue.

Next we turn to the noneconomic social effects of auto advertising. A recent study of television by G. Steiner (1963) shows that auto advertising offends the tastes of few people. Many people like the ads. And auto-manufacturer advertising is seldom accused of cheating and deceiving.

On the other hand, auto ads may well cause accidents and death by glorifying the excitement of speed and acceleration. O'Connell (1967) has collected a frightening set of auto advertisements (many of them in teen-agers' magazines) of which the following are fragmentary examples:

". . . Hulking under the 2 + 2's hood is our whacking great 4 BBL 421. Horsepower — 338. Torque — 459 lb.-ft. Blam! . . . For stab-and-steer men, there is a new 3-speed automatic you can lock in any gear. Turbo Hydra-Matic. . . . Just straighten right leg, wind tight, move lever. Repeat. Make small noises in your throat. Atta boy tiger! . . . [The 2 + 2 is] just a friendly little . . . saber-toothed pussy cat. . . ."

"A Howitzer with Windshield Wipers . . . The New Buick Skylark Gran Sport . . . The Skylark GS . . . is almost like having your own personal-type nuclear deterrent."

"Son of Gun . . . The Skylark Gran Sport . . . Ever prodded a throttle with 445-ft. of torque coiled tightly at the end of it? . . . Do that with one of these and you can start billing yourself as The Human Cannonball. . . ."

". . . If [Chevelle] . . . doesn't do for your driving what red capes do for bulls, our name isn't Chevrolet Division of General Motors."

We must now consider whether auto advertising induces overly materialistic values in Americans. Auto advertising certainly heightens American consciousness of automobiles somewhat. True, people yearn for cars even in underdeveloped countries where they are exposed to very little auto advertising. And Americans are very conscious of homes, too, even though homes are not heavily advertised. Nevertheless, our national preoccupation with cars is extraordinary, and it cannot be explained simply by our general scheme of values and interests. Perhaps advertising is partly responsible.

Advertising that heightens people's desires for material goods may be a bad thing for some people, under some circumstances. It may create unnecessary and undesirable tensions in some people. It may make some people unhappy because of what they do not have. It may reduce the spiritual content of the lives of some people. But increasing people's wants can be a good thing, too, as Knight (1935, Chapter 1) trenchantly pointed out. It may well be a major virtue of civilization that civilized people want more, and more varied, goods and pleasures than do less "civilized" people.[15] Merely wanting can add richness to lives, as can the attainment of the objects. So even if it is true that auto advertising increases people's wants, it is not at all clear that that is a bad thing, on balance. Each man must be his own social commentator when it comes to this issue.

The case of household appliances is generally similar to the case of autos. And advertising probably deserves credit for bringing about lower prices through mass production, and for stimulating product improvements (Borden, 1942, Chapter XV). Advertising can create a quick volume of sales for appliances and small durables that makes innovation profitable and thereby provides incentive to the innovator, e.g., the typewriter (Marshall, 1919, pp. 305–306).

Food Advertising

Food manufacturers spent perhaps $1.4 billion in food advertising in 1966; another $678 million was spent by wholesalers and retailers. In total, food advertising accounts for more than a tenth of all advertising.

Food ads are in good taste(!). Women learn from them, and enjoy them. Husbands and children benefit from new recipes and better cooking. Advertising may result in higher prices for branded goods, but private brands at extremely competitive prices are available in most chain stores and supermarkets. And a manufacturer's advertising investment in his brand may really help motivate the manufacturer to maintain high product quality; this argument may be ludicrous for bleach or for government-inspected aspirin, but it may make sense in discussing food. The extra price that the consumer pays for a branded food *may* be worth it to the shopper in increased confidence and reduced risk.

One sort of food advertising might bring great glory to the advertising industry by saving millions of children's lives each year and vastly improving the health of hundreds of millions of children and adults. Such advertising is already in operation and producing profits — fat ones — and will produce bigger profits in the future. I refer to the advertising for the "new proteins" — soybeans, peanuts, algae, fishflour, cottonseed, and other high-protein food products that can be made up in almost any form and to almost any taste.[16] If the three million children who die from Kwashiorkor (protein-deficiency disease) every

---

[15] "The chief thing which the common-sense individual actually wants is not satisfaction for the wants which he has, but more, and *better* wants" (Knight, 1936, p. 22).

[16] For facts on this problem see Altschul (1966) or U.S. Panel on the World Food Supply (1967) or Schaefer (1968).

year, or the millions more who survive but with stunted bodies and minds, are induced to use one to three cents worth of new protein each day, protein deficiency can be eliminated. But people must be induced to use these new proteins, because food preferences go deep. And that task is sufficiently difficult that many anthropologists and nutritionists have been skeptical about whether it could be done. However, an enterprising firm in South Africa with lots of marketing moxie, Hinds Brothers, and another firm in Singapore, have done it — and made money doing so. (The inspiring stories of these campaigns are told in Belden et al., 1964; or see Simon and Gardner, 1969.) There is no reason why the same success cannot be repeated elsewhere in the world, if sufficient thought and energy and interest are thrown into the task by indigenous and American firms.

Homogeneous Package Goods (HPG)

This section considers a group of products that includes as major examples the products in Table 11-3.

These products have many characteristics in common, including (1)

Table 11-3. Homogeneous Package Goods

	1966 Television Advertising (in millions of dollars)	1966 Total Advertising (in millions of dollars)
Soft drinks	$ 75	$ 220
Gum, candy	64	68
Soaps, cleaners, etc.	112	446
Tobacco	211	394
Beer, wine	101	222
Gasoline	67	225
Liquor	0	101
Patent drugs (excludes prescription drugs)	258	317
Perfumes, cosmetics, other toilet preparations	411	526
	$1,299 million	$2,519 million

Warning

No figure in this table should be quoted, except perhaps the total. All figures in the table are crude and are crude and are subject to *large* error because of the different (and inconsistent) sources used, the different definitions of advertising of various sources and the various adjustments made by the author of this book specifically for the special purposes of this chapter.

Sources: For total figures see general notes to Table 11-2.

Where IRS figures were not used alone, the following product-class estimates were made:

Beer: The recorded media expenditures were only $115 million for 1966 *(Advertising Age,* September 18, 1967, pp. 63-64). So I compromised between this and the IRS estimate of $302 million at $200 million. The difference between the two estimates is probably the large point-of-sale expenditure for beer.

Gasoline: See "other auto" note, Table 11-2.

Perfumes, cosmetics, and other toilet preparations: *Drug Trade News* (June 19, 1967).

Patent drugs: Drug Trade News, June 19, 1967.

Tobacco: 1964 advertising expenditures, from *Statistical Abstract,* 1967 [p.809], multiplied by 1.2.

Sources for TV estimates:

Soft drinks, gum and candy, tobacco and Patent Drugs: Drug Trade News (June 19, 1967).

Gasoline: Statistical Abstract (1967, pp. 808-809).

Soaps, cleaners, polishes: $132 million in network television, plus 13/18 (the network proportions) of the $155 million of "household equipment and supplies" in spot television *(Statistical Abstract,* 1967, pp. 808-809).

slight or no objective physical differences between the brands (autos and industrial products differ in style and physical make-up, but the products discussed in this section can hardly be distinguished even in a laboratory);[17] (2) low unit cost; (3) short time period between repeated purchases; (4) large total dollar volume for each product industry; (5) except for liquor, heavy use of television as an advertising medium;[18] and (6) large proportions of sales spent for advertising. Except for breakfast cereals all of the seven industries with the highest ratios of advertising to sales in the FTC's 1940 survey were HPGs. And the latest IRS data also show that all the HPG's are among the industries with the highest advertising-sales ratios.

This is the group of products whose advertising is most controversial, and it is treated here at considerable length. But the reader should keep the total economic importance of this group in perspective. The group's advertising is about 16 percent of all advertising, and about 1/4 of 1 percent of the Gross National Product.

[17] One of the most famous advertising men made this very clear: "There isn't any significant difference between the various brands of whiskey, or cigarettes, or beer. They are all about the same. And so are the cake mixes and the detergents, and the margarines" (Ogilvy, 1963, p. 102). And study after study has shown that consumers cannot distinguish among brands of cigarettes and beer, or even between "their" brand and other brands (e.g., Husband and Godfrey, 1934, quoted by Borden, 1942, p. 238; *Science News Letter*, 1949). Still not convinced? A study by McConnell that turns the problem around may help one understand why people will not *believe* that they cannot distinguish among actual brands. McConnell elicited reactions to various unmarked samples of beer: "One subject at the end of the experiment likened brand P to Heineken's and other European beers. On the other hand, he nick-named brand L 'T.C.P.' and regarded it as undrinkable. This was this man's perception of the quality of the two brands. Other subjects saw the brands as differing in other ways. However, the brand differences were not real — they only existed in the minds of the subjects because the beer was the same for all brands" (McConnell, 1968, p. 14).

[18] The tendency for such products as food, drugs, and soap to use broadcast media relatively more heavily than consumer durables was also true for radio before the television era, as Cassady and Williams noted (1949).

This tendency to use television heavily is even more pronounced for some subcategories than for all the products in Table 11–3 taken together, as the display below shows for a few products. (Note that some products not included in the definition of HPGs are also advertised heavily on television, e.g., some foods.)

$ Million Expenditures in 1963	Newspapers	Magazines	Television
Cereals	3.1	8.1	61.3
Detergents	1.3	4.4	92.2
Patent drugs	11.5	24.1	176.6
Hair preparations	2.4	16.6	90.4

Source: *Printers' Ink*, November 13, 1964, p. 36; July 10, 1964, p. 37; July 17, 1964, p. 27; December 4, 1964, p. 50.

Effect on Prices of HPG Advertising

Perhaps in the early stages of development, HPG advertising made possible real production economies and lower prices by increasing sales volume. But by now continued advertising does not lower the prices to the consumer of these products. Many or most of the manufacturers are multiplant firms, and the factories that make most of these products do not need to be very large to attain reasonable efficiency. (Gasoline refineries are an exception.) Together, these two factors suggest that if advertising did not exist, and if total production were divided among more and smaller firms, prices of homogeneous package goods would not need to be higher.

One must also ask whether advertising might raise HPG prices. Advertising and price are two of the variables that a marketer manipulates to achieve sales. *Ceteris paribus*, to achieve a given volume of sales, less advertising is needed if the price is low than if it is high. Similarly, a lower price is necessary to sell a given quantity of a little-advertised product than to sell the same quantity of a much-advertised product. It is reasonable to say, assuming *ceteris paribus* and putting dynamic effects aside, that more advertising for a given brand means higher prices.[19] But how much does advertising raise prices? That depends on the price line of the particular brand one buys. On the average, advertising is a relatively large part of the sales dollar for homogeneous package goods. To illustrate, beer, soft drinks, tobacco, and cleanser sellers spend more than eight to twelve times as much per dollar of sales as do auto manufacturers. Drug and cosmetic sellers may spend 20 times as much as auto manufacturers. Some patent-medicine firms spend as much as 60 percent of their total revenue on advertising.

But private-label unadvertised substitutes are available at lower prices for almost all types of homogeneous package goods: detergents, gasoline, beer, liquor. (Cigarettes are an exception.) Therefore, a shopper who wants to buy a product without also buying its advertising is generally able to do so. In this important sense, advertising does not raise prices. A person may pay $8 instead of $2.49 for a fifth of whiskey, both of which may have come from the same still (Wattell, 1954, p. 501), but he is not required to do so in order to obtain the merchandise. The types of price indices that economists usually employ to indicate the price level of a commodity are not applicable in this type of case, and there are no other concepts available that help one state what

[19] The aforementioned sentences are not inconsistent with the discussion in Chapter 2 that cites product categories in which the lower price-line brands are more advertised as well as product categories in which the opposite is true.

the effect of advertising is on the price of a product class as a whole, as long as different brands of the same quality sell at different prices.[20]

Does Advertising "Add Value" to Homogeneous Package Goods?

A popular theory (Mayer, 1958; Norris, 1960) but also a very old one (Barnes, quoted in Cherington, 1913, pp. 113–116, and probably earlier writers) has it that because the consumer has a different "image" of the advertised brand than of the unadvertised brand, he is really buying the image plus the product, and the image is what he pays the extra price for.

Perhaps the purchaser of Zilch's beer obtains more happiness from it because of his identification with the hero in its advertisement than he does from Zud's unadvertised beer. Maybe he does, but no one has proved it with an empirical test of consumer satisfaction. And when it comes to gasoline, I do not believe that the consumer gets any added value from Punt gasoline, advertised to contain secret ingredient Y which the customer thinks will give him more mileage than will Funt, especially since Funt was probably bought from the Punt refinery and rebranded.

Though there is an immediate intuitive appeal to this utility-adding theory by virtue of its apparent relationship to the basic axiomatics of economics, on further consideration the theory is seen to be tautologous or incomplete.[21] As to tautology, if one asserts that the test of whether

[20] Though his data pertain not just to HPG but rather to a wide range of consumer products, this is as good a place as any to report Backman's findings on the relationship of price to the advertising-sales ratio: ". . . no relationship between the intensity of advertising expenditures and the magnitude of price increases [since World War II]." Backman also wrote a directly contradictory statement in the same paragraph: "The most intensively advertised categories of products have tended to show smaller increases in price than less heavily advertised categories . . ." (1967, p. 144). But as I read his evidence (pp. 132–138) the former rather than the latter is true. Backman's correlations ranged from −.0970 to +.1464. Nor was any relationship shown by food products (pp. 138–141).

[21] But see Lancaster (1966a and b) whose approach is especially useful in this connection. By thinking about the attributes that the potential purchaser desires, rather than the product itself, there is no longer any paradox in the fact that a person buys something that does not give him satisfaction; clearly the purchase may not provide the attributes that the person wanted to buy and intended to buy. One can use this model to demolish the old argument, favored by sellers of established products, that, since consumers "reveal" their preference for the product already, labeling laws are unnecessary. Traditional theory may seem to lend some weight to this argument, but the present theory does not, since actual choice by consumers can no longer be regarded as revealing their preferences for characteristics — they may merely be making an inefficient choice (Lancaster, 1966b, p. 19). The idea itself is quite old, as Chipman notes (1966, p. 44), but Lancaster, and Baumol in a parallel work (1967) develop it formally and show useful applications of it.

someone gets more utility from Zilch than Zud is whether he will pay more for Zilch, it is then tautologous to say that one knows that Zilch gives more utility because he does buy Zilch at the higher price. And if "utility" is defined to be some empirical measure of one particular dimension of utility, then it is easy to conceive of many reasons why the consumer buys Zilch other than the particular dimension, no matter what it is. To illustrate, advertising may lead a girl to believe that she will get a husband with a new and expensive wig. If, to her great disappointment, the wig only repels men, it does not seem sensible to say that the advertising added utility. For another example, one may buy Zilch because Zilch's advertising made him believe that Zud was almost poisonous. In this last case it is clear that advertising might subtract value as well as adding it.[22] So there is no a priori reason to assert that advertising adds value, and no empirical tests of this proposition have yet been devised for advertising in particular or advertising in general.

Effect on Product Improvement

Advertising can help an inventor to exploit a product improvement, and therefore advertising can sometimes stimulate product improvement. But the possibility of advertising-induced improvement is doubtful for most homogeneous package goods. Gasoline may be improved. But aspirin will remain aspirin, no matter how much is spent on advertising. Nor should one expect technical improvements in cigarettes or beer due to advertising. Advertising may speed *detergent* movement, but soap has not changed much in many decades, and will not change in the future, either.

In general, the possibility of product improvement being stimulated by advertising is not a strong justification for HPG advertising.

Effect on Industrial Organization

Chapter 9 concluded that there is not much to fear from advertising as a cause of industrial concentration. There is no particular reason to believe that HPG industries are atypical in this respect.

HPG Advertising and Aggregate Demand

Earlier in the chapter it was suggested that advertising for autos may increase aggregate consumption by increasing the demand for autos. But as noted in Chapter 8, advertising certainly does not increase the total market for cigarettes or liquor very much, as Basmann (1955) and

---

[22] After writing the above I discovered that Vaughan made a similar argument about the "creation of disutility," at length and with great vigor, 40 years ago (1928, pp. 129–141).

Prest (1949) have shown, respectively. In fact, it is a commonplace among package-goods advertisers that their job is to switch customers from other brands rather than to create new users. Therefore, there is no reason to think that HPG advertising has any effect on aggregate demand.

Does HPG Advertising Waste National Resources?

Some social critics think that the money, talent, and energy that go into making advertisements should work in more "constructive" pursuits. Indeed, it probably would be a better world if we could divert funds and people from HPG advertising into more "beneficial" outlets. But of course we would have long arguments about which other uses of the resources are beneficial. In the Soviet Union it is clear that the chemical industry could use extra resources, but it is not clear that the United States chemical industry cannot obtain investment capital at a socially useful interest rate. The Soviets also are convinced that it would be beneficial to produce more autos and appliances, and other consumer goods. But the critic of HPG advertising is likely to think that the United States overemphasizes autos already. If there were a way to divert resources from HPG advertising to eradicating poverty and stamping out other social ills, we would probably all agree to the diversion. But no obvious mechanism exists that could easily accomplish this rechanneling without also disturbing much larger segments of the economy and society [23] (but see the end of this chapter for some possibilities). Galbraith's view of this problem (1952, Chapter VIII) is that though some advertising may indeed be waste, at the present stage of development a society such as the United States can well afford such waste. Analogously, a rich man may regret that much good food goes into the garbage can, but it would be foolish and uneconomic of him to try to reduce the waste. A starving pauper in India will take a different view of the situation, of course.

Does HPG Advertising Pay for Television?

HPG and other advertising does defray the costs of television, just as advertising of all kinds defrays most of the costs of magazines, newspapers, and radio.[24] This fact is chiefly of interest in measuring how much

[23] John Maurice Clark, who I think was the wisest observer of the American economic system we have had, put it this way: "Wasteful advertising is waste, not social product, though we may not know how to get rid of it without sacrificing more than we should give" (Clark, 1936, p. 50).

[24] For estimates of the relationship of advertising to the existence of the media see Borden (1942, Appendix III), Kaldor and Silverman (1948, Chapters 4 and 5), and Machlup (1962, pp. 265–275).

social waste there is in package-goods advertising. Approximately 85 percent of the advertising funds spent on television pay for entertainment for the public, i.e., only 15 percent of television time is devoted to commercials, which means that only 15 percent, or $255 million, is "pure waste" (in 1961). But advertising's support of television is not a *justification* of advertising. There are many other possible economic arrangements, including pay TV and public sponsorship of all or some stations, arrangements that would be no more costly to society in the long run. Furthermore, there is no reason to think that the particular United States–type arrangement of television networks supported by advertising results in as much variety in programming as would occur with other arrangements (P. Steiner, 1952; Rothenberg, 1962; Wiles, 1963).

Do People Dislike HPG Advertising?

G. Steiner (1963, p. 215) found that, with the exception of women's underwear, all the products whose television ads were disliked more than they were liked were homogeneous package goods: cleansers, deodorants, tobacco, drugs, and toothpaste. (However, beer and wine ads were well liked, generally.) So television advertising for this group of products generally offends people more than does advertising in other media and for other products. Paradoxically, this is why HPG advertisers use television so heavily. Unlike a magazine or newspaper that the audience can turn away from, television can almost force the viewer to watch the commercial because he cannot speed it up. Because HPG messages are almost necessarily repetitive, uninformative, and uninteresting, television's capacity to compel people to see the commercial makes television particularly useful to these products. And it is useless to ask for more pleasant television commercials. Most competent advertising men might agree that ads (for homogeneous package goods) intended to entertain are usually inferior in selling power to hard-bitten, hard-selling ads. (However, experience in the few years prior to publication of this book throws some doubt on this point of view.)

Does the Dishonesty of HPG Advertising Corrupt Our Society?

Here is the advertising man's problem: Soap X is exactly the same as everybody else's soap. What can he say that will make people want to buy Soap X?

One solution to his problem is to claim that if you use Soap X, you'll never have a wrinkle or blemish on your skin. That would surely sell soap, but it's a lie.

Another solution is to scream that Soap X has no corrosive acids in it. That's true. But the clear implication is that the competitors' products *do* contain corrosive acids. That's false. Nevertheless, this is the advertising solution chosen by many package goods.

A third solution is to find or put some unimportant but distinguishing feature into the product that you can talk about. Nylon tires make noise for the first few feet after being at rest for a while, an entirely harmless thing. Rayon tire-makers therefore pointed with pride to rayon's absence of noise as an advantage of rayon tires. You are your own judge of the honesty of this practice. The sad thing is that this practice is exactly the course of action taken by the "wise" marketer. Recent research by D. Cox (1962) even puts a theoretical foundation under this practice.

A fourth solution is to claim nothing for the product, but to give it an "image" — by associating it with happy occasions, charming people, adventure, or the like. If you've seen beer, cigarette, and soft-drink commercials on television, you know exactly what I am talking about. The nature of these "image" ads is mystifying, even to the psychologists who have been trying to understand them for years. Do you really feel younger when you drink a Pepsi, because Pepsi has told you it is a drink for those who think young? Or is it a subtle cheat and you feel no younger when you drink Pepsi than when you drink plain water? This is the question of "value added." [25]

There is another solution that has been known to work. Petrofina sold its gasoline in Texas by advertising "Pink Air" available for the tires at its stations. By making fun of gasoline additives, Petrofina won the good will of many customers. But notice that such a campaign could not succeed unless there was hogwash to debunk. And campaigns like "Pink Air" are extremely difficult to execute successfully.

Many advertising men are unhappy about package-goods advertising. One major agency head recently said that it is "dishonest" to "dif-

---

[25] The following extracts from a published interview with Morton Salt's advertising manager illuminates several of the above points:

"Your ads can't very well focus on the product, because your salt is the same as everybody's else's. But Morton does talk about its history (its current magazine campaign involves old-fashioned sepia photos to show how long Morton salt has been a favorite); it talks about its packaging ('free flowing,' 'shake 'n pour top,' moisture-proof container, etc.); and it talks about its introduction of iodized salt (to protect against goiter) many years ago, which was a real innovation in the industry.

"All of this is designed to imply a quality difference in the product, though it is the company and the packaging that is actually being sold. This year's new slogan — 'No salt salts like Morton salt salts' — follows in this tradition by implying a product quality difference where actually a packaging difference exists" [Ray McDonald, quoted in "Morton Alters Strategy in Shifting Salt Market," *Advertising Age*, March 6, 1967, p. 52].

ferentiate" identical products. The advertising man who suddenly feels remorse at wasting his life making ads is a stock figure in popular fiction, and he probably exists in the flesh in greater proportion than in most other occupations. I'd guess that his remorse often follows on a sense of corruption from package-goods advertising. On the other hand, package-goods advertising is the most exciting field of advertising professionally, because of the difficulty of legally doing the impossible and because of the great amounts of money involved.

The corruption of package-goods advertising may lead one to condemn it. But it is not the "fault" of advertising. It is inherent in the nature of the HPG industry, and criticism must therefore go beyond the advertising people to include the managers of those firms, also. Packaging, for example, has the same effect as advertising.

Some Special Cases of HPG Advertising

1. *Cigarette advertising.* The preceeding chapter finds that for each dollar of earnings from cigarettes, perhaps a hundred hours of human life are lost. It concludes that there are no economic reasons in favor of cigarette advertising, and there are excellent moral and health reasons to ban cigarette advertising completely.

2. *Patent-medicine advertising.* Some medical personnel believe that the advertising for patent medicines induces people to dose themselves when they should be seeing a doctor. Maybe so. One can only hope that the charge is not made irresponsibly by doctors who would prefer to have an increase in patients and fees. The Food and Drug Administration exists to protect the public from advertising-caused health dangers, and it has the powers to accomplish this goal.

3. *"Scare" advertising.* Does deodorant advertising scare young girls into unnecessary worry and unhappiness? No one knows. Nor does anyone know for sure that traveling in a hot crowded bus in the summer is pleasanter now than if deodorants had never been advertised.

What Policies toward HPG Advertising Are Indicated?

Aside from homogeneous package goods, much advertising gives direct benefits to the consumer and to business firms, and there may be indirect benefits in stimulating the economy and maintaining a free and progressive society. There are social abuses, of course, but the abuses are remediable by police bodies that have and exercise the power to prosecute dishonesty. Vulgarization of our values from materialistically oriented advertisements, and offenses to the esthetic sense, are perhaps the worst negative effects.

The HPG segment of advertising is a subject of a different nature.

The tough problem, of course, is how to throw out the bath water without throwing out the baby, how to kill the weeds without harming the crops. Many proposals have been advanced. They include regulation by (1) direct administration and/or legislation, (2) self-regulation and (3) taxation. Let us consider each of these briefly.

1. Banning certain types of advertising by administrative fiat or legislation certainly could eliminate certain types of advertising. But which types? Which czar would we entrust with the power to certify some advertising and prevent other advertising? A solution by czar runs counter to our entire philosophy of government.

Regulation by legislation runs into great problems when it tries to define classes of advertising that are and are not permissible. If Congress were to decide to eliminate HPG advertising, it would run into great difficulties of specifying in legislation what is and what is not within this classification. Congress might exclude food from the HPG classification, but what about soft drinks? Is an artificially sweetened soft drink a soft drink? Gasoline dosen't come in a package, though it has many other characteristics of homogeneous package goods. Regulation might allow only advertising that conveys new information. But what is "new information," and new to whom?

It is difficult to conceive of a scheme by which regulation by fiat can do the job. When there is a specific danger, such as the health-threat of tobacco, legislation can easily excise the offending advertising without destroying the rest. But the danger of tobacco advertising that legislation would aim at is the threat to health of *tobacco*, and not the evils of advertising per se.

2. Self-regulation by advertisers and agencies undoubtedly has some effect in upgrading the content of advertising, largely because it creates group pressure against the rascals. But self-regulation necessarily breaks down in the HPG industry. If a firm regulates itself not to say something untrue or meaningless about its bleach, which is chemically identical to all other bleaches (FTC vs. Procter & Gamble, 1963), what is there left for it to say?

3. Taxation is a more subtle possible method of regulating advertising. Several tax plans have been suggested.[26]

a) One plan calls for a progressively higher tax on larger amounts of advertising. This plan has the unfortunate property of taxing the firm that sells many products more than the firm that sells only one product. This might have the desirable effect of helping to break up large firms. But such a plan would also discourage the introduction of new products

---

[26] Most often no specific tax plan is suggested, and hence the problems with any tax plan are not faced, e.g., Meade (1968, p. 389).

because of the higher incremental tax cost for the firm as a whole. This is certainly a disqualifying disadvantage when seen in the perspective of the U.S. policy of stimulating innovation.

b) A progressive tax on advertising might be applied to products rather than firms. The theory of this plan — and the preceding one — is that the heaviest advertising is done by firms whose advertising is least beneficial. But a product-advertising tax also runs into major definitional problems. Are Valiant and Plymouth the same product or different products? And what about advertisements that advertise two of a firm's products together? At best, the bookkeeping problems would be very great. At worst, the tax could be frustrated completely by deliberate fragmentation of products into subtypes of products, by adding some distinguishing doodad or minor contraption.

c) Still another plan calls for higher taxes on firms that spend higher *proportions* of their sales income on advertising. This plan would certainly deal a heavy blow to patent-medicine and soap advertising. But it would also kill book and magazine publishers and other firms that sell valuable products directly from advertisements. Such a tax plan would also shift many industrial firms' selling efforts from advertising to personal salesmen, with a consequent loss of efficiency.

d) Advertising license fees are worst of all, because their effect is disproportionately greater on small firms.

None of the types of advertising tax yet suggested is a sharp enough scalpel. Rather, they all seem to mortify the healthy tissue almost as badly as that which is to be excised. (The problem is like that in political oratory. No way has yet been found to get rid of mud-slinging without proscribing free speech.)

A more subtle device has been suggested by Corden. This idea builds upon the following observations:

> . . . it can be argued with considerable conviction that by treating [English] advertising as a current cost rather than as an investment, the Chancellor is providing an interest-free loan to the advertisers. The result is a distortion of business endeavour in a socially disadvantageous way. At present there is a powerful temptation to businesses to put their money into persuading customers that their product is the best by exploiting the skills of the advertising profession rather than by actually improving their products or by reducing their production costs and prices.
>
> This is true only when advertising is actually building up an asset. If the whole benefit is felt in the year in which the advertising takes place then it is correctly treated as a current cost. Furthermore, if the advertising is only *maintaining* an asset — in other words, if advertising is being maintained at a constant rate — then the new expenditure would come out of depreciation allowances, and there would be no tax to pay on it.
>
> While it is undoubted that under the present system investment in

goodwill tends to be favoured over investment in a machine, it is difficult to see that the full logic of treating advertising as an investment expenditure could be followed through. It would have to be decided over what period advertising should be written off. Some advertising has only an immediate effect (such as most retail advertising) and should then be written off in the current year, while some could be effective at a diminishing rate ranging from one year to the lifetimes of the people on whose minds its message has impressed itself.

It can be concluded that at present advertising is being favoured only to the extent that it is an investment, and not a current cost, and in so far as the investment is not just replacing a depreciating asset. In the main a tax on advertising has to be justified by the arguments . . . that the social gain from advertising may be less than the private gain.

Such a tax would be in no way radical, for it is in principle no different from taxing many other activities and products — such as beer, wine, tobacco and entertainments — which it is not necessarily desired to prohibit, but which provide a useful source of revenue or have a value to the people who pay for these products greater than the social value the community attributes to them. It is interesting to note that all advertising is taxed in Italy (except strictly informative signs, company and tourist advertisements and official notices). Posters are taxed in Belgium. There are also local taxes on outdoor advertising in the Netherlands and Switzerland. In Switzerland pharmaceutical advertising is taxed.

One approach would be to have a direct and distinct tax on advertising. . . .

The alternative approach is no longer to allow advertising as a business expense for purposes of income and profits tax [Corden, 1961, pp. 32–34].

There is yet another alternative within this general approach, however — to allow advertising to be written off in accord with the actual facts of its immediacy or delay in effect. If the revenue produced in the first year by an expenditure for advertising really is only 25 or 50 percent of the total revenue produced in the first and succeeding years, then only 25 or 50 percent of the expenditure should then be allowed as an expense in the first year. This scheme would have the disadvantage of requiring information about the rate at which particular advertising investments in particular industries are used up. But it is by no means impossible to estimate this parameter within useful limits for most if not all industries (see, e.g., Telser, 1961; Cunningham, 1961; Palda, 1964; Simon, 1969a). If the procedure were to treat all advertising as, say, 75 percent investment beyond the current year unless a firm showed evidence of a faster depreciation rate from its own or the industry's operations, evidence on depreciation rates would be forthcoming in a hurry. Judging the evidence would be a problem for a while, but in not too long a time a set of industry guidelines would develop which would make the matter little more problematic than estimating depreciation rates for machines and buildings. (Note that the approach does not require knowing the absolute returns or profitability of given advertising expenditures. The investment *proportion* is the same for good and bad advertising. Accountants, however, would have to worry about the *absolute* value of the advertising investment when including it along with physical capital in the firm's assets.)

Perhaps the most valuable effect of this plan is *in addition* to any general diminution in advertising that might result. It would operate to diminish mostly that advertising that is least valuable socially while leaving the most socially valuable advertising untouched. To understand why, consider that if a bit of advertising tells you something that you want and need to know, the effect is likely to come soon after you see the advertisement. For example, retail advertising is generally considered socially useful, and most of its effect is on the day it appears. It helps the shopper decide where to shop that day for a given item, or whether to shop at all for the item that day. In contrast, the most-delayed-over-time effects that have been shown are in cigarettes before World War II (Telser, 1961) and liquor (Simon, 1969a), where there is (was) certainly no value at all to the consumer in coming to be "loyal" to one brand or another. Some valuable advertising is slow-acting and might be harmed, e.g., magazine-subscription campaigns, but mostly the effect can be expected to fall on the least desirable forms of advertising.

Another plan, perhaps complementary to the previous alternative and certainly not incompatible with it, is to tax [27] and/or restrict the amount of television advertising per broadcast hour, in such a way as to raise the price of television advertising. Such an action seems at first to be arbitrarily aimed at television. But television stations obviously are unlike all other advertising media in profiting from their valuable free franchise.[28] A restriction in the number of commercials per hour of programming would result in a greater number of stations, and hence would result in a wider variety of programs (P. Steiner, 1952; Rothenberg, 1962; Wiles, 1963).[29] Such a policy would not only reduce the amount of television advertising, which is surely the most odious and least valuable socially, it also would reduce in total the amount of advertising from homogeneous package goods. But this policy would cause less of a reduction in advertising for other products. Those products that now advertise largely in other media can be expected to shift to the other media more readily in response to a price rise. HPGs, which are concentrated so largely in television, would find other media

[27] A flat tax per commercial minute in prime time based upon station market size might accomplish the desired effect, but I have not analyzed this thoroughly.

relatively much less attractive, and hence would continue to use television (although less), and therefore would advertise less in total.

The objection may be raised that a diminution of television revenue would result in poorer programming. This need not be so. First of all, stations would get more revenue per commercial minute, which would partially offset the tax or reduction in advertising. Second, a very considerable drop in revenue could come out of profits and still leave the networks and stations in the black, even without reducing program costs. And, third, it is not at all clear that higher expenditures for programming mean better programs. Hollywood's most expensive epics are not demonstrably superior to many films made for much less money, both in the United States and abroad. Worry over programming should not be a disabling defect to this plan.

[28] Consider these rates of earnings that are certainly indicative of monopoly power:

Years	Total no. of stations	Broadcast revenues (millions)	Broadcast expenses (millions)	Earnings before fed. taxes (millions)
1946	10	$ .5	—[a]	—[a]
1947	15	1.9	—[a]	—[a]
1948	50	8.7	$ 23.6	($14.9)[b]
1949	98	34.3	59.6	(25.3)[b]
1950	107	105.9	115.1	(9.2)[b]
1951	108	235.7	194.1	41.6
1952	122	324.2	268.7	55.5
1953	334	432.7	364.7	68.0
1954	410	593.0	502.7	90.3
1955	437	733.7	594.5	139.2
1956	475	896.9	707.3	189.6
1957	501	943.2	783.2	160.0
1958	514	1030.0	858.1	171.9
1959	521	1163.9	941.6	222.3
1960	530	1268.6	1024.5	244.1
1961	540	1318.3	1081.3	237.0
1962	554	1486.2	1174.6	311.6
1963	565	1597.2	1254.0	343.2
1964	575	1793.3	1377.7	415.6
1965	588	1964.8	1516.9	447.9
1966	608	2203.0	1710.1	492.9

[a] No figures available.
[b] Parentheses denote loss.

Source: *TV Factbook*, 1968–69, p. 44a.

And any such tax or restriction device should include returning some of these monopoly profits to the public, perhaps in the form of support for public television.

[29] Another plan that would increase the variety of programming by increasing the number of channels is "wired city television." In this scheme all homes would be wired and channels would be rented out to anyone who wished to offer programs. See Barnett and Greenberg (1968a and b).

The above-described plan would strike differentially at some industries rather than others, e.g., the tobacco industry rather than department stores. But one might instead wish to strike differentially at the larger firms within given industries. One way to do this would be with a graduated corporate income tax. That is, a firm with a $100 million income would pay a larger proportion of income tax than a firm whose income is $10,000. (Of course, this tax would also strike differentially at entire industries whose firm size is relatively large. I believe, however, that this effect is also desirable.)

In any case, however, because any regulatory decisions about advertising must be general rather than specific, we must accept some of advertising's evils as being necessary evils.

One ray of hope shines from the consumer herself. If the buyer is willing to buy private brands when they are identical to advertised brands, she takes some of the profit out of HPG advertising, and hence she reduces the amount of valueless advertising. Supermarkets and discount houses exert pressure in this direction with their private-label merchandise. Education and sophistication increase purchases of private-label merchandise, surveys show. And indeed, in at least one industry — liquor — the major firms are very worried at the onslaught of private brands. (In New York the liquor lobby worked very hard to achieve a law that crippled private-label sales, and succeeded.)

Consumer education, by public or private agencies, is a weak suggestion, to be sure. But it does reduce the profitability of what are probably the most odious practices in advertising.

NUTSHELL SUMMARY

This is my overall assessment of advertising in the economy and society.

First, there is no question but that much of advertising is useful and important economically, and without grave danger to society; industrial advertising and department-store advertising are leading examples. In the main, no one objects to either the presence or the nature of these branches of advertising and hence there is no issue for analysis and argument.

Second, those branches of advertising which are most in dispute — advertising for such products as beer, autos, soap, and aspirin — do not seem to have much effect upon the economy in any way, direct or indirect, and hence from an economic point of view it is immaterial whether they are present or absent. (However, it must be noted that it would be operationally difficult to get rid of any branch of advertising without also getting rid of branches of advertising that are valuable.) All this implies that the economic study of advertising is not deserving of great attention except for special problems, e.g., the television rate structure. (As the reader may realize, this is not a congenial point at which to arrive after spending several years working on the subject.)

Third, it follows that if there are important issues in advertising they concern esthetics and morals, and advertising should be studied in those contexts.

APPENDICES

Appendix A

"Product Differentiation": A Meaningless Term and an Impossible Concept

Let us be clear on the importance of the term "product differentiation" and of the concept it represents. Chamberlin wrote that a key difference between his theory and that of Joan Robinson is "her rejection of 'product differentiation,'" which is "probably the most fundamental concept in monopolistic competition" (1962, p. 202). He added that "'The Differentiation of the Product' is by all odds the most difficult subject of all . . ." (1962, p. 204).[1]

To discredit the *term* "product differentiation" by showing that its use in economics is confused and misleading would not discredit the theory of monopolistic competition, though it would at least require a restatement in better terms. But to discredit the *concept* that the term tries to represent goes to the heart of the theory. The first and second sections of this appendix attempt to do both, in that order. The last section discusses where this leaves us.

[1] The concept of *group equilibrium* was Chamberlin's other main building block, and the other way in which Chamberlin thought monopolistic competition "differs both from the theory of competition and from the theory of monopoly" (Chamberlin, 1962, p. 56). But Stigler argues that this difference is illusory because Chamberlin's "group" is not a useful concept and cannot replace the concept of the industry. Stigler's analysis of the group concept concludes that if one uses the concept "in the general case we cannot make a single statement about the economic events in the world we sought to analyse" (Stigler, 1949, p. 20).

THE MEANINGLESSNESS OF "PRODUCT DIFFERENTIATION"

This is Chamberlin's definition:

A general class of product is differentiated if any significant basis exists for distinguishing the goods (or service) of one seller from those of another. Such a basis may be real or fancied, so long as it is of any importance whatever to buyers, and leads to a preference for one variety of the product over another. Where such differentiation exists, even though it be slight, buyers will be paired with sellers, not by chance and at random (as under pure competition), but according to their preferences.

Differentiation may be based upon certain characteristics of the product itself, such as exclusive patented features; trade-marks; trade names; peculiarities of the package or container, if any; or singularity in quality, design, color, or style. It may also exist with respect to the conditions surrounding its sale [1962, p. 56].

The first evidence that confusion is built into the term "product differentiation" is that masters of economic language use it confusedly. For example, Boulding writes: "In general, the more homogeneous [2] the product, the less important will selling cost be for the individual firm" (1955, p. 648). This statement is either wrong or it is a tautology. If, contrary to Chamberlin's definition, one excludes "fancied" differences and refers only to differences among products in physical composition, service, etc., then beer, pre–World War II cigarettes, household bleach, vodka, and a host of other products which are physically homogeneous have selling costs that are very important by any test. On the other hand, if one accepts Chamberlin's usage and includes fancied differences, the very existence of important selling costs for beer and the other products is a proof that the products are indeed differentiated and not homogeneous. But if so, Boulding's sentence above describes a measurement of the independent variable (homogeneity) by measuring the dependent variable (selling cost); hence, a tautology. Similar examples by eminent economists abound, but I will not bore the reader with them.

A second evidence of confusion is that various writers redefine "product differentiation" in different ways as, for example, "brand loyalty" (Weiss, 1965, p. 731), "price elasticity" (Telser, 1964, p. 557), "demand-increasing costs" (Demsetz, 1964), "cross elasticity," and "price dispersion," among others. These redefinitions differ from one another, indicating that the redefiners do not agree what "product differentiation" means.[3]

---

[2] "Differentiated product" and "homogeneous product" have been generally used as antonyms in the practice of the last 30 years.

[3] This is the semantic danger Machlup emphasizes. ". . . non-sense can be

Furthermore, if any of these other better-established terms means exactly the same thing, then "product differentiation" is unnecessary as well as confusing.

A third reason to think that "product differentiation" is a confused term is that no empirical investigator has been able to formulate an operational definition of the term for his empirical purposes. For example, Bain tried to use the concept in his classification of industries to explain concentration of sellers. But Bain offers only a subjective basis for his classification by degree of product differentiation: ". . . an appraisal of the relative 'importance' of product differentiation on the basis of various visible evidence . . ." (1959, p. 222). He lists various relevant factors such as sales-promotion costs and distinctions in design, but he does not tell how to measure and combine the various factors. And his definition is inconsistent to the extent of sometimes including advertising *à la* Chamberlin but sometimes excluding it (1959, pp. 215, 222).

Stigler (1947, p. 434) and Gort (1963, p. 58) have also employed the product-differentiation concept in empirical work, but neither provided an objective measurement. The fact that economists have not found a formal objective measurement and measure the extent of product differentiation only subjectively makes the term suspect, indeed.

The cause of the confusion is that *Chamberlin's definition is operationally circular; it is equivalent to a tautology; confusion is irremovably built into the term "product differentiation."* The definition quoted above says that differentiation is that which "leads to a preference for one variety of the product over another." This logically implies that the *only* possible operational test of whether a product is differentiated, or whether a particular aspect of a product or seller is differentiating, is a test of whether there *is* consumer preference (i.e., whether a change in the seller's offering is accompanied by a change in preference). If differentiation and preference are operationally equivalent (i.e., if there is only one measurement for the two concepts), then *preference and differentiation are, for all scientific purposes, equivalent.* If the two concepts are equivalent, then differentiation cannot sensibly be used to *explain* preference. And if the two concepts are equivalent, the new and less basic term "product differentiation" is unnecessary and dangerous. In fact it is probably the mere existence of a term with an *apparently* different meaning (Chamberlin says "leads to" rather than "is equivalent to" but the meanings cannot be different) that has led economists

shrugged off with a laugh, but multiple sense may be a real nuisance" (Machlup, 1963, p. 41).

to assume that the two terms are operationally independent; this is the root of the confusion.

To sum up, as Chamberlin defines it "product differentiation" is merely a synonym for "consumer preference." [4]

THE IMPOSSIBILITY OF A SOUND CONCEPT OF PRODUCT DIFFERENTIATION

The previous section showed that the concept of product differentiation as defined by Chamberlin is tautologous and hence useless and misleading. But is there a concept that Chamberlin was striving to describe that one can redefine and render useful?

Let us begin by guessing at Chamberlin's purposes in introducing the concept of product differentiation. First, Chamberlin sought to explain the downward-sloping price-quantity relationship that exists even in the absence of legal or natural monopoly; that is, he wished to increase the realism in economic description. Chamberlin (and others before him, as he acknowledged) observed "preferences of buyers to be distributed" in such manner that when firms and their offerings are not identical on any or all of a great many dimensions, usually no one firm will get all the customers (1962, p. 67). Because consumer preferences are not all lumped at one or several points in a preference space, the reaction to a change in a firm's price or to a change in other selling or product conditions will not be discontinuous, in contradiction to the theory of pure competition.

Chamberlin also wanted to explain a congeries of phenomena of marketing that had no place in the classical theory of competition: price dispersion within an industry, differences in spatial location, advertising and the size of expenditures for advertising, and minor

---

[4] A further (and painful) illustration of the confusion inherent in the term "product differentiation" is found in the complete contradiction in the two referees' comments sent to me by a journal. With respect to the conclusion arrived at by the above paragraphs — that "product differentiation" and "consumer preference" are synonyms — one reviewer wrote: ". . . 'product differentiation' is not, as Mr. Simon claims, literally a synonym for 'consumer preference'. Surely it would be only confusing [to use them as synonyms]. . . . This, however, is not my interpretation of Chamberlin nor is it the interpretation of anyone else I know of. . . ."

What the other reviewer says is diametrically opposite: "His [Simon's] conclusion — that 'product differentiation' means 'consumer preference' — seems completely inconsequential to me. Did it ever mean anything else?"

The difficulty is that every economist has learned the term early in his training and has used it frequently since then. Therefore one feels that one *must* understand what the term means, and therefore that the term *must* have a sensible meaning — even if it does not.

changes in products that may or may not have an obvious physical utility but that apparently shift custom among firms.

Several approaches other than the product-differentiation concept have been considered by Chamberlin and by others later. They include (1) conceptual experiments in which consumers judge the subjective difference between a pair of offerings; (2) price dispersion as a measure of preference differences; (3) price elasticity; (4) cross elasticity; (5) demand-increasing costs. Each approach grasps some part of what Chamberlin intended to do, but all fail to represent other important parts of his notion. No concept has been presented that both purifies Chamberlin's concept and is objectively measurable.

Now follows a demonstration that there *cannot* be a concept that will accomplish what Chamberlin hoped for the product-differentiation concept. We begin with the broadest description of the phenomena Chamberlin sought to understand. Imagine an n-space for each category of purchase alternatives — autos, department stores, beer, phonographs, lipstick, etc., for a given unit size [pound of bread, single refrigerator, etc.), and for a given set of competitors and competitors' policies. The dimensions of this n-space are each of the variables that might affect consumer choice. Some of the variables are easy to define and measure — price, for instance, speed of delivery, and perhaps horsepower for a car. Others are complex, such as the "image" of a beer, which may include elements of social status (lower or upper class), age (young or middle-aged), whether "square" or "hip," etc., each of which must probably be made a separate dimension of the space.[5]

Within this preference space there is for each point a "yes" or a "no," which represents the willingness of an individual to buy or not to buy at that combination of variables. For each point we can determine whether the individual prefers money or the purchase. The meaning of Chamberlin's term "differentiated" can now be understood clearly for the individual case: a store or brand is "differentiated" at any point at which there is a "yes," relative to each point at which there is a "no."

Then aggregate the observations over individuals in a market for each point in the n-space, giving a total of "yes'es" and "no's" for each point. Each combination of variables described by any point on any of Chamberlin's diagrams can now be represented by a point in this aggregate n-space. The higher the number of "yes'es," the more the "differentiation," by Chamberlin's definition. This n-space represents all the aspects of the world that Chamberlin worked with; it shows the rela-

[5] This is the sort of notion developed recently by Lancaster (1966a and b), and Baumol (1967), and mentioned in footnote 21 in Chapter 11.

tionship of purchase behavior to all objective and "fancied" aspects of a firm's offering.

Next we discuss the properties that Chamberlin hypothesized for this n-space and investigate those properties to see what can be said about them. Notice that without further assumptions [6] there is no way to predict which points within the space will have higher or lower numbers of "yes'es," i.e., no way of predicting which points are "differentiated." There is no a priori reason to believe that a movement in either direction along any of the dimensions of the n-space, *ceteris paribus* or *ceteris non paribus*, will lead to higher or lower consumer preference; i.e., we have no reason to believe that any particular movement will lead to more or less "differentiation." Therefore we have no a priori reason to say that a change in a beer's taste that makes it more like other beers will increase or decrease differentiation. Similarly with advertising: we have as yet no a priori reason to say that more advertising increases or decreases differentiation. As long as we put no separate axioms or knowledge about consumer preference into the n-space, we cannot take out any deduced knowledge.

Now we must ask (1) what restrictions we can sensibly put on the preference space in order to be able to deduce useful information from it, and (2) what restrictions a concept akin to Chamberlin's differentiation would require. It is only after we impose such restrictions (i.e., after we know something about the functional relationships within the preference space) that we can predict the effects on preference of moves of firms to various points within the space, and it is only then that we can explain those moves that do occur (e.g., explain why a firm advertises more or less).

One's mind naturally turns to the price dimension. For most purposes it is quite acceptable to place the restriction that, *ceteris paribus*, there will be more "yes" purchase decisions as price decreases.[7]

It is almost as easy to accept a restriction that an increase in speed of delivery is positively related to preference, i.e., that the speed of delivery can be considered to have a monotonically increasing functional relationship to sales volume. Under any sensible assumptions, a further

---

[6] A restriction has already been implicitly placed upon the n-space that the individuals' preferences are not unitary, i.e., that there are several different points that will be "yes" and several that will be "no." We have also assumed implicitly that the preference spaces will not be identical for all consumers. Together these simple assumptions explain perhaps the most basic phenomenon that Chamberlin was interested in — dispersion of price for a unit size of product in a given industry.

[7] However, one must consider profit rather than preference when considering optimizing solutions, and no restriction on the relation of price to profit is generally acceptable.

increase in speed of delivery or transportation will never result in a marginal decline in sales. This is so because an increase in speed of delivery will not cause any person not to buy who would otherwise buy.

Furthermore, I would argue that a similar restriction on the advertising-preference relationship is also sensible. There may be situations in which a larger quantity of a given advertising campaign will diminish sales ("yes'es") but no empirical evidence has come to light.

The class of dimensions that includes speed, service, and advertising may be thought of as making the product "better" to some or all potential customers, while making it "worse" to none. To make a product better while holding price constant is to make the product cheaper, and hence these types of changes in the product are analogous to price reductions to some or all customers. And indeed, Mrs. Robinson characterized advertising in just this way: "It may be assumed that expenditure on advertisement necessary to increase the sales of a firm may be treated as equivalent, from the point of view of the entrepeneur, to a reduction in price having the same effect upon sales" (1933). Chamberlin himself drew an analogy between product improvement and price reduction, though it is not clear whether he meant "product improvement" to be synonymous with "product differentiation."

Given such restrictions we could say that, if we assume *ceteris paribus*, a firm's offerings will have higher preference (more differentiation) at lower price, faster delivery, and more advertising. After we have imposed these restrictions we can predict changes in the dependent variable for changes in any of these independent variables.

But the situation is different with respect to those other important dimensions of consumer preference which Chamberlin includes in his definition. For example, unlike changes in price or advertising expenditures, under any but the most unrealistic assumptions such as zero elasticity, a change in spatial location or flavor will lose some customers for a firm, even though it gains others. Spatial and flavor changes make the product worse to some potential customers, and beyond some point the marginal number of worsened customers will exceed the number of bettered customers. There may be exceptional segments of the functional relationship in which a spatial change, say, may better everyone; examples include a store's move from the second to the first floor, or the move of a roadside discount house closer to the town. But this cannot continue indefinitely, as can the analogous process in the case of advertising or speed of delivery. (Of course a spatial or flavor change can still be profitable even if it causes some previous customers not to buy; the change may gain more customers than it loses and might therefore be profitable. Or if the number of customers decreases the firm may increase its profit by the higher price that will be the optimum solution for the lesser elasticity of demand.)

The important point is that beyond some point the preference function must turn downward, as the change in location or flavor becomes so great as to lose more customers than it gains. The effect of a change will therefore not necessarily raise its demand curve at every point in it. This is also true of a flavor change in beer, or a fashion change in liquor; some customers will be attracted by the change, but inevitably some will be repelled. A change may increase or decrease the slope and the height of the demand curve at any given point.

These latter dimensions (location, flavor, etc.), which are important to Chamberlin's definition, bear a U-shaped (or sometimes a monotonically decreasing) functional relationship to quantity sold. There is some point beyond which increasing "differentiation" will cause decreasing volume; for example, the store that moves too far away from its competitors must also eventually move away from its customers. But in Chamberlin's scheme of things, an increase in "differentiation" is defined as always leading to increased preference (i.e., sales volume); even the weaker requirement of increased revenue will not work.

In still other words, a change in a variable like speed of delivery or advertising is "this plus that," whereas a change in spatial location, taste, etc., is "this instead of that." This is why a beer's flavor change is not the same kind of thing as is the "quality competition" of an addition to a car's horsepower.

Therefore, many of the dimensions that Chamberlin wishes to consider cannot be restricted monotonically, a priori, as can price. And hence *it is logically impossible for there ever to be a single composite of Chamberlin's variables that can be treated as a monotonic dimension, as Chamberlin hoped for "product differentiation." Therefore we must decide that Chamberlin's product-differentiation concept is faulty, not because of faulty construction, but because it is logically impossible to construct a roughly similar concept that will achieve Chamberlin's purpose.*

In other words, unlike speed, the usual price variable, and Hotelling's distance variable, *differentiation can never be a variable that will independently explain or predict preference*, which is its primary purpose in Chamberlin's scheme. There is no function of the constituents of differentiation (those that are included in Chamberlin's definition) that will have a monotonic relationship to preference, because of the nonmonotonic relationships of the constituents to preference. Therefore no variable can be constituted to represent Chamberlin's notion of differentiation that will permit *general* statements about the effects of higher or lower values of the variable, without specific outside knowledge of the constituent functions in the particular situation.

AFTER "PRODUCT DIFFERENTIATION," WHAT THEN?

If we jettison the concept of product differentiation, what have we lost? There are two issues to discuss, product differentiation as an independent variable in economic investigation, and product differentiation as an explanation of the downward-sloping demand curve of firms that do not qualify as monopolists under earlier definitions of the term "monopoly." We shall discuss the latter matter first.

It seems to me that the concept of product differentiation is not really necessary for an economics that accepts a downward-sloping demand curve. Perhaps it is easiest if we begin economic discourse by stating only that when a man has goods to sell, the normal apparatus for him (or for economists) to use to understand his situation is a downward-sloping demand curve, which is the natural state of affairs in a world in which many dimensions of products affect the preferences of buyers and in which the preferences of individual buyers are scattered throughout the aggregate preference n-space. To establish the exact shape of the demand curve — or more generally, to determine the functional relationship between purchases for a firm's product and all the relevant dimensions — is a problem in business management and market research. It is reasonable to consider the competitive almost-horizontal demand curve as a limit case of *physical* identity of the goods of many other sellers. This solution does not require us to consider the normal case as a resolution of competitive and monopolistic "forces," or as a situation "in which monopolistic and competitive elements are blended," as Chamberlin puts it. As Mrs. Robinson suggested, we can ignore the ideal case of perfect monopoly and its vertical demand curve, to which not even a rough approximation has ever been seen in the real world; and we can abandon to courts of law the discussion of whether or not "monopoly" exists. We can merely assume that a seller has some market discretion to adjust price and output without discontinuous results, except for the special case in which his discretion is so exceedingly small as to have the appearance that we call perfect competition.

Without making an explicit argument of this sort, various writers do proceed in exactly this fashion. Stigler, for example, in the second edition of *The Theory of Price*, does not mention "product differentiation," though he does categorize firms with varying degrees of market power into monopolies and nonmonopolies. But that distinction could be abandoned by Stigler with the loss of nothing more than a few sticks of type.[8] Samuelson (1st ed.) discusses the subject in this way also, though he attaches the label "monopolistic competition" to the in-between cases. Indeed, this is exactly the usage that Sraffa proposed in his famous 1926 article, to which Mrs. Robinson points as the fount of her work.

With respect to product differentiation as an independent variable that predicts various aspects of a firm's market behavior, the outlook is not so sanguine. I think we must acknowledge a forced *demarche* from technical esthetics: we have not found a single concept of product differentiation that will explain any or all market behavior, and we should not expect to find such a concept in the future.

This writer is inclined to think that purchasing depends upon so very many different factors, operating in all directions, that a consideration of them must require so many variables that generalization beyond the unit of the firm, or at most the industry, is impossible. In fact, we do not yet have in the literature a convincing analysis of the effect of even one of these variables, except perhaps spatial location, upon demand for any given firm's product. Until we can make such statements at the specific level, any more general statement is surely folly.

SUMMARY

1. (*a*) The term "product differentiation" often is used in confusing descriptions of economic phenomena, or tautologically, or both. (*b*) It has been explicitly used as a synonym for many other terms which are not themselves synonyms. (*c*) The strongest evidence of its confusion is that the term has never been made operational, and when it has been used empirically, its measurement has been subjective.

2. Chamberlin's definition of "product differentiation" is tautological. The term is made synonymous with preference, but Chamberlin tries to use the concept to explain preference phenomena, including the downward-sloping demand curve.

3. None of the other concepts that have been offered as identical with product differentiation — price dispersion, price elasticity, etc. — fits Chamberlin's purposes and the rest of his system.

4. No operational definition that fits Chamberlin's purposes for "product differentiation" is possible. The dimensions of which product differentiation is to be composed — speed, taste, spatial location,

---

[8] It may be significant that Stigler's first edition contained a chapter on "Imperfect Competition" which did employ the term and concept of "product differentiation."

etc. — are not all monotonically related to preference, and hence a combination of them cannot be monotonically related to preference. Therefore no a priori restrictions can be placed upon the composite variable, and it consequently lacks predictive or explanatory power.

5. Both economic theory and empirical economic investigation can get along nicely without a variable like product differentiation — as they must.

Appendix B

The Advertising Ratio and Marginal Returns to Advertising[1]

INTRODUCTION

The proportion that advertising expenditures bear to sales (the advertising ratio) has been used in several studies of the advertising response function, including the work of Kolliner, Mitchell, Sandage and Bernstein, and Stigler. However, the results are quite contradictory. The survey of manufacturers by Sandage and Bernstein indicated that the larger firms have smaller advertising-sales ratios (1956). Kolliner's survey concluded that larger advertisers have lower ratios of advertising-selling expense (1963). Stigler found no correlation between the "optimum firm size" and the advertising-sales ratio (1958). Mitchell found that for almost all classes of retailers, the larger stores had higher advertising-sales ratios (1941). McNair's data on department stores showed smaller ratios for smaller stores before World War II, but since then the pattern has been more mixed; McNair explains the change by the shift to branch stores (1939–62).

The review in Chapter 1 of a great deal of evidence *other* than from studies of advertising ratios — including experimental data and econometric analysis — led to the conclusion that *for a given firm advertising a given product*, there are no increasing returns to advertising; i.e., marginal returns to advertising diminish monotonically. However, that chapter tried to exclude overall corporate data, which is what the studies mentioned in the paragraph above contained, and which this appendix will discuss.

[1] The empirical work in this appendix was drawn from an earlier article by Julian L. Simon and George H. Crain (1966).

At first thought it seems that the advertising ratio of firms of various sizes can tell much about the relationship of advertising to size. But upon reflection it becomes clear that the advertising ratio tells nothing about the relationship of advertising to economies of scale or to market power except possibly by way of telling something about the simpler question of whether there are any increasing returns to advertising. The latter is the only question on which the advertising ratio can possibly throw any light. And it can only be informative on that question if several assumptions can reasonably be made, as follows.

Begin with a little model of the firm that advertises:

(B1) Quantity sold $= f_1$ (price, advertising, other promotion)

(B2) Production cost $= f_2$ (quantity) $= f_3$ (labor, materials, capital)

(B3) Profit $=$ (quantity) (price) $-$ production cost.

Now, if price is the same for all firms in the industry, one might consider that

(B4) Sales $=$ (quantity) (price) $= f_4$ (advertising, other promotion).

But this last assumption may not be reasonable, because price might be lower (or higher) for the smaller firms in an industry, or for those that advertise less. To the extent that relationship (B4) does not hold, simple cross-sectional studies of the relationship between firm size and advertising ratio (of the sort done previously and also done here) cannot mean much.

A further necessary assumption for such studies is that the amounts spent for advertising and other promotion are independent — which they almost certainly are not. But if they were, one might consider that

(B5) Sales $= f_5$ (advertising).

What, then, might it signify if one were to find one pattern or the other, that larger firms have higher or lower advertising ratios? Begin with the former. First assume further that production cost is proportional to quantity produced,

(B6) Production cost $=$ (quantity) (constant per-unit cost).

If it is found that the larger the firm, the higher the advertising ratio, then if equation (B5) is a good approximation, there must be decreasing returns. This would also suggest that the larger firm is at a disadvantage. On the other hand, if production cost is a decreasing function of quantity, then the larger firm might have a higher advertising ratio and still be more efficient than the smaller firm, i.e., there might still be economies of scale if the advertising ratio increases with size. In casual language, if the larger firm can produce much cheaper, it pays for it to spend considerably more for advertising per unit for the marginal unit sold, and hence more for the average unit sold.

Or, if price is higher for the larger firm, its advertising ratio might be higher without proving anything at all about either marginal returns or economies of scale.

On the other hand, now, let us consider what it might mean if the advertising ratio were found to be *lower* for larger firms. If equation (B5) is a reasonable assumption, price and other promotion being the same for all firms in the industry, it would be rather extraordinary to find larger firms with lower advertising ratios, because that would almost surely mean that they stopped advertising too soon; i.e., it would apparently mean that they had chosen advertising budgets in which marginal cost is lower than average cost (though peculiarly-shaped advertising response functions could make this explanation not true). Of course it is also hypothetically possible that production costs are higher for the larger firm, in which case the larger firm would reasonably have a lower advertising ratio than a smaller firm, but this is unlikely. So if one does observe a lower advertising ratio for larger firms it probably indicates that price and other promotion are different for the larger firms than for the smaller, e.g., more reliance by the larger firm on the sales force and less on advertising. Another quite likely explanation is that the firms in the larger size category sell different products than the smaller firms, which may well happen within the IRS three-digit system.

After the above discussion the reader may have no interest whatever in cross-sectional studies of the relationship between the advertising ratio and firm size. Nevertheless, we shall now look at these data to see what, if any, patterns they show, if only to check whether previously reported cross-sectional patterns are correct.

A word about why ratio data have been used in advertising studies. Ratio data have been used only because advertising figures are commonly available only in the form of ratios, or in aggregated form which then forces the reduction to ratios. (The IRS 1960–61 *Source Book of Income* data used in this paper is an example of the latter.) It is trade secrecry that prevents disclosure of dollar data. Hence, the superb ground-breaking article (now forgotten) by Sidney Sherman in the 1900 *Journal of the American Statistical Association* employed the advertising ratio as a major analytical tool for a general study of advertising. For other examples, Kaldor and Silverman (1948), and Telser (1962), have studied the relationship of industry concentration to the industry advertising ratio. Mitchell related the advertising ratio of retailers to size of city and size of firm (1941). Jastram used advertising ratio data in his investigation of stability of advertising expenditures in oligopolized industries (1949). Bain (1957), Lewis (1954), the FTC in the Procter & Gamble-Clorox case (1963), and many others have related the ratio to various product characteristics. Borden's massive study (1942) used the advertising ratio ubiquitously.

The ratio data that are provided by trade magazines and trade associations can sometimes be useful to business firms, because firms have special qualitative knowledge of their industries and their competitors which helps them put meaningful interpretations on the ratios. A firm can estimate the amount of personal selling by its rivals, for example, which renders the advertising ratio more informative. The advertising ratios of a firm's competitors can also be used as helpful yardsticks for its own expenditure decisions. (Of course, managers often misuse ratio data and base wrong decisions upon them. For example, the ratio given by trade sources is always for advertising and sales in year t, which must be misleading in those industries in which the effect of advertising is heavily lagged — cigarettes and beer, for example).

Economists are certainly not barred from having specific qualitative knowledge of an industry. But because economists usually wish to speak about many industries at once in an attempt to find general patterns of behavior, and also because economists wish to render all data quantitative and comparable, it is less likely that artful interpretation will be applied by economists to particular ratios to bring out their hidden meanings. We must therefore consider the usefulness of the advertising ratio for objective, quantitative investigations.

THE SAMPLE DATA

The studies by Mitchell, Sandage and Bernstein, Kolliner, and McNair used sample-survey data on advertising ratios. A combination of advertising data from checking bureaus and sales data from annual reports was used by Shuford (1961). Sample-survey data suffer badly from inadequate sampling frames (complete lists of firms in various industries are not available) and nonresponse bias (firms that don't advertise are less likely to reply) and differences in the definition of advertising. An interesting illustration of the extraordinary extent of nonresponse bias (or sampling bias) is found in Borden's juxtaposition of Census of Manufacturers data, data from a Survey of the Association of National Advertisers, and Dun & Bradstreet data, summarized in Table B-1.

Checking-service data on advertising expenditures typically represent something over half of what a firm actually spends because many advertising media are not checked by the checking services; the proportion varies greatly with a given firm's choice of where it spends its advertising dollars.

The IRS data used in the present study have the advantage of comprehensiveness, in that they include every tax return within an industry. They also have the definitional advantage that the sales data are as reported for current tax purposes, and the advertising expenditures are those that are claimed as expenses. The firms in each of the 218 SIC three-digit classes are divided into 13 asset-size classes as follows; (1) zero assets, (2) zero–$50,000, (3) $50M–$100M, (4) $100M–$500M, (5) $500M–$1MM, (6) $1M–$2.5MM, (7) $2.5MM–$5MM, (8) $5MM–$10MM, (9) $10MM–$25MM, (10) $25MM–$50MM, (11) $50MM–$100MM, (12) $100MM–$250MM, (13) over $250MM.

Table B-1. Advertising-Sales Ratios for Shoe Manufacturers
Estimated by Various Sources (in percentages)

	1933	1934	1935
Census of Manufacturers	0.18% (n unknown)	– –	0.26% (n unknown)
Association of National Advertisers Survey	4.0 (n = 6)	4.3 (n = 8)	4.0 (n = 9)
Dun & Bradstreet Survey, 17 profitable firms	– –	1.4 (n = 17)	– –
Dun & Bradstreet Survey, 10 not-profitable firms	– –	2.2 (n = 8)	– –

Source: Borden, 1942, pp. 372-373.

We took a systematic sample of every other industry, moving down the SIC code (with a few exceptions). The 109 industries that fell into the sample represent $422 billion (52.4 percent of total) business receipts, $4,624 thousand (51.1 percent of total) advertising, and 639,469 firms. Difficulties caused by the nature of the data will be discussed as we analyze the data.

We shall employ several approaches as discussed in sections A–D below.

A. Simple Correlation of Advertising Ratio to Size of Firm

Our first approach follows these steps:

1. For each size class in each industry (e.g., bakery products, firms with assets of $500,000–$1,000,000 compute the advertising ratio (advertising/total sales $= A_i/S_i$). The number of firms in the category does not directly affect the computed ratios.

2. For each industry compute simple correlations between the mean sales S_i (and separately, mean assets W_i) per firm in each size class, and the ratio of advertising/sales (also the ratio of advertising/assets) in that size class. Size classes with zero total assets were omitted from the analysis. These simple correlations — r_{s_i} and r_{w_i} — are the basic units in much of the analysis that follows.

(At first it seemed difficult to decide which industry-size-groups to exclude from the analysis as being empty. Obviously we had to exclude cells that contained no firms. A little less obviously, we excluded cells whose firms had a total of zero assets, on the grounds that they are only paper firms. But what about cells containing only firms that had assets and sales, but did no advertising? Quite obviously, advertising was not responsible for their sales. Nevertheless, we include such cells because they do not differ qualitatively from other cells, some of which may contain a great many firms that also do no advertising, and that overall have a very low — but positive — advertising ratio.[2] This decision points up the tenuousness of possible inferences concerning the relationship of advertising to sales, based on this type of data.)

3. Compute the mean correlation across industries. The values obtained were

$$\frac{1}{109} \sum_{j=1}^{109} r_{s_i} = .09 \text{ (s.d.} = .45\text{), and}$$

$$\frac{1}{109} \sum_{j=1}^{109} r_{w_i} = .07 \text{ (s.d.} = .40\text{).}$$

The means are small compared to their standard deviations.

4. The distribution of r_{s_i} is shown in Table B-2.[3]

There are two possible interpretations of these data: (1) The advertising ratio rises with size in about half the industries and declines in the other half; or (2) the data are not competent to support conclusions about this matter. In either case, however, we may consider these data as a refutation of the conclusions about this relationship based on similar approaches to similar data (Koliner, 1963; Sandage and Bernstein, 1956).

[2] Lee Preston told us that he considers this an error in judgment. Whether or no, the next section avoids the question by considering each pair of size-classes separately.

[3] The significance of any particular correlation coefficient does not matter. We are here interested in the direction of the relationships, not their intensity.

Table B-2.   Distribution of Correlations r_{s_i} between Assets and the Ratio
(Advertising to Sales) for the Various Industries

r_{s_i}		Number of Cases
+.90 to 1.0	. . .	5
.80 to .90	. . .	7
.70 to .80	. . .	9
.60 to .70	. . .	4
.50 to .60	. . .	6
.40 to .50	. . .	3
.30 to .40	. . .	6
.20 to .30	. . .	10
.10 to .20	. . .	8
0 to .10	. . .	0
−.10 to 0	. . .	0
−.10 to − .20	. . .	12
−.20 to − .30	. . .	11
−.30 to − .40	. . .	11
−.40 to − .50	. . .	6
−.50 to − .60	. . .	2
−.60 to − .70	. . .	4
−.70 to − .80	. . .	4
−.80 to − .90	. . .	0
−.90 to −1.0	. . .	0

B. Increases versus Decreases between Pairs of Size Classes

Our approach in section A above describes relationships over the entire range of sizes of firms. However, the true relationship might be that of an S-curve in which there are first decreasing then increasing advertising ratios. A correlation coefficient could mask the presence of such relationship.

To search out such possible S-curve relationships we computed the differences between the ratios for each pair of succeeding size classes, e.g.,

$$\frac{\text{advertising}}{\text{sales}} \text{ (size class 1) minus } \frac{\text{advertising}}{\text{sales}} \text{ (size class 2),}$$

$$\frac{\text{advertising}}{\text{sales}} \text{ (size class 2) minus } \frac{\text{advertising}}{\text{sales}} \text{ (size class 3), etc.}$$

We then added up the number of increases and the number of decreases from each size class to the next size class, as shown in Table B-3. A "+" indicates an increase from the smaller to the larger size group, with the size groups increasing from 1 to 13. The number of observations in each group is considerably less than 109 due to the varying numbers of empty cells in the various size groups.

Table B-3. Comparison of Advertising-Sales Ratio
between Pairs of Asset Size-Groups

Between Groups	Positive (+)	Negative (−)
(1-2)	26	26
(2-3)	31	49
(3-4)	43	39
(4-5)	44	39
(5-6)	52	34
(6-7)	57	44
(7-8)	51	47
(8-9)	49	45
(9-10)	40	36
(10-11)	28	33
(11-12)	22	25
(12-13)	12	19

Again the data do not show us a mean decrease in the ratio between any pair of successive size classes where theory would lead us to predict economies of scale, that is, at the smaller end of the size distribution. Again the data are consistent with hypotheses of (1) increasing ratios in some industries, decreasing in others, and (2) incompetence of the data.

In our inspection of various neighborhoods of the total size range, it might be that the absolute size classification obscures differences that might appear if we looked at relative size relationships in the various industries. In other words, if there are points of decreasing ratios in the steel industry and in the retail jewelry industry, the point is surely between a smaller pair of size classes in the jewelry industry than in the steel industry.

The SIC categories with which we are working lump together many very different types of economic activities. Nevertheless, perhaps even a slight decrease in heterogeneity will illuminate the situation. We therefore identified the size class with the largest number of firms in each industry and compared advertising ratios between it and the next smaller size class, and between it and the next higher class. The results are shown in Table B-4. Once more the data show no effects worthy of explanation.

C. The Effect of the Extent of Advertising in an Industry

If some consistent relationships can be found between subclasses of firms, it might help us to assess the value of our basic data — and hence to choose between the hypotheses (1) that there are, indeed, no relationships between the advertising ratio and size, and (2) that the data are incompetent. As a first possibility let us consider whether there are different sorts of relationships between advertising ratio and size of firm in industries that use advertising heavily compared to industries that do little advertising. If heavy-advertising-use and light-advertising-use industries behave differently with respect to advertising, a statistical trade-off might explain the appearance of an overall zero relationship.

Table B-4. Comparison of Advertising-Sales Ratio of Model Size-Groups with Next Smaller and Next Larger Asset Size-Groups

Next smaller size-group higher ratio than most-numerous group Next larger size-group higher ratio than most-numerous group	= 16
Next smaller size-group higher ratio than most-numerous group Next larger size-group lower ratio than most-numerous group	= 18
Next smaller size-group lower ratio than most-numerous group Next larger size-group higher ratio than most-numerous group	= 12
Next smaller size-group lower ratio than most-numerous group Next larger size-group lower ratio than most-numerous group	= 24

We can test for this possibility by correlating the advertising ratios for industries taken as wholes, with the correlations of size and advertising ratio within the industries. More specifically, with the observed results:

$$\text{correlation of } \frac{\sum_{j=1}^{n \le 13} \left(\frac{A_{j,i}}{S_{j,i}} \right)}{n \le 13} \text{ with } r_{si} = -.03 \text{ and}$$

$$\text{correlation of } \frac{\sum_{j=1}^{n \le 13} A_{j,i}}{\sum_{j=1}^{n \le 13} S_{j,i}} \text{ with } r_{si} = +.06,$$

where $A_{j,i}$ = advertising expenditures for the j*th* size-group in the i*th* industry, $S_{j,i}$ = sales, $n \le 13$ = number of non-zero size-groups in the particular industry.

The extent of use of advertising by an industry apparently does not help explain its particular relationship between size of firm and extent of advertising.[4]

---

[4] Preston suggested considering consumer-goods industries separately. Arranging the industries by amount of advertising, as we have done here, covers some of the same ground, however.

D. The Effect of Numbers of Competitors

Following the general argument of Section C, the relationships might be different in industries with very different market structures. We therefore correlated the total number of firms in the industry with the correlation coefficient of the advertising ratio with size of firms, as follows:

$$\text{correlation of } \sum_{j=1}^{n \le 13} F_{ji} \text{ with } r_{si} = +.06, \text{ and}$$

$$\text{correlation of } \sum_{j=1}^{n \le 13} \sqrt{F_{ji}} \text{ with } r_{si} = -.04,$$

where F_{ji} is the number of firms in asset size-group j in industry i. Again the results are astonishing in their blankness. Not even to get interesting but spurious relationships is unusual.

DISCUSSION

Given only the data and the results shown above, one simply cannot draw even the slightest hint of a conclusion about marginal returns to advertising. Reasons why this might be so were discussed earlier in this appendix. But there are still other reasons why the data may not be meaningful in this connection.

1. Structural changes in an industry that are not revealed by IRS statistics can cause changes in the advertising ratio. Such a structural shift is apparent in Table B-5, which shows the advertising-sales ratio for various classes of department stores in the years 1938–40 and 1962. Whereas in 1938–40 the ratio data are consistent with a hypothesis of economies of scale, the 1962 data show a different pattern. To understand such phenomena one must go below the ratio data. McNair, who has lived close to these data for many years, explains the shift by the structural shift to branch suburban stores.

2. The model that underlies the study of advertising efficiency by relating size-class to advertising ratio is that the group of firms for whom advertising is more efficient will have more sales produced per dollar of advertising. This assumes that all firms advertise to the margin.

But one size-class of firms may not advertise to the margin. Small firms, for example, may not understand advertising measurement very well, and hence they may be particularly cautious (though the effect of ignorance could be in the other direction). If this size-class does not approach the margin, its advertising ratio will be lower than if the firm

Table B-5. Ratio Advertising to Sales for Department Stores

Sales Volume Groups	1938	1939	1940	1962
Under $500M	.0360	.0330	.0300	
500M to 1MM	.0382	.0406	.0350	
1MM to 2MM	.0399	.0390	.0397	.0390
2MM to 5MM	.0458	.0450	.0413	.0292
5MM to 10MM	.0423	.0411	.0314	.0293
10MM and over				
(1962 10MM to 20MM)	.0433	.0434	.0405	.0336
20MM to 50MM				.0279
50MM and over				.0277

Source: Data for 1938-1940 from NRDGA, quoted by D. M. Edwards and W. H. Howard, *Retail Advertising and Sales Promotion* (rev. ed.) 1943. Data for 1962 from Malcolm P. McNair, *Operating Results for Department and Specialty Stores in 1962.*

went to the margin. This could be another influence on the advertising ratio which is not related to efficiency, but which helps render ratio data uninterpretable as an index of efficiency.

Taking all the above into account, it is our opinion that advertising-ratio data alone are not competent to serve as the basis for any general investigation of the economics of advertising.[5]

[5] The behavior of advertising expenditures in the depression cf the 1930s is an example of how advertising ratio data can be misleading. If one looks at the proportion of net sales spent for advertising by department (and specialty) stores from, say, 1929 to 1944, the highest ratio occurred in 1932 (McNair, 1944, as seen in Figure 3-7). This suggests that advertising "intensity" rose in the depths of the depression. But if one looks at the absolute amount spent for advertising by department stores, one sees that it dropped sharply from a high in 1929 to a low in 1933, and was almost as low in 1932 as in 1933 (Weld, 1940, p. 20, as seen in Figure 3-4). This shows that the use of ratio data alone would almost surely lead a researcher to the wrong conclusion.

Appendix C

The Effect of Advertising Competition on the Diffusion of Innovations[1]

This appendix is included in the book for two reasons. First, it may be of interest to students of the economics of marketing. Second, it illustrates how the advertising industry and its data can be used to study proportions of general interest in economics.

Griliches made a considerable advance in understanding the diffusion of economic innovations when he showed that the absolute relationship of revenue to cost explains much of the spread of hybrid corn (1957). But a different sort of explanation than Griliches offered is needed for the case considered in this chapter.

The "January White Sale" is now a universal event in the calendar of department stores. Towels, sheets, and other "white goods" are used evenly throughout the year, and they are not sold much as gifts. Therefore, white goods are ideal merchandise to offer on special sale during the slow season that follows Christmas. (The "August White Sale" has the same low-marginal-cost rationale.)

Clearance sales in January were well established in New York City at least as early as 1886 and probably long before, and white goods were major items in those sales. (The category at that time included underwear also.) But it was not until 1900 that Bloomingdales and Wanamakers both titled their sales "White Sale." Then, in quick succession, the other department stores followed.

[1] By Julian L. Simon and Leslie Golembo. This appendix originally appeared under the title, "The Spread of a Cost-Free Business Innovation." The authors are grateful to the Illinois State Historical Library and to its director, Clyde C. Walton, for great courtesy in providing microfilms of Illinois newspapers.

Unlike the spread of such innovations as hybrid corn or coke use in the blast furnaces (Temin, 1964), there is no incremental out-of-pocket cost to a merchant who conducts a white sale in place of the "January Clearance Sale" he would otherwise conduct. The advertising cost is the same, assuming he uses the same amount of newspaper space, and the goods are much the same, though he may concentrate more heavily on white goods. Apparently the innovation is successful by some standard meaningful to merchants because it has continued in New York City since its beginning and has caught on and continued elsewhere. Nor can mere habit explain it, because the cost accounting of retail merchants is sufficiently simple, and sales response is measured with sufficient ease and immediacy, so that profitable promotional practices are quite distinguishable from unprofitable practices.

Given that the January white sale is a good thing, and given that merchants in other cities were aware of it (evidence for which will be shown shortly), what was the time and space pattern of the innovation's spread?

The pattern of diffusion for some U.S. cities [2] is shown in Table C-1. The data were developed from retrogressive inspection of newspaper advertisements.

Table C-1. White Sale Adoption Pattern in Various Cities

City	Year first store adopted 1	Year second store adopted 2	Total number of stores advertising in newspaper 3
New York	1900	1900	30 (1900)
St. Louis	1903	1905	21 (1903)
Chicago	1910	1918	22 (1910)
Los Angeles	1906	1912	21 (1906)
San Francisco	1908	1917	19 (1908)
Peoria, Ill.	1901	1916	11 (1901)
Springfield, Ill.	1915	1916	12 (1915)
Rockford, Ill.	1935	1935	10 (1935)
Jacksonville, Ill.	1933	1936	5 (1933)
Mattoon, Ill.	1933	1936	6 (1933)
Joliet, Ill.	1936	1936	9 (1936)

The table shows considerable variation. For example, Schipper and Block ran Peoria's first white sale in 1901. This change from the usual January "Odds and Ends Sale," or "Leftover Sale," or "Clearance

---

[2] The sample for the big cities was chosen to get a geographic spread, subject to the availability of newspapers. The middle-sized cities in Illinois were chosen to scatter across the state.

Sale" was neither casual in motive nor trivial in execution. Schipper and Block ran this copy in their advertisement:

White, clean and fresh as the new born century itself is the storeful of merchandise that greet those who come here today. Annual White Sales is one of the notable evolutions in 19th Century merchandising. It is planned for nearly 6 months ahead — at times when goods are cheapest. It is by far the most notable feature in our business year, transforming as it does, a naturally dull period into a busy one; give us a chance to become acquainted — and prove to you the wonderful buying power a big store possesses.

Much of the small-city data are immediately explained by Montgomery Ward's (and later Penney's) national policy of an annual white sale beginning in 1933, which accounted for the first white sale in Joliet (1936), Mattoon (1933), Rockford (1935), and Jacksonville (1933). The independents, and Penney's too, quickly responded everywhere. This wave of adoption clearly shows that the white sale is an effective device. Ward's skipped one year in some cities (e.g., Jacksonville in 1935), but since then the event has been almost invariable for Ward's, Penney's, and most other stores.

One possible determinant of the spread of an innovation is geographical contiguity, whose rationale is the "two-step flow of influence" in which neighbors talk to each other chainwise. This model does not seem appropriate to the white sale case because there is little day-to-day communication among store-owners (or executives) across communities. However, being a neighbor of a city that had adopted fluoridation made it more likely that the city would also adopt fluoridation (Crain, 1966), a fact which gives some support to the model. But distance alone does not seem to explain the observed white sale pattern. San Francisco and Los Angeles are farther from New York than are Chicago and St. Louis, but they were not noticeably slower to adopt the practice. And certainly those two California cities were much ahead of most of the smaller Illinois cities that were closer to New York. A bigger sample, holding other variables constant, might reveal distance as having some influence, but probably not enough influence to make it a truly important variable.

Communication of knowledge of the innovation is not likely to be important either. In many cases, the advertisements mentioned white goods as such several years before the store or city reached the criterion of having the major headline announce "White Sale." For example, in 1905 the Hamburger Department Store in Los Angeles used the words "White Fair" within its January clearance sale advertisement; also in 1905 Siegel Cooper in Chicago devoted almost a page to "white goods," but it was not until 1910 that the headline "January White

Sale" appeared. And in 1906 Hess Brothers in Rockford wrote "Come to our fancy white goods basement" at the bottom of their "January Clearance Sale" advertisement. (Interestingly, it was 1935 before there was any further mention of "white goods" in Rockford stores' advertisements.)

The cultural variables frequently adduced by sociologists to explain diffusion are not very relevant in this case either. Department-store merchants in middle-sized and large cities are hardly fettered by the ties of traditional culture that may [3] affect responses of farmers in underdeveloped countries. This view of the adaptability of the merchants is supported by the showing that once the innovation was used by one store in a city, the second (and other) stores responded without delay — in both small cities as well as large — indicating that culture did not prevent quick response.

The difference between big and middle-sized cities is obviously important in an explanation and requires interpretation. Size itself has some effect in that there are more stores in large cities, and hence the probability of one of them taking up the innovation is greater in the larger city. But mere numbers can explain very little because the number of department stores advertising in the big cities is not very much greater in the big cities, as column (3) in Table C-1 shows. Lumping the numbers of stores in the big-city versus small-city classes indicates that the number of stores in the big cities does not explain the early acceptance of the innovation.

The most reasonable explanations we can offer of these data showing differences by city size are two:

1. There may be a difference in the nature of the competition in big versus small cities. There being smaller numbers of stores in the small cities means that there is more competitive interaction among the stores; each store is relatively more affected by a move of a single competitor where the numbers are smaller. This greater interdependence suggests more caution and conservatism through greater fear of retaliation. If this explanation holds, and if it generalizes to other innovations, it suggests that the general belief in the quickening effect of competition on economic activity is indeed well placed.

2. Another possibility is that the executives in bigger stores are simply keener merchandisers and quicker to act. This is supported by the finding that big cities adopted fluoridation earlier than smaller cities (Crain, 1966). (But against this is the fact that once a single store in the small city began the innovation the others were quick to act also.) This second explanation of the acceptance of an innovation (white sales) is

---

[3] Or may not (see Schultz, 1964).

in harmony with the Schumpeter-Galbraith hypothesis about the creation of innovations, that is, that large firms are more inventive than small ones. Clearly, however, their explanations for invention do not apply here: larger benefits accruing to the larger firms from market control, ability of the larger firm to self-insure itself with a whole series of successes and failures, and the high investment cost of invention. Furthermore, a comparison of bigger to smaller is dangerous if the curve is likely to be U-shaped — as this one is. If indeed bigger stores in bigger cities accept innovations faster because of scale, this comparison might well be taking place at the *lower* end of the meaningful absolute range of firm magnitude. That is, *even* bigger stores might be slower to accept.

The decision about which of these two explanations is better, or whether both forces have influence, awaits a larger sample and study of other innovations — especially the August white sale.

Appendix **D**

A Bibliographical Essay on Some Sources of Data in Advertising [1]

Reader, beware. This appendix offers clues, not inclusiveness. It covers some topics more throughly than others. And the listings on any one sort of data are usually only a few examples from ongoing series. Furthermore, the coverage for the years since 1963 is much more thorough than for the years before 1963. The reader who wants a historical series will have to back-track from the contemporary data. Nevertheless, it is hoped that this appendix is helpful and better than nothing.

From one point of view the researcher in the economics of advertising is well off. The data available to him are plentiful as compared with other industries. One reason for this is that the basic facts about advertising — how many advertising messages are sent out by various advertisers — are public, out in the open. One can watch a competitor's advertising and record what he does, and the competitor cannot conceal the broad outlines of his advertising efforts. This naturally has led to the rise of commercial organizations that measure all firms' advertising, and these published measurements are basic data for the researcher.

Several of the standard texts do an excellent job of listing these commercial services. Probably the most recent and comprehensive is Bogart (1967, Chapter 10 and pp. 324–327). An older book which also gives a comprehensive listing is Burton (1959, Chapter XXIII). Although some of the publications in Burton are now out of print, they are

[1] This appendix benefited from the assistance of Eleanor Blum, who wrote some of it. She should not be held responsible for any of its many shortcomings, however. Seymour Banks was good enough to correct and up-date several of the data-source descriptions, and his wording has been used in such places without further note. Estelle Popkin also contributed several very helpful pieces of information.

still available in agencies and libraries and are useful historically. A number are also described in Blum (1963, and currently being updated). The reader may also want to consult the chapter on "Competitive Advertising Expenditures" in Brown, et al. (1957, Chapter 12). There is also a good section, "Advertising Expenditures and Activity for Companies and Products," in *Media Analysis Principles and Practices*, a mimeographed publication of Leo Burnett Company, presently being rewritten, which may or may not be available upon request. Two excellent articles are by Daly (1963) and Ziegler (1964), though not completely up to date as of now.

Also, the researcher is fortunate that the field has an exceptionally good trade journal, *Advertising Age* (*AA* hereafter), which publishes excerpts of most of the data of value that are available anywhere. Many of the data we mention are in *AA*. In the past, data in each issue could be located through an index to the issue, but unfortunately this index has recently been gutted of its informative function, perhaps to insure that readers go through the issue from start to finish.

In spite of these advantages, advertising data can be hard to come by, especially complete data. The purpose of this appendix is to lead the researcher to some of the more obscure sources of information and to point out certain gaps in the field.

Advertising Expenditures by Firms and Brands

In England expenditure data for firms and brands have been compiled for over 30 years by the *Statistical Review of Press Advertising*. In the United States, however, there are several organizations that collect this type of data, and they have changed from time to time; the areas of their coverage have changed also.

For newspapers, *Media Records* (Media Records, Inc., 370 Seventh Avenue, N.Y.) compiles data by individual firm and by brand as it appears throughout the year in almost 400 newspapers (more in the past), and presents it in detailed form. Millican summarized the forms in which the data were presented as of 1962:

Media Records Quarterly Blue Book: Linage record of 420 [380 as of 1969] newspapers in 140 cities, by classification, accumulative year to date quarterly; linage used by each. Covers 75 percent of the total daily circulation, and 92 percent of total Sunday circulation in the United States.

Monthly City Report is compiled for newspaper publishers in each city showing a complete record of each advertiser's use of linage in all the newspapers in that city for the past month and accumulative year to date total.

Quarterly City Report of General and Automotive Advertising shows amount of space used by every individual General and Automotive advertiser in each paper in the city for the accumulated 3, 6, 9 and 12 months' periods respectively.

Annual City Report is identical with monthly city report except carries accumulated twelve months' figures for each Display account in Retail, General, Automotive, and Financial Advertising.

Retail Advertising Performance Report lists in descending order according to city population size, all cities measured, showing for each total Retail linage of the eight most important subclassifications of Retail advertising for current month.

First Fifty Report lists leading papers for Retail, General, Automotive, Financial, Department Stores, Classified and Total Advertising. Since 1930.

Chain Store Report is an annual report of chain store linage in newspapers of each Media Records city in which chain had retail outlets.

Advertising Trend Chart. Monthly. 52 city base, January 1928, to date, for the following classifications: Retail General, Automotive, Financial, Total Display, Classified, Department Store, and Total Advertising.

Other monthly reports and special services available upon request (Millican, 1962).

Although the *Media Records* data are very useful, the coverage is far from complete — not all newspapers are covered, and coverage differs each year. Another difficulty is that firms whose expenditures in a given medium are not large are not mentioned in the published data. (The minimum changes from year to year.) A yearly abridgment of the data, *Expenditures of National Advertisers in Newspapers* (Bureau of Advertising of the American Newspaper Publishers Association, 485 Lexington Ave., New York) lists amounts spent by those national advertisers who invested $25,000 or more in newspapers measured by *Media Records.* The Bureau of Advertising also has begun recently to publish a monthly newspaper advertising report which gives percentage changes in revenue for national, retail, classified and total for the report month versus the same month a year previous and for the current and previous year's totals to date. It also contains seasonally adjusted annual advertising revenues in millions of dollars for the same four classifications. Finally, it gives percentage changes in general and automotive linage from 14 cities as measured by Media Research for the report month and year to date versus the corresponding periods of the previous year. This may be obtained from the Research Department, Bureau of Advertising, ANPA.

For consumer magazines: Leading National Advertisers (P.O. Box 525, Norwalk, Conn.) prepares for Publishers Information Bureau (575 Lexington Ave., New York) a compilation by advertiser of the expenditures in more than 100 of the largest consumer magazines.

For television: Two formerly allied firms compete in the production of network television activity and expenditure data. Both Leading National Advertisers and Broadcast Advertisers Reports (formerly LNA-BAR) monitor ABC, CBS, and NBC broadcasts and estimate expenditures for the advertisers and individual brands. BAR recently began to prepare a spot-television expenditure report on the basis of one week's monitored data per month in each of the top 75 markets. The data are projected to a monthly figure and cumulated quarterly. The Rorabaugh report was produced by LNA until January 1, 1969. It estimated spot-television expenditures in all markets on the basis of station logs. Currently, Rorabaugh estimates only TV spot expenditures for markets not monitored by BAR.

These services are well known, expensive, and difficult for libraries to obtain unless connected with an advertising agency, a fact which can make it difficult for researchers to obtain them. Less well known and much less expensive is LNA's *National Advertising Investments* which abridges data in PIB, LNA-BAR and Rorabaugh. All companies investing in these media $20,000 or more in the first six months, and $25,000 or more in the twelve month period, are included. Media covered are approximately 100 of the consumer mass magazines; five newspaper supplements; net time and program expenditures on the three major TV networks; and spot TV expenditures on 400 stations. The tables preceding this data are also useful. One table ranks the 100 top advertisers, giving comparative figures covering five years, another table shows the ten top-ranking companies in each of the four media. The data in *National Advertising Investments* are nowhere near as detailed as the data in the more comprehensive services, but they will often serve the researcher's purpose.

For radio: "Since 1966, Radio Expenditure Reports, a firm located in Larchmont, N.Y., has compiled for the Radio Advertising Bureau (RAB) quarterly data on advertisers' expenditures on network and national spot ratio. These reports contain a complete list, arranged by product category, of national spot advertisers (companies and some brands) and their estimated expenditures. Also the top 100 national spot advertisers are listed alphabetically with expenditures broken down by brand. Network advertisers' expenditures are listed by company and brand." [2]

For business publications: *The Rome Report of Business Publication Advertising* (Rome Research Company, 1960 Broadway, New York), formerly *Brad Vern's Report*, gives the expenditures of hundreds of companies which placed advertising in 630 business publications. A similar publication, more condensed and not so well known but which nevertheless lists much of the same data is *Leading Advertis-*

[2] Estelle Popkin, letter of August 5, 1969.

ers in Business Publications (American Business Press, Inc., Business Press Advertising Bureau, Information Division, 205 E. 42nd St., New York). Since 1950 it has provided advertising expenditures by company for the majority of the periodicals having their primary listing in Standard Rate & Data's *Business Publication Rates & Data.* The 1967 edition contains data on almost 2,500 advertisers investing $35,000 or more.

Standard Directory of Advertisers (National Register Publishing Co., 5201 Old Orchard Road, Skokie, Ill.), a classified guide to 17,000 corporations, occasionally gives advertising appropriations. Generally only the total amount is given, although sometimes there is a breakdown by media.

Thus, a great deal of raw data exists. But the data are not complete, even for any given brand in any one medium. Brands whose expenditures in a given medium are small are not mentioned in the published data. (The minimum amount which merits inclusion changes from year to year.) A good discussion of the difficulties in obtaining complete data is Ziegler (1964, p. 122), which tells what supplementary steps must be taken to gather comprehensive broadcast data. Brown, Lessler and Weilbacher (1957, Chapter 12) discusses the problems in connection with both print and broadcast media.

The researcher who wants to know the total expenditure for one or more particular firms must compile the expenditures from each medium separately. This is a great nuisance, and sometimes downright impossible, because one often cannot lay one's hands on all this data in even the best library. The totals were published, however, for the "100 largest" or "125 largest" advertisers each year, for many years by *Printers' Ink* (PI hereafter) which has recently become *Marketing/ Communications,* and then by *AA* (e.g., August 26, 1968, the 13th year in the *AA* series. However, these data are most frustrating and can be misleading for several reasons. First, they are for firms and not for brands or products; second, the measured expenditures include some media expenditures one year and exclude the media the next year — e.g., radio and farm magazines; third, the retrospective data exclude years for which the firm was not in the top 100 (or 125, or whatever). The recent *AA* run-downs also include data from company balance sheets where possible, and although this is helpful in estimating total advertising and sales, this kind of data is of far more interest to businessmen than to academic students of the advertising industry. (The data on the 100 or the 25 largest advertisers in *particular* media, carried in the same annual issue of *AA* as the "125 largest" is even more ubiquitous and even less useful.)

Advertising Expenditures by Industries

The academic researcher has two further difficulties: aggregating into industries, and getting data on past years.

For most industries no one organization pulls together the expenditures of the various firms, either in particular media or all together. There are certain welcome exceptions. *Advertising Age* carries data for automobiles (e.g., June 2, 1967, p. 42; September 18, 1967, p. 63; September 9, 1968, p. 106; January 2, 1966, p. 62; October 9, 1961, p. 70). The *Printers' Ink* "Battle of the Brands" series in 1964 and 1965 gives data for one or more years for razor blades, pet foods, insurance, hair products, frozen foods, gas and oil, cereals, detergents, coffee and business machines. Products sold in drugstores get the best coverage of all, compiled in *Drug Trade News* and carried in a June issue each year since 1956 (e.g., June 18, 1956, p. 24 ff.). *Merchandising Week* is another useful source, with data on the various classes of major and minor appliances and consumer electronics goods (e.g., June 14, 1965, July 19, 1965; May 31, 1965). Each year Travel Research International publishes data on major public carriers and selected travel services in U.S. media. And the Magazine Advertising Bureau makes available the expenditures in various media of states and leading associations (e.g., Air Transport Association). All of these compilations contain data both by industry and by individual brand. Data for a few industries are broken down by media in *Survey of Current Business* and *Statistical Abstract*. The product breakdown of industrial advertising in business publications is compiled by American Business Press and published in *Industrial Marketing* (e.g., July, 1968, pp. 66–70). *National Advertising Investments* (page 12 of the January–June 1968 issue compares January–June 1968 vs. the same period in 1967; page 9 of the January–December 1968 issue compares January–December 1968 vs. 1967) has a table which summarizes industry class expenditures for the current and preceding year. (The data include only expenditures of firms that spent at least $35,000 in the year.)

The researcher can get some idea about various industry expenditures from data published by the Internal Revenue Service in *Statistics of Income* and in the unpublished (but available on microfilm) *Source Book of Statistics of Income. Advertising Age* presents these data yearly for many industries as ratio of sales. But again the definitions of the industries are not always what is desired. More troublesome still, the Internal Revenue Service definition of advertising expenditures, from tax returns, often produces estimates far from those obtained by checking services, and the differences are predictable neither in size nor even in direction.

Very detailed monthly and yearly linage data have been provided for many years on individual department store items — e.g., towels — by the *Neustadt Red Book of Seasonal Patterns*, sold by George Neustadt Statistical Advertising. Average prices for past years are also included.

National Total Advertising Expenditure — U.S.

In light of these problems at the firm and industry levels, it is not surprising that the aggregate statistics for the United States are less than perfectly reliable or meaningful. The trouble is compounded by the lack of coverage for some media (which change from year to year), such as point-of-purchase advertising, and the casual coverage of others, such as direct mail, which is estimated from Post Office data on mail volume. The first regular compilation of aggregate data was by L. D. H. Weld under the auspices first of *Printers' Ink* and later the McCann-Erickson Advertising Agency. The handiest source for this series back to 1867 is *Historical Statistics of the U.S.*, and from 1958 onwards, the current *U.S. Statistical Abstract*. The problems of working with these data, plus some attempts to patch them up for particular purposes, have been discussed by other writers. The interested reader should consult Borden (1942, Appendices I and II), Backman (1967, pp. 161–167) and Blank (1963). Recently Yang has tried to improve the aggregate estimates by working with both the *purchases* of advertising as measured by the IRS tax data on reported advertising expenses and the *sales* of advertising, from IRS data on the advertising media, and then reconciling the two. These estimates are available back to 1947, and are discussed in Yang (1965).

Foreign Advertising Expenditure Data

Data for other nations can be useful to test a hypothesis if American data are not available. Such data may also be interesting for comparative studies, to see whether the same or different patterns are found in different sorts of countries.

To our knowledge the British *Statistical Review of Press Advertising* provides the only comprehensive set of firm data for any single country. Various industry compilations are made from time to time by the *Statistical Review*, and the *Advertising Quarterly* now publishes annual estimates of advertising expenditure in the United Kingdom, including media and product breakdowns (e.g., Summer, 1968, pp. 72–76) in which are given total expenditures from 1952 to 1967 as a proportion of national income and consumption. Also given are expenditures by medium for 1960 and 1964–67. Some product breakdowns are given in these sources and also in *Advertising Age*'s annual "International Section" (e.g. June 17, 1968).

Kaldor and Silverman (1948) contains many sorts of useful data (except on firms) for England as of 1935, 1938, and before World War II. And a brief article by Abrams (1952) surveys major English advertising data sources. In addition to these sources, Silverman (1951) provides many data up to 1948, and Scott (1951) summarizes various data from 1934 to 1949.

Considering more aggregated data now, in 1960 the International Advertising Association began a series which surveys (as best it can) the aggregate expenditures in various countries, presenting media and product breakdowns for some countries. This series is now included in the December issue of *International Advertiser*. And *Advertising Age* each year publishes a roundup of the world advertising situation, including data from some sources different from those of the International Advertising Association. Needless to say, the statistics for various countries suffer from various defects of varying degrees of severity.

One of the best sources for international data is *The Advertising Agency Business Around the World* (5th ed. New York: American Association of Advertising Agencies, 200 Park Ave.), which contains reports from advertising agency associations and agency leaders in 40 countries. Data varies by country, probably according to figures available. Media breakdowns for many of the countries are included.

"International Advertising Expenditures," Appendix III, in Dunn (S. Watson Dunn, *International Handbook of Advertising*, New York: McGraw-Hill, 1964) gives advertising expenditures for 36 countries, broken down by media. Footnotes to each table show the various sources of data.

Amounts of Advertising in the Various Media

We have discussed how data for the various media are used to estimate aggregate expenditures. However, these data are sometimes of interest for themselves. In addition to the sources already mentioned, both *Survey of Current Business* and the back of *PI (Marketing/Communications)* give the most current figures, including monthly estimates. *Business Statistics* goes into even more detail, giving both dollar figures and statistically adjusted indices. The latest edition (1967) should be considered the basic source for all aggregate and major-media expenditure data. Even more important, the descriptions of the sources of the data (found in the back of the book) are the most comprehensive and detailed listings available, past and present. This is where the researcher should begin his search for most advertising data.

The *Directory of Specialized Media*, prepared by Ted Bates and Company, New York, gives a standardized report — description, geographic availability, audience data, costs, advertiser acceptance (users) and suppliers — on a wide (and wild) variety of media — spectaculars, skywriting, truck posters, handbills, matchbooks, shirtboards, milk containers, shopping carts, hotel TV, commuter-clock spectaculars, ethnic, outdoor, etc., etc.

Estimates for the "unmeasured" media are occasionally made by their own trade publications, e.g., *Premium Practices*, and often picked up by *AA* (e.g., September 23, 1968, p. 50 for premiums, p. 102 for trading stamps). The Transit Advertising Measurement Bureau publishes estimates for that medium and for advertisers in it each year. Aggregates are in *AA* (e.g., November 29, 1965). The *Census of Manufacturers* is another source of data on media receipts (e.g., the 1958 and 1963 data in *AA*, September 13, 1965). Linage data for middle-western newspapers are given monthly and retrospectively in the Inland Daily Press Association's *Bulletin*.

Sometimes, too, the researcher needs to know data for a specific media vehicle — a television network or station, or a given magazine. Data on pages of advertising each month and cumulatively through the year in most consumer and farm magazines are a monthly feature of *Advertising Age*. So, too, are network billing figures originating from LNA-BAR. *Media Records* gives linage figures for specific newspapers. And *Editor and Publisher* publishes yearly advertising linage figures from more than 700 newspapers not covered by *Media Records*. (The May 24, 1969, issue gives these data as well as some republished *Media Records* data.) *Broadcasting Yearbook* contains data from the Federal Communications Commission on billings of television stations in a number of countries (e.g., 1969 edition, p. A-128ff.).

For individual business publications, *Industrial Marketing* carries a rich collection of information each year (e. g., July 1968, pp. 65–72). It gives annual data both in pages and in dollars, retrospective to 1955 and also 1950 and 1945; dollar volume by field, such as power and power utilities, for 1955 and also 1950 and 1945; and expenditures by Standard Industrial Classification groups in 1966 and 1967. Also, each issue gives total advertising volume in business publications monthly and cumulatively in terms of pages, and breaks the data down by types — industrial, "class," and so on — as well as by individual publications.

Estimates of total industrial advertising volume, made by American Business Press, appear in *Advertising Age* (e.g., June 20, 1966, p. 84).

A report on Yellow Pages advertising expenditure (a nontrivial half-billion dollars in 1963) appeared in *Media/Scope* (February 1964, pp. 48–51).

Advertising Rates and Circulation

The prices of advertising in the various domestic and foreign media are readily available through a number of sources. The Standard Rate & Data Series (SRDS) covers most of the major media. It provides comprehensive data on most vehicles in major media, including each type of offer made by the vehicle. (For an example, see the *New York Times* rate display shown on pp. 148–9.) Separate publications cover daily U.S. newspapers, weekly papers audited by ABC, spot and network radio and television, consumer magazines (including newspaper-distributed ones), farm publications, business publications, direct mail, and transit advertising. All broadcasting stations and print media which accept advertising on a large scale are included.

A microfilm record spanning forty-five years, of all media rates and data compiled and published by Standard Rate and Data Service, Inc., (SRDS) [is in] the Mass Communications History Center of the State Historical Society of Wisconsin. . . . The 730 reels of 16 mm. microfilm contain more than a million pages of information. . . . [The] Society will maintain a continuing record of media information by microfilming annually the January and July issues of all SRDS publications which will be donated to the Center by the firm [SHSW Press release].

The Audit Bureau of Circulation provides quarterly circulation figures for newspapers and magazines, and the American Research Bureau does so for broadcast media. Information about both rates and circulation is generally comprehensive but varies according to medium, as does the frequency; the series for major media like broadcasting, magazines and daily newspapers are issued bimonthly. International editions are available for Canada, England, France, Italy, Mexico and West Germany. However, because ABC audits so few weekly newspapers, coverage here is far from complete, but fortunately can be supplemented by the annual *National Directory of Weekly Newspapers* (American Newspaper Representatives, Inc., 404 Fifth Ave., New York). SRDS also has international editions for Canada, England, France, Italy, Mexico and West Germany.

Data on circulation and rate trends for some major media are collected from time to time by the Association of National Advertisers, Inc. (155 East 44th St., New York). *Magazine Circulation and Rate Trends* began in 1940 under the title *Magazine Circulation Analysis* and is continuous through 1967; *Business Publication Circulation and Rate Trends* began in 1946 and is continuous through 1966; *Newspa-*

per Circulation and Rate Data also began in 1946 and is continuous through 1968; *Television Circulation and Rate Trends* began in 1959 and is continuous through 1968; *Outdoor Advertising Circulation and Rate Trends* began in 1959 and is continuous through 1966. All five series are updated irregularly at periods varying from one to four years.

Further information on outdoor advertising rates can be found in three other references, each of which is annual: *Outdoor Rate and Market Service* (Outdoor Advertising Association of America, 24 West Erie St., Chicago); *Outdoor Buyers Guide*, sections II, IV and V (Institute of Outdoor Advertising, 625 Madison Ave., New York); and *Poster Rate Book* (v. 1–2), (National Outdoor Advertising Bureau, Inc., 711 Third Ave., New York). The first of these contains information on markets, districts, cities and towns, including coverage intensities, service costs and poster discount plans. The second tells outdoor rates and markets in Section II, discount plans in Section IV, and TAB circulation Audits in Section V. The third gives rates and allotments in over 10,000 U.S. towns and markets.

Circulation '68, published annually since 1962 by American Newspaper Markets, Inc., compiles data on the geographic distribution of newspapers, i.e., the circulation by newspapers and major magazines in various states, counties, and metropolitan areas.

Radio Programming Profile (BF Communication Services, Inc., 341 Madison Ave., New York) gives audience and program data for a number of radio stations. It is up-dated by quarterly supplements. Coverage includes only the AM stations in the country's top 100 markets.

The considerable amount of change in television prices from week to week is shown in *AA* (February 27, 1967, p. 20). In contrast, the prices listed for magazines and newspapers are fairly firm, but prices for large blocks of advertising in all media, and especially television, are subject to considerable haggling. Therefore published rates may be misleading. Further price sources have been listed in Chapter 6.

Advertising price data should support many kinds of studies of price behavior of interest to students of industrial organization, e.g. studies of prices in markets of different degrees of concentration and at different points on the business cycle. The course of advertising rates taken together is shown by indexes of media cost formerly in *Printers' Ink* and now in *Media/Scope*. A survey of such rates from 1940 to 1965 and an analysis of them is in Backman (1967, Appendix B).

Advertising Audience Breakdowns

The *audiences* of advertising media are of great importance for advertisers, and hence the media have spent a lot of money providing audience data. This topic is therefore a voluminous one. It will not be covered here because it is well covered at length elsewhere. A large number of studies are done for particular media and their markets. Many of the current ones are listed in *Advertising Age*'s yearly "Market Data Section," e.g., May 20, 1968, the 21st such yearly section, while others are available upon application to the particular media.

Audiences are also measured more broadly by a variety of organizations for the various media. Rundowns are given in Burton (1959, Chapter 23) and Bogart (1967, Chapter 10 and p. 326). And all of Lucas and Britt's book (1963) is about this topic.

Consumer Market and Magazine Report (Daniel Starch and Staff, Boston Post Road and Beach Avenue, Mamaroneck, N.Y.), popularly known as the Starch Report, annually publishes a demographic and product rundown on readership for about 100 mass consumer magazines. W. R. Simmons and Associates Research, Inc. (235 East 42nd St., New York) has since 1963 published annual reports on readership of approximately 40 mass consumer magazines, each report differing somewhat from the others both in title and content. *Brand Rating Index* also supplies useful audience data of this sort.

Sales Data

Many advertising studies require sales data as well as advertising data. Industry and aggregate sales data require an entire bibliography of their own. Most information comes from government sources, including income-tax data and censuses of business. A magnificent source for the number of steel items of various types sold yearly (e.g., bicycles) is in *Steel* magazine (e.g., March 27, 1961, the 13th annual).

Data on sales of individual brands and firms are harder to come by. For those commodities that are taxed or licensed directly, e.g., cars, cigarettes, liquor and beer, data are sometimes available. *AA* usually manages to find and publish these, often picking them up from other trade sources. *PI* also has run a series of articles entitled "Battle of the Brands" (e.g., on cereal, June 24, 1966) which has compiled some brand-share data over time. Other sources are purchase panels, some of which are commercial (e.g., Nielsen, Pulse, Trendex and Sales-Area Marketing Inc.) while others are run by particular media in their own areas for the benefit of their advertisers (e.g., *Chicago Tribune*, *Milwaukee Journal*, and Scripps-Howard papers in various cities). Brand-usage studies are done for particular products in particular geographic and media categories by the media. Many are listed as available in *AA*'s "Market Data Section" (e.g., May 20, 1968), but you are not likely to be able to get either a comprehensive picture of the present or a historical picture of the past from these piecemeal sources.

Miscellaneous

The above paragraphs have attended mostly to on-going series or still-current compilations. Now we shall briefly list some valuable special compilations, followed by a variety of statistics relating more or less tangentially to the advertising business.

1. Data on the billings of the largest agencies, both in the United States and world-wide, are compiled annually, by *AA* (e.g., February 26, 1968, p. 34 ff., and March 25, 1968, p. 45 ff.). These data can support such studies as whether small or large agencies grow faster.

2. Billings of advertising agencies in each main city and for various types of agency activity are compiled from the Census Bureau and published in *AA* (e.g., August 2, 1965, pp. 79, 86, 115.)

3. *The World of Advertising* (*AA*, January 15, 1963) was a useful supplement of *AA* which pulled together many pieces of data found elsewhere.

4. Comparative advertising agency income accounts are published yearly in *AA* (e.g., August 12, 1968, p. 44), including a ten-year retrospective picture. The income accounts are also broken by size of agency (e.g., *AA*, Jan. 2, 1967; *World of Advertising*, Jan. 15, 1963, p. 50). The nature of agency operations is also illuminated by the balance sheets of publicly-owned agencies (e.g., Foote-Cone-Belding, in *AA*, August 2, 1965; Wells, Rich, Greene, in *AA*, August 26, 1968, p. 254; Grey, in *AA*, August 30, 1965, p. 32). Stock prices of agencies and other advertising-related businesses are published weekly in the back of *AA*.

5. Crum (1927) compiled enormous amounts of data up to the 1920s on various categories of newspaper advertising. Most of it does not seem to be very useful today, however.

6. Advertising agency salaries are released from time to time by one or another employment agency catering to the advertising industry, and reported in *AA* (e.g., by Jack Baxter, *AA* Supplement, *World of Advertising*, January 15, 1963, p. 387).

7. *Advertisers' Guide to Marketing* was from 1954 to 1965 a most valuable annual supplement of *PI*, republishing data published earlier in the year in *PI*. But as *PI* began going downhill, both generally and from the point of view of statistical publication, the annual also began to carry less and less information of value.

8. *AA* is a wonderful trade journal and is certainly a great boon to

the researcher, publishing most of the data of value that are available anywhere which do not require too much space. It is unfortunate that the index was recently gutted of its informative function.

9. *Television Factbook* yearly presents various data pertaining to television, including (in the 1968–69 issue):

a) Television ownership. Broken by 1967 market geography and by color, multiset, UHF (pp. 21a, ff.); by size rank (pp. 40a, ff.), by states and countries (pp. 65a, ff. 1946–68, pp. 56a–57a).

b) Television station aggregate financial data, 1946–66 (pp. 44a). By market, 1961–66 (pp. 45a, ff.).

c) CATV subscribers, by market (p. 57a).

d) TV time sales, 1949–66 (pp. 55a).

e) TV set production and sales, 1946–67 (pp. 55a, 58a, 62a); tube sales, 1947–67 (p. 59a); sales to dealers (pp. 609, 61a).

10. The number of television sets in use in various countries in the world is picked up from the USIA and other sources by *AA* (e.g., May 31, 1965, p. 69, and June 26, 1967).

11. Radio data may be found in *Television Factbook*, too:

a) Radio set production, 1922–1967 (p. 58a); sales (p. 62a).

b) Radio station aggregate financial data, 1946–66 (p. 54a).

12. The percentages of sales spent in 1955 for advertising in eight media for 521 major companies, summarized into industries (e.g., gasoline and oil), are in a *Printers' Ink* publication (1957, pp. 53–61).

13. *Standard Directory of Advertising Agencies* (National Register Publishing Co., 5201 Old Orchard Road, Skokie, Ill.), an annual, lists all agencies in the United States, with top personnel, and accounts carried, and in some cases approximate billings. This is especially useful for charting the development of an agency. (To find out which agency a given company uses, consult a companion volume mentioned previously, *Standard Directory of Advertising.*)

Finally, here are some references that I have either never been able to lay my hands on or to which I have not gone back recently enough to be able to give more than a casual note, but that may turn out to be useful:

1. Presbrey (1929, pp. 259, 590 ff., and chapter LXIII) gives 19th century expenditure estimates.

2. Crowell Publishing Co. (1925) contained a wealth of early 20th century data on national advertising.

3. Curtis Publishing Co. (annual) gave data on leading advertisers for the years before and after 1920.

4. Seiden, Martin H., *CATV Sourcebook*, Thurmont, Md.: TAB Books (1965) has 28 detailed tables on television and microwave.

5. *Relative Costs of Local Display Advertising in the Daily Newspapers of the U.S.*, published by Retail Ad Cost Research Inc., Washington, D.C., contains milline rates for all American dailies, milline rates for and percentage of coverage of city zone and retail trade zone populations and milline rates for r.o.p. color advertising.

Appendix E

Needed Research in the Economics of Advertising

1. The last pages of Chapter 11 concluded that most, if not all, of the issues in the economics of advertising are not important from a social point of view. This is not to say that advertising itself is not important. But one feels no need to question its most important aspects. And those aspects of advertising that are most subject to question are not very crucial socially. If this conclusion is correct, then research in the economics of advertising is not likely to be of first-rank importance.

Consider the matter from another point of view. What is most important about an economy is how efficiently it produces. Societies that produce efficiently are rich; those that produce inefficiently are poor. Advertising mostly affects consumption, and the smaller part of advertising that goes to producers (i.e., industrial advertising) is questioned by no one, nor is it likely to be. So there is little relationship between advertising and the economy's productivity.

2. Under one set of circumstances consumption is crucial, however. This is the case of Keynsian unemployment of resources. And if such circumstances might be otherwise allowed to occur in the future in industrialized countries, then advertising might indeed be important. Chapter 8 concludes that advertising is not likely to have any important effect on total consumption, but that conclusion is based on flimsy evidence and could be wrong. Therefore, further research on this question might be important. But the question is a tough one to attack empirically. One approach might be to subject an experimental group of people to artificially low levels of advertising, by means of a system like the Milwaukee Advertising Laboratory that blocks out commercials in a randomly chosen subsample of its panel. Or, one might greatly raise the advertising intensity level of an experimental group. Then one could compare the total consumption of the control and experimental groups.

(An ethical question might arise here, however, as with many other tests. Should one manipulate people's lives this way?)

3. Without doubt it is crucial to the field of the economics of promotion to create a reasonably comprehensive set of expenditure statistics for advertising. As of now we have only (*a*) estimates of aggregate advertising, (*b*) the total expenditures of the various media, (*c*) expenditures by various gross industries (the IRS statistics), and (*d*) scattered collections of the expenditures of various firms in various media. Furthermore, the various sets of data do not always correspond well to each other because of differences in definitions and differences in data-collection methods.

What is needed is for someone to try to put all the available data together into some sort of national pattern. On the one hand, data sould be presented broken down as finely as possible, i.e., the expenditures of each firm or brand in each medium. Then the firms should be totaled by industry. This is the sort of thing that has been done admirably by *Drug Trade News* for all the products sold in drugstores, except that many important media are not covered. Then the totals for industries as estimated from checking data should be compared with the IRS data for industries. Then these estimates totaled should be compared and adjusted with total advertising estimates from the expenditures in media. This work has been done for the aggregates by Yang (the "Advertising Age" series) but the estimates for firms and industries have not been fitted into the aggregate estimates.

All this is a formidable task and I'm not sure that the necessary talent and effort would not be better devoted to other scientific tasks. But I am sure that until this work gets done the study of the economics of advertising will be hampered badly.

Even if other studies of the working of the advertising mechanism in the economy are not crucially important, they may be interesting and useful. Without further ado here are a few such studies. (Some of these have been referred to in the body of the text above.)

4. The elasticity of demand for aggregate advertising with respect to an advertising price index needs to be estimated, as do also the elasticities of demand of the various media, e.g. television (see the discussion in Chapter 3).

5. The rate structures in radio, magazines, and outdoor advertising harbor all kinds of interesting phenomena, just as did television and newspapers (see Chapter 6).

6. Industry studies of the advertising-agency industry, or of the entire advertising industry, of the sort that have been done on cigarettes, aluminum, etc., should be worth doing.

7. The interrelationship of advertising and various other forms of promotion needs attention, e.g., to what extent do advertising and personal selling substitute for one another?

8. The rise of the "drummer" along with the rise of manufacturing and national markets in the United States would be interesting both historically and theoretically.

9. Only a portion of the hypotheses about the effect of demand, cost, and competitive variables on advertising expenditures given in Chapters 2 to 4 have been tested. Tests of others may falsify the hypotheses (or may verify them, as I prefer to think they will).

10. Several detailed case studies in depth of the process by which firms set advertising appropriations *à la* Cyert et al. (1956) would tell much about decision-making in general as well as about the advertising-appropriation decision.

11. A study of the extent to which firms selling the same products in different countries spend high and low proportions of their advertising dollars in the same media, e.g. television, would tell much about the extent to which advertising practice is institutionally and historically determined, or is determined by the inherent nature of the products themselves. A comparison of U.S. and U.K. data should be reasonably straightforward.

12. The relative seasonal and cyclical volatility of retail versus national advertising is worth studying (see pp. 88–89 above).

13. Two studies that badly need repeating in different forms are Zielske (1959) and Politz (1960). (See Chapter 1 for comment on what needs to be done differently with the Politz study.)

14. The proportion of local to total advertising linage in newspapers varies with the size of the city, as do the total amounts of local and (especially) national advertising. These phenomena deserve investigation.

There is still another sort of research using advertising data, however. One may use advertising data to illuminate general questions in economic theory. The reason for choosing to work with advertising data is that so much information is so available and so good. The study of the effect of monopoly in prices in the second part of Chapter 6 is a modest example. A few other examples I have done are: a study of the diffusion of new innovations, in this case the January white sale (Appendix C); an investigation of frequency of changes of their advertising rates for magazines with changes and weaker monopolistic positions to test the theory of the kinky oligopoly curve (Simon, 1969b); and a study of the size distribution of advertising agencies in various countries to see what relationship there is between size of country and extent of industrial concentration.

Here are a few other such studies that someone might find it interesting to do:

15. Shopping patterns have long interested economists, especially location theorists. One can use advertisements as a permanent and easy-to-consult record of where people shop. For example, advertisements for Reno dentists in Elko, Nevada, classified telephone directories tell something about where people in Elko go to get their teeth fixed.

16. Another way to exploit the printed-record quality of advertising is to examine changes in purchases during a society's history, or to examine differences between societies. One can see that patent medicines are sold in particular sorts of places and times. One may also study changes in attitude over time, as Dornbusch and Hickman (1959) did with a content analysis of advertisements in the United States over several decades.

Bibliography

The bibliography that follows is composed of two sorts of items. It includes those books and articles that are referred to in this book; and it also includes other works on the economics of advertising, excluding works written from the managerial point of view, that I believe have some scholarly merit. This second sort of item is included because I hope that this bibliography can save time for future writers on these subjects.

Sherman (1900) includes a bibliography of early works on advertising. And Chamberlin (1962) has many references related to monopolistic competition. Other relevant bibliographies are those of Wales and Ferber (1963), Bylund et al. (1962), Dailey (1963), Perloff (1962), Revzan (1951, 1963), and Wolfson (1963).

Abrams, Mark. 1952. "Statistics of Advertising." *Journal of the Royal Statistical Society* 115 (pt. 2): 258–264.

Ackley, Gardner. 1961. *Macroeconomic Theory*. New York: Macmillan.

Adams, Henry Foster. 1916. *Advertising and Its Mental Laws*. New York: Macmillan.

Advertising Age, the National Newspaper of Marketing. 1930+. New York: Advertising Publications.

Agnew, Hugh E., and Warren B. Dygert. 1938. *Advertising Media*. New York: McGraw-Hill.

Alderson, Wroe. 1963. "Administered Prices and Retail Grocery Advertising." *Journal of Advertising Research* 3 (March): 2–6.

Altschul, Aaron M. 1966. "A Look at the World Protein Situation." *Soybean Digest* 26, No. 8 (May): 15, 16, 19–20.

American Association of Advertising Agencies. 1964. *Newspaper Rate Differentials*.

American Newspaper Publisher's Association, Retail Department. 1962. *Annual Timetable of Retail Opportunities*. New York: ANPA.

Ando, Albert, and Franco Modigliani. 1963. "The 'Life Cycle' Hypothesis of Saving: Aggregate Implications and Tests." *American Economic Review* 52 (March): 55–84.

"Antitrust Implications of Network Television Quantity Advertising Discounts." 1965. *Columbia Law Review* 65 (November): 460–502.

Ashby, William Ross. 1963. *An Introduction to Cybernetics*. New York: Wiley.

Association of National Advertisers. 1964. *Newspaper Circulation Rate Trends.* New York, (August).

Backman, Jules. 1967. *Advertising and Competition.* New York: New York University Press.

Bain, Joe Staten. 1948. "Price and Production Policies." In Howard Sylvester Ellis, ed. *A Survey of Contemporary Economics.* Philadelphia: Blakiston, 129–173.

———. 1951. "Relation of Profit Rate to Industry Concentration: American Manufacturing, 1936–40." *Quarterly Journal of Economics* 65 (August): 293–324.

———. 1956a. "Advantages of the Large Firm: Production, Distribution, and Sales Promotion." *Journal of Marketing* 20 (April): 336–346.

———. 1956b. *Barriers to New Competition, Their Character and Consequences in Manufacturing Industries.* Cambridge, Mass.: Harvard University Press.

Baran, Paul A. 1957. *The Political Economy of Growth.* New York: Monthly Review Press.

Barber, William J. 1961. *The Economy of British Central Africa.* Stanford: Stanford University Press.

Barfod, Borge. 1940. "The Theory of Advertising." *Econometrica* 8:279–280.

Barnett, Harold J., and Edward Greenberg. 1968a. "The Best Way to Get More Varied TV Programs." *Trans-Action* 5 (May): 39–45.

———, and Edward Greenberg. 1968b. "On the Economics of Wired City Television." *American Economic Review* 58 (June): 503–508.

Basmann, Robert L. 1955. "An Application of Several Econometric Techniques to a Theory of Demand with Variable Tastes." Ph.D. thesis, Iowa State University.

Bassie, V. Lewis. 1958. *Economic Forecasting.* New York: McGraw-Hill.

Baster, Albert S. J. 1935. *Advertising Reconsidered. A Confession of Misgiving.* London: P. S. King.

Bauer, Peter T., and Basil S. Yamey. 1957. *The Economics of Underdeveloped Countries.* Chicago: University of Chicago Press.

Bauer, Raymond, and M. G. Field. 1962. "Ironic Contrast: US and USSR Drug Industries." *Harvard Business Review* 40, No. 5 (October): 89–97.

Baumol, William J. 1959. *Business Behavior, Value and Growth.* New York: Macmillan.

———. 1967. "Calculation of Optimal Product and Retailer Characteristics: The Abstract Product Approach." *Journal of Political Economy* 75 (October): 674–685.

———, R. E. Quandt, and H. T. Shapiro. 1964. "Oligopoly Theory and Retail Food Pricing." *Journal of Business* 37 (October): 346–363. 363.

Becknell, James C., and Robert W. McIsaac. 1963. "Test Marketing Cookware Coated with 'Teflon.' " *Journal of Advertising Research* 3 (September): 2–8.

Belden, Gail Chester, et al. 1964. *The Protein Paradox; Malnutrition, Protein-Rich Foods, and the Role of Business.* Boston: Management Reports.

Bishop, Frank Patrick. 1944a. *The Economics of Advertising*. London: Hale.

————. 1944b. *The Ethics of Advertising*. London: Hale.

Blair, John M. 1965. "Statement." Hearings Before the Sub-Committee on Anti-Trusts and Monopoly. In *Economic Concentration, Part IV. Concentration and Efficiency, 89th Congress*, p. 1538.

Blake, H. M., and J. A. Blum. 1965. "Network Television Rate Practices: A Case Study in the Failure of Social Control of Price Discrimination." *Yale Law Journal* 74, No. 8 (July): 1339–1401.

Blank, David M. 1962. "Cyclical Behavior of National Advertising." *Journal of Business* 35 (January): 14–27.

————. 1963. "A Note on the Golden Age of Advertising." *Journal of Business* 36 (January): 33–38.

————. 1968. "Television Advertising: The Great Discount Illusion, or Tonypandy Revisited." *Journal of Business* 41 (January): 10–38.

Blum, Eleanor. 1963. *Reference Books in the Mass Media*. Urbana: University of Illinois Press.

Bogart, Leo. 1967. *Strategy in Advertising*. New York: Harcourt, Brace & World.

Borden, Neil Hopper. 1937. *Problems in Advertising*, 3rd ed. New York: McGraw-Hill.

————. 1942. *The Economic Effects of Advertising*. Chicago: Irwin.

———— et al. 1946. *National Advertising in Newspapers*. Cambridge, Mass.: Harvard University Press.

Boulding, Kenneth Ewart. 1941. *Economic Analysis*. New York: Harper.

————. 1955. *Economic Analysis*, 3rd ed. New York: Harper.

————. 1963. *The Image; Knowledge in Life and Society*. Ann Arbor: University of Michigan Press.

Braithwaite, Dorothea. 1928. "The Economic Effects of Advertisement." *The Economic Journal* 38 (March): 16–37.

Brems, Hans. 1948. "The Interdependence of Quality Variations, Selling Effort, and Price." *Quarterly Journal of Economics*. 62 (May): 418–440.

————. 1951. *Product Equilibrium Under Monopolistic Competition*. Cambridge, Mass.: Harvard University Press.

————. 1952. "Employment, Prices and Monopolistic Competition," *Review of Economics and Statistics* 34, No. 4 (November): 314–325.

————. 1957. "Input-Output Coefficients as Measures of Product Quality." *American Economic Review* 47 (March): 105–118.

————. 1958. "Price, Quality, and Rival Response." In Mary Jean Bowman, ed. *Expectations, Uncertainty, and Business Behavior: A Conference Held at Carnegie Institute of Technology, October 27–29, 1955*. New York: Social Science Research Council, 1958. Also in Max Kjaer-Hansen, *Readings in Danish Theory of Marketing*. Copenhagen: Harcks, 1966, 149–159.

————. 1959. *Output, Employment, Capital and Growth: A Quantitative Analysis*. New York: Harper.

Brink, Edward Loren, and William T. Kelley. 1963. *The Management of Promotion: Consumer Behavior and Demand Situation*. Englewood Cliffs, N.J.: Prentice-Hall.

Britt, Steuart H. 1956. "Study Indicates Effective Magazine Ad May Be Repeated Without Loss of Readership." *Advertising Age* 27 (May 14): 63–64.

Broadcasting. Yearbook Issue. Annual. Washington: Broadcasting Publications.

Brown, George H. 1953. "Brand Loyalty — Fact or Fiction?" *Advertising Age* 24 (January 26): 75–76.

———. 1964. "Measuring the Sales Effectiveness of Alternative Media." In *Proceedings of the Seventh Annual Conference.* New York: Advertising Research Foundation.

Brown, Lyndon Osmond, R. S. Lessler, and W. M. Weilbacher. 1957. *Advertising Media: Creative Planning in Media Selection.* New York: Ronald.

Brown, Suzanne. 1964. "The January and August White Sales." Term paper, University of Illinois.

Buchanan, N. S. 1942. "Advertising Expenditures: A Suggested Treatment." *Journal of Political Economy* 50 (August): 537–557.

Bullen, H. J. 1961. "1961 Industrial Ad Budgets — How Big, What Goes Into Them?" *Industrial Marketing* 46 (January): 31–39.

Burnett, Leo, Co. Inc. 1961. "Media Analysis Principles and Practices." Chicago: Burnett. Mimeo.

Burns, Arthur F. 1954. "Wesley Mitchell and the National Bureau." 29th Annual Report, 1949. Collected in A. F. Burns, *The Frontiers of Economic Knowledge.* Princeton: National Bureau of Economic Research, 1954.

Burton, Philip Ward. 1959. *The Profitable Science of Making Media Work.* New London: Printers' Ink.

Burtt, Harold Ernest. 1938. *Psychology of Advertising.* Boston: Houghton Mifflin.

Bylund, Bruce H., Robert Hostetter, and William C. Tomlinson. 1962. "Consumer Behavior: An Annotated Bibliography with Special Emphasis on Food." University Park, Pa.: Agricultural Experiment Station. Mimeo.

"Can Mathematics Pick a Good Media Schedule?" 1962. *Printers' Ink* 279 (May 11): 56–58.

Carr-Saunders, Alexander Morris, P. Sargant Florence, and Robert Peers. 1942. *Consumers' Co-operation in Great Britain: An Examination of the British Co-operative Movement,* 3rd ed. London: Allen and Unwin.

Cassady, Ralph, Jr., and Robert M. Williams. 1949. "Radio as an Advertising Medium." *Harvard Business Review* 27 (January): 62–78.

Caves, Richard E. 1964. *American Industry: Structure, Conduct, Performance.* Englewood Cliffs, N.J.: Prentice-Hall.

Chamberlin, Edward. 1962. *The Theory of Monopolistic Competition: A Reorientation of the Theory of Value.* Cambridge. Mass.: Harvard University Press.

———. 1964. "The Definition of Selling Costs." *Review of Economic Studies* 31 (January): 59–64.

Cherington, Paul Terry. 1913. *Advertising as a Business Force: A Compilation of Experience Records.* Garden City, N.Y.: Doubleday, Page.

————. 1925. "The Economics of Advertising: Discussion." *American Economic Review Supplement* 15 (March): 36–38.

Chipman, John S. 1966. "Allocation and Distribution Theory — Discussion." *American Economic Review* 56 (May): 45–47.

Clark, Colin. 1940. *The Conditions of Economic Progress.* London: Macmillan.

Clark, Fred E. 1925. "An Appraisal of Certain Criticisms of Advertising." *American Economic Review Supplement* 15 (March): 5–13.

Clark, John Maurice. 1936. *Preface to Social Economics; Essays on Economic Theory and Social Problems.* New York: Farrar and Rinehart.

Clement, Wendell E. 1963. "Some Unique Problems in Agricultural Commodity Advertising." *Journal of Farm Economics* 45 (February): 183–194.

————, P. L. Henderson, and C. P. Eley. 1965. "The Effect of Different Levels of Promotional Expenditures on Sales of Fluid Milk." Washington: U.S. Department of Agriculture, Economic Research Service.

Coffin, Thomas E. 1963. "A Pioneering Experiment in Assessing Advertising Effectiveness." *Journal of Marketing* 27, No. 3 (July): 1–10.

Collins, George Rowland. 1948. "The Advertising Appropriation and the Business Cycle." Ph.D. thesis, New York University.

Collins, N. R., and L. E. Preston. 1966. "Concentration and Price-Cost Margins in Food Manufacturing Industries." *Journal of Industrial Economics* 14 (July): 226–242.

Columbia Law Review, 1965. See "Antitrust Implications of . . . Advertising Discounts."

Comanor, William S., and Thomas A. Wilson. 1967. "Advertising Market Structure and Performance." *Review of Economics and Statistics* 49 (November): 423–440.

Conference on Price Research, Committee on Price Determination. 1943. *Cost Behavior and Price Policy.* New York: National Bureau of Economic Research.

Copeland, Morris A. 1925. "The Economics of Advertising: Discussion." *American Economic Review Supplement* 15 (March): 38–41.

Copland, B. D. 1958. *The Study of Attention Value; A Review of Some Available Material.* London: Published on behalf of the Institute of Practitioners in Advertising by Business Publications.

Corden, Max. 1961. *A Tax on Advertising?* Fabian Society Research Series 222. London: Fabian Society.

Cox, Donald F. 1961. "Clues for Advertising Strategists." *Harvard Business Review* 39 (September–October 1961): 160–176, and 39 (November–December 1961): 160–182.

————. 1962. "Information and Uncertainty: Their Effects on Consumers' Product Evaluation." DBA thesis, Harvard, 1962.

Cox, Reavis, in association with Charles S. Goodman and Thomas C. Fichandler. 1965. *Distribution in a High-Level Economy.* Englewood Cliffs, N.J.: Prentice-Hall.

Crain, Robert L. 1966. "Fluoridation: The Diffusion of an Innovation Among Cities." *Social Forces* 44 (June): 467–476.

Crowell Publishing Co. 1925. *National Markets and National Advertising.* New York: Crowell.

Crum, William Leonard. 1927. *Advertising Fluctuations: Seasonal and Cyclical.* Chicago: Shaw.

Cunningham, Ross M. 1956. "Brand Loyalty: What, Where, How Much?" *Harvard Business Review* 34, No. 1 (January–February): 116–128.

————. 1961. "Customer Loyalty to Store and Brand." *Harvard Business Review* 39, No. 6 (November–December): 127–137.

Curtis Publishing Co. Annual. *Leading Advertisers.* Philadelphia: Curtis.

Cyert, Richard Michael, and James G. March. 1963. *A Behavioral Theory of the Firm.* Englewood Cliffs, N.J.: Prentice-Hall.

————, H. A. Simon, and D. B. Trow. 1956. "Observation of a Business Decision." *Journal of Business* 29 (October): 237–248.

Dailey, Edward. 1963. "Advertising and Promotion of Agricultural Products, Annotated Bibliography." Lafayette, Indiana: Cooperative Extension Service. Mimeo.

Daley, James B., Jr. 1963. "Services that Measure Competitive Advertising Expenditures." *Media/Scope* 7 (May): 57–58; 62–66.

Dean, Joel. 1951a. "Cyclical Policy on the Advertising Appropriation." *Journal of Marketing* 15 (January): 265–273.

————. 1951b. "How Much to Spend on Advertising." *Harvard Business Review,* 29 (January): 65–74.

————. 1951c. *Managerial Economics.* New York: Prentice-Hall.

De Grazia, Sebastian. 1962. *Of Time, Work, and Leisure.* New York: Twentieth Century Fund.

Demsetz, Harold. 1964. "The Welfare and Empirical Implications of Monopolistic Competition." *Economic Journal* 74 (September): 623–641.

Dhrymes, Phoebus J. 1962. "On Optimal Advertising, Capital and Research Expenditures under Dynamic Conditions." *Economica* N.S. 29 (August): 275–279.

Dorfman, Robert, and Peter O. Steiner. 1954. "Optimal Advertising and Optimal Quality." *American Economic Review* 44, No. 5 (December 1954): 826–836. Reprinted in Frank Bass, ed. et al., *Mathematical Models and Methods in Marketing.* Homewood, Ill.: Irwin, 1961.

Dornbush, Sanford, and L. Hickman. 1959. "Other-directedness in Consumer-Goods Advertising: A Test of Riesman's Historical Theory." *Social Forces* 38 (December): 99–102.

Downs, Anthony. 1957. "An Economic Theory of Political Action in a Democracy." *Journal of Political Economy* 65 (April 1957): 135–150. Reprinted in Earl Hamilton et al., eds., *Landmarks of Political Economy.* Chicago: University of Chicago Press, 1962.

Due, John Fitzgerald. 1959. "Monopolistic Competition and the Incidence of Special Sales Taxes." In Richard Abel Musgrave and C. S. Shoup, *Readings in the Economics of Taxation.* Homewood, Illinois: Irwin, 1959, 340–376. Originally in John Fitzgerald Due, *The Theory of Incidence of Sales Taxation.* New York: Kings Crown Press, 1942.

Duffy, Ben. 1951. *Advertising Media and Markets,* 2nd ed. New York: Prentice-Hall.

Economists Advisory Group. 1967. *The Economics of Advertising.* London: Advertising Association.

Edwards, Charles Mundy, Jr., and W. H. Howard. 1943. *Retail Advertising and Sales Promotion.* Rev. ed. New York: Prentice-Hall.

Else, P. K. 1966. "The Incidence of Advertising in Manufacturing Industries." *Oxford Economic Papers* New Series 18 (March): 88–105.

Emmett, Boris, and John Jeuck. 1950. *Catalogues and Counters*. Chicago: University of Chicago Press.

Farley, John. 1964. " 'Brand Loyalty' and the Economics of Information." *Journal of Business* 37 (October): 370–381.

Federal Reserve 7th District. "Departmental Distribution of Apparel and Department Store Sales." April 1960, March 1962, April 1964. Mimeo.

Federal Reserve Bank of Chicago, Research Department. Annual. *Departmental Sales at Department Stores*. Chicago.

F.T.C., Proctor and Gamble case. See U.S., Federal Trade Commission, 1963.

Ferber, Robert. 1962. "Research on Household-Behavior." *American Economic Review* 52, No. 1 (March): 19–63.

———, and P. J. Vendoorn. 1962. *Research Methods in Economics and Business*. New York: Macmillan.

Ferguson, James M. 1963. *The Advertising Rate Structure in the Daily Newspaper Industry*. Englewood Cliffs, N.J.: Prentice-Hall.

———. 1964. "Advertising and Competition in the Liquor Industry." Mimeo.

———. 1965. "Advertising Investment and the Theory of Entry." Mimeo.

Firestone, O. J. 1967. *The Economic Implications of Advertising*. Commissioned by the Institute of Canadian Advertising. London: Methuen.

Forrest, Dorsey. 1949. *Advertising Practices of Ohio Retailers*. Columbus: Bureau of Business Research, College of Commerce and Business Administration, Ohio State University.

Forrester, Jay W. 1959. "Advertising: A Problem in Industrial Dynamics." *Harvard Business Review* 37, No. 2 (March–April): 100–110.

Fourt, Louis A., and Joseph W. Woodlock. 1960. "Early Prediction of Market Success for New Grocery Products." *Journal of Marketing* 25, No. 2 (October): 31–38.

Frank, Ronald E. 1962. "Brand Choices as a Probability Process." In Ronald E. Frank, et al. eds., *Quantitative Techniques in Marketing Analysis*. Homewood, Ill.: Irwin, 372–389.

Frey, Albert Wesley. 1955. *How Many Dollars for Advertising?* New York: Ronald.

Friedman, Laurence. 1961. "Game-Theory Models in the Allocation of Advertising Expenditures." In Frank Bass, ed., et al., *Mathematical Models and Methods in Marketing*. Homewood, Ill.: Irwin, 220–244.

Friedman, Milton. 1953. "The Methodology of Positive Economics." In his *Essays in Positive Economics*. Chicago: University of Chicago Press, 3–43.

———. 1957. *A Theory of the Consumption Function: A Study by the National Bureau of Economic Research*. Princeton: Princeton University Press.

Gaeddert, Orlan M. 1961. "Two Techniques for Estimating Sales Response to Advertising with Examples from the Cigarette Industry." M.A. thesis, New York University.

Galbraith, John Kenneth. 1952. *American Capitalism, the Concept of Countervailing Power*. Boston: Houghton Mifflin.

Gavin-Jobson Associates, Inc. Annual. *Liquor Handbook*. New York: Gavin-Jobson.

Geertz, Clifford. 1963. *Peddlers and Princes: Social Change and Economic Modernization in Two Indonesian Towns*. Chicago: University of Chicago Press.

Geller, Max A. 1952. *Advertising at the Crossroads*. New York: Ronald.

General Media and Copy Research Co. "A Profile of Outdoor Advertising Readers." (No date.) Mimeo.

George Neustadt, Inc. *The Neustadt Redbook of Seasonal Patterns, 1963*. New York, Neustadt, 1964 and annual.

Gilboy, E. W. 1931–32. "Demand Curves by Personal Estimate." *Quarterly Journal of Economics* 46: 376–384.

Gill, Samuel E. 1961. "New Findings in Continuity and Duplication." *Advertising and Selling* 24 (February): 19–21.

Gillman, Leonard. 1950. "Operations Analysis and the Theory of Games: An Advertising Example." *Journal of the American Statistical Association* 45 (December): 541–545.

Godfrey, Milton L. 1962. "Media Selection by Mathematical Programming." Talk given to Institute of Management Sciences.

Gold, Jack A. 1964. "Testing Test Market Predictions." *Journal of Marketing Research* 1 (August): 8–16.

Goldman, Marshall I. 1960. "Product Differentiation and Advertising: Some Lessons from Soviet Experience." *The Journal of Political Economy* 68, No. 4 (August): 346–357.

———. 1963. *Soviet Marketing: Distribution in a Controlled Economy*. New York: Free Press of Glencoe.

Gore, Budd. 1956. *How to Budget Advertising for Bigger Volume, More Profits*, 1st ed. New York: Retail Department, Bureau of Advertising, ANPA.

Gort, Michael. 1963. "Analysis of Stability and Change in Market Shares." *Journal of Political Economy* 71 (February): 51–63.

Gray, Roger W., and Roice Anderson. 1962. "Advertised Specials and Local Competition Among Supermarkets." *Food Research Institute Studies* 3 (May): 125–140.

Greenhut, Melvin. 1963. *Microeconomics and the Space Economy; the Effectiveness of an Oligopolistic Market Economy*. Chicago: Scott Foresman.

Greyser, Stephen A., and R. A. Bauer. 1966. "Americans and Advertising: Thirty Years of Public Opinion." *Public Opinion Quarterly* 30 (Spring): 69–78.

Griliches, Zvi. 1957. "Hybrid Corn: An Exploration in the Economics of Technological Change." *Econometrica* 25, No. 4 (October): 501–522.

———. 1961. "A Note on Serial Correlation Bias in Estimates of Distributed Lags." *Econometrica* 29 (January): 65–73.

Haase, Albert Ericssen. 1931. *The Advertising Appropriation, How to Determine It and How to Administer It*. New York: Harper.

Hahn, Frank H. 1959. "The Theory of Selling Costs." *Economic Journal* 69 (June): 293–312.

Haldeman-Julius, Emanuel. 1928. *The First Hundred Million.* New York: Simon and Schuster.

Harris, Emerson P. 1893. "The Economics of Advertising." *Social Economist* 4 (March): 171–174.

Harris, Ralph, and Arthur Seldon. 1962. *Advertising and the Public.* London: Published for the Institute of Economic Affairs by Deutsch.

Hatcher, James Gregson. 1942. "An Investigation of Time Consumed in Selling at Retail, in Independent Stores of a Small Town, Nationally Advertised Products as Compared with Unadvertised or Little Advertised Products." M.S. thesis, University of Illinois, Urbana.

Hauk, James G. 1965. "Research in Personal Selling." In George Schwartz ed., *Science in Marketing.* New York: Wiley, 213–249.

Henderson, Peter Louis, and Sidney E. Brown. 1961. *Effectiveness of a Special Promotional Campaign for Frozen Concentrated Orange Juice.* U.S. Department of Agriculture, Marketing Research Report No. 457. Washington: U.S. Department of Agriculture, Agricultural Marketing Service, Market Development Research Division.

Herskovits, Melville Jean. 1952. *Economic Anthropology; A Study in Comparative Economics,* 2nd rev. ed. New York: Knopf.

Hicks, John R. 1962. "Economic Theory and the Evaluation of Consumers' Wants." *Journal of Business* 35 (July): 256–263.

Hoffman, Robert M. 1963. "The 20-second Commercial." *Media/Scope,* 7 (July): 72, 74, 76.

Holdren, Bob R. 1960. *The Structure of a Retail Market and the Market Behavior of Retail Units.* Englewood Cliffs, N.J.: Prentice-Hall.

Hollander, Sidney, Jr. 1949. "A Rationale for Advertising Expenditures." *Harvard Business Review* 27 (January): 79–87.

Hoos, Sidney. 1959. "The Advertising and Promotion of Farm Products: Some Theoretical Issues." *Journal of Farm Economics* 41 (May): 349–363.

Hotchkiss, George Burton. 1925. "An Economic Defense of Advertising." *American Economic Review Supplement* 15 (March): 14–22.

————, and Richard B. Franken. 1927. *The Measurement of Advertising Effects; A Study of Representative Commodities Showing Public Familiarity with Names and Brands.* New York: Harper.

Hotelling, Harold. 1929. "Stability in Competition." *Economic Journal* 39 (March): 41–57.

House Beautiful. Promotion literature (no date).

Howard, John A. 1957. *Marketing Management, Analysis and Decision.* Homewood, Ill.: Irwin.

Hurwicz, Leonid. 1950. "Least-Squares Bias in Time Series." In Koopmans Tjalling ed., *Statistical Inference in Dynamic Economic Models.* New York: Wiley, 365–383.

Husband, Richard W., and Jane Godfrey. 1934. "An Experimental Study of Cigarette Identification." *Journal of Applied Psychology* 18 (April): 220–223.

International Advertising Expenditures. 1960. New York: International Advertising Association.

Jastram, Roy W. 1949a. "Advertising Outlays Under Oligopoly." *Review of Economics and Statistics* 31 (May): 106–109.

————. 1949b. "Advertising Ratios Planned by Large-Scale Advertisers." *Journal of Marketing* 14 (July): 13–21.

————. 1955. "A Treatment of Distributed Lags in the Theory of Advertising Expenditure." *Journal of Marketing* 20 (July): 36–46.

Jessen, R. J. 1961. "A Switch-Over Experimental Design to Measure Advertising Effect." *Journal of Advertising Research* 1 (March): 15–22.

Johnson, Harry G. 1960. "The Consumer and Madison Avenue." *Current Economic Comment* 22 (August 1960): 3–10. Reprinted in Perry Bliss, ed., *Marketing and the Behavioral Sciences, Selected Readings*. Boston: Allyn and Bacon, 1963, 115–125.

Jorgenson, Dale W. 1963. "Capital Theory and Investment Behavior." *American Economic Review Supplement* 53 (May): 247–259.

Kaldor, Nicholas. 1950. "The Economic Aspects of Advertising." *Review of Economic Studies* 18, No. 1: 1–27.

————, and Rodney Silverman. 1948. *A Statistical Analysis of Advertising Expenditure and of the Revenue of the Press*. Cambridge, England: University Press.

Kapp, Karl William, and Lore L. Kapp eds. 1949. *Readings in Economics*. New York: Barnes and Noble.

Kefauver, Estes, with the assistance of Irene Till. 1965. *In A Few Hands; Monopoly Power in America*. New York: Pantheon Books.

Kelvin, Reginald Peter. 1962. *Advertising and Human Memory*. London: Business Publications.

Keyser, O. A. 1947. "A Counter-Cyclical Fund for Advertising." *Advertising Agency Magazine* 40 (April): 34.

Kindleberger, Charles Poor. 1958. *Economic Development*. New York: McGraw-Hill.

Kjaer-Hansen, Ulf. 1963. *Trends in Danish Advertising Expenditures*. Copenhagen: Danish Sales and Advertising Association.

Knight, Frank Hyneman. 1936. *The Ethics of Competition and Other Essays*, 2nd ed. New York: Harper.

————. 1965. *The Economic Organization*. New York: Harper & Row.

Kolens, Carole. 1964. "Study of Newspaper Advertising Elasticities." Term paper, University of Illinois.

Kolliner, Sim A., Jr. 1963. "New Evidence of Ad Values." *Industrial Marketing* 48 (August): 81–84.

Kotler, Philip. 1964. "Toward An Explicit Model for Media Selection." *Journal of Advertising Research* 4 (March): 34–41.

Koyck, Leendert Marinus. 1954. *Distributed Lags and Investment Analysis*. Amsterdam: North-Holland.

Kuehn, Alfred A. 1961. "A Model for Budgeting Advertising." *Journal of Business*, (April 1961). Reprinted in Frank Bass, ed., et al., *Mathematical Models and Methods in Marketing*. Homewood, Ill.: Irwin, 1961, 302–353.

————. 1962. "Consumer Brand Choice — A Learning Process?" In Ronald E. Frank ed., et al., *Quantitative Techniques in Marketing Analysis*. Homewood, Ill.: Irwin, 390–403.

————. 1962. "How Advertising Performance Depends on Other Marketing Factors." *Journal of Advertising Research* (March): 2–11.

Kuznets, Simon Smith, assisted by Elizabeth Jenks. 1953. *Shares of Upper Income Groups in Income and Savings.* New York: National Bureau of Economic Research.

Labour Party Commission of Enquiry into Advertising. 1966. *Report.* London: Labour Party. Chairman: Rt. Hon. Lord Reith.

Lancaster, Kelvin. 1966a. "A New Approach to Consumer Theory." *Journal of Political Economy* 14 (April): 132–57.

————. 1966b. "Change and Innovation in the Technology of Consumption." *American Economic Review* 56 (May): 14–23.

Landes, David S. 1952. "Bankers and Pashas: International Finance in Egypt in the 1860's." In William Miller ed., *Men in Business: Essays in the History of Entrepreneurship.* Cambridge, Mass.: Harvard University Press, 23–70.

Leblang, Paul. 1962. "The Effect of Merchandise, Price, and Weather on Department Store Advertising." Ph.D. thesis, New York University.

Lee, Alec M. 1962. "Decision Rules for Optimal Media Scheduling: Static Campaigns." *Operational Research Quarterly* 13, No. 3 (September): 229–242.

————, and A. J. Burkart. 1960. "Some Optimization Problems in Advertising Media Planning." *Operational Research Quarterly* 11, No. 3 (September).

Lees, D. S. 1968. "An Economist Looks at Advertising." *The Advertising Quarterly* No. 16 (Summer): 9–15.

Lees, F. A., and C. Y. Yang. 1966. "The Redistributional Effect of Television Advertising." *The Economic Journal* 76 (June): 328–336.

Leibenstein, Harvey. 1966. "Allocative Efficiency vs. 'X-Efficiency.' " *American Economic Review* 56 (June): 392–415.

Leiter, Robert D. 1950. "Advertising, Resource Allocation, and Employment." *Journal of Marketing* 15 (October): 158–166.

Leser, Conrad E. V. 1941. "Family Budget Data and Price-Elasticities of Demand." *Review of Economic Studies* 9 (November): 40–57.

Lever, E. A. 1947. *Advertising and Economic Theory.* London: Oxford University Press.

Levinson, Horace C. 1953. "Experience in Commercial Operation Research." *Operations Research* 1 (February): 220–239.

Lewis, Edwin H. 1954. "Sales Promotion Decisions." *Business News Notes.* University of Minnesota, No. 18 (November): 1–5.

Liquor Handbook. New York: Gavin-Jobson, annual.

Lucas, Darrell Blaine, and Steuart H. Britt. 1950. *Advertising Psychology and Research.* New York: McGraw-Hill.

————, and Steuart H. Britt. 1963. *Measuring Advertising Effectiveness.* New York: McGraw-Hill.

Lund, John V. 1947. *Newspaper Advertising.* New York: Prentice-Hall.

Lyon, Herbert C., and Julian L. Simon. 1968. "The Price Elasticity of Demand for Cigarettes Estimated from Quasi-Experiments." *American Journal of Agricultural Economics* 50, No. 4 (November): 888–895.

Machlup, Fritz. 1962. *The Production and Distribution of Knowledge in the United States.* Princeton: Princeton University Press.

————. 1963. "Marginal Analysis and Empirical Research." *American*

Economic Review 36 (September 1946), 519–554. Reprinted in his *Essays in Economic Semantics,* ed. by Merton H. Miller. Englewood Cliffs, N.J.: Prentice-Hall, 1963, 147–190.

Maffei, Richard B. 1960. "Brand Preferences and Simple Markov Processes." *Operations Research* 8 (March–April): 210–218.

Malinowski, Bronislaw. 1961. *Argonauts of the Western Pacific; An Account of Native Enterprise and Adventure in the Archipelagoes of Melanesian New Guinea.* New York: Dutton.

———. 1964. *Crime and Custom in Savage Society.* Patterson, N.J.: Littlefield, Adams.

Mann, H. M., J. A. Henning, and J. W. Meehan, Jr. 1967. "Advertising and Concentration: An Empirical Investigation." *Journal of Industrial Economics* 16, No. 1 (November): 34–45.

Margolis, Charles. 1947. "Traceable Response as a Method of Evaluating Industrial Advertising: A Case Study." *Journal of Marketing* 12 (October): 202–210.

Marshall, Alfred. 1919. *Industry and Trade; A Study of Industrial Technique and Business Organization; and of Their Influences on the Conditions of Various Classes and Nations.* London: Macmillan.

———. 1961. *Principles of Economics.* Ninth variorium ed. New York: Macmillan.

Mason, Edward Sagendorph. 1964. *Economic Concentration and the Monopoly Problem.* New York: Atheneum.

Matthews, John B., R. D. Buzzell, T. Levitt, and R. E. Frank. 1964. *Marketing: An Introductory Analysis.* New York: McGraw-Hill.

May, Charles D. 1963. "Selling Drugs by 'Educating' Physicians." *ETC.: A Review of General Semantics* 20 (May 1963): 31–69. Also in *Journal of Medical Education* 36 (January 1961): 1–23.

Mayer, Martin. 1958. *Madison Avenue, USA.* New York: Harper.

McConnell, J. Douglas. 1968. "Testing Brand Loyalty and Beer Quality." *Marketing Insights* (October 21): 14–16.

McGarry, Edmund D. 1958. "The Propaganda Function in Marketing." *Journal of Marketing* 23 (October): 131–139.

McGraw-Hill, Sales Service Department, Sales Information Division. (No date.) *Color and Size of Space in Advertising.* New York.

McHale, Henry P. 1964. "A Research Study to Test the Hypothesis, on the Average for Motion Picture Theater Firms in Illinois, Duopolists Advertise More in their Home Town Newspapers than Monopolists do in Theirs." Term paper, University of Illinois.

McNair, Malcolm P. Annual. *Operating Results of Department and Specialty Stores.* Boston: Harvard Business School.

Meade, J. E. 1968. "Is the 'New Industrial State' Inevitable?" *Economic Journal* 78 (June): 372–392.

Media/Scope. "What is the Best Length for a TV Commercial?" 8, No. 10 (October): 63–66.

Meissner, Frank. 1961. "Sales and Advertising of Lettuce." *Journal of Advertising Research* 1 (March): 1–10.

Meyer, John Robert, and Edwin Kuh. 1957. *The Investment Decision: an Empirical Study.* Cambridge, Mass.: Harvard University Press.

Mickwitz, Gösta. 1959. *Marketing and Competition, the Various Forms of Competition at the Successive Stages of Production and Distribution.* Helsinki.

Mills, Harland D. 1961. "A Study in Promotional Competition." In Frank Bass, ed., et al., *Mathematical Models and Methods in Marketing.* Homewood, Ill.: Irwin, 245–301.

Mindak, William A., Andrew Neibergs, and Alfred Anderson. 1963. "Economic Effects of the Minneapolis Newspaper Strike." *Journalism Quarterly* (Spring): 213–218.

Mitchell, Walter, Jr. 1941. "How Retail Advertising Expenditures Vary with Sales Volume and Size of City." *Dun's Review* 49 (January): 13–20.

Mitchell, Wesley Clair. 1937. *The Backward Art of Spending Money and Other Essays.* New York: McGraw-Hill. Reprinted, New York: A. M. Kelley, 1950.

Modigliani, Franco. 1966. "The Life Cycle Hypothesis of Saving, the Demand for Wealth and the Supply of Capital." *Social Research* 33 (Summer): 160–217.

———, and Richard Brumberg. 1954. "Utility Analysis and the Consumption Function: An Interpretation of Cross-Section Data." In Kenneth K. Kurihara, ed., *Post-Keynesian Economics.* New Brunswick: Rutgers University Press, 383–436.

Morgan, J. N. 1954. "Factors Relating to Consumer Saving When It is Derived As A Net-Worth Concept." In Lawrence Robert Klein ed., et al., *Contributions of Survey Methods to Economics.* New York: Columbia University Press.

Morgenstern, Oskar. 1963. *On The Accuracy of Economic Observations.* 2nd ed. Princeton: Princeton University Press.

Moriarty, William Daniel. 1923. *The Economics of Marketing and Advertising.* New York: Harper.

National Retail Merchants Association, Controllers' Congress. 1957. *Departmental Merchandising and Operating Results.* New York.

———. 1963. *Operating Results of Department and Specialty Stores.* New York: Annual.

Nelson, Paul Edwin, and Lee E. Preston. 1966. *Price Merchandising in Food Retailing: A Case Study.* Berkeley: Institute of Business and Economic Research, University of California.

Nelson, Ralph, 1964–65. See U.S., Senate, 1964–65.

Nerlove, Marc, and Kenneth J. Arrow. 1962. "Optimal Advertising Policy Under Dynamic Conditions." *Economica* N.S. 29 (May): 129–142.

———, and F. V. Waugh. 1961. "Advertising without Supply Control: Some Implications of a Study of the Advertising of Oranges." *Journal of Farm Economics* 43 (November): 813–837.

Neustadt. See George Neustadt, Inc.

Nicholls, William Hord. 1951. *Price Policies in the Cigarette Industry; A Study of "Concerted Action" and its Social Control, 1911–50.* Nashville: Vanderbilt University Press.

Norris, Vincent Paul. 1960. "Advertising and the Consumption Function: A Theoretical Approach." Ph.D. thesis, University of Illinois, Urbana.

O'Connell, Jeffrey. 1967. "Lambs to Slaughter." *Columbia Journalism Review* 6 (Fall): 21–28.

Ogilvy, David. 1963. *Confessions of an Advertising Man.* New York: Atheneum.

Operating Results of Department and Speciality Stores. See National Retail Merchants Association, Controllers' Congress.

Ortengren, John. 1961. "Statistical Analysis of the Role of Advertising Expenditure in the American Economy." Ph.D. thesis, Syracuse University.

Oxenfeldt, Alfred Richard. 1950. "Consumer Knowledge: Its Measurement and Extent." *Review of Economics and Statistics* 32 (November): 300–314.

———. 1964. *Marketing Practices in the 'TV Set Industry.* New York: Columbia University Press.

Ozga, S. A. 1960. "Imperfect Markets through Lack of Knowledge." *Quarterly Journal of Economics* 74 (February): 29–52.

Palda, Kristian S. 1964. *The Measurement of Cumulative Advertising Effects.* Englewood Cliffs, N.J.: Prentice-Hall.

———. 1966. "The Hypothesis of a Hierarchy of Effects: A Partial Evaluation." *Journal of Marketing Research* 3 (February): 13–24.

Palmer, Allan V. 1964. "Forecasting Advertising Expenditures in the Cigarette Industry." Talk given to American Marketing Association, December 28–30, 1964.

Parsons, Talcott, and Neil J. Smelser. 1956. *Economy and Society; A Study in the Integration of Economic and Social Theory.* Glencoe, Ill.: Free Press.

Pease, Otis. 1958. *The Responsibilities of American Advertising; Private Control and Public Influence, 1920–1940.* New Haven: Yale University Press.

Perloff, Robert. 1962. "A Selected Bibliography of Consumer Psychology." Lafayette, Ind.: Department of Psychology. Mimeo.

Peterman, John Larsen. 1965. "The Structure of National Time Rates in the Television Broadcasting Industry." *Journal of Law and Economics* 8 (October): 77–131.

Phillips, Almarin. 1962. *Market Structure, Organization, and Performance; An Essay on Price Fixing and Combinations in Restraint of Trade.* Cambridge, Mass.: Harvard University Press.

Polanyi, Karl, C. M. Arensberg, and H. W. Pearson, eds. 1957. *Trade and Market in the Early Empires: Economies in History and Theory.* Glencoe, Ill.: Free Press.

Politz (Alfred) Research, Inc., New York. Media Studies in 1956, 1958, and 1960. Published by *Reader's Digest*, 1956; *Saturday Evening Post*, 1958; *Reader's Digest, Saturday Evening Post, Life,* and *Look*, 1960.

———. 1960. "The Rochester Study," sponsored by the *Saturday Evening Post.* New York.

———. 1964. "Reach and Frequency." New York: *Look* Magazine. Not published.

———. 1965. *A Study of Advertising Effects in Modern Medicine.* New York: Politz.

Poffenberger, Albert Theodor. 1932. *Psychology in Advertising,* 2nd ed. New York: McGraw-Hill.

Potter, David Morris. 1960. *People of Plenty; Economic Abundance and the American Character.* Chicago: University of Chicago Press, 1954. Reprinted in Charles Herald Sandage and V. Fryberger, *The Role of Advertising; A Book of Readings.* Homewood, Ill.: Irwin, 1960.

Presbrey, Frank Spencer. 1929. *The History and Development of Advertising.* Garden City, N.Y.: Doubleday, Doran.

Prest, Alan R. 1949. "Some Experiments in Demand Analysis." *Review of Economics and Statistics* 31 (February): 33–49.

Preston, Lee E. 1963. *Profits, Competition and Rules of Thumb in Retail Food Pricing.* Berkeley: Institute of Business and Economic Research, University of California.

―――. 1968. "Advertising Effects and Public Policy." Paper presented to American Marketing Association, Denver, August 28–20, 1968. In Robert L. Ling, ed., *Marketing and the New Science of Planning.* Chicago: American Marketing Association, 1968, 558–566.

Printers' Ink. 1957. *Presenting and Justifying Your Advertising Budget. Printers' Ink* Portfolio for Planning No. 8. Pleasantville: N.Y.

Quinn, Francis X. ed. 1963. *Ethics, Advertising and Responsibility.* Westminster, Md.: Canterbury Press.

Quinn, Theodore Kinget. 1953. *Giant Business: Threat to Democracy; the Autobiography of an Insider.* New York: Exposition Press.

Ramsdell, Sayre M. 1931. "How Philco Doubled Sales During the Depression." *Printers' Ink* 157 (October 22): 17–19.

Rasmussen, Arne, 1952. "The Determination of Advertising Expenditure." *Journal of Marketing* 16 (April): 439–446.

Redfield, Robert. 1950. *A Village That Chose Progress; Chan Kom Revisited.* Chicago: University of Chicago Press.

Reeves, Rosser. 1961. *Reality in Advertising.* New York: Knopf.

Reid, Margaret G. 1962. "Consumption, Savings, and Windfall Gains." *American Economic Review* 52 (September): 728–737.

Reith Commission. *Report of a Commission into Advertising.* See Labour Party Commission of Enquiry into Advertising.

Revzan, David A. 1951, 1963. *A Comprehensive Classified Marketing Bibliography.* Berkeley: University of California; 1951, Parts I and II, and 1963, Supplements.

Roberts, Harry V. 1947. "The Measurement of Advertising Results." *Journal of Business* 20 (July): 131–145.

Robinson, Joan. 1933. *The Economics of Imperfect Competition.* London: Macmillan.

Rothenberg, Jerome. 1962. "Consumer Sovereignty and the Economics of Television Programming." *Studies in Public Communication* No. 4 (Autumn): 45–54.

Rothschild, Kurt W. 1942. "A Note on Advertising." *Economic Journal* 52 (April): 112–121.

Rottenberg, Simon. 1952. "Income and Leisure in an Underdeveloped Economy." *Journal of Political Economy* 60 (1952): 95–101. Reprinted in E. J. Hamilton et al., *Landmarks in Political Economy.* Vol. 2. Chicago: University of Chicago Press, 1962.

Rudolph, Harold J. 1936. *Four Million Inquiries from Magazine Advertising.* New York: Columbia University Press.

Samuelson, Paul Anthony. 1947. *Foundations of Economic Analysis.* Cambridge, Mass.: Harvard University Press.

Sandage, Charles Harold. 1948. *Radio Advertising for Retailers.* Cambridge: Mass.: Harvard University Press.

———, and S. R. Bernstein. 1956. "Questionnaire Study of Advertising Ratios." *Advertising Age* 27 (January 30): 51–56.

———, and V. Fryburger eds. 1960. *The Role of Advertising; a Book of Readings.* Homewood, Ill.: Irwin.

Schaefer, Arnold E. 1968. "Nutritional Aspects of the World's Food Needs." In *The Land-Grant University and World Food Needs.* Urbana: University of Illinois, College of Agriculture, 13–26.

Science News-Letter. See "Without Knowing the Brand . . . ," 1949.

Schlaifer, Robert. 1959. *Probability and Statistics for Business Decisions; An Introduction to Managerial Economics Under Uncertainty.* New York: McGraw-Hill.

———. 1961. *Introduction to Statistics for Business Decisions.* New York: McGraw-Hill.

Schoenberg, Erika H. 1933. "The Demand Curve for Cigarettes." *Journal of Business* 6 (January): 15–35.

Schumpeter, Joseph Alois. 1934. *The Theory of Economic Development; An Inquiry Into Profits, Capital Credit, Interest and the Business Cycle.* Cambridge, Mass.: Harvard University Press.

Schwab, Victor O. 1948. "What 92 Split-Run Ads Tell Us." *Advertising Agency Magazine* 41 (April): 33–34, 60–64; and 41 (May): 38, 74.

———. 1950. "Successful Mail-Order Advertising." In Roger Barton, ed., *Advertising Handbook.* New York: Prentice-Hall, 597–615.

Schwartzman, David. 1959. "The Effect of Monopoly on Price." *Journal of Political Economy* 67 (August): 352–362.

Scott, James D. 1943. "Advertising When Buying is Restricted." *Harvard Business Review* 21, No. 4: 443–454.

Scott, Jesse. 1951. "The Changing Pattern of British Advertising." *World's Press News* (July 6): 5–6, 86.

Schultz, Theodore. 1964. *Transforming Traditional Agriculture.* New Haven, Conn.: Yale University Press.

Shaffer, James D. 1959. "Information About Price and Income Elasticity for Food Obtained from Survey Data." *Journal of Farm Economics* 41 (February): 113–118.

———. 1964. "Advertising in Social Perspective." *Journal of Farm Economics* 46 (May): 387–397.

Shakun, Melvin. 1965. "Advertising Expenditures in Coupled Markets: A Games-Theory Approach." *Management Science* 11 (February): B42–B47.

Sherman, Sidney A. 1900. "Advertising in the United States." *Journal of the American Statistical Association* 7 (December): 119–162.

Sherrard, Alfred. 1951. "Advertising, Product Variation, and the Limits of Economics." *Journal of Political Economy* 59 (April): 126–142.

Shoemack, Harvey R. 1965. A Study of How the Amount of Newspaper Advertising Done by Movie Houses is Affected by the Number of Movie Houses, the Population, and the Newspaper Circulation, in Selected Illinois Towns." Term paper, University of Illinois.

Shone, R. M. 1935. "Selling Costs." *Review of Economic Studies* 2: 225 ff.

Shryer, William A. 1912. *Analytical Advertising*. Detroit: Business Service Corporation.

Shuford, Donald Beam. 1961. "A Study of the Firm's Advertising Expenditure." Ph.D. thesis, University of Illinois, Urbana.

Silcock, Thomas H. 1947. "Professor Chamberlin and Mr. Smith on Advertising." *Review of Economic Studies* 15, No. 1: 34–39.

Silverman, Rodney. 1951. *Advertising Expenditure in 1948*. London: The Advertising Association.

———. 1955. "Advertising Costs in Monopolistic Competition." In J. K. Eastham, ed., *Economic Essays in Commemoration of the Dundee School of Economics, 1931–1955*. Perthshire: Coupar Angus, 85–103.

Simon, Julian L. 1965a. "A Simple Model for Setting Advertising Appropriations." *Journal of Marketing Research* (August): 285–292.

———. 1965b. *"How to Start and Operate a Mail-Order Business."* New York: McGraw-Hill.

———. 1966. "The Price Elasticity of Liquor in the U.S. and a Simple Method of Determination." *Econometrica* 34 (January): 193–205.

———. 1968a. "The Health Economics of Cigarette Consumption." *Journal of Human Resources* 3, No. 1 (Winter): 111–117.

———. 1968b. "The Relationship between Cigarette Smoking and Life Expectancy." Mimeo.

———. 1969a. "The Effect of Advertising on Liquor Brand Sales." *Journal of Marketing Research* 6 (August): 301–313.

———. 1969b. "The Kinky Oligopoly Curve Re-examined." *American Economic Review* 59 (December): 971–975.

———. 1970. The Management of Advertising. Englewood Cliffs, N.J.: Prentice-Hall, (forthcoming).

———, and George H. Crain. 1966. "Is the Statistic (Advertising/Sales) Useless for the Study of Economies of Scale and Other Purposes?" *Journal of Advertising Research* 6 (September): 37–43.

———, and David M. Gardner. 1969. "The New Proteins and World Food Needs." *Economic Development and Cultural Change* 17 (July): 520–526.

Simon, Leonard S., and Melvin R. Marks. 1965. "Consumer Behavior during the New York Newspaper Strike." *Journal of Advertising Research* 5 (March): 9–17.

Smith, H. 1935. "The Imputation of Advertising Costs." *Economic Journal* 45 (December): 682–699.

Smith, Henry. 1947. "Advertising Costs and Equilibrium: A Reply." *Review of Economic Studies* 15, No. 1: 40–41.

Smithies, Arthur. 1942. "The Stability of Competitive Equilibrium." *Econometrica* 10 (July–October): 258–274.

"Smoking and News." 1963. *Columbia Journalism Review* 2 (Summer): 6–12.

Sponsor Services, Inc. *All Media Evaluation Study*. New York.

Spratlen, Thaddeus Hayes. 1962. "An Appraisal of Theory and Practice in the Analysis of Sales Effort." Ph.D. dissertation, Ohio State University.

Sraffa, Piero. 1926. "The Laws of Returns Under Competitive Conditions." *Economic Journal* 36 (December): 535–550.

Starch, Daniel. 1956. "How Well Do People Read Long Advertisements?" *Tested Copy: Highlights from the Starch Advertisements* (May).

———. 1959a. "Analysis of 12 Million Inquiries. I: How Size, Color, Position, and Location Affect Inquiries." *Media/Scope* (January): 23–27.

———. 1959b. "Analysis of 12 Million Inquiries. II: How Thickness of Issue, Season, Affect Inquiries." *Media/Scope* (February): 30–43.

———. 1959c. "Analysis of 12 Million Inquiries. III: How Types of Offers, Products, and Coupons Affect Inquiries." *Media/Scope* (March): 40–44.

———. 1959d. "How Does Repetition of Advertisements Affect Readership?" *Media/Scope* 3 (November): 50–51.

———. 1961a. "What Is the Best Frequency of Advertisements?" *Media/Scope* 5 (December): 44–45.

———. 1961b. *Measuring Product Sales Made by Advertising.* Mamaroneck, N.Y.: Starch and Staff, circa 1961.

———. 1963. "No Papers: What Effect on Sales?" *Printers' Ink* 284 (August 23): 47–48.

Statistical Abstract. See U.S., Bureau of the Census.

Steiner, Gary Albert. 1963. *The People Look at Television; A Study of Audience Attitudes.* New York: Knopf.

———. 1966. "The People Look at Commercials: A Study of Audience Behavior." *The Journal of Business* 39 (April): 272–304.

Steiner, Peter O. 1952. "Program Patterns and Preferences, and the Workability of Competition in Radio Broadcasting." *Quarterly Journal of Economics* 66 (May): 194–223.

Stewart, John Benjamin. 1964. *Repetitive Advertising in Newspapers: A Study of Two New Products.* Boston: Harvard University, Graduate School of Business Administration.

Stigler, George Joseph. 1946. *The Theory of Price.* New York: Macmillan. 3d edition, 1966.

———. 1947. "The Kinky Oligopoly Demand Curve and Rigid Prices." *Journal of Political Economy* 55 (October): 432–449.

———. 1949. "Monopolistic Competition in Retrospect." In his *Five Lectures on Economic Problems.* London: Longmans, Green.

———. 1952. "The Case Against Big Business." *Fortune* (May).

———. 1958. "The Economies of Scale." *Journal of Law and Economics* 1 (October): 54–71.

———. 1961. "The Economics of Information." *Journal of Political Economy* 69 (June): 213–225.

Stone, Robert F. 1955. *Successful Direct Mail Advertising and Selling.* New York: Prentice Hall.

Strong, Edward K. 1914. "The Effect of Size of Advertisements and Frequency of Their Presentation." *Psychological Review* 21 (March): 136–152.

Taplin, Walter. 1959. "Advertising Appropriation Policy." *Economica* N.S. 26 (August): 227–239.

———. 1960. *Advertising; A New Approach.* London: Hutchinson.

———. 1961. *The Origin of Television Advertising in the United Kingdom*. London: Pitman.

Taylor, C. J. 1963. "Some Developments in the Theory and Application of Media Scheduling Methods." *Operational Research Quarterly* 14, No. 3 (September).

Taylor, Frederic Wilfred. 1934. *The Economics of Advertising*. London: Allen & Unwin.

Television Fact Book. 1965. Washington, D.C.: Radio News Bureau, 1965 ed.

Telser, Lester G. 1961. "How Much Does It Pay Whom to Advertise?" *American Economic Review* 51 (May): 194–205.

———. 1962a. "The Demand for Branded Goods as Estimated from Consumer Panel Data." *The Review of Economics and Statistics* 44 (August): 300–324.

———. 1962b. "Advertising and Cigarettes." *Journal of Political Economy* 70 (October): 471–499.

———. 1964. "Advertising and Competition." *Journal of Political Economy* 72 (December): 537–562.

———. 1966. "Supply and Demand for Advertising Messages." *American Economic Review* 56, No. 2 (May): 457–466.

———. 1968. "Economics of Advertising." In *International Encyclopedia of the Social Sciences*. 2nd ed. 1:106–111.

Temin, Peter. 1964. "A New Look at Hunter's Hypothesis about the Antebellum Iron Industry." *American Economic Review* 54 (May): 344–351.

Tennant, Richard B. 1950. *The American Cigarette Industry; A Study in Economic Analysis and Public Policy*. New Haven, Conn.: Yale University Press.

Towers, Irwin M., Leo A. Goodman, and Hans Zeisel. 1962. "A Method of Measuring the Effects of Television Through Controlled Field Experiments." *Studies in Public Communication* No. 4 (Autumn): 87–110.

———, Leo A. Goodman, and Hans Zeisel. 1963. "What Could Nonexposure Tell the TV Advertiser?" *Journal of Marketing* 27, No. 3 (July): 52–56.

Travel Research International, Inc. 1967. *Resort and Tourist Advertising Expenditures of Individual States in Measured Media within the United States, 1966* and annual. New York.

Tull, Donald S. 1955. "A Re-examination of the Causes of the Decline in Sales of Sapolio." *Journal of Business* 28 (April): 128–137.

———. 1956. "An Examination of the Hypothesis that Advertising Has A Lagged Effect on Sales." Ph.D. thesis, University of Chicago.

U.S., Bureau of the Census. *Statistical Abstract of the United States*.

U.S., Department of Agriculture. 1963. *Yearbook, 1963: A Place to Live*. Washington: Government Printing Office.

U.S., Federal Trade Commission. 1944. *Report of the Federal Trade Commission on Distribution Methods and Costs, Part V, Advertising as a Factor in Distribution*. Washington: Government Printing Office.

———. 1963. *United States of America before Federal Trade Commission in the Matter of Procter and Gamble Company*. A Corporation Docket No. 6901.

————. No date. Bureau of Economics. "Report on Cigarette Advertising and Output." Washington: Mimeo.

U.S., Internal Revenue Service. Annual. *Source Book of Income*. Washington: Microfilm.

U.S., Panel on the World Food Supply. 1967. *The World Food Problem: A Report*. Washington: Government Printing Office.

U.S., Senate, Committee on Commerce. 1965. *Cigarette Labeling and Advertising Hearings*. 89th Congress, 1st session, on S.559 and S.547. Washington: Government Printing Office.

U.S., Senate, Committee on the Judiciary, Subcommittee on Antitrust and Monopoly. 1958. *Administered Prices: Automobiles*. Pursuant to S.Res. 231, 85th Congress, 2nd session. Washington: Government Printing Office.

————. 1961. *Administered Prices: Drugs*. Pursuant to S.Res. 52, 87th Congress, 1st session. Senate Report No. 448. Washington: Government Printing Office.

————. 1957–63. *Administered Prices, Hearings*. 85th Congress, 1st session; 88th Congress, 1st session. Pursuant to S.Res. 57 and others. Washington: Government Printing Office.

————. 1964–65. *Economic Concentration. Hearings*. 88th Congress, 2nd session, 89th Congress. Testimony by Ralph Nelson and Leonard Weiss. Washington: Government Printing Office.

————. 1967. *Possible Anticompetitive Effects of Sale of Network TV Advertising. Hearings*. 89th Congress, 2nd session. Pursuant to S.Res. 191. Washington: Government Printing Office.

U.S. Surgeon General's Advisory Committee on Smoking and Health. 1964. *Smoking and Health; Report of the Advisory Committee to the Surgeon General of the Public Health Service*. Washington: Government Printing Office.

Vaile, Roland Snow. 1927. "The Use of Advertising During Depressions." *Harvard Business Review* 5 (April): 323–330.

————. 1931. "The Effects of Advertising During Depressions." *Printers' Ink* 154 (January 1): 41–44.

————. 1955. "Science Applied to Advertising." *Journal of Marketing* 20 (July): 48–49.

Vaughan, Floyd Laman. 1928. *Marketing and Advertising: An Economic Appraisal*. Princeton: Princeton University Press.

Verdon, Walter A., Campbell R. McConnell, and Theodore W. Roesler. 1968. "Advertising Expenditures as an Economic Stabilizer: 1945–64." *Quarterly Review of Economics and Business* 8 (Summer): 7–18.

Vidale, M. L., and H. B. Wolfe. 1957. "An Operations-Research Study of Sales Response to Advertising." *Operations Research* 5, No. 3 (June): 370–381. And in Frank Bass, ed., et al., *Mathematical Models and Methods in Marketing*. Homewood, Illinois: Irwin, 1961, 357–377.

Wagner, Louis C. 1941. "Advertising and the Business Cycle." *Journal of Marketing* 6 (October): 124–135.

Wales, Hugh G., and Robert Ferber. 1963. *A Basic Bibliography on Marketing Research*. 2nd ed. Chicago: American Marketing Association.

Wattell, Harold R. 1953. "The Whiskey Industry: An Economic Analysis." Ph.D. thesis, New School for Social Research, New York.

Waugh, Frederick V. 1959. "Needed Research on the Effectiveness of Farm Products Promotion." *Journal of Farm Economics* 41 (May): 364–376.

Weber, Max. 1961. *General Economic History*. New York: Collier.

Weilbacher, W. M. 1960. "The Qualitative Values of Advertising Media." *Journal of Advertising Research* 1 (December): 12–17.

Weinberg, Robert Stanley. 1960a. *An Analytical Approach to Advertising Expenditure Strategy*. New York: Association of National Advertisers.

———. 1960b. "Sales and Advertising of Cigarettes." In *Minutes of the Third Meeting of the Operations Research Discussion Group*. New York: Advertising Research Foundation.

Weir, Walter. 1968. Quoted by *Advertising Age* (April 15): 8.

Weiss, Leonard, 1964–65. See U.S., Senate, 1964–65.

Weld, L. D. H. 1937. "Advertising and Retail Trade." *Printers' Ink* 180 (August 12): 49–55.

———. 1940. "Newspaper Advertising Volume As Influenced by Sales of Department Stores." *Printers' Ink* 192 (July): 19–22.

Wellman, Harry R. 1939. "The Distribution of Selling Effort Among Geographic Areas." *Journal of Marketing* 3 (January): 225–239.

"What Is the Best Length for a T.V. Commercial?" 1964. *Media/Scope*, 8 (October): 63–66, 112–116.

Wheatley, John J. 1968. "Influence of Commercial's Length and Position." *Journal of Marketing Research* 5, No. 2 (May): 199–202.

Wiles, P. 1963. "Pilkington and the Theory of Value." *Economic Journal*, 73 (June): 183–200.

Wilhelm, Ross Johnston. 1963. "A Psychological-Economic Model of Advertising-Sales Effort." Ph.D. thesis, University of Michigan.

Williams, Raymond. 1960. "The Magic System." *New Left Review* No. 4 (July–August): 27–32.

Williamson, Oliver E. 1963. "Selling Expense as a Barrier to Entry." *Quarterly Journal of Economics* 77 (February): 112–128.

Winick, Charles. 1962. "Three Measures of the Advertising Value of Media Context." *Journal of Advertising Research* (June): 28–33.

"Without Knowing the Brand Smokers Have No Preference." 1949. *Science News-Letter* 55 (May 21): 324.

Wold, H. 1964. "On the Definition and Meaning of Causal Concepts." Paper given at the Entretiens de Monaco, May 21–27.

Wolfe, Harry Deane, J. K. Brown and G. C. Thompson. 1962. *Measuring Advertising Results*. New York: National Industrial Conference Board.

Wolfson, Joel. 1963. *Consumer Behavior: An Annotated Bibliography with Special Emphasis on the Food Purchase Situation*. 2nd ed. East Lansing, Mich.: Department of Agricultural Economics. Mimeo.

The World of Advertising. 1963. Chicago: *Advertising Age*, supp. 34, No. 3 (January 15).

Yancey, Thomas Alexander. 1957. "Some Effects of Selling Effort and

Product Quality in a Dynamic Macroeconomic Model." Ph.D. thesis, University of Illinois, Urbana.

Yang, Charles Yneu. 1964. "Variations in the Cyclical Behavior of Advertising." *Journal of Marketing* 28, No. 2 (April) : 25–30.

———. 1966. "Advertising and the Economy." Mimeo.

———. 1965. "Input-Output Concept is Basis of Improved Estimates on Advertising Expenditures in the U.S." *Advertising Age* 36 (March 29): 79–84.

Zangwill, Willard I. 1965. "Media Selection by Decision Programming." *Journal of Advertising Research* 5 (September): 30–36.

Zentler, A. P., and Dorothy Ryde. 1956. "An Optimum Geographical Distribution of Publicity Expenditure in A Private Organisation." *Management Science* 2, No. 4 (July 1956): 337–352. Reprinted in Frank Bass, ed., et al., *Mathematical Models and Methods in Marketing*. Homewood, Ill.: Irwin, 1961.

Ziegler, Isabel. 1964. "Procuring Competitive Information." *Media/Scope* 8 (December): 122.

Zielske, Hubert. 1959. "The Remembering and Forgetting of Advertising." *Journal of Marketing* 23 (January): 239–243.

Zingler, Ervin K. 1940. "Advertising and the Maximization of Profit." *Economica* N.S. 7 (August): 318–321.

Index

1970.

DATE DUE

OCT 2 9 2002			
			PRINTED IN U.S.A.